1989

David R. Strü

Criminal Justice and Law Enforcement Books

of

WEST PUBLISHING COMPANY

St. Paul, Minnesota 55102

October, 1977

CONSTITUTIONAL LAW

Maddex's Cases and Comments on Constitutional Law by James L. Maddex, Professor of Criminal Justice, Georgia State University, 816 pages, 1974. Maddex's 1976 Supplement.

CORRECTIONS

Burns' Corrections—Organization and Administration by Henry Burns, Jr., Professor of Criminal Justice, University of Missouri–St. Louis, 578 pages, 1975.

Kerper and Kerper's Legal Rights of the Convicted by Hazel B. Kerper, Late Professor of Sociology and Criminal Law, Sam Houston State University and Janeen Kerper, Attorney, San Diego, Calif., 677 pages, 1974.

Killinger and Cromwell's Selected Readings on Corrections in the Community, 2nd Edition by George G. Killinger, Chairman, Board of Pardons and Paroles, Texas and Paul F. Cromwell, Jr., Director of Juvenile Services, Tarrant County, Texas, about 400 pages, 1978.

Killinger and Cromwell's Readings on Penology—The Evolution of Corrections in America by George G. Killinger and Paul F. Cromwell, Jr., 426 pages, 1973.

Killinger, Cromwell and Cromwell's Selected Readings on Issues in Corrections and Administration by George G. Killinger, Paul F. Cromwell, Jr. and Bonnie J. Cromwell, San Antonio College, 644 pages, 1976.

Killinger, Kerper and Cromwell's Probation and Parole in the Criminal Justice System by George G. Killinger, Hazel B. Kerper and Paul F. Cromwell, Jr., 374 pages, 1976.

Krantz' The Law of Corrections and Prisoners' Rights in a Nutshell by Sheldon Krantz, Professor of Law and Director, Center for Criminal Justice, Boston University, 353 pages, 1976.

Model Rules and Regulations on Prisoners' Rights and Responsibilities, 212 pages, 1973.

Rubin's Law of Criminal Correction, 2nd Edition (Student Edition) by Sol Rubin, Counsel Emeritus, Council on Crime and Delinquency, 873 pages, 1973.

Rubin's 1977 Supplement.

CRIMINAL JUSTICE BOOKS

CORRECTIONS—Continued

Smith & Berlin's Introduction to Probation and Parole by Alexander B. Smith, Professor of Sociology, John Jay College of Criminal Justice and Louis Berlin, Chief, Training Branch, New York City Dept. of Probation, 250 pages, 1975.

CRIMINAL JUSTICE SYSTEM

Kerper's Introduction to the Criminal Justice System by Hazel B. Kerper, 558 pages, 1972.

Senna and Siegel's Introduction to Criminal Justice by Joseph J. Senna and Larry J. Siegel, both Professors of Criminal Justice, Northeastern University, about 600 pages, 1978.

Study Guide to accompany Senna and Siegel's Introduction to Criminal Justice by Roy R. Roberg, Professor of Criminal Justice, University of Nebraska-Lincoln, about 200 pages, 1978.

CRIMINAL LAW

Dix and Sharlot's Cases and Materials on Basic Criminal Law by George E. Dix, Professor of Law, University of Texas and M. Michael Sharlot, Professor of Law, University of Texas, 649 pages, 1974.

Ferguson's Readings on Concepts of Criminal Law by Robert W. Ferguson, Administration of Justice Dept. Director, Saddleback College, 560 pages, 1975.

Gardner and Manian's Principles, Cases and Readings on Criminal Law by Thomas J. Gardner, Professor of Criminal Justice, Milwaukee Area Technical College and Victor Manian, Milwaukee County Judge, 782 pages, 1975.

Heymann and Kenety—The Murder Trial of Wilbur Jackson: A Homicide in the Family by Philip Heymann, Professor of Law, Harvard University and William Kenety, Instructor, Catholic University Law School, 340 pages, 1975.

Loewy's Criminal Law in a Nutshell by Arnold H. Loewy, Professor of Law University of North Carolina, 302 pages, 1975.

CRIMINAL PROCEDURE

Davis' Police Discretion by Kenneth Culp Davis, Professor of Law, University of Chicago, 176 pages, 1975.

Dowling's Teaching Materials on Criminal Procedure by Jerry L. Dowling, Professor of Criminal Justice, Sam Houston State University, 544 pages, 1976.

Ferdico's Criminal Procedure for the Law Enforcement Officer by John N. Ferdico, Assistant Attorney General, State of Maine, 372 pages, 1975.

Israel and LaFave's Criminal Procedure in a Nutshell, 2nd Edition by Jerold H. Israel and Wayne R. LaFave, 372 pages, 1975.

Johnson's Cases, Materials and Text on The Elements of Criminal Due Process by Phillip E. Johnson, Professor of Law, University of California, Berkeley, 324 pages, 1975.

CRIMINAL PROCEDURE—Continued

Kamisar, LaFave and Israel's Cases, Comments and Questions on Basic Criminal Procedure, 4th Edition by Yale Kamisar, Professor of Law, University of Michigan, Wayne R. LaFave, Professor of Law, University of Illinois and Jerold H. Israel, Professor of Law, University of Michigan, 790 pages, 1974. Supplement Annually.

Uviller's the Processes of Criminal Justice—Adjudication by H. Richard Uviller, Professor of Law, Columbia University, 991 pages, 1975.

Uviller's the Processes of Criminal Justice-Investigation by H. Richard Uviller, 744 pages, 1974.

EVIDENCE

Klein's Law of Evidence for Police by Irving J. Klein, Professor of Law and Police Science, John Jay College of Criminal Justice, 416 pages, 1973.

Markle's Criminal Investigation and Presentation of Evidence by Arnold Markle, The State's Attorney, New Haven County, Connecticut, 344 pages, 1976.

Rothstein's Evidence in a Nutshell by Paul F. Rothstein, Professor of Law, Georgetown Law Center, 406 pages, 1970.

INTRODUCTION TO LAW ENFORCEMENT

More's The American Police—Text and Readings by Harry W. More, Jr., Professor of Administration of Justice, California State University at San Jose, 278 pages, 1976.

Police Tactics in Hazardous Situations by the San Diego, California Police Department, 228 pages, 1976.

Schwartz and Goldstein's Law Enforcement Handbook for Police by Louis B. Schwartz, Professor of Law, University of Pennsylvania and Stephen R. Goldstein, Professor of Law, University of Pennsylvania, 333 pages, 1970.

Sutor's Police Operations—Tactical Approaches to Crimes in Progress by Inspector Andrew Sutor, Philadelphia, Pennsylvania Police Department, 329 pages, 1976.

JUVENILE JUSTICE

Cromwell, Killinger, Sarri and Solomon's Text and Selected Readings on Introduction to Juvenile Delinquency by Paul F. Cromwell, Jr., George G. Killinger, Rosemary C. Sarri, Professor, School of Social Work, The University of Michigan and H. N. Solomon, Professor of Criminal Justice, Nova University, about 525 pages, 1978.

Faust and Brantingham's Juvenile Justice Philosophy: Readings, Cases and Comments by Frederic L. Faust, Professor of Criminology, Florida State University and Paul J. Brantingham, Professor of Criminology, Florida State University, 600 pages, 1974.

Fox's Law of Juvenile Courts in a Nutshell by Sanford J. Fox, Professor of Law, Boston College, 286 pages, 1971.

Johnson's Introduction to the Juvenile Justice System by Thomas A. Johnson, Professor of Criminal Justice, Washington State University, 492 pages, 1975.

Senna and Siegel's Cases and Comments on Juvenile Law by Joseph J. Senna, Professor of Criminal Justice, Northeastern University and Larry J. Siegel, Professor of Criminal Justice, Northeastern University, 543 pages, 1976.

CRIMINAL JUSTICE BOOKS

MANAGEMENT AND SUPERVISION

More's Criminal Justice Management: Text and Readings, by Harry W. More, Jr., 377 pages, 1977.

Souryal's Police Administration and Management by Sam S. Souryal, Professor of Criminal Justice, Sam Houston State University, 462 pages, 1977.

Wadman, Paxman and Bentley's Law Enforcement Supervision—A Case Study Approach by Robert C. Wadman, Rio Hondo Community College, Monroe J. Paxman, Brigham Young University and Marion T. Bentley, Utah State University, 224 pages, 1975.

POLICE–COMMUNITY RELATIONS

Cromwell and Keefer's Readings on Police-Community Relations, 2nd Edition by Paul F. Cromwell, Jr., and George Keefer, Professor of Criminal Justice, Southwest Texas State University, about 500 pages, 1978.

PSYCHOLOGY

Parker and Meier's Interpersonal Psychology for Law Enforcement and Corrections by L. Craig Parker, Jr., Criminal Justice Dept. Director, University of New Haven and Robert D. Meier, Professor of Criminal Justice, University of New Haven, 290 pages, 1975.

VICE CONTROL

Ferguson's the Nature of Vice Control in the Administration of Justice by Robert W. Ferguson, 509 pages, 1974.

Uelman and Haddox' Cases, Text and Materials on Drug Abuse Law by Gerald F. Uelman, Professor of Law, Loyola University, Los Angeles and Victor G. Haddox, Professor of Criminology, California State University at Long Beach and Clinical Professor of Psychiatry, Law and Behavioral Sciences, University of Southern California School of Medicine, 564 pages, 1974.

CORRECTIONS IN THE COMMUNITY:
Alternatives to Imprisonment
Selected Readings

SECOND EDITION

by

GEORGE G. KILLINGER
Chairman, Texas Board of Pardons and Paroles

and

PAUL F. CROMWELL, Jr.
Director of Juvenile Services
Tarrant County, Fort Worth, Texas

and

Adjunct Professor—Institute of Urban Studies
The University of Texas at Arlington

CRIMINAL JUSTICE SERIES

WEST PUBLISHING CO.
St. Paul • New York • Los Angeles • San Francisco
1978

Library of Congress Cataloging in Publication Data

Killinger, George Glenn, 1908–   comp.
  Corrections in the community.
  (Criminal justice series)
    1. Corrections—Addresses, essays, lectures. 2. Halfway houses—Addresses,
essays, lectures. 3. Probation—Addresses, essays, lectures. 4. Parole—Addresses,
essays, lectures. I. Cromwell, Paul F., joint comp. II. Title. III. Series.
HV9275.K54   1978   364.6'08   77–17632
ISBN 0–8299–0155–8

PREFACE

This book was designed to fill what heretofore has been a significant gap in the literature. Developed as a text or supplement to other texts in Probation and Parole, it incorporates the newly emerging phenomenon of Diversion and Community Based Corrections, therefore offering the reader, whether student or practitioner, a comprehensive view of corrections outside the prison.

In recent years in the United States an increasing emphasis has been placed upon the development of community oriented correctional programs. For the most part correctional institutions have been located outside metropolitan areas, with the inmates isolated from the community and from normal community activities. Increased knowledge in corrections has pointed to the need for closer ties between offenders and their families and community.

It appears, furthermore, that imprisonment as a method of correction has assumed too great a role in dealing with the offender. Increasing utilization of probation and parole illustrate the major trend away from institutional confinement. Within the past decade additional programs and methods have been developed, either as alternatives or supplements to confinement in correctional institutions.

Diversion is increasingly being suggested as a viable alternative to traditional processing of offenders through the criminal justice system. Diversion refers to formally organized efforts to utilize alternatives to initial or continued induction into the justice system. It implies halting or suspending formal criminal or juvenile justice proceedings against a person who has violated a statute in favor of processing through a non-criminal disposition or means.

Programming Alternatives to Imprisonment

This chapter reviews the history and practice of Diversion and presents major papers, each a comprehensive and exhaustive study of the process. This second edition explores the origins of diversion and identifies the major operational and philosophical problems associated with the movement and various programs of Diversion currently in use and suggests further means by which Diversion may be utilized.

Community treatment programs, other than probation and parole, for offenders are still in an early stage of development. Programs now in use or suggested include: Halfway Houses, Work or Study Release, Furloughs and Probation Hostels. The concept is summarized by the Task Force on Corrections of the President's Crime Commission (1967):

> The general underlying premise for the new directions in corrections is that crime and delinquency are symptoms of failure and disorganization of the community as well as the individual offender. In particular, these failures are seen as depriving offenders of contact with institutions (of society) that are basically responsible for assuring the development of law abiding conduct . . ..

> The task of corrections, therefore, includes building or rebuilding solid ties between the offender and the community, integrating or re-integrating the offender into community life—restoring family ties, obtaining employment and education, securing in a larger sense a place for the offender in the routine functioning of society. This requires not only efforts directed toward changing the individual offender, which has been almost the exclusive focus of rehabilitation, but also mobilization and change of the community and its institutions.

Efforts are being made by a number of states and the Federal Government to develop ways to reestablish offenders into the community through community treatment programs. This volume undertakes to analyze this trend in American corrections. The contributors include some of the leading authorities in criminal justice; correctional administrators, members of the judiciary, the bar and the academic community.

Probation

The basic idea underlying a sentence to probation is very simple. Sentencing is in large part concerned with avoiding future crimes by helping the defendant learn to live productively in the community against which he has offended. Probation proceeds on the theory that the best way to pursue this goal is to orient the criminal sanction toward the community setting in those cases where it is compatible with the other objectives of sentencing. The emergence of probation during the last half of the 19th Century marked a definite advance in the disposition and treatment of the offender. Over the years the concept has been expanded far beyond that envisioned by its founders.

In this chapter the origins and evolution of probation services are traced. Problems of supervision, the Pre-sentence Report, counseling and probation revocation are considered.

PREFACE

Parole

Almost every offender who enters a correctional institution is eventually released. The only relevant questions are: When? Under what conditions? Parole is the predominant mode of release for prison inmates today, and it is likely to become even more so. Parole resembles probation in a number of aspects. In both, information about an offender is gathered and presented to a decision making authority with the power to release him to community supervision under specific conditions. If he violates those conditions, the offender may be placed in, or returned to, a correctional institution. Parole, however, differs from probation in a significant way. Parole implies that the offender has been incarcerated in a correctional institution before he is released, while probation usually is granted by a Court in lieu of any kind of confinement.

This chapter will review the origins of parole and analyze methods of parole supervision, procedures, and the use of parole in association with other community programs. The current crisis in parole and the move to abolish parole as a means of release is analyzed and opposing viewpoints are presented.

A major purpose of this book is to provide for college students a collection of original material from professionals in the field of corrections. In comparison with a book written by one author, a compendium has the advantage of placing before the reader exactly what an author had to say on his subject and provides a wider range of knowledge than can be gained by a single author in a lifetime.

The editors wish to thank the authors and publishers who kindly consented to the reprinting of their work in this book.

GEORGE G. KILLINGER
PAUL F. CROMWELL, JR.

Austin, Texas
November, 1977

*

TABLE OF CONTENTS

TABLE OF CONTENTS

†

CORRECTIONS
IN THE COMMUNITY

CHAPTER ONE

PROGRAMMING ALTERNATIVES TO INCARCERATION

INTRODUCTION

Until recently probation and parole have been the only visible and "sanctioned" forms of community based corrections. *Diverson* has been utilized informally and unofficially at all stages of the criminal justice process without being identified and labeled. *Diversion* refers to efforts to utilize alternatives to initial or continued processing into the justice system. To qualify as diversion, such efforts must be taken prior to adjudication. Diversion implies halting or suspending formal criminal or juvenile justice proceedings against a person who has violated a statute, in favor of processing through a noncriminal disposition or means.

A further extension of community corrections is the use of the community treatment facility or halfway house. Dissatisfaction with incarceration as a means of correction has grown to a point where some states have almost completely abolished incarceration for some classes of offenders. In other states, experimental programs have been successful enough that once-overcrowded prisons and reformatories are now unused. A major force in this movement has been the growth of the halfway house movement. Initially, such programs were conceived for offenders "halfway out" of institutions, as a means of easing the stresses involved in transition from rigid controls to freedom in the community. Recently, the halfway house has come to be viewed as a potential alternative to imprisonment, and thus, a program for those "halfway in" between probation and prison.

In the past decade, a number of experimental community programs have been set up in various parts of the country, differing substantially in content and structure, but all offering greater supervision and guidance

1

than the traditional probation and parole programs. The new programs take many forms ranging from the more familiar foster homes and group homes to halfway houses, "guided group interaction" programs and intensive community treatment. As such, they offer a set of alternatives between regular probation supervision and incarceration, providing more guidance than probation services commonly offer without the disruptive effects of total confinement. They also enrich the alternatives available to parole supervision. The growth and prominence of these programs are perhaps the most promising developments in corrections today.

This chapter presents the reader with various perspectives of diversion, community treatment facilities and an adjunct of each, the increasing use of restitution by the offender to the victim of his crimes. Opposing viewpoints are presented and analyzed in order that the reader may gain a comprehensive understanding of these forms of community corrections.

THE DIVERSION OF OFFENDERS *

Diversion is increasingly being suggested as a viable alternative to traditional processing of offenders through the criminal justice system. This article is in two parts. The first segment attributes the current emphasis on diversion to three factors: (1) increasing recognition of deficiencies in the nonsystem of justice, (2) rediscovery of the ancient truth that the community itself significantly impacts upon behavior, and (3) growing demands of the citizenry to be active participants in the affairs of government. The second section identifies major unresolved problem areas in the diversion process, such as the absence of guidelines for diversion fiscal complexities, political and social issues, inadequate and uneven community resources, lack of assessment or evaluation of diversion programs, and the need for redefining traditional roles.

I. ORIGINS OF DIVERSION

Although there is considerable discussion and writing by academicians, administrators, and researchers about the system of criminal and/or juvenile justice, the United States does not have a single system of justice. Each level of government, indeed each jurisdiction, has its own unique system. These many "systems"—all established to enforce the standards of conduct believed necessary for the protection of individuals and the preservation of the community—are a collectivity of some 40 thousand law enforcement agencies and a multiplicity of courts, prosecution and defense agencies, probation and parole departments, correctional institutions and related community-based organizations. It is clear that

* Robert M. Carter, "The Diversion of Offenders", *Federal Probation*, December, 1972. Reprinted with permission.

our approach to criminal and juvenile justice sacrifices much in the way of efficiency and effectiveness in order to preserve local autonomy and to protect the individual.

The many systems of justice in existence in the United States in the early 1970's are not the same as those which emerged following the American Revolution. Indeed this 200-year evolution has not been uniform or consistent; some of the innovations and changes in our systems have been generated by judicial decisions and legislative decrees; others have evolved more by chance than by design. Trial by jury and the principle of bail, for example, are relatively old and date back to our European heritage in general and the English Common Law in particular. Probation and parole began in the 19th century and the juvenile court is a 20th century innovation.

Coupled with the numerous criminal and juvenile justice arrangements in the United States and their uneven development is the separation of functions within the systems. There are similar components in all systems ranging from apprehension through prosecution and adjudication to correction. Although in fact interwoven and interdependent one with the other, these components typically function independently and autonomously. This separateness of functions, which on one hand prevents the possibility of a "police state," on the other leads to some extraordinary complex problems. Not the least of these is that the systems of justice are not integrated, coordinated, and effective entities, but rather are fragmented nonsystems with agencies tied together by the processing of an increasing number of adult and juvenile offenders. These nonsystems are marked by an unequal quality of justice, inadequate fiscal, manpower and training resources, shortages in equipment and facilities, lack of relevant research and evaluation to provide some measure of effectiveness and, until recently, a general indifference and apathy on the part of the public which the systems were designed to serve.

Society Itself Contributes to Criminal Behavior

Society deals with crime in a manner which reflects its beliefs about the nature and cause of crime. Many centuries ago, for example, when crime was believed to be the product of the possession of the mind and body by an evil spirit, the primitive response was simple: drive the devil out of the body by whatever means were available for such purposes. The American tradition as relates to the etiology of crime has focused, until recently, upon the individual as a free agent—able to choose between good and evil and aware of the differences between right and wrong. Our "treatment" of crime accordingly reflected the simplistic notion that criminality was housed solely within the psyche and soma of the offender. Regardless of whether the prevalent philosophy was revenge, retaliation, retribution or rehabilitation, the individual was seen as being of primary importance.

We have long assumed that the criminal or delinquent either willfully disregards legitimate authority by his illegal acts or suffers from some personal defect or shortcoming. There is much to learn, however, about the mysteries by which a society generates abnormal responses within its own circles. But this has become increasingly apparent: Society itself contributes significantly to such behavior. Indeed, it is the self-same social structure expressing its force and influence in an ambivalent manner which helps create on one hand the conforming individual—the person respectful of the social and legal codes—and on the other the deviant and lawbreaker who are disrespectful of the law. We have only recently become aware that crime and delinquency are symptoms of failures and disorganization of the community as well as of individual offenders. In particular, these failures may be seen as depriving offenders of contact with those social institutions which are basically responsible for assuring the development of law-abiding conduct.

Note, for example, that it has become increasingly common to discuss the "decline in respect for law and order." In every quarter, and with increasing intensity, we hear that the citizenry, for reasons as yet unclear, is not only failing to honor specific laws, but also displays a mounting disregard for the "rule of law" itself as an essential aspect of the democratic way of life. But even as this concern is echoed, it is not clear that we are all agreed as to what is meant by "decline in respect for law and order" or precisely to whom or to what we are referring. It may be that a large amount of what we observe and label as "disrespect for law" in a wide range and diversity of communities is in fact a normal reaction of normal persons to an abnormal condition or situation.

As knowledge expands to recognize the role of society in the creation of deviance, justice systems themselves will be modified. The implementation of knowledge, of course, always lags behind the development of knowledge.

Mass Disaffection by Large Segment of Population

Concurrent with the recognition that (1) the justice system is but a nonsystem and (2) the community itself has an enormous impact upon the crime problem, there has been—particularly within the past decade—the emergence of mass disaffection of a large segment of our population. This disaffection with the American system is often described in terms which suggest that citizens are not involved in decision-making and are acted upon by the government rather than impacting upon government. The disaffection has been manifested in many communities and in various ways.

We have, for example, been witness to mass civil disorder unparalleled in recent times. We have seen our young people in revolt against the war in Vietnam, the grape industry, selective service, marihuana laws, prison administration, presidential and congressional candidates, Supreme Court nominees, and Dow Chemical. We have observed rebellion against

the establishment ranging from burning ghettos and campuses everywhere to looters in the North, freedom riders in the South, and maniacal
bombers from East to West. Young and old, black and white, rich and
poor have withstood tear gas and mace, billy clubs and bullets, insults and
assaults, jail and prison in order to lie down in front of troop trains, sit-in
at university administration buildings, love-in in public parks, wade-in at
nonintegrated beaches and lie-in within legislative buildings. The establishment has been challenged on such issues as the legal-oriented entities
of the draft, the rights of Blacks to use the same rest-rooms and drinking
fountains as whites, the death penalty, and free speech. Young people
have challenged socially oriented norms with "mod" dress and hair styles,
language, rock music, end psychedelic forms, colors, and patterns. We
have seen the emergence of the hippy and yippy, the youthful drug
culture, black, yellow, red, and brown power advocates, and organizations
such as the Panthers, Women's Lib, the Third World Liberation Front,
and the Peace and Freedom Party.

But this disaffection or unrest is not restricted to youth alone.
Increasingly, adults are rebelling against the system. One need look no
further than the recent slowdowns, work stoppages, and strikes of such
tradition-oriented groups as police and fire officials, military personnel,
social workers, school teachers, and indeed even prison inmates. Adult
participation in protest has generally been more moderate than that of
youth; some have been through membership in political organizations of
a left wing orientation; others have joined conservative right wing
organizations such as the Birch Society or Minutemen. Millions of
Americans protested against the political establishment by voting for a
third or fourth party or not voting at all in the last Presidential election.

Movement Toward Diversion

These three phenomena—recognition that the community impacts
significantly upon behavior, the uncertainty as to the effectiveness or
quality of justice in the nonsystem of justice, and the growing desire of
the citizenry for active relevant and meaningful participation in every
area of governmental affairs and community life—are moving the responses to the challenge of crime in a new direction. This direction is
typically referred to as "diversion" and relates specifically to movement
away from the justice system. It is most likely a prelude to "absorption"
.   .   .   a process in which communities engage a wide variety of
deviant behavior without referral to or only minimum interaction with
the traditional establishment agencies.

Diversion is justice-system oriented and focuses upon the development of specific alternatives for the justice system processing of offenders. The diversion model and its application has been generated from a
belief that the control of crime and delinquency would be improved by
handling criminals and delinquents outside the traditional system. Diversion is also predicated upon the reported effects of the "labeling" process

and the impact of the "self-fulfilling prophecy." Whether diversion, at long range, is more effective than the established justice system and whether the "labeling" and "self-fulfilling" phenomena are operationally significant is unclear. These uncertainties do not dictate against diversion models, but rather should serve to restrain unbounded enthusiasm based upon belief and emotion rather than fact.

Absorption may be defined generally as the attempts of parents, peers, police, schools, and neighborhoods to address social problems—including those of crime and delinquency—by minimizing referral to or entry into one or more of the official governmental agencies designated to handle those manifesting deviant behavior. If there has already been a referral, absorption involves the removal of the transgressor from the official processes by offering solutions, techniques or methods of dealing with him outside of the usual agency channels. Absorption is not restricted to the criminal offender or delinquent. It is, for example, equally applicable to deviants within the educational process. Absorption is adaptive behavior within the community in which alternative strategies are developed for coping with social problems. These involve the extensive use of community and personal resources.

II. DIVERSION: SOME PRACTICAL/OPERATIONAL ISSUES

There are issues about diversion—involving both philosophy and practice—which demand in depth examination. Failure to address these completely interwoven issues is likely to result in diversion efforts which are every bit as fragmented and disjointed as those justice system practices which, in some measure, led to the diversion movement. Rather clearly, there is a need to explore operational aspects of diversion, examine the community, its role and resources and determine the latent and manifest impact of diversion on the justice system. These requirements are in fact, mandates for assessment and evaluation. There is an explicit need to: (1) Determine the guidelines and standards which define those eligible or ineligible for diversion, those agencies which are appropriate to receive those who are diverted, and programmatic activities of the agencies which receive diverted cases; (2) identify or develop, and mobilize, resources in a community, determine techniques for increasing community "tolerance" levels, enhance the delivery system for these resources and make more equitable the availability of resources to diverse types of communities; (3) determine the impact of diversion practices on the justice systems over-all as well as their component parts and examine the need for possible administrative, organizational and legal changes; (4) prepare a complete methodology for evaluating the effectiveness of diversion, keeping in mind that being "progressive" is not synonymous with being "successful."

The need for diversion guidelines is critical. Without some minimum standards for practice and procedure and general concensus or agreement on philosophy, there is a distinct possibility that diversion may become the source of continuing and substantial inequities. Basic questions—such as who is (or is not) to be diverted, by whom, on what basis, and to what programmatic activities—should be answered by some shared understandings. Without such common understandings, the justice system—through increased use of nonsystematic diversion—may become more confused, autonomous, and fragmented.

Some minimum standards are needed, for example, to guide the *selection of individuals* for diversion. Diversion practices may be exclusionary and identify types of offenders who are deemed ineligible, such as those with a history of violence or felony offenders. Or practice may be permissive and allow that all offenders who will benefit from nonjustice system treatment are to be considered eligible, regardless of other considerations. Diversion may be restricted to adjudicated offenders, or it may include nonadjudicated offenders. If the former, diversion is from the system after entry; if the latter, diversion is an alternative to entry into the system. Both raise substantial legal issues.

Determinations as to time frames are required, i. e., the optimum time for diversion, the length of time or duration of diversion, and so on. Guidelines are also needed as to actions to be taken if the person diverted fails to comply with the actual or implied conditions of diversion or if it appears that the diversion plan is inappropriate.

Meaningful standards are necessary, for the *selection of agencies* to receive those who are diverted. Diversion need not necessarily be made to private agencies; it may be appropriate for there to be diversion to those public agencies which normally have been either minimally or not at all concerned with the offender population. And it may be appropriate for diversion to be to individuals rather than agencies. The selection of agencies requires community inventories which in turn may indicate the need for new private and/or public agencies or combinations/consortiums/conglomerates of established agencies which address needs of offenders.

Of equal significance is the complex and politically sensitive problem of sifting through a wide variety of potential diversion agencies including those with "unusual" or nontraditional characteristics such as those with an ex-offender or ex-addict staff. Underlying many of these guidelines are fiscal considerations—including possible requirements for subsidies to agencies which handle those who are diverted. A delicate issue arises from public support of private agencies in terms of performance objectives and standards, constraints and expectations. The subsidy issue is made even more complex as the need arises to determine which public agency at what level of government pays the subsidies to these new partners in the justice system.

There is, of course, a requirement to examine the *programmatic activities* of the agencies which receive diverted offenders. While an inventory of these various programs and some estimate of their effectiveness are essential to rational diversion practice, a basic question emerges as to whether offenders should be diverted if appropriate (or at least similar) programs exist within the justice system. And if such programs already exist in the justice system, the advantages, if any, which accrue by transfer of these programs and clientele to community-based, nonjustice system organizations must be established.

The movement of programs and offenders to nonjustice system organizations will require new roles for justice and nonjustice system personnel. As an example, the probation or parole officer realistically might be required to become a catalyst and seek to activate a community and its caretakers to absorb the offender as a member of that community. This would require a complete knowledge of community resources and diagnosis of clientele needs. There would be an emphasis on reducing the alienation of the offender from his community by impairing the continued maintenance of a criminal identity and encouraging a community identity. The officer would no longer find employment for the offender, but instead direct him into the normal channels of job seeking in the community. Residential, marital, medical, financial or other problems would be addressed by assisting the offender engage those community resources which deal with these problem areas. This new role, then, might be one of insuring a process of community, not correctional absorption. Again illustrating interrelationships of these issues, note that the "new role" phenomenon itself raises questions about training for and acceptance of the role and methods or techniques of implementation.

Imbalance in Community Resources a Problem

Other issues arise as one examines the role and resources of the community. Not at all insignificant is the complex issue of imbalance among communities to accept cases which are diverted and to provide necessary services and resources. Some communities have distinct economic advantages over others—and it is clear that diversion has an economic, as well as a motivation base. Middle- and upper-class communities and their citizens, socially and economically secure, often have internal financial resources available to mobilize a wide range of agencies of diversion or specialized services ranging from psychiatric care through private schools. The differences in resource levels need scrutiny, for it would be socially disastrous to deny diversion to those who are economically disadvantaged; diversion cannot be restricted to the affluent. Without action to balance resource requirements with the capacity of delivering services, the poor and the disadvantaged will continue to flow into and through the justice agencies.

A parallel community-based problem occurs where there is a low community tolerance for diversion. How is community tolerance to be increased? A simple demonstration of need may be insufficient. Numerous examples of low or non-tolerance may be cited ranging from open through latent resistance and hostility directed against self-help groups and agency halfway houses. And besides the very difficult "how," there is the related question of "who" is responsible for dealing with community fears and anxieties. Is every justice agency seeking to divert offenders responsible for its own resource development or is some overall plan among cooperating justice agencies more rational? And again, as one question leads to another, if a plan is necessary, who designs and implements it, and how are activities financed and monitored?

Diversion Will Result in Significant Changes

Although changes in justice systems are inevitable consequences of an increased use of diversion, there is a distinct probability that the changes will be both unplanned and unsystematic. These changes may range from administrative and organizational restructuring and modification in procedure and policy on one hand through major changes in the populations which are serviced by the justice systems on the other.

As justice agencies become partners with communities, there may be requirements in all agencies for organizational change to include new bureaus or divisions of "community service." This would require new personnel or reassignment of personnel, development and acceptance of new roles such as those of diagnostician and/or catalyst, innovative training, perhaps additional funding and different kinds of facilities, and new understandings within the agencies and communities themselves. Permanent linkages with community organizations may be required. Traditional pyramid, hierarchical organizational models may have to be flattened. New information systems will be required, and continuing involvement or monitoring of diverted cases may be desirable.

The large scale diversion of offenders—either from or after entry into the justice system—may have other consequences for the justice agencies. If, for example, substantial numbers of offenders are diverted by local law enforcement to community-based agencies, there will be, in all likelihood, reduced inputs to prosecution, adjudication and correctional agencies. Lessened inputs will alleviate some of the backlog in the judicial system and reduce caseload pressure in probation and parole and size of institutional population. While these occurrences are desirable, at some point in time the bureaucratic instinct for survival may be threatened. Reactions protective of the establishment may set in. Of greater significance, however, is that increased diversion may leave the justice system with a unique clientele of hardened, recalcitrant, difficult offenders who seem unlikely to "make it" in the community. These offenders may have complex problems requiring long-range treatment and they may represent a major threat to and be rejected by their communities. In addition to creating major management problems, these offenders will require new and different programs, facilities and staff for treatment. In short, extensive diversion may not only "threaten" the justice establishment, it may change the justice system population and alter the system itself.

Planning and Evaluation Necessary

There are yet other important aspects of diversion which require attention—planning and evaluation. A lack of mid-range and strategic planning and systematic evaluation has long been a major defect in justice operations from law enforcement through corrections. The movement toward diversion of offenders mandates that planning and evaluation not be "tacked on" to operational processes, but rather be built-in, continually [...]

[...] The questions about planning a[...] [...]e established, funds must be m[...] [...]ardware must be obtained, m[...] [...]neated. Without such plan- ni[...] [...]at diversion practices will pr[...] [...]rity and consistency.

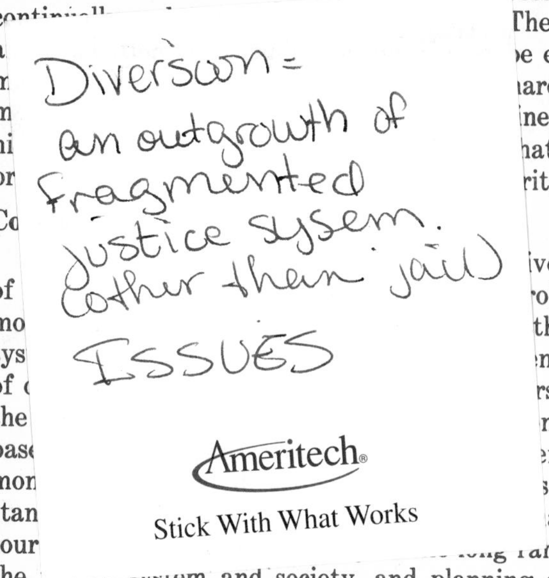

Co[...]

[handwritten note: Diversion = an outgrowth of Fragmented Justice system. (other than jail)]

[handwritten: ISSUES]

[Ameritech logo — Stick With What Works]

of [...] [...]version and identified some mo[...] [...]oblems associated with the sys[...] [...]th of a fragmented justice of [...] [...]nt, the increasing demands the [...] [...]rs of government including base[...] [...]mmunity is an appropriate mor[...] [...]en as there is increasing stan [...] [...]sing need for guidelines, sour[...] [...]ation of the role and re- [...] [...]ong range impact of diversion on the justice system and society, and planning and evaluation.

Diversion is both a challenge and an opportunity. As a potentially major mechanism of the justice system, diversion requires considered attention. Although changes in our justice systems are indicated, rapid movement to untested and ill-defined alternatives is inappropriate.

ISSUES AND REALITIES IN POLICE DIVERSION PROGRAMS *

With the publication of the reports of the President's Commission on Law Enforcement and Administration of Justice in 1967, the word "diversion"—with attendant variations in definition and practice—came into vogue. By 1971, enough discussion and planning of juvenile diversion programs had taken place to permit an assessment of diversion issues facing law enforcement agencies willing to consider involvement in these programs. Within the next five years, enough experience in carrying out police diversion programs for juveniles was logged to permit an assessment both of those issues identified in 1971 and of certain realities as they have appeared since. This paper will comment on both the 1971 issues and the current realities.

* Malcolm W. Klein, *Crime and Delinquency*, Oct. 1976. Reprinted by permission of the National Council on Crime and Delinquency.

In an extensive paper written in 1971,[1] I listed eleven issues that were directly pertinent to police juvenile diversion programs. Nine of these seem worthy of review and updating now. In addition, another five issues have emerged in a review of current police diversion programs and will be treated here.

We start with definitions of *diversion* and *referral* as these terms are used here:

. ☞ By *diversion* we shall mean "any process employed by components of the criminal justice system (police, prosecution, courts, correction) to turn suspects and/or offenders away from the formal system or to a 'lower' level of the system."[2]

By *referral* we shall mean "any process by which a diverting agent initiates the connection of the diverted suspect or offender to another agent or agency, usually within the offender's community. Thus referral goes beyond the most common police diversion practice of 'station adjustment,' 'warning,' or 'counsel and release,' in which the youngster is released without further significant action. A police officer who *refers* a youngster takes active steps to attach that youngster to someone else for preventive, rehabilitative, or reintegrative purposes."[3]

Thus one can divert either *without* a referral to a community agency or *with* a referral. Even with a referral, there is no guarantee of either an initial or a lasting contact between youth and agency.

As we turn now to discuss the initial 1971 issues and then the emerging issues, these definitions and distinctions will assume considerable importance.

1971 ISSUES

1. *Appropriateness.*—In the earlier paper, nine pages were devoted to arguments for and against the appropriateness of diversion activities to the enforcement mandate. The point is now moot; almost every police department diverts some portion of its arrested juvenile population. Further, diversion *with referral* is now a common practice. In one large metropolitan area investigated by the writer and his colleagues, 33 out of 49 departments said they were involved in referral activities in 1974, and regional plans existed to add to that number in 1975. Police have clearly decided that diversion and referral *are* appropriate to their mandate.

1. Prepared originally as curriculum material for a training program for Juvenile Bureau Commanders, the paper has since appeared as Section VII: Malcolm W. Klein, "Issues in Police Diversion of Juvenile Offenders: A Guide for Discussion," in Gary B. Adams et al., eds., *Juvenile Justice Management* (Springfield, Ill.: Charles C. Thomas, 1973), pp. 375–422, and in Robert M. Carter and Malcolm W. Klein, eds., *Back on the Street: The Diversion of Juvenile Offenders* (Englewood Cliffs, N.J.: Prentice-Hall 1975), pp. 73–104.

2. Klein, supra note 1, p. 376.

3. Ibid.

2. *Separatism.*—Is it best or most "proper" for the police to remain somewhat separate from the community and other components of the formal justice system such as the courts and probation? A system, after all, can be conceived of either as coordinated but separate units or as integrated units. Diversion involvements, interestingly, are being employed in both ways.

In some instances we find police diversion programs bringing about greater integration. Within the system, the most common form this takes is the placement of probation or court intake personnel within the police department to bring about mutually agreeable decisions on who shall be diverted. With respect to the community, we find numerous instances of police seeking out and activating more referral resources and, usually, developing feedback systems between community agencies and themselves. The follow-through and accountability thus achieved clearly increase the level of police/community integration.

By way of contrast, we also find programs which rather explicitly divert and refer to place the responsibility for the referred youngster in someone else's hands, usually a community agency. The police thus "wash their hands" of responsibility via diversion. Typically, this approach is accompanied by a short fuse on repeat offenders; one police contact or one referral is all that is allowed before the filing of a petition.

3. *Court Decisions.*—By 1971, decisions expanding the rights of juveniles—especially the *Gault* decision—set the stage for police to handle juvenile offenders more like adults, even though *Gault* did not pertain directly to police operations. Diversion procedures have abetted this trend by opening up referral as an acceptable disposition for cases which won't meet the rigors of a court test but seem to the police officer to require more than simple release. Noncriminal and first-offense cases can be expected to be dismissed by court, intake, and prosecution officials. Referral of such cases to a community agency has come along to give the appearance, and perhaps the reality, of an alternative disposition effective in reducing recidivism.

4. *Normalization.*—This term refers to the reaction to an act as if it were "normal" (for the circumstances, the times, etc.). Many acts, while technically delinquent, are altogether normal for developing adolescents and can, therefore, in the view of many, be overlooked by police. The development of more diversion/referral programs has, if anything, reduced normalization responses by police because there is now less of a distinction between acting and not acting, between normalizing and arresting or booking. Referral to community resources is now a more salient alternative for officers who previously could not justify *formal* arrest procedures but would like to respond to minor delinquency.

5. *Diversion Criteria.*—To increase the number of youngsters diverted away from the justice system, a true diversion program must *by definition* reach for its clients further into the pool of arrestable, booka-

ble, petitionable offenders. Since this means the release of a greater proportion of serious cases, criteria other than the seriousness of the instant offense come more into play. One would expect greater reliance to be placed on prior record, family situation, and judgments of "treatability." In particular, the client's and his parents' attitudes toward participation in an agency program have become crucial to the discretionary decision to divert.

6. *Community Tolerance.*—The point was made in the 1971 paper that greater diversion requires either an already tolerant community, willing to absorb these youngsters, or greater activity by the police diverters toward creating a sufficient tolerance level. Our earlier interviews made it abundantly clear that most juvenile officers defined such activity (the activation of community absorption or deliberate attempts to increase tolerance for the presence of diverted offenders) as beyond the proper role of the police. A number went further, saying that it was inappropriate to law enforcement or even that it defeated enforcement goals.

Now, however, we find many police diversion programs *featuring* a pro-active police role in the community. Tied in very directly with the ethos which has led to greater numbers of police-community relations programs, we find officers urging agencies to accept diverted offenders, helping to establish new agency programs, and even organizing (as well as seeking grant funds for) multi-community diversion and referral programs. Under some diversion programs, police are almost literally going out into the community and "drumming up business." To the extent that this is true, it represents a significant departure from recent traditions.

7. *Absorption Mechanisms.*—The earlier paper summarized the characteristics of community agencies pertinent to the police (in their own view) as falling under the headings of *acceptability, suitability, availability,* and *accountability.* No particular change has taken place in the first three: police views of what makes a good referral agency have not changed substantially. However, making more referrals has led a number of diverting departments—but clearly not all of them—to institute procedures to make agencies account for what happens to the referred offender. This means offender-agency contacts in most cases, and in some it includes treatment plans and follow-through as well. In a few programs, some including purchase-of-service arrangements, it even means reporting by the agencies to the police on behavioral outcomes such as school performance and recidivism. Departments which insist upon agency accountability are protecting themselves against a new source of frustration while at the same time taking responsibility for their own involvements. Departments involved in diversion that are *not* concerning themselves with accountability can hardly be said to be taking their new activities very seriously.

8. *Old Stigma for New.*—The issue raised here was whether avoidance of delinquent or criminal labels via diversion might not lead via referral to new labels of disturbed, mentally ill, and so on. Most of the referral agencies employed by the police belong to mental health, welfare, or special education systems which can also stigmatize their clients. Let the reader ask whether, as a youngster, he would rather have been thought of as a "sick kid" than as a "bad kid."

On this issue, we have detected no growth in concern or resolution since the 1971 paper. The questions of alternative stigma, the substitution of one for the other, the impact of other stigma on recidivism or other subsequent behaviors, or the moral implications inherent here simply have not taken substantive form in police diversion programs. At this point, there simply is too little concern or too much of a presumption that psychological "help" *offered* is help *received.*

9. *The Impact of Stigmatization.*—Almost all diversion programs assume, indeed aver, that avoidance of the unnecessary stigmatization which accompanies processing through the juvenile justice system will help to prevent the furtherance of delinquent careers. But proposals for diversion programs have seldom sought supportive evidence (at best they would find conflicting evidence), and the programs ordinarily make only feeble *pro forma* attempts to collect such evidence from their own activities. Program funders and program administrators alike are at fault here, at fault for years of inexcusable waste.

This brings us up to date on previously identified issues. A fair summary might be that diversion is leading police departments into a somewhat broader focus in the handling of delinquents, breaking down some old inhibitions to some extent, but that this trend is tentative and still superficial. It would take little to swing the pendulum back.

Whether or not the pendulum does swing back may depend a good deal on additional issues that have emerged from a review of several dozen diversion programs undertaken by the writer and his colleagues. Five of these will be mentioned, and the reader will readily see that they are both interconnected and clearly related to the 1971 list.

CURRENT REALITIES

1. *Resource Location.*—An issue that seems to symbolize important value orientations is whether the referral resource—usually a counselor or referral agent—should be located physically within the police department or within a community setting. More pertinent to smaller departments with fewer potential referral cases, this issue revolves around control of the counselors, maintenance of a stance of deterrence versus rehabilitation, direct accountability, and avoidance of justice system stigmatization.

In-house systems take several forms. A juvenile or other police officer may receive special training in counseling and then be assigned the counselor role. A social worker may be hired on departmental (or grant) funds to serve the counselor function, reporting to or under the supervision of a police official. A social worker from a community agency may be physically placed within the department but retains his paid position in the agency. Finally, in a rare instance, the police department may operate its own "agency," staffed by officers and counselors paid by departmental (or grant) funds. This "agency" is usually located somewhere other than at police headquarters.

There is also a variation of the in-house approach in which the diversion role is one of a referral agent only, referring offenders to outside agencies but not doing any counseling at all. This is really closer to the typical external system, wherein police refer offenders either to one of a series of agencies or to a "clearing house" which does the final referring. In most of these instances, the counselors are paid by and responsible to their own agencies. If police want to increase accountability to the department, they may work out purchase-of-service arrangements whereby agency fees for counseling of diverted offenders are controlled by the police.[4]

2. *Locus of Control.*—The internal vs. external placement of diversion counselors is closely related to the question of where administrative control (and accountability) should be lodged. The police either apprehend or take over control of juvenile offenders. In making discretionary judgments about case dispositions, they believe that their decisions may deter further delinquency or, conversely, have no deterrent effect at all. Because they have faith in their judgments, they don't want deterrent effects "blown" by someone else—such as agency or probation personnel—who may not share their views. Thus many police in diversion programs seek as much control over the counseling operation as possible. Failing this, they want to be in a position to "blow the whistle" on ineffective counseling by withdrawing support, funds, or the client population.

For their part, many community agencies are nervous about police or justice system control. They fear regimentation, a narrow focus on recidivism rather than more general personal adjustment, and stigmatization of their own programs by association with enforcement officials. Many counselors and agency administrators believe further that some youngsters will shy away from a police-connected program and that others will fail to establish good rapport with the counselors for fear of having their acts reported to the police.

There are other problems as well, touching upon autonomy, value orientations, mutual trust, local governmental and political practices, and so on. The end point of each, however, seems to be program control. Each program now in existence has had to resolve this issue, sometimes with ease and sometimes after considerable struggle. Which view is

---

4. There are two basic variations. The first is a straight fee-for-service agreement. The second is a split fee, part on acceptance of the offender-client and part payable upon "success" (for example, no recidivism for six months).

"right" or "wrong," if we are to judge by program impact, cannot be known until impact data have been carefully designed and collected.

3. *Diversion or Business as Usual.*—Three operational meanings of diversion have surfaced in the past few years. The first involves an expansion of the released population by diverting away from court. That is, cases ordinarily slated for petitions are instead released (usually with referrals). This is "true" diversion above and beyond that normally undertaken.

The second operational meaning is referral, where diversion and referral are synonymous terms. The emphasis is on initiating and increasing the numbers of offenders referred for counseling or other help. This meaning is not "true diversion," in that it does not involve diverting more offenders *away from* the justice system, although it does nevertheless imply a departure from past practices. To that extent, it is new.

The third and by no means uncommon meaning of the term "diversion" is the minor referral operation that some police departments have been using for several years. In some instances it may have meant a few referrals a month; with the advent of federal funds, this is suddenly called "diversion" and entitles the department to participate in spending those funds. On occasion this is done unwittingly, with no fraudulent intent. In some instances we suspect that funders are being deliberately misled; in others, there is the distinct possibility that they are in on the game, sacrificing legislative intent for local strategy. It is in instances such as these that strict attention to the *definition* of diversion and referral would help keep the lines straight and the strategies aboveboard.

4. *The "Bumped" Client.*—In most instances, police diversion programs do not organize new referral agencies. Rather, they refer offenders to acceptable agencies already operating in the community, agencies with an established track record. In many instances, the referred offender presents a different profile from the usual agency client and, of course, constitutes an additional caseload. What, then, happens to the "ordinary" or usual clientele of these agencies?

We have undertaken no analysis of this question, nor have we seen any. However, observation in several agencies and the design of at least one regional plan in our purview suggests that many ordinary clients are being "bumped" or given less treatment or inferior treatment in favor of the diverted offenders. This is particularly true—and perhaps almost exclusively true—of agencies entering into purchase-of-service agreements. When agencies are paid to take on offender clients, they may reasonably be expected to heed the desires of the payer. When asked to comment on this problem, one program funder/planner responded "That's the way the cookie crumbles." The comment speaks for itself; the bumped client usually can't.

5. *Funding and Stability.*—Most of the formal police diversion programs are supported primarily by special federal or state funds, though

often with a small local "match." These funds will not long be used for these purposes: pilot projects are eventually terminated, funding priorities change, and political exigencies shift. So the question arises: will the police continue to participate in diversion/referral programs once they must depend on municipal funding alone?

While an analysis of past programing in the juvenile field does not make us hopeful, somewhat clearer evidence is available. A new program trying to move from outside to inside funding must compete with other priorities and it must establish itself within the permanent departmental structure. As to competition, we find little in our survey of existing diversion programs to suggest that they are anything but low priority items. Juvenile matters are rather low on the police totem pole; diversion gets low priority even within that status.

Second, in very few departments have we detected *structural* changes to accommodate diversion. In most instances, new units are not established, additional staff are not assigned, work routines are not substantially altered, lines of supervision are not shifted, etc. This is significantly less true of large departments but it is nonetheless the dominant pattern. *Diversion has been appended rather than incorporated.* Among the police, we predict for it a short, inconclusive life.

PREDICTING THE EFFECTS OF PRETRIAL INTERVENTION PROGRAMS ON JAIL POPULATIONS *

County jail populations throughout the country have been increasing at an alarming rate. The resulting overpopulation of the jails has been a concern of law enforcement personnel and taxpayers alike. One response to the dilemma has been to construct either new or expanded jail facilities. Planning for these facilities is usually based on the assumption that the jail population will continue to steadily increase each year at a rate consistent with increments in prior years. This response not only ignores changes in detention policies which could potentially reduce jail populations, but also has several possible negative consequences. First of all, historically this resolution of expanding or building new facilities has tended to result in a further increase of the jail population. It is well known that, regardless of the size of a facility, the creators of a setting can rapidly acquire enough persons to reach capacity. A second negative consequence is that this kind of shortsighted response to the immediate crisis serves to divert a community's energies from developing and implementing innovative solutions that might permanently decrease jail

* Ronald Roesch, *Federal Probation*, December 1976. Reprinted by permission.

populations.　Sarason[1] has expanded on the notion that buildings serve to distract attention from other solutions.　He states:

> .　.　.　the unexamined assumption that buildings are necessary is a bar to the recognition of the relationship between values, resources, and public policy.　Put in another way: in the area of human service putting up new buildings tends to perpetuate the problem of limited resources, contributes to the inadequate services they ordinarily provide, and separates the setting from the larger society.[2]

It seems clear that the decision to construct a new facility is not usually based on a careful evaluation of all potential alternatives.　Once the decision has been made other alternatives will undoubtedly not be implemented since money and other resources will be used to create and maintain the larger facility.　Also, the necessity of justifying the need for a facility by keeping the population close to capacity runs counter to alternatives which serve to potentially decrease the jail population.　For example, alternatives to traditional bail practices such as increased use of release on recognizance, pretrial diversion, and expediting criminal case disposition are three possible alternative solutions for confronting the problem of increasing jail populations.　This article demonstrates a method by which the short-term and long-term effects of these three alternatives on the jail population can be predicted.　While there are other reasons for implementing these programs, such as the positive effects for defendants, reduced recidivism and so on, this article deals only with the predictable and measurable effects that implementation of the above three alternatives could have on pretrial jail populations.

RELEASE ON RECOGNIZANCE

Release on recognizance (ROR) programs were initiated to provide alternatives to cash bail with obvious advantages to indigents and others unable to raise the funds for release.　A method developed by the Vera Institute of Justice[3] has been shown to be a useful tool for increasing the use of ROR without a subsequent increase in the rate of failure to appear in court.[4]　The release recommendation is based on an assessment of a defendant's prior record, family and community ties, health, employment or school information and length of residence in the community.　The verified information is scored by assigning numerical weights to each area and, depending on the total score, a recommendation for release or detainment is made.　It was recently estimated that over 150 similar

1.　S. B. Sarason, *The Creation of Settings and the Future Societies.*　San Francisco: Jossey-Bass, 1972.

2.　Id., p. 160.

3.　C. Ares, A. Rankin, and H. Sturz, "The Manhattan Bail Project: An Interim Report on the Use of Pretrial Parole," *New York University Law Review,* 1963, 38, 67–95.

4.　M. T. Nietzel and J. T. Dade, "Bail Reform as an Example of a Community Psychology Intervention in a Criminal Justice System," *American Journal of Community Psychology,* 1973, 1, 238–247.

projects have been implemented throughout the country.[5] The National Center for State Courts[6] recently published a review of the effects of pretrial release programs. They cited an unpublished national survey of 20 cites conducted by Wayne Thomas. This survey showed that between 1962 and 1971, the number of defendants released on noncash bonds rose from less than 5 percent to about 23 percent. Concurrently, the number of defendants released by all possible methods increased from about 47 percent to 67 percent for felony defendants, while released misdemeanor defendants increased from 60 percent to 72 percent. Clearly, bail reform has had an impact on jail populations.

PRETRIAL DIVERSION

Pretrial diversion programs attempt to intervene at an early point with defendants by diverting some, usually low risk, defendants out of the legal system. Increased use of pretrial diversion has been recommended by the American Bar Association,[7] the Corrections Task Force of the National Advisory Commission on Criminal Justice Standards and Goals,[8] and numerous other groups and organizations. It is estimated that there are about 50 such programs presently in operation.[9] Most of these programs focus on first and in some cases second offenders, charged with less serious offenses. Thus, these programs divert offenders who would most likely receive probation if they were normally processed through the courts. However, the intervention, usually through referral to community resources, occurs much earlier and perhaps more importantly, successful participants do not have a record of conviction. It should be noted that, unlike bail alternative programs, there is little empirical support that pretrial diversion is an effective alternative,[10] largely because of a lack of appropriate control groups. Nevertheless, a pretrial diversion program may have an important effect on jail populations.

5. See the President's Commission, *The Challenge of Crime in a Free Society*, Washington, D.C., 1967, p. 131; P. B. Wice, *Freedom for Sale: A National Study of Pretrial Release*. Lexington, Massachusetts: Lexington Books, 1974.

6. National Center for State Courts, *An Evaluation of Policy Related Research on the Effectiveness of Pretrial Release Programs*. Denver, Colorado: National Center for State Courts, 1975.

7. American Bar Association Commission on Correctional Facilities and Services, *Diversion From the Criminal Justice System*, Washington, D.C., 1972.

8. Report of the Corrections Task Force of the National Advisory Commission on Criminal Justice Standards and Goals.

9. R. Rovner-Pieczenik, *Pretrial Intervention Strategies: An Evaluation of Policy-Related Research and Policymaker Guidelines*. Washington, D.C.: American Bar Association, 1974.

10. J. Mullen, K. Carlson, R. Earle, C. Blew, and L. Li, *Pretrial Services: An Evaluation of Policy Related Research*, Cambridge, Massachusetts: Abt Associates, 1974; R. Roesch, "Pretrial Interventions in the Criminal Justice System," in T. R. Sarbin and L. Hessol (eds.), *Crime in a Class Society*, New York: Human Sciences Press, 1976, in preparation.

EXPEDITING DISPOSITION

A third method for lowering a jail population is to decrease the length of time between arrest and disposition. For example, in Clark County, Nevada, the average pretrial length of stay was 186 days in 1974. If this time interval were reduced the effect on the average daily population would be substantial. The *Courts Guidelines* of the National Advisory Commission on Criminal Justice Standards and Goals[11] has recommended a 60-day maximum time from arrest to trial. If 30 days additional time is considered necessary for the sentencing process, then a total of 90 days (plus the length of trial) from arrest to final disposition would be appropriate. Hickey[12] has recently detailed several methods for reducing delay. Some methods are costly, such as increasing the judicial and prosecution staff. Other methods involve minimal costs. For example, plea bargaining is the most frequent method of case disposition in most communities. Prosecutors, however, typically wait until just prior to the scheduled trial date to enter into negotiation with the defendant and/or defense attorney. Defendants unable to obtain release must remain incarcerated during this period. The plea bargaining process could be moved up without increasing the prosecution staff. The major obstacle to this change is that the immediacy of trial may be facilitative of plea bargaining. The influence of this issue can be evaluated if the practice were implemented.

The utility of each of these alternatives will vary from community to community. It would be useful to have estimates of their impact on present and future jail populations so that appropriate planning of facility and program needs can be made. A method for obtaining these estimates is presented below. It should be emphasized that this article is intended to illustrate a potential model for considering the effects of pretrial alternatives on jail populations. The model and results presented here should not be considered a definitive statement of these effects but rather should be used to facilitate collection of similar data in other communities. Several design limitations weaken the generalizability of the findings of this study. These issues are reviewed and methods for improving the data collection are discussed so that future studies can serve to extend the utility of the planning model.

METHOD

Subjects.—Subjects were unsentenced defendants in two county jail systems located in Harris County, Texas (Downtown Jail), and Clark County, Nevada. The Harris County population was drawn largely from

11. *Courts Task Force Report.* National Advisory Commission on Criminal Justice Standards and Goals, Washington, D.C., 1973.

12. W. L. Hickey, "Depopulating the Jails," *Crime and Delinquency Literature*, 1975, 7, 234–255.

Houston, while Clark County received most of its population from Las Vegas. Unsentenced defendants were defined as those who were under investigation, awaiting trial, or awaiting sentencing. In Clark County the total number of subjects was 73 which represented approximately 25 percent of the total unsentenced population. The total sample in Harris County was 400 which represented approximately 50 percent of the total unsentenced population.

Questionnaire.—A 69-item self-administered questionnaire was given to presentence defendants in both facilities as part of a survey of local jails conducted by the National Clearinghouse for Criminal Justice Planning and Architecture.[13] The questionnaire contained all of the items from the Manhattan Bail Project Interview, as well as other background information necessary to determine diversion eligibility and length of detention. Presentence defendants volunteered to complete the questionnaire. All data were collected in 1 day.[14] The questionnaire data were not verified.

Procedure.—The criteria developed by the Manhattan Bail Project[15] were used to determine release on recognizance (ROR) eligibility. Each of five areas (prior record, residence, health, family and community ties, and employment or educational history) is assigned a numerical score. For example, being employed full-time for 1 year or more would receive a score of 4. Scores for each area are added; a score of 6 or more is needed for an ROR recommendation. Regardless of the total score, only those defendants who were charged with misdemeanors or nonviolent felonies and who were residents of the county in which they were incarcerated were considered eligible for a recommendation.

Pretrial diversion eligibility was determined by the following criteria: A defendant had to be charged with a misdemeanor or nonviolent felony. Further, a prior felony conviction would exclude a defendant from eligibility.[16] Finally, all eligible defendants had to be residents of the county in which they were incarcerated. These eligibility criteria are consistent with the quantifiable criteria used in many diversion projects. They do not take into account less tangible factors such as subjective selection criteria used by project staff and defendant motivation. Zimr-

13. During 1974 and 1975 the National Clearinghouse developed comprehensive master plans for the State of Nevada and for Harris County, Texas. The data used in this study were collected as part of these plans.

14. A more precise estimate of the effects of the three programs could be obtained by administering the questionnaire at several time intervals.

15. Vera Institute of Justice, "The Manhattan Bail Project," In *Programs in*

Criminal Justice Reform. New York: Vera Institute of Justice, 1972.

16. The criteria for diversion eligibility vary considerably from project to project. "No prior felony convictions" was chosen to illustrate the use of this method; other more or less stringent criteria can be employed. This is also true for calculating length of stay prior to trial. Longer time intervals could be substituted to show how different time intervals affect the jail population.

ing,[17] for example, found that 14 percent of the defendants eligible for the Manhattan Court Employment Project rejected participation. Thus, the diversion estimates may be slightly inflated.

A 90-day average length of incarceration prior to sentencing was used as the standard for estimating the effects of reducing the delay between arrests and disposition. This average includes 60 days prior to trial (or other disposition) and an additional 30 days for sentencing. The proposed length was then compared with the average length of incarceration for the sample population. Suppose, for example, that the presentence average length of incarceration was 180 days for a population of 400 presentence defendants. Reducing this to 90 days would result in doubling the number of defendants that could be held in the facility during the 180-day period.

The potential impact of the three interventions was determined separately for each county population. Two population forecasts are necessary to estimate the effects of the interventions. The first forecast is an estimate of the jail population given no changes in existing detention practices. The following procedure was used to calculate this figure. The average daily unsentenced population was obtained for each jail for the years 1970 to 1973, inclusive. In order to determine the incarceration rate in relation to the county population, the U.S. Bureau of Census statistics were consulted for each county. The incarceration rate for each year (1970–1973) was then found by dividing the average daily unsentenced jail population by the county population. This ratio is an incarceration rate per number of citizens in the population. Future jail needs were then estimated by applying the average incarceration rate for the 4-year period to estimates of the county population for the years 1975, 1980, 1985, and 1990. This forecast of the future unsentenced populations is thus based on data that reflect the existing detention practices in that it is based on the current length of incarceration between arrest and sentencing, pretrial release alternatives and the rate of incarceration. Changes in these practices would be expected to alter these projections. This revised projection was found by applying the percentage of unsentenced defendants who qualified for each of the three interventions to the estimated jail populations projected to 1990. These estimates were calculated separately for each intervention. Finally, the cumulative impact of implementing all three interventions concurrently was determined. This cumulative impact on the presentence jail population was determined by first considering ROR eligibility, then diversion, and finally reducing court delay. Eligibility for one form of release excluded consideration from subsequent ones so that no defendant was counted twice.

17. F. E. Zimring, "Measuring the Impact of Pretrial Diversion From the Criminal Justice System," *University of* *Chicago Law Review,* 1974, 41, 224–241.

RESULTS

An ROR project in Clark County would have a minimal effect on the unsentenced population (figure 1). The average daily population was about 284 unsentenced defendants in 1975, a figure which is expected to reach 443 by 1990. This population would be reduced only about 8 percent if an ROR project were introduced.

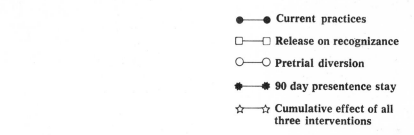

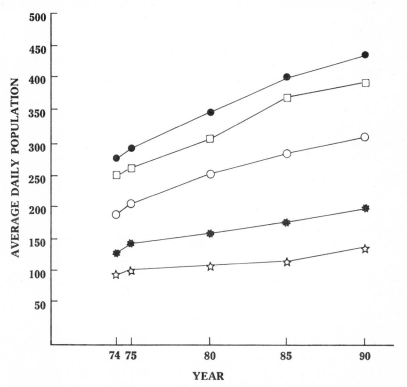

Figure 1. County jail population projections for Clark County, Nevada, comparing the predicted unsentenced population reduction resulting from three pretrial interventions with the population expected if no changes in incarceration practices occur.

[B6771]

The reduction in Harris County is more significant (figure 2). In 1975 Harris County had an unsentenced average daily population of 881, with 1,605 defendants expected by 1990. ROR could potentially reduce this population by about one-third.

Pretrial diversion was found to have a large impact on both jail populations. In 1975 there was an average of 284 unsentenced defendants in the Clark County jail. This population could be immediately reduced to 206, if diversion were available as an alternative (figure 1). By 1990 this would suggest a reduction of 27 percent in the unsentenced population. Harris County shows a similar decrease. Instead of the estimated 1,605 defendants in jail by 1990 there would be 1,186, a decrease of 26 percent.

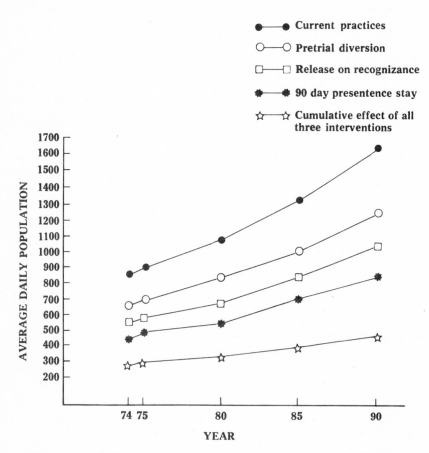

Figure 2. County jail population projections for Harris County, Texas, comparing the predicted unsentenced population reduction resulting from three pretrial interventions with the population expected if no changes in incarceration practices occur.

[B6772]

Reducing the length of time between arrests and final disposition would obviously be expected to have an effect on the unsentenced population. Figure 1 shows the expected reduction in Clark County, assuming a total of 90 days between arrests and disposition. The estimate clearly shows a substantial reduction in the unsentenced population. This was also found to be true in Harris County (figure 2).

The population projections thus far assumed each intervention was implemented independent of the remaining interventions. However, one could also analyze the effects on the unsentenced population if all three interventions were implemented in the sequential fashion suggested above, (i. e., if ROR is not granted then consider diversion; if both ROR and diversion are not granted then consider reducing length of incarceration prior to sentencing). Figure 1 shows this effect for Clark County. As expected all three programs operating at the same time has a dramatic effect on the population. The 1990 average daily population would drop from 443 to only 260, a difference of 41 percent. The Harris County population could potentially be only one-third the size it is currently predicted to reach (figure 2).

DISCUSSION

Several cautions need to be considered regarding the subjects used in this analysis. Since the questionnaires were completed on a voluntary basis the results are possibly unrepresentative of the presentence population. The questionnaire return rates of 25 and 50 percent are low and should be increased in future studies. Furthermore, the information on which the predictions were based was unverified, which could result in inflated estimates. Of course, this potential source of error can be evaluated by verifying the information of a random sample of the total subjects. Finally, the predicted reductions resulting from each intervention, and especially the reduction expected given concurrent availability of all three alternatives, assumes optimal conditions rarely met in practice.

Given these cautions the analysis of unsentenced defendants incarcerated in Clark (Nevada) and Harris (Texas) County jails showed that many inmates could potentially be released via three pretrial interventions that are presently in operation throughout the country. Each intervention was shown to have measurable effects on the present and future unsentenced populations. It seems clear that such programs can be effective alternatives to jail construction since they minimize the number of persons held prior to trial and/or sentencing.[18]

18. The Harris County projections were recently presented in a class action suit brought by Harris County jail inmates challenging the unnecessary detention and resulting overcrowded conditions in the jail. The judge ruled in favor of the inmates and issued a court order for the increased use of ROR and other pretrial programs which could potentially decrease the jail population. Furthermore, the judge, in response to some local officials' contention that a new or expanded facility was needed to meet the problems of overcrowding,

The three interventions chosen for this analysis had similar effects in both counties, with the exception of a release on recognizance program intervention which had a minimal effect on the Clark County population. It appears that those persons eligible for ROR had already obtained their release through more traditional methods. However, this is not to say that ROR would not be a useful program in Clark County. Many defendants could have depleted their financial resources when they obtained release through a bail bondsman. This could result in an increased necessity for public defenders, at a considerable cost to the County.

One of the major obstacles to increasing the use of alternatives to construction is simply that many communities have not considered these alternatives as possible solutions. This may be due to the fact that decisionmakers are unaware of the potential impact of these alternatives on jail populations. Thus, decisions are made to construct new facilities because construction is the most obvious solution. This article has illustrated that several interventions can be implemented which will tend to decrease the number of defendants requiring detention prior to sentencing. Implementing and operating these interventions are far less expensive than incarceration, especially considering the cost of new construction. Communities planning for future jail needs should follow the lead of Harris County, Texas, in demanding the exploration of all possible solutions to the jail population crisis. At a minimum, Federal and/or State guidelines should be developed to assist communities in evaluating their options.[19] These guidelines could prove to be a significant factor in the creation of a more rational, empirical, and innovative approach to the problems of overcrowding in today's jails.

WILL DIVERSION REDUCE RECIDIVISM? *

Arrests of persons under the age of eighteen have doubled over the past eight years. Individuals between twelve and eighteen make up only one-tenth of the total population but account for nearly one-fourth of all persons arrested. Of all persons arrested for serious offenses, nearly half are under eighteen.[1]

ruled that no construction could take place until alternatives to construction had been fully explored.

19. The National Clearinghouse for Criminal Justice Planning and Architecture, an agency funded by LEAA, has served this function for several years when communities requested assistance or Federal funds for new construction. However, if funds for jail construction come from local or State re-sources the Clearinghouse would not usually be involved. Therefore, guidelines for these communities need to be established.

* Richard J. Lundman, *Crime and Delinquency*, Oct. 1976. Reprinted by permission of the National Council on Crime and Delinquency.

1. *Uniform Crime Reports* (Washington, D.C.: Department of Justice, 1971).

In addition to the recent increase in delinquent behavior, the demographic characteristics of delinquents appear to be changing. Official delinquency statistics affirm that delinquents are disproportionately male, lower class, in a racial minority, and urban in residence, but recent study of undetected delinquents suggests expansion of the demographic correlates of delinquency.[2] Although some of the evidence is mixed,[3] it now appears that serious delinquents are also female, middle class, in the ethnic majority, and rural in residence.

Law enforcement, social service, and federal agencies have been involved in a variety of attempts to prevent delinquent behavior or control the apparent increases in delinquent behavior by all types of juveniles. These attempts have been diverse in nature but uniform in outcome. Thus, attempts have been made to control or prevent delinquency by involving juveniles with caseworkers,[4] psychotherapists,[5] counselors,[6] and detached gang workers[7]; still others have involved juveniles in control or prevention projects emphasizing altered school environment,[8] recreation,[9] employment,[10] or creation of neighborhood antidelinquency groups.[11] But our own research[12] and the research of others[13] lead to the

2. See J. Short and F. Nye, "Extent of Unrecorded Delinquency—Tentative Conclusions," *Journal of Criminal Law, Criminology and Police Science,* November-December 1958, pp. 296–302.

3. See M. Gold, "Undetected Delinquent Behavior," *Journal of Research in Crime and Delinquency,* January 1966, pp. 27–46.

4. For example: C. Berleman and T. Steinburn, "The Execution and Evaluation of a Delinquency Prevention Program," *Social Problems,* Spring 1967, pp. 413–23; D. Braxton, "Family Casework and Juvenile First Offenders," *Social Casework,* February 1966, pp. 87–92; and R. Downing, "A Cooperative Project at an Elementary School and a Family Agency," *Social Casework,* November 1959, pp. 499–504.

5. For example: M. Stranahan and C. Schwartzman, "An Experiment in Reaching Asocial Adolescents through Group Therapy," *Annals,* March 1959, pp. 46–52.

6. For example: L. Berkowitz and J. Chwast, "A Community Center Program for the Prevention of Dropouts," *Federal Probation,* December 1967, pp. 36–40; E. Powers and H. Witmer, *An Experiment in the Prevention of Delinquency* (New York: Columbia University Press, 1951).

7. For example: J. Gandy, "Preventive Work with Street Corner Groups: Hyde Park Youth Project, Chicago," *Annals,* March 1959, pp. 107–16.

8. For example: W. Reckless and S. Dinitz, *The Prevention of Juvenile Delinquency* (Columbus, Ohio: Ohio State University Press, 1972).

9. For example: R. Brown and D. Dodson, "The Effectiveness of a Boys' Club in Reducing Delinquency," *Annals,* March 1959, pp. 47–52.

10. For example: M. Friedman and E. Cohen, "Delinquency, Employment, and Youth Development," *Federal Probation,* December 1962, pp. 45–49.

11. For example: S. Kobrin, "The Chicago Area Project—a 25-Year Assessment," *Annals,* March 1959, pp. 19–29.

12. R. Lundman, P. McFarlane, and F. Scarpitti, "Delinquency Prevention: A Description and Assessment of Projects Reported in the Professional Literature," *Crime & Delinquency,* July 1976, pp. 297–308.

13. P. Lejins, "The Field of Prevention," in W. Amos and C. Wellford, eds., *Delinquency Prevention* (Englewood Cliffs, N.J.: Prentice-Hall, 1967); J. Stratton and R. Terry, *Prevention of Delinquency: Problems and Programs* (London: Macmillan, 1968); M. Dixon, inescapable conclusion that nearly all past attempts at delinquency control or prevention have failed.

Given this history of failure, correctional administrators have been preoccupied with the tasks of discovering and implementing "new" prevention and control strategies.[14] Diversion from the juvenile justice system is the newest of these strategies.

> Only a few years ago, most American chief probation officers used the words "research" and "breakthrough" if they wanted good marks from their superiors and their colleagues. . . . Now the word is "diversion" and it is diversion programs that win the accolades.[15]

The appeal of new strategies is such that twenty-three statewide diversion programs had been implemented by 1971, ten more were planned for 1972, and ten additional states were expressing interest in developing diversion programs.[16] The passage of the Juvenile Justice and Delinquency Prevention Act of 1974 should result in a further increase in diversion programs since one condition for the funding of state and local projects is establishment of diversion programs. Thus it is not unreasonable to predict a sharp increase in the number of diversion efforts in the near future.

The increase in diversion programs makes the concerned observer curious about their nature and their probable effectiveness in achieving stated goals. It appears appropriate, therefore, to undertake a preliminary evaluation of diversion programs. After a brief description of these programs, this paper will identify their sociological origins. Specific attention will then be given to the symbolic interactionist origins of labeling theory, early labeling informed research, and recent labeling research. The paper concludes by assessing certain of the implications and problems of diversion programs.

DIVERSION PROGRAMS

Diversion of persons from the juvenile and criminal justice systems is an old practice.[17] Numerous studies of the police, for instance, indicate

An Evaluation of Policy-related Research on the Effectiveness of Juvenile Delinquency Prevention Programs (Nashville, Tenn.: George Peabody College for Teachers, 1974).

14. Stratton and Terry, op. cit. supra note 13, p. 2.

15. D. Cressey, *Diversion from the Juvenile Justice System* (Washington, D.C.: U.S. Govt. Printing Office, 1974), p. 1.

16. R. Gemignani, "Diversion of Juvenile Offenders from the Juvenile Justice System," in P. Lejins, ed., *Criminal Justice Monograph: New Approaches to Diversion and Treatment of Juvenile Offenders* (Washington, D.C.: U.S. Govt. Printing Office, 1973), p. 36.

17. R. Smith, "Diversion: New Label— Old Practice," Lejins, op. cit. supra note 16, p. 39.

that they routinely divert more people than they arrest.[18] What, then, distinguishes diversion programs from past practices?

First, diversion is a legal procedure which presumably differs from the informal decisions made by members of juvenile justice systems in the course of their work. Formal procedures replace the previously arbitrary exercise of discretion.

Second, diversion programs can be distinguished from informal pre-adjudication dispositions by reference to a well-articulated awareness of the potentially stigmatizing consequences of formal processing. The following observation is found in a work advocating diversion programs:

> Young persons whose controlling ties to the school have been weakened, who thereby acquire a history of misbehavior, becoming subject to the repeated intervention of the juvenile justice system, are rendered increasingly vulnerable to delinquency through a process of building up of stigmatizing labels.[19]

Similarly, Robert L. Smith, Chief of Planning for the California Youth Authority, offered the following argument in support of diversion programs:

> The deeper an offender penetrates the existing criminal justice system and the more frequently he is recycled through it, the greater is the probability that he will continue his criminal career.[20]

Finally, Robert J. Gemignani, Commissioner of Youth Development and Delinquency Prevention, DHEW, observes:

> A great deal of interest has legitimately been generated over the process of labeling, particularly the labeling that attaches a stigma. The process of searching for an approach to eliminate the negative labeling of youth leads directly to those agencies and institutions which apply the labels, most notably the schools, welfare departments, juvenile courts, employment services, and some private agencies that stress eligibility determinations.[21]

A third source of distinction is found when one examines what is done to, with, or for the diverted juvenile. In the past, juveniles fortunate enough to avoid formal processing were either immediately released by the police or disposed of after a brief, informal lecture.[22] Diversion programs differ in that once diversion had occurred, the juve-

18. D. Black and A. Reiss, "Police Control of Juveniles," *American Sociological Review*, February 1970, pp. 63–77.

19. K. Polk and S. Kobrin, "Delinquency Prevention through Youth Development," Washington, D.C., DHEW Publication No. (SRS) 72–26013, 1972, p. 29.

20. Smith, supra note 17, p. 48.

21. Gemignani, supra note 16, p. 33.

22. For example: C. Werthman and I. Piliavin, "Gang Members and the Police," in D. Bordua, ed., *The Police* (New York: John Wiley, 1967).

nile is to be provided with some type of formal assistance. This assistance, however, is seen as problematic since any assistance can conceivably result in stigmatization. The solution which appears to have been arrived at involved creation of broadly based programs serving the needs of a variety of juveniles—delinquents being but one type. Polk and Kobrin suggest:

> To cope with the problem it is necessary to develop mechanisms to divert troublesome youth from the juvenile justice system. To be effective, these mechanisms should be designed to increase youth participation in activities that forge legitimate identities by (a) avoiding their segregation into groups made up solely of stigmatized and troubled individuals, and (b) enlarging their opportunities, as members of mixed groups. . . .[23]

Gemignani offers a similar solution:

> The problem still to be addressed is how to provide alternative youth services that do not label by their presence in the community. [Youth Development and Delinquency Prevention Administration's] comprehensive youth services systems, with a wide range of participants, not just delinquent or predelinquent youth, offer a viable alternative.[24]

SOCIOLOGICAL ORIGINS OF DIVERSION PROGRAMS

This section suggests that the labeling perspective in sociology contributed to diversion programs. It begins with a brief natural history of the labeling perspective, reviews early labeling research, discusses the specific connections between labeling theory and diversion programs, and concludes with a review of recent labeling research.

Natural History of Labeling Theory

That the symbolic interactionist tradition provided the conceptual basis for the emergence of labeling theory can best be demonstrated by considering its views of the nature of social objects and the self.

The "social object" is one of the concepts central to symbolic interactionism. Blumer[25] has noted that the process of making social objects involves perceptual indication and that "to indicate something is to extricate it from its setting, to hold it apart, to give it a meaning, or in Mead's language, to make it into an object." Elsewhere he notes that social actors live in worlds of symbols and objects and observes that this "bland statement becomes very significant when it is realized that . .

23. Polk and Kobrin, supra note 19, pp. 20–30.

24. Gemignani, supra note 16, p. 33.

25. H. Blumer, "Society as Symbolic Interaction," in A. Rose, ed., Human Behavior and Social Processes (Boston: Houghton Mifflin, 1962), p. 182.

objects are human constructs and not self-existing entities with intrinsic natures."[26]

A second concept central to symbolic interactionism is the self, which, says Mead, "arises in the process of social experiences and activity; that is, develops in the given individual as a result of his relation to the process as a whole and to other individuals within that process."[27] Socialization is understood as a continuous process involving internalization of the designatory action of others. The social actor becomes conscious of self as an object having particular characteristics by thinking of self from the standpoint of significant others. An actor's sense of self is thus built up across time, remains relatively constant in the face of consonant designatory actions, and may be altered, modified, or replaced with change in the designatory actions of others.

Despite the now clear implications of these conceptualizations for deviance theory, labeling theory remained dormant although "anticipated"[28] on more than one occasion. Polsky[29] has pointed out that the notion of the self-fulfilling prophecy is the "labeling dictum writ small." Tannenbaum[30] spoke of the negative consequences of "tagging" delinquents, and Lemert[31] introduced the notion of secondary deviation.

Then, in 1963, Becker presented his insightful labeling analysis of deviance. In a now classic and oft-quoted statement he extended the symbolic interactionist understanding of social objects to the problem of defining social deviance:

> Social groups create deviance by making the rules whose infraction constitutes deviance, and by applying those rules to particular people and labeling them as outsiders. From this point of view, deviance is not a quality of the act the person commits, but rather a consequence of the application by others of rules and sanctions to an "offender." The deviant is one to whom that label has successfully been applied; deviant behavior is behavior that people so label.[32]

All objects, including social deviance, are given meaning and value.

The symbolic interactionist understanding of the self was extended to account for the negative effects of labeling. "One of the most crucial

26. H. Blumer, "Sociological Implications of the Thought of George Herbert Mead," *American Journal of Sociology,* March 1966, p. 539.

27. A. Strauss, ed., *G. H. Mead on Social Psychology* (Chicago: University of Chicago Press, 1965), p. 212.

28. For a discussion of theoretical anticipation see R. Merton, *On Theoretical Sociology* (New York: Free Press, 1967), pp. 13 ff.

29. N. Polsky, *Hustlers, Beats and Others* (Chicago: Aldine, 1967), p. 198.

30. F. Tannenbaum, *Crime and the Community* (New York: Columbia University Press, 1938), p. 19.

31. E. Lemert, *Social Pathology* (New York: McGraw-Hill, 1951), pp. 54 ff.

32. H. Becker, *Outsiders: Studies in the Sociology of Deviance* (New York: Free Press, 1963), p. 9.

steps in the process of building a stable pattern of deviant behavior is likely to be the experience of being caught and publicly labeled." [33] Labeling, it is argued, results in alteration of an actor's sense of self because of change in the designatory action of others aware of the label. The change is thought to be a consequence of internalization of a deviant image of self.

Early Research

Denzin [34] observed at the start of this decade that labeling formulations had not been subjected to systematic critical analysis. Of the research which had been done, however, most was supportive of labeling notions. In law formulation, for example, earlier accounts of laws of theft,[35] prohibition,[36] and sexual psychopathology [37] were marshaled in support of labeling assertions. Contemporary research efforts in vagrancy law [38] and support law [39] served to substantiate labeling definitions of deviance.

Others studied the nature of the social reaction to labeled deviants. Nunnally,[40] Scheff,[41] and Whatley,[42] for example, examined social reactions to the mentally ill and found evidence of negative stereotyping. In an influential study Schwartz and Skolnick [43] reported that involvement in the criminal justice system interfered with employment. Rubington and Weinberg [44] assembled over fifty articles supportive of labeling theory in a widely adopted deviance reader.

In the period following Becker's initial formulations, then, one can find a number of studies apparently supportive of labeling theory. What must be recognized, however, is that these studies were supportive of selected dimensions of labeling theory (e. g., law formulation). A central

33. Id., p. 31.

34. N. Denzin, "Rules of Conduct and the Study of Deviant Behavior," in J. Douglas, ed., *Deviance and Respectability* (New York: Basic Books, 1970), p. 120.

35. J. Hall, *Theft, Law and Society,* 2nd ed. (Indianapolis: Bobbs-Merrill, 1952).

36. A. Sinclair, *Prohibition: The Era of Excess* (Boston: Little, Brown, 1962).

37. E. Sutherland, "The Diffusion of Sexual Psychopath Laws," *American Journal of Sociology,* September 1950, pp. 142–48.

38. W. Chambliss, "A Sociological Analysis of the Law of Vagrancy," *Social Problems,* Summer 1964, pp. 67–77.

39. K. Eckhardt, "Social Change, Legal Controls, and Child Support," unpub. Ph.D. dissertation, Department of Soci-ology, University of Wisconsin, 1965; K. Eckhardt, "Deviance, Visibility, and Legal Action: The Duty to Support," *Social Problems,* Spring 1968, pp. 470–77.

40. J. Nunnally, *Popular Conceptions of Mental Health* (New York: Holt, Rinehart and Winston, 1961).

41. T. Scheff, *Being Mentally Ill: A Sociological Theory* (Chicago: Aldine, 1966).

42. C. Whatley, "Social Attitudes toward Discharged Mental Patients," *Social Problems,* Spring 1959, pp. 313–20.

43. R. Schwartz and J. Skolnick, "Two Studies of Legal Stigma," *Social Problems,* Summer 1964, pp. 133–42.

44. E. Rubington and M. Weinberg, *Deviance: The Interactionist Perspective* (New York: Macmillan, 1968).

labeling argument—namely, that labeling is a cause of career deviance—had not been systematically examined.

Diversion Programs

It was during this period that diversion programs emerged, pervaded by inadequately examined labeling conceptions of social deviance. The importance of labeling notions is suggested by the earlier discussion of diversion programs. Nonetheless, it would be helpful to establish the connection between labeling theory and diversion programs in as clear a manner as possible. Smith's justification of diversion programs is an example:

> The structural and procedural systems that society has established to deal with its problem segments have . . . built-in patterns that tend to be self-defeating. First, the offender is identified and labeled. As he is labeled, certain sanctions are imposed; a certain critical stance is assumed. The sanctions and stance tend to convince the offender that he is a deviant, that he is different, and to confirm any doubts he may have had about his capacity to function in the manner of the majority. Further, as the label is more securely fixed, society's agencies, police, school, etc., lower their level of tolerance of any further deviance.[45]

Diversion programs, in short, were informed by labeling theory and emerged at a time when the results of empirical examinations of labeling notions were generally supportive. As a consequence, there was reason to believe that diversion programs would lower recidivism rates—i. e., lower the probability of career deviance. The problem, however, is that these programs were launched in the absence of adequate empirical examination of the labeling framework. This issue is addressed in the next section.

Recent Research

As noted, study of labeling assertions and formulations has, until very recently, been less than systematic. Moreover, examination of the central labeling assertion—that labeling is a cause of career deviance—has been even less frequently examined.

Review of the available literature reveals four recent examinations of the basic labeling assertion.[46] The first and second concern the

45. Smith, supra note 17, p. 44.

46. W. Gove, "Societal Reaction as an Explanation of Mental Illness: An Evaluation," *American Sociological Review*, October 1970, pp. 872–83; W. Gove and P. Howell, "Individual Resources and Mental Hospitalization: A Comparison and Evaluation of the Societal Reaction and Psychiatric Perspectives," *American Sociological Review*, February 1974, pp. 86–100; S. Fisher, "Stigma and Deviant Careers in School," *Social Problems*, Summer 1972, pp. 78–83; J. Foster, S. Dinitz, and W. Reckless, "Perception of Stigma following Public Intervention for Delinquent Behavior," *Social Problems*, Fall 1972, pp. 202–09.

relations between labeling and mental illness and hence permit only direct assessment of diversion programs. The third and fourth concern labeling and delinquency and hence permit direct assessment.

Gove reviewed the extent to which available evidence in the sphere of mental illness supported a variety of labeling assertions. Of interest to us is whether labeling someone as mentally ill, distinct from other factors, increased the probability of career deviance. Gove observed:

> The available evidence indicates that when former patients continue to have difficulty, these difficulties are generally due to the person's confronting a troubled situation or to some psychiatric disorder, and not to the social expectations of others.[47]

Later, Gove and Howell re-addressed the same issues, with special attention to psychiatric versus labeling explanations of entry into "the role of mentally ill." They concluded that the available evidence and their own data failed to support the labeling explanation.

Fisher examined the effects of delinquent labeling on school performance. Labeled subjects were matched with nonlabeled subjects and the two groups were compared. In addition, the preprobation academic averages of the labeled juveniles were compared with their postprobation averages.

> It appears that improper weighting has been given to the label or, at the very least, insufficient attention has been given to the various kinds and contexts of deviance to assess properly the relevance of one of its known characteristics, namely labeling and negative societal response thereto. Our data argue for a more careful empirical exploration of the relation between deviants and conventionals in a variety of social and institutional contexts. Once cumulative data of this kind have been collected and assessed .   .   . it will be possible then to deal with the more important issue of whether or not labeling theory is a proper area of independent theoretical attention, or an area to be superseded by more traditional areas of sociological theory.[48]

Foster et al. reach an essentially similar conclusion. They interviewed 196 male juveniles within thirty days of arrest to determine their perceptions of stigma following intervention for delinquent behavior. The juveniles were quizzed about the effects of labeling on interpersonal relations and social structural opportunities. The authors concluded:

> So far as labeling theory is concerned .   .   . little empirical evidence can be found to support the notion that delinquent boys who have encountered public intervention actually *perceive at the time of intervention* the negative effects attributed to stigma. .   .   .[49]

47. Gove, supra note 46, p. 882.   49. Foster et al., supra note 46, p. 208.

48. Fisher, supra note 46, p. 83.

Although additional study is clearly in order, the results of recent research suggest that labeling is possibly not as consequential as originally indicated by labeling theorists. Specifically, there now exists reason to believe that deviant careers do not inevitably or frequently follow from public identification of the subjects as deviant.

EVALUATION

This section undertakes a preliminary evaluation of diversion. First, it gives attention to the economic and humanitarian advantages of diversion. Next, it suggests that diversion units are being created in the absence of careful assessment of the effects of past practices and the results of recent research. Third, it argues that proponents of diversion have failed to assess the disadvantages of diversion. The essential conclusion drawn is that diversion units are not likely to reduce recidivism or correct existing abuses.

Economic and Humanitarian Advantages

Compared with formal processing, diversion is a significantly less expensive method of attempting to solve the problem of juvenile delinquency. Baron et al.,[50] for example, report that diversion is only about one-tenth as expensive as regular intake, and Gemignani [51] estimates that by 1977 "almost $1.5-billion could be saved . . . by the adoption of a [national] strategy of diversion."

Diversion is also far more humane than formal processing. The nonperson status granted the juvenile in court [52] and the clearly arbitrary exercise of power over the lives of children by court personnel [53] generate mistrust and hatred of the system. Incarceration in even the best institution is necessarily less than humane since it inevitably involves deprivations [54] not encountered by the diverted juvenile.

In addition to these advantages, however, proponents maintain that widespread diversion can reduce juvenile recidivism and correct existing problems. The problem is that the effects of past practices, the results of recent research, and the disadvantages of diversion all fail to support this contention.

Past Practices and Recent Research

Diversion programs are being implemented in the absence of adequate study of the effects of past practices. As noted, diversion is an old

50. R. Baron, F. Feeney, and W. Thornton, "Preventing Delinquency through Diversion: The Sacramento County Diversion Project," *Federal Probation*, March 1973, pp. 13–19.

51. Gemignani, supra note 16, p. 10.

52. A. Platt, *The Child Savers* (Chicago: University of Chicago Press, 1969).

53. D. Matza, *Delinquency and Drift* (New York: John Wiley, 1964).

54. G. Sykes, *The Society of Captives (Princeton, N.J.: Princeton University Press, 1958).*

practice. Police officers have regularly warned and released more juveniles than they have arrested, while probation officers have routinely placed juveniles on informal probation as an alternative to the filing of a petition for a formal hearing. Despite this informal diversion, the juvenile crime rate has continued to increase. Thus one can at least question the adequacy of the assertion that formal diversion results in a decrease in juvenile recidivism.

The results of recent labeling research also call the adequacy of this argument into question. This research suggests that programs which rely on diversion to reduce recidivism are not likely to be any more successful than other types of programs. Even if diversion is coupled with extensive efforts at individual or group treatment, the results of previous prevention and control programs provide little reason for optimism. The conclusion tentatively drawn from these data is that diversion is not likely to have a significant impact on the rate of criminal deviance by juveniles.

Disadvantages of Diversion

In addition to failing to reduce recidivism, diversion may magnify rather than correct existing problems. Inadequate attention, for example, has been given to the results of recent research by proponents of the deterrence perspective. Contrary to earlier research, which indicated little or no relationship between sanctioning and rates of criminal deviance,[55] recent research indicates that the *certainty* of punishment correlates inversely with rates of criminal deviance.[56] Moreover, there exists controversial evidence that the severity of punishment may also deter criminal deviance.[57] Although the relations among deterrence, diversion of juveniles, and rates of criminal deviance are unspecified, the possibility exists that diversion programs could result in an increase in the general rate of criminal deviance.

Another potential disadvantage of widespread diversion is an increase in the number of juveniles under the control of the state. One of the reasons that police and intake officers avoid formal action is their awareness of the harshness and general ineffectiveness of the juvenile justice system.[58] Diversion programs, however, *promise* to temper harshness and be more effective. As a consequence, those charged with

55. See, for example, L. Savitz, "A Study in Capital Punishment," *Journal of Criminal Law, Criminology and Police Science*, September-October, 1958, pp. 347–54; also H. Bedau, ed., *The Death Penalty in America* (Garden City, N.Y.: Anchor-Doubleday, 1964).

56. J. Gibbs, "Crime, Punishment and Deterrence," *Southwestern Social Science Quarterly*, March 1968, pp. 515–30; C. Logan, "General Deterrent Effects of Imprisonment," *Social Forces*, September 1972, pp. 64–73.

57. W. Chambliss, "The Deterrent Influence of Punishment," *Crime and Delinquency*, January 1966, pp. 70–75; L. Gray and D. Martin, "Punishment and Deterrence: Another Analysis of Gibbs's Data," *Social Science Quarterly*, March 1969, pp. 389–95.

58. I. Piliavin and S. Briar, "Police Encounters with Juveniles," *American Journal of Sociology*, September 1964, pp. 206–14.

decision-making may be less reticent to take formal action. As was the case with introduction of indeterminate sentences,[59] the result could be an increase in the number of juveniles under the control of the state.

Attention must also be given to the potential disadvantages associated with increasing the discretionary power of certain members of juvenile justice bureaucracies—principally, intake officers. This increase in discretion is not necessarily a cause for alarm although a large body of literature holds that the potential for abuse is clearly present. Thus, studies of the police,[60] defense attorneys,[61] and judges [62] all report the discriminatory and arbitrary exercise of power over the lives of children. Specifically, variables such as social class, sex, age, majority/minority status, and, especially, demeanor all appear to relate to the decision rendered. Unless precautions are taken to insure application of universalistic rather than particularistic criteria, diversion will magnify rather than alleviate existing abuses.

Another potential disadvantage of diversion is that juveniles may be diverted to treatment in advance of formal adjudication as delinquent. True diversion means that the diverted juvenile is free to choose treatment or refuse it.[63] When other than true diversion occurs, the limited due process protections extended juveniles in *Gault* are threatened as they may receive treatment without trial.[64]

Diversion programs also deflect attention from analysis of the cause of delinquent behavior.[65] Diversion units operate to prevent or reduce secondary deviation (i. e., recidivism) and thus fail to attend to the causes of the primary deviation which brought the juvenile to the attention of the diversion unit. Since we lack adequate descriptive data about the day-to-day lives of delinquents [66] and, therefore, usable theories of the causes of delinquency, concentration of attention on secondary deviation is another disadvantage of diversion.

The point, then, is that in addition to not reducing recidivism, diversion units also possibly magnify existing problems. It would seem that proponents of diversion must begin the process of balancing the economic and humanitarian advantages of diversion with these and other disadvantages. This should have been done before diversion programs were widely implemented. This task now deserves immediate attention.

59. S. Rubin, "Illusions of Treatment in Sentences and Civil Commitments," *Crime and Delinquency.* January 1970, pp. 206–14.

60. See Piliavin and Briar, supra note 58; Black and Reiss, supra note 18.

61. See Platt, op. cit. supra note 58.

62. See Matza, op. cit. supra note 53.

63. Cressey, op. cit. supra note 15, p. 3.

64. P. Tappan, "Treatment without Trial," *Social Forces*, March 1946, pp. 306–11.

65. Cressey, op. cit. supra note 15, pp. 33–35.

66. Becker, op. cit. supra note 32, pp. 166 ff.

Conclusion

These and other problems would appear to cloud the future of diversion. At this juncture, it is difficult to predict whether diversion programs will prevent or control delinquency, take their place alongside other unsuccessful strategies, or be found effective with only certain types of offenders. As long as delinquency remains a major social problem, practitioners will continue to embrace new strategies. Past efforts, recent research, and unresolved problems, however, suggest that this embrace will be momentary since it is unlikely that diversion units will reduce recidivism or correct existing abuses.

OVERVIEW OF ISSUES RELATING TO HALFWAY HOUSES AND COMMUNITY TREATMENT CENTERS *

A. HALFWAY HOUSES—A HETEROGENOUS CONCEPT

The term *halfway house* or *community treatment center* does not convey a homogeneous meaning. Halfway houses are as varied and different from each other as "closed" institutions such as jails, prisons, training schools and mental hospitals vary among and between themselves.

There is no single definition or description which can possibly be devised at this time which would adequately encompass the wide range of facilities which call themselves or which are called halfway houses or community treatment centers.[1]

Intake criteria, length of stay, treatment goals, target population serviced, services offered, quantity and quality of staffing, physical plant, physical location, and numerous other factors are so diverse that a unified, capsulized definition is virtually impossible.[2]

For example, there are in existence today, halfway houses or community treatment centers for the psychiatric patient, the neglected child, the delinquent child (the latter two are variously called halfway houses, group homes and even group foster homes), the adult public offender—both misdemeanant and felon—for the homeless adult with social or adjustment problems, and for individuals with specialized problems such as drug abuse, alcoholism and mental retardation.

The point is that each type of halfway house or community center mentioned above differs, often widely, from others which logically could be grouped in the same type.

---

* John M. McCartt and Thomas Mangogna, *Guidelines and Standards for Halfway Houses and Community Treatment Centers*, United States Dept. of Justice, L.E.A.A. Publication, May, 1973.

1. *"Halfway Houses: Community-Centered Corrections and Treatment"*, Oliver J. Keller and Benedict S. Alper; D. C. Heath & Co., pp. 11 and 12.

2. Keller and Alper, op. cit., pp. 13 and 14.

One reason halfway houses have developed in this manner was to meet varying needs for different target populations and communities. A second, and more valid reason, is that with no standards or guidelines to follow, halfway houses reflected the personal treatment and other philosophies of their founders or directors.[3] To establish a halfway house ten or even five years ago was a formidable task for anyone, whether the facility was privately or publicly sponsored. Those who assumed the responsibility were usually driving, energetic, creative and individualistic. In an area of practice which was very new to the modern correctional field, and which demanded the kind of qualities listed above, homogeneity could not be expected. Indeed, even at this stage of development, diversity—as wide as it is currently—should be viewed as an asset rather than a liability. Differing ideas, programs, goals, treatment modalities, staffing patterns and techniques need to be implemented; however, there is a desperate need for their evaluation. More will be said of evaluation later.

Suffice it to say now that there has been little of it in the halfway house and community treatment center field, as is true of most other areas of corrections.[4] As diverse as they currently are, halfway houses provide a rich and fertile ground for research in the area of community corrections.[5]

In the short period of time that halfway houses have been a part of the correctional scene, many have evolved rapidly into highly sophisticated programs. The evolution probably has taken place more out of necessity to meet ever-increasing demands for services for varying groups of clientele, and the demonstrated need for those services, as well as a change in our correctional approach.[6]

The halfway house whose average length of stay is thirty days is undoubtedly serving as a "way station" for its clientele, more than anything else. On the other hand, halfway houses whose average length of stay is a year to eighteen months are probably serving groups with specialized problems, such as drug abuse and alcoholism. The first type of house mentioned probably has little or no "program", as such. The second, more often than not, uses various modifications of "therapeutic community" techniques. Most halfway houses, with the exception of

3. Keller and Alper, op. cit., p. 123.

4. "The Continuum of Corrections", H. G. Moeller, *Annals of the American Academy of Political and Social Science,* January, 1971, p. 86.

5. For a broad discussion on the topic of correctional research, see *Crime and Delinquency,* Vol. 17, No. 1, January,

1971, in which the entire issue is devoted to the problem.

6. *"Administration of Justice in a Changing Society",* A Report of Developments in the United States—1965–70, prepared for the Fourth United Nations Congress on the Prevention of Crime and Treatment of Offenders, p. 7. Cf. Moeller, op. cit., p. 82.

those just noted and those serving juveniles, usually have their clients in residence from eighty to one hundred and twenty days.[7]

Some halfway houses and community treatment centers have as few as six to eight residents, while others may have as many as eighty. "A small population is an essential characteristic of the halfway house idea, and is found almost universally." "Most authorities maintain that a population of approximately twenty is close to ideal, permitting informal and close interaction among the residents." [8]

B. THE HALFWAY HOUSE IN THE CRIMINAL JUSTICE SYSTEM—WHERE DOES IT BELONG?

It was noted earlier in this report that the early halfway houses were relatively isolated from the correctional staff and facilities providing them with releasees. They were not considered a part of the correctional or criminal justice system.[9] Some halfway houses in existence today are still somewhat isolated from the "system" and indeed, prefer to remain so. Some community-based services, such as the Youth Services Bureau concept, as formulated by the National Council on Crime and Delinquency, insist on remaining not only independent of, but apart from, the juvenile justice system.[10]

Vasoli and Fahey note that in comparison to its forebears, the halfway house of today is more frequently closely coordinated with and even a part of the correctional system.[11] It is common knowledge that the criminal justice system as it exists today, and even components within that system, such as corrections, are too fragmented, and thus lose much of their effectiveness. Increasingly, reference is made not to the "system" but to the "nonsystem". It also has been recognized that there have been histories of barriers between institutional and community programs themselves, such as probation and parole, which are frequently administered by different agencies.[12]

As the Task Force on Corrections notes, "It is clear that new community programs must be integrated into the main line of corrections,

7. See Question No. 6 in Appendix F, Section II of the questionnaire sent to halfway houses throughout the United States. It was considered to be "essential" by the majority of respondents that the length of a client's stay should be determined on a case-by-case basis. Therefore, the figures eighty to one hundred and twenty days are not viewed as a recommendation, only as a report of widespread current practice.

8. Keller and Alper, op. cit., p. 12. Cf. U. S. Bureau of Prisons, *"Trends in the Administration of Justice and Correctional Programs in the United States"*, a Report prepared for the Third United

Nations Congress on the Prevention of Crime and Treatment of Offenders, U. S. Government Printing Office, Washington, D.C., 1965, p. 34.

9. Vasoli and Fahey, op. cit., p. 293.

10. Sherwood, Norman, "The Youth Services Bureau: A Key to Delinquency Prevention", *National Council on Crime & Delinquency*, Paramus, New Jersey, 1972, pp. 8, 16 and 17.

11. Vasoli and Fahey, op. cit., p. 294.

12. "Task Force Report: Corrections", op. cit., p. 6. Cf. Moeller, op. cit., p. 87.

if they are to succeed and survive." [13]   This would seem to support the contention made earlier in this report that the self-containment and isolation of the early halfway houses was one of several factors leading to their failure to survive.

By grants and contracts awarded to both public and private agencies, governmental funding bodies have fostered the phenomenal growth of halfway houses. As a practical stipulation of most grants and contracts, cooperation with other agencies, especially correctional agencies, is required. Such cooperation is an absolute necessity if halfway house programs are to have any measure of success, much less survive. More will be said of cooperative relationships later, but it is noted here to emphasize the fact that halfway houses, no matter who operates them, must have solid ties with other segments of the criminal justice system, and corrections in particular.

Keller and Alper consider halfway houses organizationally related to corrections.[14] Controversy about where halfway houses "belong" in the organizational structure of the system have arisen among and between public agencies as they have become involved in their establishment and operation.[15] The most reasonable viewpoint offered on this controversy seems to be that, "Despite differing views, it probably matters little whether the management of a center falls under the sponsorship of a public or private agency, or in fact, becomes part of the responsibilities of a probation, parole or correctional institution administrator. Of far greater importance are the quality of the programs offered, the competence and integrity of the center's staff and the working relationships between the center and the correctional agencies that use the resources." [16]

The issue, therefore, does not seem to be which agency, public or private, should operate halfway houses, but:

1.   Are halfway houses, public or private, a part of the correctional system?

2.   If they are part of the correctional system, what is their function in relationship to that system?

For public agencies, we can be safe in answering the first question in the affirmative. For private agencies, the majority seem to view themselves as part of the correctional system, but this view is by no means unanimous. As a practical matter, those private agencies who wish to remain isolated from the system will find it increasingly difficult, not only to survive as an increasing amount of public funds go to support privately operated programs, but also will find that the services they

13.   "Task Force Report: Corrections", op. cit., p. 44.

14.   Keller and Alper, op. cit., p. 15.

15.   Moeller, op. cit., p. 87.

16.   "The Residential Center: Corrections in the Community", United States Bureau of Prisons, Department of Justice, Washington, D.C.

could offer to the offender will be severely restricted because of their isolation. As the early halfway houses did, they will undoubtedly continue to service only those released from institutions. In isolation, they will be unable to participate in the "more positive and dynamic role for community treatment centers" that is "a hopeful substitute for the large prison".[17] Furthermore, they will be unable to assist the offender by offering many services now being delivered by halfway houses over and above the traditional "transitional facility" concept.

If halfway houses, public or private, are truly to be a part of the criminal justice system and serve their clientele most effectively, then strong relationships must be developed with the other components of the system—both at the administrative and line staff levels. This means the whole spectrum of the justice system: chiefs of police and police officers, prosecutors, defense attorneys (especially public defenders), jails, judges, probation and parole authorities (both adult and juvenile), workhouses, houses of detention, prisons and reformatories, training schools and other community treatment center programs in the same geographical area. Here we have spoken only of the relationships which must be developed within the system. Many other community relationships need to be developed also.[18]

At this point, a question should be asked: "Why corrections in the community?" Our communities are conditioned to the "correctional process" taking place elsewhere. Corrections is too frequently equated with prisons. Unfortunately, notions of punishment still underlie much of the community's attitude toward corrections,[19] and the symbol of punishment is prison.

Although most offenders currently incarcerated in our prisons are from large metropolitan areas, the prisons themselves are usually located away from urban areas. The original reasons for establishing these institutions in remote locations were diverse. To a large extent, those reasons are now outdated, i. e., the communities' interest in banishing the offender to a remote locale, the desire of rural legislators to provide public employment for their constituents and the belief that a rural setting was beneficial and salutary for individuals reared in cities, are just a few.[20]

Two factors, of which many unfamiliar with the field of corrections are unaware, however, are that only about one-third of all offenders are in institutions, while two-thirds are already under supervision in the community,[21] and that approximately 95% of all offenders committed to penal institutions are eventually released and returned to the community.

17. "Administration of Justice in a Changing Society", op. cit., p. 69.

18. "The Residential Center: Corrections in the Community", op. cit., p. 11.

19. "Task Force Report: Corrections", op. cit., p. 2.

20. Ibid., p. 4.

21. Ibid., p. 1.

Even though two-thirds are in the community under supervision, the treatment afforded them is more illusion than reality.[22]

Crime and delinquency are symptoms of failure and disfunctioning of the community as well as of the individual offender.[23] The community has its share of responsibility to bear for the conditions conducive to crime and as a result must share in the "responsibility to deal with the results of these conditions".[24] With the recognition that traditional penal institutions have not adequately performed their rehabilitative functions, community programs such as halfway houses are being developed in order to reduce the flow of individuals into those institutions.[25] While institutional populations have been showing a decrease in many areas of the country, community-based treatment programs are showing a considerable increase.

The best opportunity for successful integration or reintegration of the offender seems to lie in the community itself.[26]

The field of mental health has paved the way for corrections by establishing community-based programs whose aims are to ease the patient's transition back into the community and to prevent their removal from it in the first place, if possible.[27] Adequately trained personnel and other resources which only the community can offer with any degree of quality or quantity are essential for the rehabilitative process. Physicians, dentists, psychiatrists, psychologists, social workers, para-professionals, including indigenous personnel, teachers, vocational counselors, and other personnel, are not to be found in sufficient numbers in places other than metropolitan areas. Resources such as schools, diverse vocational training courses and employment opportunities, mental health centers, recreational opportunities and not least of all, family and friends, are also located in metropolitan areas.

It was noted earlier that we have spoken only of relationships which the halfway house must develop with other components of the criminal justice system, but that many other community resources and relationships must also be developed. To provide a successful and viable program for its clients as well as to achieve its purpose as a community-based program, a halfway house must develop strong relationship with a host of non-correctional or criminal justice agencies, public and private, as well as various citizen and neighborhood groups.

Vocational rehabilitation agencies, including vocational training centers, public and private, medical and mental health facilities, schools, including colleges and universities as well as centers for adult and juvenile basic education, agencies providing family counseling and recrea-

22. Ibid., p. 4.

23. "Task Force Report: Corrections", op. cit., p. 7.

24. Keller and Alper, op. cit., p. 108.

25. Ibid., p. 110.

26. "The Residential Center: Corrections in the Community," op. cit., p. 1.

27. Keller and Alper, op. cit., p. 5.

tional facilities, chambers of commerce, labor unions, the news media (radio, television, press), employers, civic and fraternal groups such as the Lions, Rotary Clubs, U. S. Jaycees, citizen groups interested in the criminal justice field such as the Alliance for Shaping a Safer Community, and various neighborhood improvement and association groups, are just a few samples of the type of community agencies, groups and resources with which halfway houses must develop strong relationships.

A key function of corrections today is to help the offenders avail themselves of the variety of services they need in order to take advantage of the opportunity structure which they have previously lacked, or to open doors to services which have been denied them in the past.[28]

Therefore, those who work in corrections must develop the knowledge and skill it requires to see that those services are made available to the offender.[29] The answer to the question: "Why corrections in the community?" should now be obvious. The next issue we need to address is the function and place of halfway houses or community treatment centers in relation to the correctional system.

C. THE FUNCTION AND PLACE OF THE HALFWAY HOUSE IN THE CORRECTIONAL SYSTEM

Traditionally, the early halfway houses, including those founded fifteen to twenty years ago, served the parolee or mandatory releasee from penal institutions almost exclusively. Some halfway houses or community treatment centers, however, have developed rather sophisticated programs, and have broadened not only the scope of services they offer, but also the target populations being serviced. Corrections is moving away increasingly from traditional methods of confinement, and community-based programs are being utilized in numerous ways as the appropriate alternatives. Halfway houses or community treatment centers are being developed rapidly and as the range of alternatives for courts and correctional officials broadens for the treatment of the public offender, such alternatives will be increasingly utilized in preference to traditional methods.[30]

As corrections becomes increasingly more community-based, the range of possible alternatives available to our courts and correctional officials will offer a flexibility for the treatment of the offender hitherto unknown to corrections, and will allow for the flow of offenders from one alternative to another, as need dictates.[31]

28. Moeller, op. cit., p. 84.

29. For a discussion of the availability of community resources in conjunction with correctional agencies, see Mandall, Wallace, "Making Corrections a Community Agency", Crime & Delinquency, Vol. 17, July, 1971.

30. "Administration of Justice in a Changing Society", op. cit., p. 7.

31. "Task Force Report: Corrections", op. cit., p. 11.

While the place of halfway houses or community treatment centers has not been decided from an organizational standpoint for either public or private agencies,[32] the present and possible future functions of such facilities have become increasingly clear. As indicated above, many halfway houses are serving a much wider target population and are being utilized for many other purposes than just the parolee or mandatory releasee. Starting with the traditional populations served by halfway houses, we will list the current uses of community-based residential treatment facilities.

1. Mandatory Releasee and Parolee

The mandatory releasee or parolee who is in need of a transitional center, and the range of services it offers (see Standards Nos. 10, 11 and 12 under "Program") has always been and still is being served by the community treatment center. The rationale for servicing this population has been to ease their transition back into free society and to buffer the many negative effects of their period of incarceration and isolation from the community.

Until the recent past, parolees were usually received directly upon release from the institution. One innovation, however, recently formalized by Federal law for Federal parolees, is the use of halfway houses for the parolee who is already "on the street", but who is having difficulty in his adjustment and perhaps stands the risk of revocation. Instead of waiting for failure, and sending such an offender back to the institution, the alternative to send him to community treatment centers for more intensive treatment and supervision, while keeping him in the community, is now available. While we are unaware of any state or local jurisdictions which have such formal provisions written into statute or ordinance, parole officers at those levels are using community treatment centers informally for this purpose already. Here is one added alternative to the traditional options of parole or reinstitutionalization.

2. The Probationer

Many halfway houses are increasingly accepting persons placed on probation. Probationers are referred to a halfway house under two sets of general circumstances: First, the court may consider the individual too much of a risk to simply place him on probation to be supervised by an already overworked probation officer, who will be unable to give the needed time and attention to the prospective probationer. At the same time, the court may recognize that the individual in question does not need incarceration in the traditional institutional setting. Therefore, the court may choose to stipulate that, as a condition of probation, the individual agree to participate in a halfway house or community treatment center program. This stipulation takes place prior to the time the person is placed on probation. The alternative just described has been

---

32. Moeller, op. cit., p. 82.

practiced informally by courts and probation officers at all jurisdictional levels throughout various parts of the United States for the past few years. Its use has been dependent largely upon the intake policies of a given halfway house and whether they have been willing to accept such potential probationers.

Second, an individual may have been placed on probation already, but like the parolee described earlier, may be experiencing adjustment problems in the community, and running the risk of revocation. Rather than revoke an individual in such a situation, the court or probation officer may refer him/her to a halfway house. Again, intensity of treatment and supervision is much greater, but the benefits of remaining in the community are maintained. The Federal government has also passed legislation formalizing the procedure for utilizing halfway houses for probationers in the situation just described. This alternative is also being utilized informally by many state and local courts and probation officers.

3. The Pre-releasee

For several years, Federal law, and more recently, the laws of several states, have allowed for the release of prisoners to halfway houses or community treatment centers prior to their actual mandatory release or release on parole. The period of time for which an individual is released under this provision ranges from thirty to one hundred and twenty days, although some jurisdictions allow for pre-release status for up to six months. While the pre-release of such individuals is considered an administrative transfer from one "institution" to another "institution", the pre-releasee receives the benefit of community-based treatment and supervision *prior* in time to the mandatory release or parole. Therefore, when the pre-releasee reaches mandatory release or parole status, he has had the opportunity of working through many of the problems of adjustment, and utilizing the necessary community resources, such as vocational training, employment placement, psychiatric and medical resources, housing, re-establishing family and other community ties, with which the parolee or mandatory releasee newly released to a halfway house is just beginning to cope. Many halfway houses, public and private, are accepting pre-releasees from Federal and state referral sources.

4. Study and Diagnostic Services to Offenders

Depending on their level of sophistication, many halfway houses are now capable of offering study and diagnostic services to courts. Such services are rendered prior to final disposition in court. It was mentioned earlier that the court may consider an individual too great a risk to place on probation and yet recognizes that the individual does not need incarceration and, therefore, stipulates that they enter a halfway house program as a condition of probation. The court may be able to arrive at this conclusion based on information provided by the pre-sentence report.

Study and diagnostic services, however, is a more formalized method of assisting the court to arrive at a final disposition, especially when the pre-sentence investigation cannot provide enough information about special problematic areas facing the offender. In such instances, the court of jurisdiction may place the offender in a halfway house or community treatment center for "study and observation" for a sixty-to-ninety-day period. During this time, a complete battery of psychiatric or psychological tests are administered, as well as psychiatric or psychological interviews with an accompanying assessment; a complete social history is also developed along with an assessment of the offender's prior record, if any; vocational and/or employment history, assessment and potential, and a record of the individual's progress and behavior while at the halfway house. A prognosis and recommendation is submitted to the court for its consideration for final disposition. Upon completion of study and diagnostic services, the individual may be placed on probation and/or possibly required to remain in the community treatment center, either as a condition of probation with the provisions of the "split sentence" * procedure, or sent to a more traditional correctional institution.

While study and diagnostic services have been utilized with community treatment centers primarily by the Federal justice system, there is much promise that such services will be rendered to offenders at the state and local levels if "correctional center complexes" as described in the *Task Force Report on Corrections* are constructed in metropolitan areas.[33]

5. The Juvenile—Neglected and Delinquent

Halfway houses, or group homes, as they are often called, are being utilized increasingly for the child who is neglected or delinquent. The establishment of such group homes has been increasing at an extremely rapid pace. Many times in the past, the neglected child was placed in detention facilities or training schools along with delinquent children, simply because there were no other resources to draw upon. Without any violation of the Juvenile Code, a child could, in effect, be incarcerated. Not enough foster parents are available to care for these children, and as a result, group homes have been established to meet this pressing need.

Group homes for the delinquent child are serving several purposes. First, they give the court of jurisdiction an alternative to incarceration if the child does not respond to the supervision of his probation officer or social worker. This prevents the child from being sent to training schools, which often are ill equipped to meet the child's needs. A child may be in residence in such a home for well over a year. The child's inability to care for himself, secure gainful employment, and be exclusively responsible for his own welfare, often makes a longer length of stay in a group home necessary.

---

* That sentence in which the offender is initially committed for a brief period prior to supervision on probation.

33. "Task Force Report: Corrections", op. cit., p. 11.

Second, the group home may be used as a short-term facility for the delinquent child while community resources are brought to bear on the root of his problems, such as family difficulties which may be resolved by intensive counseling in a relatively short period of time.

Third, the group home is also used as a "halfway out" facility for children who have been incarcerated and do not have an adequate home plan.

The group home may be used flexibly as one of many alternatives for the delinquent child. Community correctional centers seem to be approaching reality more quickly for the juvenile delinquent than for the adult offender. Relatively small institutions with greater security but also intensive treatment for the hyper-aggressive child are being established in metropolitan areas, in lieu of "training schools" located in rural areas. In addition to regular probation supervision, intensive treatment units are being established for children still living in their own homes. Intensive treatment units may have a ratio of one social worker or counselor for every six to ten children. The establishment of group homes in conjunction with the other alternatives listed above will give courts of jurisdiction tremendous flexibility to move the child from one component of the "system" to another as need or progress dictates. It should be noted that all of the alternatives listed above would be based in the community.

6. Use of Halfway Houses for Individuals with Special Difficulties, such as Drug Abuse, Alcoholism and Psychiatric Problems

Halfway houses or community treatment centers are being utilized for target populations with special difficulties such as drug abuse, alcoholism or psychiatric problems. Due to the nature of the problems being treated, the length of stay in such centers is usually much longer than in those servicing the general offender population, often for as long as eighteen months. Many, perhaps most such centers, utilize one form or another of the therapeutic community technique. Especially in the case of drug abuse and alcoholism, such centers are frequently staffed by individuals who have experienced and successfully worked through the problem. In many such centers, professionally trained personnel who have not experienced the problem being treated, were often excluded from the staffing pattern as a matter of treatment philosophy. However, there is evidence that professionally trained staff are now being accepted more readily as a part of the treatment team. Because of the nature of the difficulties experienced by drug abusers and alcoholics, many of them have passed through our criminal justice system. This has occurred usually as a direct result of their problems.

7. Use of Halfway Houses for Individuals Released on Bail Prior to Final Disposition

We have been speaking of some of the traditional and more recent uses and functions of the halfway house in relation to the correctional system. What are some other innovative uses which may be made of halfway houses? What other functions may it serve in the correctional system?

Bail reform has been spreading rapidly in the United States. Federal and many state and local jurisdictions have enacted bail reform measures. Although innocent until proven guilty, it is known that most individuals accused of crimes are from lower socio-economic groups,[34] and cannot afford ten per cent of the bail set by the court, which is usually required by professional bondsmen. As a result, the poor remain in jail to await final disposition while those more affluent are able to obtain their release.

To remedy the inequity of this situation, "Recognizance Bond" legislation has been and still is being enacted in various parts of the nation. If the individual meets certain criteria, he may be released upon his own signature, promising to reappear in court on the appropriate date. This provision does away with the need for the accused to produce a certain amount of cash or property for his bail.

One of the usual standard requirements is that the individual have roots in the community in which he stands accused, i. e., family, friends, job, etc. Many accused individuals, however, have poor family ties, and poor work histories, which are often the result of educational and cultural deprivation. Not meeting some of the basic criteria, they are excluded from the use of recognizance bond and must await final disposition in jail. The bad effects of this situation have been expounded by governmental commissions, hearings by committees of Congress, and state legislatures, and several publications in professional journals and books.

The halfway house should consider the possibility (and some already have) of providing services to an individual enabling him to become eligible for recognizance bond. At a minimum, this would include providing shelter and supervision prior to final disposition. However, whether the accused is found guilty or not, they are usually in need of a range of services which the halfway house is often in a position to provide, directly or indirectly. Medical, dental, psychological and psychiatric services, individual and group counseling services, vocational evaluation and counseling services, as well as employment placement services, can all be provided to the accused who has not been found guilty, but who is in need of such services. The delays which occur between the time of arrest and final disposition are often lengthy, ranging from six months to a year or more. Even if the process is speeded up, and the time from arrest to final disposition is reduced to two or three months, there is still much that can be accomplished during this period of time.

34. "Task Force Report: Corrections", op. cit., p. 2.

The next point is obvious: as most halfway houses deliver their range of services between an eighty to one hundred and twenty day period, a question should be asked: Why not intervene on the client's behalf long before final disposition, and why not deliver needed services prior to final disposition?

If the accused are found not guilty, they are in a much better position after the delivery of these services to pursue a more meaningful and constructive life. In one sense, this approach might be considered crime prevention in the true sense of the word. If the accused is found guilty, a range of services has been delivered already which may well affect the outcome of final disposition, e. g., probation rather than incarceration. In this instance, the halfway house would be in a position to offer valuable information to the court even before a pre-sentence investigation commences. The progress (or lack of it) of the individual found guilty could be reviewed with the court of jurisdiction as well as the investigating probation officer.

Additional or continued treatment plans could be formulated prior to the time of sentencing and if the person is to be placed on probation, made a part of the probation treatment plan. Even if the person is to be incarcerated, the services rendered, progress made, and information obtained need not be wasted, but could be shared with institutional treatment staff to help them formulate a plan for treatment with the client while he is incarcerated. Even if incarcerated, the fact that the individual was willing to avail himself of needed services while on recognizance bond could have a positive effect on how quickly he is released back into the community.

Few halfway houses have experimented in this area, but it seems to be a fertile ground for new uses of the halfway house.

8. Use of the Halfway House for Diversion from the Criminal Justice System

Halfway houses or community treatment centers can be utilized in the future to divert individuals from the criminal justice system. The question of diversion has been discussed in criminal justice circles for some time. Some that were formerly arrested and convicted repeatedly for an offense such as public intoxication are now being diverted from the criminal justice system in some jurisdictions.

When it is realized that in 1965, one-third of all the arrests in the United States were for the offense of public drunkenness, the magnitude of the problem of processing these individuals through the criminal justice system can be appreciated. The burden on police departments, courts, prosecutors, probation and parole officers and jails, as well as other penal institutions, is tremendous.[35]

---

35. "Task Force Report: Drunkenness",
op. cit. p. 1.

The criminal justice system seems to be ineffective to alter the behavior of the chronic alcoholic and to meet his underlying medical and social problems. The "system" only served to remove the publicly intoxicated individual from public view.[36] *The Task Force Report on Drunkenness* states that, "The commission seriously doubts that drunkenness alone (as distinguished from disorderly conduct) should continue to be treated as a crime."[37]

A general trend seems to be developing in the United States to restrict the scope of the criminal sanction by removing those statutes which tend to regulate the private moral conduct of individuals. Channeling through the criminal justice system those who have committed "victimless crimes" gravely dissipates the resources at the command of that system.

Time, energy, manpower, financial and other resources are diverted from coping with the type of offenses that threaten a community most, and affect the quality of life of its citizens, i. e., various forms of violence and theft.[38]

If alternative mechanisms are established to deal with victimless crimes, not only is the individual diverted from the criminal justice system, and relieved of the burden of the lasting stigma which is the result of the formal adjudication process, but a greater opportunity exists for obtaining the desired results of rehabilitation.[39]

The Board of Trustees of the National Council on Crime and Delinquency has issued a policy statement in support of abolition of victimless crime statutes.[40] There are also a substantial number of individuals at both the juvenile and adult offender levels, who could be diverted from the justice system, well before the point of sentencing, to alternative treatment programs.[41] As far as juveniles are concerned, this is certainly the thrust of the Youth Service Bureau as espoused by the National Council on Crime and Delinquency.

Legislation has been enacted already by the Federal government permitting drug abusers, for instance, to commit themselves voluntarily for treatment. Federal legislation also allows drug abusers who have been apprehended to be committed for treatment with the consent of the United States Attorney. If the individual successfully completes treatment, criminal charges against him are dropped.

In some areas of the United States, it is the policy of local police departments to take those who are publicly intoxicated to detoxification

36. "Task Force Report: Drunkenness", op. cit., p. 3.

37. Ibid., p. 4.

38. "Administration of Justice in a Changing Society", op. cit., p. 10.

39. Ibid., p. 11.

40. "Crimes without Victims—A Policy Statement", Board of Trustees, National Council on Crime and Delinquency, *Crime and Delinquency*, Vol. 17, No. 2, April, 1971.

41. "Task Force Report: Corrections", op. cit., p. 22.

centers for treatment, rather than charging them with such petty offenses as disorderly conduct and vagrancy. If the person arrested consents to treatment, charges are not brought against him.

Halfway houses as well as public health facilities can be utilized to divert and treat a substantial number of people such as alcoholics, drug abusers, and petty offenders who are currently being channeled through our criminal justice system. Obviously, not all such persons will want treatment, and in those instances, the mechanisms have been created to protect the individual and the community. With the proper legislation, halfway houses can be the focal point of a whole new direction for the diversion of individuals from the criminal justice system.

To return to an issue raised earlier would now be appropriate: if halfway houses serving the offender (primarily the privately-operated halfway houses) do not consider themselves a part of the correctional system, and if they do not establish cooperative relationships with correctional and other agencies but prefer to remain relatively isolated, they will be limiting the scope of their services and seriously restricting their participation in future innovative programs. We see this as being true for two reasons:

1. Correctional authorities will be increasingly hesitant to refer individuals to a house or center which does not have some type of cooperative relationship with them, especially as the numbers of such centers grow and the authorities have alternative houses or centers to which they may turn.

2. Without such cooperative relationships, which in themselves make a house or center a part of the correctional system, in fact if not by law, public funds will be increasingly difficult to obtain, whether by grant or contract with public agencies. Relying solely on private sources of income, the vast majority of private halfway houses would have extreme difficulty not only in offering a wide range of quality services to meet the varying needs of its clientele but also in simply surviving. Those who would suffer most, of course, would be the clientele halfway houses are serving, and the community of which both the client and the halfway house are a part.

COMMUNITY CORRECTIONS: A STATE OF TURMOIL *

The American correction scene is in an unstable and transitional state. Not since the 1790's, when the correctional institution developed as a refuge in which to place criminal offenders, has the field of corrections undergone such pronounced policy changes. In the 1970's another radical change in correctional policy originated; this change is characterized by a

* Richard P. Seiter, *Proceedings* of the One Hundred and Fifth Annual Congress of Correction of the American Correctional Association, Louisville, Ky.1975.

movement back to keeping the offender in the community rather than isolating him in a prison.

The growing realization of the egregious and dysfunctional effects of institutionalization in the rehabilitation of offenders has produced an excrecence of community correctional programs. This present emphasis on community corrections is based on the proposition that in order to relieve society of the crime problem (in the long run), the problem must be attacked at its origin—the community. Therefore, efforts are being made to reintegrate ex-offenders into the culture in which they will be living following their release from correctional supervision.

However, community corrections must now become accountable. Such programs are being called upon to prove they have and can produce better results than the institutional treatment of offenders. To date, few evaluations have shown community programs are effective than their institutional counterparts. This is in part due to the non-systemic approach taken in the development of such programs.

Therefore, it may be suggested that a rational policy analysis be supplied to the present surge of community corrections. Some have perhaps advocated community corrections as a panacea for offender reintegration without carefully analyzing the clients, his needs and capabilities, and available services and programs to fulfill these needs. Community correctional administrators should not be subject to the pitfalls that, due to a lack of analysis and evaluation, have perplexed correctional programs for years.

The importance of evaluation and systematic policy analysis (especially in developing programs such as community corrections) cannot be underestimated. The President's Commission on Law Enforcement and Administration of Justice indicated an acute awareness of this need:

> The most conspicuous problems in corrections today are lack of knowledge and unsystematic approach to the development of programs and techniques . . . .
>
> . . . Failure to attempt really systematic research and evaluation of various operational programs has led to repetitive error. Even more, it has made it impossible to pinpoint the reasons for success when success did occur.[1]

A salient example of the present problem of non-rational policy analysis in community corrections is reflected in a statement taken from an LEAA technical assistance publication regarding halfway houses:

> However, halfway houses must also commence qualitative research on the effectiveness of their programs. This is necessary both because those in the field of corrections and governmental funding agencies are increasingly inquiring into the quality of

---

1. President's Commission on Law Enforcement and Administration of Justice, *Task Force Report: Corrections*, U.S. Government Printing Office, Washington, D.C., 1967 (p. 13).

K. & C. Corr. In Comm.–CrJS Pamph.—3

such programs, and also because halfway house administrators cannot afford to base programmatic judgments on "cumulative experience" or "intuition." Virtually the whole field of criminal justice has always been in this position. Halfway houses must avoid this vicious circle of perpetuating something which may well be ineffective or not changing a program which is not as effective as it could be.[2]

Before the question of whether community-based correctional programs are effective can be answered, a coordinated approach to planning and policy making must be developed. Utilizing evaluations as feedback mechanisms to the policy-making process, administrators and evaluators can combine knowledge to further the development of correctional programs. Only in the past year has the National Institute of Law Enforcement and Criminal Justice attempted to formulate answers regarding program success.[3]

Although the author is in agreement with the underlying theory and alleged economic benefits of community correctional programs, there is doubt that these programs can reach the potential possible when policies are subjected to a rational decision-making process. Without evaluation and accountability, it is possible that historians will look back upon the era of the 1970's as a period of yet another ineffective attempt at reform in corrections, which later resulted in a return to the previous over-use of institutions.

UTILIZING EVALUATIONS TO DETERMINE PROGRAM EFFECTIVENESS

As previously argued, evaluations should be an integral element in policy making for developing community correctional programs. Although more evaluations of programs are presently being completed than at any other time in the history of modern corrections, it is believed that many of these evaluations have little, if any, effect in the determination of program policy.

In order to determine truly whether community based corrections is effective, it is important to be aware of several methodological considerations in the evaluation of criminal justice programs. Poor design of a program evaluation can lead to inconclusive or invalid results.

While designing the valuative methodology, it is important to determine program objectives. Program effectiveness should be judged through a measurement of its ability to accomplish prescribed objectives.

2. McCartt, John M., and Mangogna, Thomas, J., *Guidelines and Standards for Halfway Houses and Community Treatment Centers*, U.S. Government Printing Office, Washington, D.C., 1973 (pp. 33–34).

3. Recently within NILECJ, a National Evaluation Program was developed. The emphasis of the project is to determine what is known regarding the success of criminal justice programs, while

Simon contends that to measure organizational effectiveness, it is essential to look at a set of goals.[4] McCartt and Mangogna further discuss the importance of goals in evaluation:

> Evaluation must measure the outcome of the program and services in relation to the agency's stated purpose and goals. Program and service effectiveness must be measured by recognized evaluation techniques, and when possible, by formal research.[5]

After program goals have been identified and enunciated, the evaluator must develop an appropriate evaluative design for testing program effectiveness. The design must be structured to allow the effected experimental treatment to be measured and program effectiveness tested. This necessitates operationally defining and examining the experimental variable, while controlling for the effect of extraneous variables.

The classic design for evaluations is the true experimental design, a model using both an experimental and control group randomly selected from the target population. Weiss writes, "The essential requirement for the true experiment is the randomized assignment of people to programs."[6] Utilizing random assignment to experimental and control groups assumes any uncontrolled variables will affect the groups equally, and any difference in outcome can therefore be attributed to the experimental variable.

Evaluators in criminal justice programs should attempt to utilize a true experimental design whenever it is possible to do so without altering operational program practices to the extent that the evaluated program bears little resemblance to the program that will operate after completion of the evaluation. The evaluator therefore needs to be well versed in the powers and restrictions involved in utilizing a true experimental design.

However, there are valid situations in which evaluators of criminal justice programs are unable to utilize true experimental designs. Evaluators are often asked to conduct an ex post facto study to determine program effectiveness. In this situation, there is no possibility to randomize groups, and the evaluator must resort to the use of a quasi-experimental design.

Quasi-experimental designs do not satisfy the strict methodological requirements of the experimental design, but can be quite useful and powerful when the researcher is aware of the specific variables for which the chosen design does not control. Weiss contends:

constructing evaluative designs to fill gaps in the state of the art.

4. Simon, Herbert A., "On the Concept of Organizational Goals," *Administrative Science Quarterly* 9 (June 1964): 1–22.

5. McCartt, John M., and Mangogna, Thomas J., *Guidelines and Standards for Halfway Houses and Community Treatment Centers*, U.S. Government Printing Office, Washington, D.C., 1973 (p. 33).

6. Weiss, Carol H., *Evaluative Research: Methods of Assessing Program Effectiveness*, Prentice Hall, Inc., Englewood Cliffs, N.J., 1972 (p. 67).

Quasi-experiments have the advantage of being practical when conditions prevent true experimentation. But they are in no sense just sloppy experiments. They have a form and logic of their own. Recognizing in advance what they do and do not control for, and the misinterpretation of results that are possible, allows the evaluator to draw conclusions carefully. Quasi-experiments, in their terms, require the same rigor as do experimental designs.[7]

A frequently utilized and practical design for criminal justice evaluations is the non-equivalent control group design. In the non-equivalent control group design, there is no random assignment to experimental and control groups, but groups with similar characteristics are used as controls. Nonrandomized controls are generally referred to as "comparison groups." Comparison groups are often chosen by matching factors between groups. Prediction methods can also be used to weight important variables of the experimental group in developing comparable groups.

A statistical technique infrequently used due to its complexity and tedious calculation, but with relevant application to social research, is analysis of covariance. Analysis of covariance combines the most important factors of matching and prediction. With this technique, the evaluator can select the matching variables to be used as covariates, and is also provided the attributes of prediction in that these covariates are weighted according to their importance to outcome.

Analysis of covariances involves two basic steps. Initially, the selected control variables are correlated against the sets of outcome scores to determine their relationship to outcome. After determination of the effect of each control variable on outcome, means of outcome scores are adjusted to reflect the effect of the control variables. In effect, control variables are correlated with original or "raw" outcome scores to determine their effect on the score, each control variable weighting is applied to the raw score to predict what this score would be if the groups were equal in regards to the control variables, and the raw scores are then adjusted to reflect an equalization of the groups and allow comparison of the adjusted scores.[8]

The determination of program effectiveness is also affected by the choice of outcome measures. In the selection of outcome measures to test program effectiveness, several factors should be considered. Glaser notes that:

No definition of success can be useful unless methods of measuring its attainment are sufficiently precise, valid, and reliable to

7. Weiss, Carol H., *Evaluative Research: Methods of Assessing Program Effectiveness*, Prentice Hall, Inc., Englewood Cliffs, N.J., 1972 (pp. 67–68).

8. Logan, Charles, "Evaluative Research in Crime and Delinquency," *Journal of Criminal Law, Criminology, and Police Science* 63 (September 1972): 378–387.

warrant confidence that they improve the quality of knowledge available for guiding policy makers.[9]

Throughout the last 50 years in corrections, evaluators have relied on and principally utilized recidivism rates to measure the success of a program. Recidivism is usually measured in terms of rearrest, reconviction, or reimprisonment. Evaluations of correctional programs utilizing these indicators have failed conclusively to identify programs that reduce recidivism. Martinson, after an extensive analysis of correctional program effectiveness, has concluded that "nothing works."[10] A recent review of halfway houses has also lead to the conclusion that halfway houses are no more effective than other traditional methods of correction. In fact, the authors conclude:

> In terms of recidivism, the measuring rod traditionally used for determining the effectiveness of correctional programs, halfway house programs do not appear to have produced significantly better results than many community supervision programs, and in fact, in some instances have demonstrated a rather inferior performance.[11]

The deficiencies of recidivism as an outcome measure are important. Perhaps the most serious problem in the use of recidivism as an outcome measure is the forced dichotomous choice; recidivism classifies each offender as either a "success" or a "failure," rather than grading them on a continuous scale to measure "progress." Glaser emphasizes this point:

> Any measure of the success of a people-changing effort which fails to take into account variations in the degree to which a goal has been obtained, and instead classifies all the research subjects as either successes or failures, is thereby limited in its sensitivity as an index of variations in the effectiveness of alternative programs and policies.[12]

Another problem in the use of recidivism indicators is that they are a negative measurement of criminal actions, and do not consider positive behavior or "adjustment." Therefore, a treatment program would not receive credit for developing acceptable living patterns within offender clients unless criminal behavior were totally eliminated. The reintegrative model mandates an additional measure of positive behavior. Since

9. Glaser, Daniel, *Routinizing Evaluation: Getting Feedback on Effectiveness of Crime and Delinquency Programs,* Department of Health, Education, and Welfare, Washington, D.C., 1973 (p. 16).

10. Martinson, Robert, "What Works?—Questions and Answers About Prison Reform," *Public Interest,* no. 35 (Spring 1974): 22–55.

11. Sullivan, Dennis C.; Seigel, Larry J., and Clear, Todd, "The Halfway House,

Ten Years Later: Reappraisal of Correctional Innovation," *Canadian Journal of Criminology and Corrections* 16 (April 1974): 188–197.

12. Glaser, Daniel, *Routinizing Evaluation: Getting Feedback on Effectiveness of Crime and Delinquency Programs,* Department of Health, Education, and Welfare, Washington, D.C., 1973 (p. 22).

correctional programs seek to replace negative-valued behavior with positive behavior, outcome measures should include both types of indicators, sensitive enough to detect slighter progressive changes in the individual.

Correctional philosophy appears to be shifting from the rehabilitative to the reintegrative model. O'Leary and Duffee have summarized four models of correctional policy as presented Figure 1.[13]

Figure 1. Models of Correctional Policies

		Emphasis on the Community	
		Low	High
Emphasis on the Offender	High	Rehabilitation (Identification Focus)	Reintegration (Internalization Focus)
	Low	Restraint (Organizational Focus)	Reform (Compliance Focus)

[B6528]

Halfway house operations fit best into the reintegrative model. The reintegrative model provides the offender alternatives of behavior while in the community rather than isolated in a prison. O'Leary and Duffee have written:

> Emphasis on the community does not mean simply a stress on maintaining its values but in promoting changes as well within its institutional structure to provide opportunities for offenders and reduce systematic discrimination because of economic and cultural variances.[14]

Reintegration is not perceived as an overnight change, but the gradual adoption of socially-acceptable behavior as such behavior is practiced and reinforced. John Conrad, in describing the reintegrative model, has written:

13. For detailed description of these four models, see O'Leary, Vincent, and Duffee, David, "Correctional Policy—A Classification of Goals Designed for Change," *Crime and Delinquency* 17 (October 1971): 278–283.

14. O'Leary, Vincent, and Duffee, David, "Correctional Policy—A Classification of Goals Designed for Change," *Crime and Delinquency* 17 (October 1971): 382.

"Where this model is applied, the process will be the internalization of community standards." [15]

The development and utilization of a continuous scale to include both positive and criminal behavior has been used in an evaluation of Ohio halfway houses. This outcome measure ("relative adjustment") is also based on the offender's personal characteristics and, in that sense, compares him only with his own expected behavior. The relative adjustment measure of outcome should remedy many of the problems in the use of traditional outcome measures described above.

ARE HALFWAY HOUSES EFFECTIVE?

There are several diverging thoughts regarding the effectiveness of halfway houses. To date, there has been little conclusive evidence from which to develop statements of empirical program success or failure. Although it is generally accepted that we have not yet comprehensively evaluated the effectiveness of halfway houses, a brief review of completed halfway house evaluations has suggested that they are no more effective at reducing recidivism than other community supervision programs.[16]

In order to further evaluative knowledge and administrative practices regarding halfway houses, a study of the programs, policies, and effectiveness of Ohio adult halfway houses has been conducted. Initially, demographic, offense, and other data were gathered indicating the types of offenders presently being placed in halfway houses and the services provided to them. After examination of the policy and operations of Ohio halfway houses, the evaluation focused on the effectiveness of the present halfway house operations in reintegrating offenders.

For the evaluation, both an experimental and comparison group were chosen. The experimental group of clients from the ten included houses is made up of 236 subjects including parolees (144), probationers (31), and federal offenders on pre-release status (61). The comparison group includes 404 parolees released from Ohio institutions during 1973. The assignment of clients to halfway houses based on their perceived need for services has made it impossible to develop a true experimental design utilizing random assignment into control or experimental groups. Therefore, a quasi-experimental design was chosen and efforts made to control statistically for selection biases.

To identify and control for the acknowledged halfway house selection process, comparisons were made between the experimental and comparison groups on demographic data, criminal records, employment history,

15. Conrad, John P., "Reintegration: Practice in Search of Theory," in *Reintegration of the Offender into the Community,* National Institute of Law Enforcement and Criminal Justice, Washington, D.C., 1973 (p. 13).

16. Sullivan, Dennis C.; Seigel, Larry J.; and Clear, Todd, "The Halfway House, Ten Years Later: Reappraisal of Correctional Innovation," *Canadian Journal of Criminology and Corrections* 16 (April 1974): 188–197.

and previous alcohol or drug use.   Using z-scores to test for significant differences between group characteristics and utilizing the .05 probability level, the following statistically significant differences were found between the groups:

1. The comparison group has a higher percentage of Blacks.
2. The halfway house group has a higher rate of juvenile delinquency.
3. The halfway house group was younger at the age of their first offense.
4. The halfway house group has twice as many prior offenses as the comparison group.
5. The halfway house group has more offenses as adults.
6. The halfway house group has more felony offenses.
7. There are more multiple offenders in the halfway house group.
8. There are more victimless crime offenders among the halfway house group.
9. The comparison group had previously been employed a higher percentage of their lives.
10. A higher percentage of the halfway house group has an identified drug problem.

Since there are significant and theoretically important differences between the halfway house experimental and the comparison groups, analysis of covariance was used to correct for the differences and permit comparisons of outcome between groups.   This technique measures the effect of the independent variables on the dependent variables, and statistically corrects for the difference and effect by calculation of adjusted outcome scores.

The relative adjustment (RA) outcome criterion mentioned above has also been utilized for this evaluation.   The RA model has two major components.   The first component is a continuous criminal behavior outcome criterion.   So as not to rely totally on negative or deviant behavior parameters, additional factors defined as "acceptable adjustment patterns" have also been included in a graduated scale of relative adjustment.   Scores of positive and criminal behavior, when combined with the second component of RA (the utilization of analysis of covariance to correct for the relative differences in the groups), make up the "relative adjustment" outcome indicator utilized in this study.

The recidivism index used in the present analysis is an ordinal ranking of the severity of offenses as prescribed by the Ohio Criminal Code.   The Code was developed after consultation with criminal justice experts and passed by the Ohio General Assembly; severity assignments are therefore assumed to be valid.   Table 1 illustrates the severity categories and assigned scores for offenses.

Table 1. Criminal Behavior Severity Index

Offense Category	Score
Aggravated murder	−11
Murder	−10
1st degree felony	−9
2nd degree felony	−8
3rd degree felony	−7
4th degree felony	−6
1st degree misdemeanor	−5
2nd degree misdemeanor	−4
3rd degree misdemeanor	−3
4th degree misdemeanor	−2
Violator at large	−1
Technical violation	−0.5

A second element in the development of the total outcome criterion is the construction of a scale of "acceptable living patterns." The reintegrative correctional model does not assume a sudden change in behavior but rather movement away from criminal behavior and toward acceptable societal behavior. Therefore, an adjustment scale should be included as well as a recidivism scale. Several items generally considered to demonstrate "acceptable societal behavior" are presented in Table 2. These are not a complete list of success indicators, but merely selected factors which represent adjustment within the community.

Table 2. Acceptable Behavior Scale

Score	Adjustment Criterion
+1	Employed, enrolled in school, or participating in training program for more than 50 percent of follow-up period.
+1	Held any one job (or continued in educational or vocational program) for more than six-month period during follow-up.
+1	Attained vertical mobility in employment, education, or vocational program. This could be raise in pay, promotion of status, movement to better job, or continuous progression through educational or vocational program.
+1	For last half of follow-up period, individual was self supporting and supported any immediate family.
+1	Individual shows stability in residency. Either lived in same residence for more than six months or moved at suggestion or with agreement of supervising officer.
+1	Individual avoided any critical incidents that show instability, immaturity, or inability to solve problems in socially acceptable manner.
+1	Attainment of financial stability. This is indicated by individual living within means, opening bank accounts, or meeting debt payments.
+1	Participation in self-improvement programs. These could be vocational, educational, group counseling, alcohol or drug maintenance programs.
+1	No illegal activities on any available records during follow-up period.
+1	Individual making satisfactory progress through probation or parole periods. This could be movement downward in level of supervision or obtaining final release within reasonable period.

The construction of this adjustment scale was also subjected to tests for validity and reliability. To validate the scale, a panel of experts was consulted. Numerous parole and probation officers, criminal justice researchers, former members of the Ohio Citizens' Task Force on Corrections, and other correctional professionals were consulted to determine items generally considered an indication of acceptable adjustment. To test the reliability of the scale, several individuals were asked to score an individual's adjustment criteria. This "debugging" exercise resulted in the formulation of certain standards for scoring and led to consistent scoring of the outcome index.

Utilizing analysis of covariance to correct for differences between the experimental and comparison groups, comparisons have been made between "adjusted" scores. Since the groups are statistically comparable, differences in the adjusted scores represent the effect of the experimental variable (the halfway house experience).

Although the original experimental group totaled 236 persons, RA scores do not represent the outcome for all individuals. Outcome data was unavailable for approximately 10 percent of the cases, due to missing or incomplete records. However, there appeared to be no pattern for records being incomplete or missing, and the remaining sample for which records were available is assumed to be a valid representation of the total experimental group.

While scores for acceptable behavior have been assigned positive values, scores for criminal behavior were assigned negative values and the two scores combined as "relative adjustment." Therefore, the higher the relative adjustment score, the more favorable the adjustment outcome. The difference between the adjusted scores for the halfway house and

Table 3. Relative Adjustment Scores

House Name	Half-way House Group N	Unadjusted Scores		Adjusted Scores		Level of Sig-nifi-cance
		Half-way House	Com-pari-son	Half-way House	Com-pari-son	
Aggregate Group	196	2.385	0.744	3.398	0.253	.01
Alvis	20	0.775	0.744	1.970	0.685	.98
Bridge	12	3.667	0.744	6.137	0.670	.23
Denton	32	2.375	0.744	4.177	0.601	.28
Fellowship	8	4.500	0.744	5.453	0.725	.21
Fresh Start	11	3.455	0.744	3.701	0.737	.29
Helping Hand	38	2.421	0.744	3.498	0.642	.23
Talbert McMillan	18	2.167	0.744	4.587	0.636	.47
Talbert Wesley	25	3.000	0.744	5.098	0.614	.18
Talbert for Women	17	1.559	0.744	3.732	0.652	.69
Vander Meulen	15	1.700	0.744	2.979	0.696	.66

comparison groups is indicated by the level of significance value. Data in Table 3 illustrate the relative adjustment of the halfway house and comparison groups.

The aggregate adjusted score for the halfway house group is 3.398, while the comparison group score is 0.253; there is a significant difference between the scores of the two groups at the .01 level of significance. In terms of outcome, halfway house residents have significantly more favorable scores, suggesting that halfway houses are more effective at assisting ex-offenders in their reintegration to the community than the traditional modality of aftercare treatment.

These data also indicate the unadjusted and adjusted scores for each individual house, as well as the comparison group. In each case, the relative adjustment score for the halfway house group was higher than the score for the comparison groups. Partially because the sample size of several houses is quite small (thus lowering the degrees of freedom for calculation of statistical significance), no separate house shows a statistically significant difference when compared to the comparison group. When comparing the adjusted scores between the houses and the comparison group, one can note that several houses contribute positively to the significant difference between the aggregate halfway house and the comparison group scores.

Within the components of the RA indicator, adjusted and unadjusted scores for the two groups on the criminal behavior severity index are presented in Table 4. The higher the score, the more severe and/or frequent the offense and therefore the less favorable the group score.

Table 4. Criminal Behavior Scores *

House Name	Halfway House Group N	Unadjusted Scores		Adjusted Scores		Level of Significance
		Halfway House	Comparison	Halfway House	Comparison	
Aggregate Group	213	1.772	3.358	1.190	3.665	.001
Alvis	21	2.690	3.358	2.096	3.389	.64
Bridge	12	2.167	3.358	0.195	3.416	.54
Denton	37	1.730	3.358	0.460	3.474	.14
Fellowship	8	0.750	3.358	+ 0.225	3.377	.25
Fresh Start	14	0.786	3.358	0.685	3.361	.14
Helping Hand	40	1.650	3.358	0.912	3.431	.10
Talbert McMillan	22	1.273	3.358	+ 0.148	3.435	.13
Talbert Wesley	26	1.615	3.358	0.132	3.453	.17
Talbert for Women	18	1.861	3.358	+ 0.031	3.442	.33
Vander Meulen	15	2.967	3.358	1.981	3.394	.82

* Criminal behavior scores are all negative, except those marked +.

As can be seen from data in Table 4, there is a statistically significant difference between scores of the halfway house and comparison groups. Halfway house residents committed fewer and less severe offenses during the one-year outcome analysis than the comparison group, suggesting that halfway houses are effective in reducing the criminal behavior of residents.

The acceptable behavior scores have also been presented as a separate criterion of relative adjustment. It is now possible to examine the effect of halfway houses in assisting the ex-offender in developing acceptable behavior indicators. Data in Table 5 illustrate the scores for the comparison and halfway house groups in terms of positive behavior factors.

The aggregate and individual adjusted scores for halfway house residents are generally higher than the score for the adjusted comparison group. However, the difference in the aggregate scores for the groups is not statistically significant. Although this prevents rejecting the null hypothesis and drawing conclusions, the halfway house group has in general scored higher than the comparison group.

Table 5. Acceptable Behavior Scores

House Name	Halfway House Group N	Unadjusted Scores		Adjusted Scores		Level of Significance
		Halfway House	Comparison	Halfway House	Comparison	
Aggregate Group	196	4.311	4.101	4.708	3.909	.42
Alvis	20	3.600	4.101	4.199	4.072	.46
Bridge	12	5.833	4.101	6.332	4.087	.04
Denton	32	4.375	4.101	4.839	4.065	.61
Fellowship	8	5.250	4.101	5.228	4.102	.28
Fresh Start	11	4.455	4.101	4.896	4.089	.69
Helping Hand	38	4.158	4.101	4.526	4.067	.91
Talbert McMillan	18	3.722	4.101	4.419	4.070	.59
Talbert Wesley	25	3.680	4.101	5.258	4.066	.34
Talbert for Women	17	3.529	4.101	3.878	4.087	.43
Vander Meulen	15	4.667	4.101	4.960	4.091	.47

Examination of relative adjustment scores for the Ohio halfway houses provides evidence that such houses are effective treatment modalities to supplement traditional offender dispositions. Not only do halfway house clients significantly reduce their expected level of criminal behavior, but they also improve their ability to function in society in an acceptable pattern of behavior.

SUMMARY AND CONCLUSIONS

It is important to attempt to determine what the findings presented above say for the effectiveness of community based corrections. A statistically significant difference was found between the experimental and comparison groups. This, of course, indicates that halfway houses are more effective than traditional prison-parole methods of reintegrating ex-offenders.

But what differentiates Ohio halfway houses (examined in this evaluation) from other houses in which studies have indicated no or little success compared to traditional methods? Are we to assume that Ohio halfway houses must operate differently, have better personnel, or have discovered the extra something that turns criminal offenders into law-abiding citizens? This, of course, is not the case.

It appears that there is much similarity in the operations of halfway houses across America, and dedicated and qualified personnel can be found at each facility. What differentiates the results of this and previous evaluations might well be the evaluative methods and outcome measures utilized.

The problems in the utilization of a dichotomous measure of recidivism have already been pointed out. Martinson has also concluded that correctional programs (when evaluated using recidivism) do not work.[17] It is quite possible that recidivism is so insensitive that no single program can significantly effect recidivism.

It is also important to control for selection processes and differences between the experimental and comparison groups. Several evaluations do not rigidly control for such differences, and inconclusive and perhaps invalid results can occur.

Perhaps we have been too quick to indict our correctional system. It is possible that for years we have attempted to evaluate programs with the wrong tools. Findings of the evaluation of Ohio halfway houses seem surprisingly positive, but perhaps the outcome is no different from several previously studied programs.

This analysis certainly cannot lead to an absolute conclusion that community corrections is effective, but it does emphasize a new evaluative dimension, and perhaps in a small way contradict all the previous negative findings regarding community programs. The important conclusion from this analysis is that more appropriate methods of evaluation need to be developed, and a systematic approach toward correctional policy making initiated.

17. Martinson, Robert, "What Works?— Questions and Answers About Prison Reform," *Public Interest*, no. 35 (Spring 1974): 22–55.

THE HALFWAY HOUSE AND OFFENDER REINTEGRATION *

It has long been known that the greatest rate of post-release failures occur within the first sixty days.[1] Only within the past few years, however, have correctional authorities realized that something must be done to enable inmates to bridge the gap between prison and freedom. The most comprehensive ᵗreatment program within the institution may meet with complete failure if it does not provide for this transition. Too often the newly released individual is simply placed on the street upon release with little or no preparation for the role of free-world citizen.

Ideally the preparation of the offender for his return to the free world should begin the moment he enters the correctional process. The transition from prison to community life, if it is to be a smooth re-assimilation, must be preceded by treatment programs which are unique to the particular inmate and dedicated to the singular purpose of providing that individual with the necessary strengths to succeed on the outside.

One of the reasons for the lack of release preparation in the past has been the lack of understanding of the psychological and social mechanisms at work in the mind of the released inmate. The public conception that release from prison is an end—a goal—is often inaccurate.

Robert Lindner has suggested that the moment of release is a time of apprehension and self-examination, of discomfort and questioning, of self-doubt, inadequacy, inferiority, and fear of the future and the unknown.[2]

More true to life than the layman's consensus is the following account of an inmate of his release from prison in Texas:

> It was the day I had been waiting for eight years. I felt self-conscious in my new suit and stiff new shoes. As I walked through the front door of the institution, past the highly polished brass bars and down the front steps to freedom I realized just how scared I was. I had heard from others what to expect but I knew things would be different with me. It was five blocks to the bus station and as I walked them I began to feel stares from passers-by and I knew that they knew I was a convict. It was a feeling and whether they really knew or not, I knew, and thought they knew.
>
>   The bus trip to Houston wasn't bad except that I felt, again, terribly self-conscious. When a woman sat down beside me I forced myself not to look at her. She smiled at me once but I turned my head, afraid that my status would show on my face.

* Paul F. Cromwell, Jr., *Texas Journal of Corrections*, June 1976.

1. Baker, "Preparing Prisoners for Their Return to the Community," 30 *Federal Probations*, 43 (1966).

2. Linder, Robert, *Stone Walls and Men* (Odyssey Press, New York), 1946, p. 470.

At the bus terminal in Houston I felt lost. Everything had changed in eight years. The town was larger, busier and the telephone book was twice its previous size. I looked for the names of several friends in it but they were not there, and then I realized; all my friends were in prison, not here.

I went into a restaurant of a large department store and sat down. I wasn't hungry, but was searching for a friendly face, a kind word or just a smile. The waitress, expressionless and tired looking, dropped a menu in front of me. I ordered coffee and a piece of pie, half ate it, and left. No smile, no kind word; just efficiency.

I walked away; unconsciously drifting back to the old neighborhood. Within a few hours I was again among friends. Within a few days I had made connections and taken my first heroin in eight years.

I'm back again. Looking forward to release. I wonder if it will be the same next time. I know it will be, but I'm still anticipating the next time.

As in this case, the releasee too often appears outside the gates with no family, no friends. He has lost contact with free society. This loss is engendered by the lock-step routine of prison life. The institutionalizing process of prison robs him of initiative; makes him dependent. He leaves the institution and enters the free world in much the same condition as a new born infant leaves the security of the womb and enters the world, kicking and screaming in protest. The releasee, unlike the newborn, often finds a rejecting or apathetic world. He is scared, dependent; psychologically naked, and often in attempting to pick up the threads of a past life returns to the environment he once found most comfortable; his former criminal subculture.

Anthropologist Ruth Benedict has discussed continuities and discontinuities in cultural conditioning.[3] The term "continuities" refers to training which gradually prepares an individual to move from one role to another with a minimum of strain, thus helping to prevent maladjustment in the new role. The transition from childhood to an adult role is an example of this process.

Discontinuity occurs when the training in one role develops patterns which are dysfunctional in a subsequent role. The released inmate faces a discontinuity of conditioning. With seemingly purposeful training we condition the inmate to become institutionalized. He awakens at a certain hour, goes to meals on signal, reports to work assignments when told, showers in the evening at a predetermined time, takes part in highly structured recreational and educational programs and retires, again at a specific time. He may learn a vocational trade and become highly skilled

3. Benedict, Ruth, "Continuities and Discontinuities in Cultural Condition-   ing," *Psychiatry*, Vol. I (1938), pp. 161–167.

or improve his academic background yet in all this he is rigidly scheduled, tightly controlled and given almost no initiative nor the opportunity to make choices or decisions.

The roles of inmate and free-world citizen are strongly differentiated. A "Good" inmate is highly tractable and assumes little responsibility in decision making; a successful free-world citizen assumes responsibility, makes the proper decisions and choices and determines his own schedules and activities. An individual in one role must revise his behavior from almost all points of view when he assumes the second role.

Dr. Benedict Alper recently told a group of correctional administrators of a man who had spent nineteen years in a correctional institution:

> He told an audience to whom I introduced him that one of the hardest things for him to learn to do when he got out was to open a door. If he came to the door of an office or a private home, or a lavatory, or a station, or wherever it might be that he found himself facing a door, his first reaction was to stand there and wait for somebody to open it. For nineteen years he had never turned a knob or lifted a latch, he had to wait on the pleasure and the keys of somebody else to do that. And so he said to his audience, "What is for you in private life the easiest thing to do—to open a door and walk through—is for a person who has been conditioned to confinement the hardest thing to relearn." It took him several weeks before he got over that conditioned feeling of having to stand stockstill when he came to a door to wait for somebody else to open it. I know of no more forceful illustration of the "theoretical" reason for alternatives to present dealing with convicted offenders.

Reconditioning to the free world must become as important a task to correctional personnel as is conditioning the newly arrived inmate to prison life.

The necessity of abrupt revision of behavior brings about a form of cultural shock to the released inmate. Thus, our thesis; *The prison does not adequately furnish support to the individual as he progresses from role to role.* Even the most well-developed treatment program, if totally contained within the institution, will lack one ingredient essential to an inmate's success after release. The missing factor is contact with the community and family.

The discontinuity between prison house and free world can be and must be relieved by a planned program of transition. Several states and federal institutions have introduced innovative programs to aid the releasee in making the transition with a minimum of role strain and cultural shock. One such program is the *Community Treatment Center* concept developed by the United States Bureau of Prisons.

The Community Treatment Centers provide a program of *graduated release*, which permits the resident to solve his social and his economical problems piecemeal and reduces prospects of finding himself in desperate circumstances soon after release. Graduated release reduces the tension and anxiety and most importantly the shock of an abrupt release. It also creates a continuity of roles consistent with a maximum adjustment upon final release. The dichotomy between imprisonment and freedom loses some of its distinction, thus causes the released inmate to move from role to role with greater ease.

An essential element of graduated release is a concomitant program of *graduated responsibility*. As the inmate is continuously conditioned toward responsible social participation, the standards of conduct expected of him should be adapted to his capacity. It is of special interest that society demands almost perfection of behavior from the newly released offender, the person least apt to be capable of such a high standard. From the "normal" citizen we easily forgive minor and temporary deviances from the norm. Petty transgressions such as overindulgence in alcohol, tardiness in paying debts, family arguments, and occasional absenteeism on the job are regarded little concern, yet any of these on the part of the released offender are considered as "proof" that the offender has not been properly rehabilitated. Expectation of immediate adaptation to the normative structure is not consistent with the concept of graduated release. Therefore, minor deviations should be viewed as natural and should be expected and even programmed within the structure of the post-release period. The goal should be growth, not total and immediate normative adherence. The responsibility for growth is with the releasee, the responsibility of requiring growth with the supervising agency.

THE HALFWAY HOUSE EXPERIENCE

The typical correctional Halfway House is a private, non-profit facility offering contract services to local, state and federal authorities. Residents usually are received from one of three major sources: the courts, penal institutions or probation or paroling authorities as alternatives to revocation and incarceration.

A typical facility provides a supervised and structured residence for the client for periods ranging from 30 days to six months. Counselors provide center residents with a supervised environment, help them find jobs and give them needed guidance and support. Family problems and special difficulties, such as drug addiction and alcoholism get special attention. Individual counseling and group sessions are available for clients on a regular basis. These counseling sessions focus upon general problems of readjustment and specific areas of concern.

Staff are trained to recognize and understand the degree to which the success of the post-release period depends upon the resident's ability to adjust to new social and cultural conditions which will be encountered upon final release. The treatment program therefore is oriented toward providing these strengths and insights which will facilitate the adjustments.

PHASES OF ADJUSTMENT

During his tenure with two major halfway house programs, the author observed and delineated four phases through which a halfway house resident tends to pass during a 90–120 day stay at the facility.

OBSERVER PHASE

Upon release from the institution and entry into the Center, the average resident maintains himself as a somewhat detached spectator. This period of detachment is analogous to the situation a child is confronted with on his first days in a new school. The surroundings and people are new and somewhat mystifying. After a few days the expectations and rules of the place become familiar, strange faces gain names and more a comfortable feeling develops.

The staff should be especially sensitive to the feelings of the resident during the Observer Phase for this is the time during which the foundation must be laid for the remainder of his stay and during which his specific treatment needs should be identified, and a treatment modality designed specifically for his needs.

INVOLVEMENT PHASE

Upon successful resolution of the Observer Phase the resident usually enters a period of involvement. His first steps into the free world culture are experienced. Job hunting and home visits on weekends and evenings may bring about the first serious adjustment problems. Attempts at family reintegration often create severe anxieties. The resident often realizes that many of his preconceptions about release were false. The liabilities and stigma of his conviction and incarceration make themselves readily apparent when searching for employment and housing.

Staff members must be aware of the potential problems inherent in the Involvement Phase and work toward maximum supportive counseling at this time. The emphasis of both group and individual counseling is toward guidance and support in resolving these anxieties and frustrations.

COMING TO TERMS

If resolution of the Involvement Phase is successful, the resident enters a stage of adjustment which enables him to function with minimal problems and anxieties. He spends less time in the Center and the thrust of this period is toward maximum community involvement.

PRE–RELEASE

At a point two to three weeks previous to final release, problems often reappear which have been latent during the Coming to Terms Phase. Final release is looked forward to with both anticipation and apprehension. Counselors again must watch for indications of anxiety. Problems may again erupt which were seemingly resolved weeks before. Even in its openness, the Center has institutionalizing qualities and the fear of leaving is often present. The institutionalizing quality is illustrated by the number of ex-residents who seek housing in the immediate vicinity of the Center and who almost daily return to visit staff members. Not only anxieties, but behavior problems often manifest themselves and the Pre-Release Phase may be a period of frustration for both resident and staff.

Maximum awareness of the potential hazards at each stage of adjustment allows the staff to anticipate and prepare the resident to resolve those problems. Re-assimilation into the free world community is thus facilitated and role conflict reduced.

The Community Treatment Center concept is, of course, only one of several options available to corrections to ease the transition from prison to the community. Re-assimilation into the free world community is thus facilitated and role conflict reduced.

The Community Treatment Center concept is, of course, only one of several options available to corrections to ease the transition from prison to the community. Work release, study release, furloughs, and increased use of parole all aid in the reduction of "release shock" and subsequent recidivism.

THE PRISON OF THE FUTURE

Daniel Glaser has predicted that the prison of the future will maintain extensive links with community organizations. "Churches, social and fraternal organizations, service clubs, hobby groups, professional or trade associations, as well as societies and persons aiding each other in the control of vices (e. g., Alcoholics Anonymous), will participate in the prison more actively than heretofore."[4] Such cooperation should go far toward the goal of providing for each releasee the ability to move from the role of prisoner, with its attendant handicaps, to the role of the useful, productive citizen.

Summary

The released inmate, contrary to popular myth, greets his freedom with fear and trepidation. Anxiety-ridden, he may drift back into old and familiar patterns of delinquent activities and to the comfort of past criminal acquaintances.

Due to the critical nature of the post-release period the onus is upon correctional authorities to provide comprehensive preparation for the inmate's release into the community. Traditional programs such as

4. Glaser, Daniel, "The Prison of the Future," from *Crime In the City*, (Harper & Row Publishers, 1970), p. 262.

institutional pre-release do not provide for gradual transition from total confinement to total freedom. This abrupt role change by the inmate creates a form of cultural shock which manifests itself in high recidivism rates. This phenomenon has been termed "discontinuity of conditioning." The role behavior required of a free world citizen is strongly differentiated from that of the inmate culture. The inmate's conditioning within the institution prepares him to play a submissive role with little opportunity for individual initiative. Free world success requires a degree of autonomy, initiative, and assumption of responsibility.

A successful pre-release program must provide a gradual transition from one role to another and should be accomplished outside the institution. A graduated release program can most efficiently provide this necessary element of the total rehabilitative process. Essential elements of graduated release are: (1) an in-community setting, (2) close supervision, (3) allowance for expected deviations from the norm, (4) releasee growth in responsibility and capabilities, and (5) a gradual programmed transition from total confinement to absolute release. Only in this manner may the released inmate experience continuity of roles consistent with successful adjustment to free world expectations.

STANDARDS FOR COMMUNITY-BASED PROGRAMS *

Legislation should be enacted immediately authorizing the chief executive officer of the correctional agency to extend the limits of confinement of a committed offender so the offender can participate in a wide variety of community-based programs. Such legislation should include these provisions:

1. Authorization for the following programs:
   a. Foster homes and group homes, primarily for juvenile and youthful offenders.
   b. Prerelease guidance centers and halfway houses.
   c. Work-release programs providing that rates of pay and other conditions of employment are similar to those of free employees.
   d. Community-based vocational training programs, either public or private.
   e. Participation in academic programs in the community.
   f. Utilization of community medical, social rehabilitation, vocational rehabilitation, or similar resources.
   g. Furloughs of short duration to visit relatives and family, contact prospective employers, or for any other reason consistent with the public interest.

* National Advisory Commission on Criminal Justice Standards and Goals, *Report on Corrections,* 1973.

2. Authorization for the development of community-based residential centers either directly or through contract with governmental agencies or private parties, and authorization to assign offenders to such centers while they are participating in community programs.

3. Authorization to cooperate with and contract for a wide range of community resources.

4. Specific exemption for participants in community-based work programs from State-use and other laws restricting employment of offenders or sale of "convict-made" goods.

5. Requirement that the correctional agency promulgate rules and regulations specifying conduct that will result in revocation of community-based privileges and procedures for such revocation. Such procedures should be governed by the same standards as disciplinary proceedings involving a substantial change in status of the offender.

COMMENTARY

The most dramatic development in corrections in the United States over the last several years is the extension of correctional programing into the community. Probation and parole have always involved supervision in the community; now institutional programs located in the community provide a gradual diminishment of control leading toward parole and outright release.

Work-release programs that allowed the committed offender to work in the community by day and return to the institution during nonworking hours began in Wisconsin for misdemeanants in 1913 and have spread through many States on the felony level. Approximately 31 States have some work-release authority. Federal prisoners were provided work-release opportunities by the Prisoner Rehabilitation Act of 1965.

Offenders participating in employment programs should continue to be protected against economic exploitation. Most work-release laws require that prisoners receive equal wages and work under employment conditions equal to those of free employees.

The flexibility of community-based programs is limited only by the availability of community resources and the imagination of correctional administrators. Employment opportunities are only one example. Legislation should authorize correctional agencies to utilize any community resource with reasonable relation to efforts to reintegrate the offender into the community on release.

Full utilization of community resources may require more from the legislature than authorization. Present laws which prohibit the sale of "prison-made goods" are, in some States, sufficiently ambiguous as applied to community-based programs as to require clarification. Some occupations regulated by government may prohibit employment of felons unless pardoned, which would curtail utilization of offenders prior to their outright release. Although it may be useful to list specific programs in authorizing legislation for clarification, an open-ended provision allowing experimentation should be provided.

Temporary furloughs likewise should be authorized for a wide variety of reasons. Most States have furlough laws allowing incarcerated individuals to attend a funeral of a relative or to visit a sick or dying family member. These programs should be expanded to include family visits, seeking employment and educational placements, and other reasons consistent with the public interest. Since furloughs for family visitation are controversial in some locations, the legislature should specifically authorize such a program.

Contemporary correctional thinking is that offenders will be given gradual responsibility and more freedom until parole or outright release. Thus, each new decrease in control is a test for eventual release. A violation of trust at any one stage of the process inevitably will affect the date when the offender will be paroled. Decisions that revoke community-based privileges thus have a substantial impact on an offender's liberty. Procedural safeguards should be required in revocation of community-based privileges.

THE USE OF RESTITUTION *

The idea that the offender should make restitution as part of the penalty for wrongdoing was entrenched in primitive law systems.[1] Its historical de-emphasis, most scholars suggest, was a consequence of the development of strong centralized authority in England following the Norman invasion, the separation of criminal and civil law, and the state's superseding interest in the outcome of criminal proceedings.[2]

While weakened, the notion of restitution as a sanction for criminal wrongdoing was never entirely lost. Its use was advocated by Sir Thomas More, Jeremy Bentham, Herbert Spencer, Raffaele Garofalo, Enrico Ferri, and others.[3] More recent advocates include Giorgio del

* Burt Galaway. *Crime and Delinquency*, Jan. 1977. Reprinted by permission of the National Council on Crime and Delinquency.

1. See, for example, Stephen Schafer, *The Victim and His Criminal* (New York: Random House, 1968, pp. 7–38; Richard E. Laster, "Criminal Restitution: A Survey of Its Past History and an Analysis of Its Present Usefulness," *University of Richmond Law Review*, Fall 1970, pp. 71–98, also in Joe Hudson and Burt Galaway, eds., *Considering the Victim: Readings in Restitution and Victim Compensation* (Springfield, Ill.:

Charles C. Thomas, 1975), pp. 19–28, 311–31; E. Adamson Hoebel, *The Law of Primitive Man* (Cambridge, Mass.: Harvard University Press, 1954).

2. See especially, Schafer, op. cit. supra note 1, and Laster, supra note 1.

3. Thomas More, *Utopia* [1516] (J. C. Collins ed., 1904), pp. 23–24; Jeremy Bentham, "Political Remedies for the Evil of Offenses" [1838], in Hudson and Galaway, op. cit. supra note 1, pp. 29–42; Herbert Spencer, "Prison Ethics" [1892], in Hudson and Galaway, op. cit. supra note 1, pp. 71–84; Raffaele Garo-

Vecchio, Stephen Schafer, Albert Eglash, Kathleen Smith, and Burt Galaway and Joe Hudson.[4] It has received limited attention in the past fifty years in the ideology of criminal justice and correction (at least as expressed in published form), but its use as a probation condition has been authorized in statutes and has been reflected in the practice of courts ordering restitution as a condition of probation. Unfortunately the extent of this practice is not known, its rationale is not clearly articulated, and there appears to be little interest among correctional practitioners in considering its impact or examining its role in criminal justice.

Recent policy statements may indicate some shift in thinking. The National Advisory Commission's standard on "sentencing the nondangerous offender" states that the offender should not be imprisoned, if among other favorable circumstances, he "has made or will make restitution . . . to the victim . . . for the damage or injury . . .,"[5] and it recommends that a fine not be imposed when it would interfere with the offender's ability to make restitution.[6] The second edition of the Model Sentencing Act explicitly recognizes restitution as a sanction to be used alone or in conjunction with other sanctions.[7] Restitution is recognized in standards enunciated by the American Bar Association[8] and was explicitly recommended as an alternative to imprisonment by the 1972 Annual Chief Justice Earl Warren Conference on Advocacy in the United States.[9] The Canadian Law Reform Commission is advocating use of

falo, "Enforced Reparation as a Substitute for Imprisonment" [1914], in Hudson and Galaway, op. cit. supra note 1, pp. 43–53; Enrico Ferri, *Criminal Sociology* (Boston: Little, Brown, 1917), pp. 498–520.

4. Giorgio del Vecchio, "The Problem of Penal Justice," in Hudson and Galaway, op. cit. supra note 1, pp. 85–101; Stephen Schafer, *Compensation and Restitution to Victims of Crime* (Montclair, N.J.: Patterson Smith, 1970); Albert Eglash, "Creative Restitution: A Broader Meaning for an Old Term," in Hudson and Galaway, op. cit. supra note 1, pp. 284–90; Albert Eglash, "Creative Restitution: Some Suggestions for Prison Rehabilitation Programs," *American Journal of Correction,* November-December 1958, pp. 20–22, 34; Paul Keve and Albert Eglash, "Payments on a 'Debt to Society,'" *NPPA News,* September 1957, pp. 1–2; Kathleen Smith, *A Cure for Crime: The Case for the Self-Determinate Prison Sentence* (London: Duckworth, 1965); Burt Galaway and Joe Hudson, "Restitution and Rehabilitation: Some Central Issues," *Crime and Delinquency,* October 1972, pp. 403–10;

Burt Galaway and Joe Hudson, "Sin, Sickness, Restitution—Toward a Reconciliative Correctional Model," in Hudson and Galaway, op. cit. supra note 1, pp. 59–70.

5. National Advisory Commission on Criminal Justice Standards and Goals, *Corrections* (Washington, D.C.: U.S. Govt. Printing Office, 1973), Standard 5.2, p. 151.

6. Id., Standard 5.5, p. 162.

7. Council of Judges, National Council on Crime and Delinquency, "Model Sentencing Act" (2nd ed.), *Crime and Delinquency* October 1972, § 9, p. 357, and commentary, pp. 358–59.

8. Herbert S. Miller, "The American Bar Association Looks at Probation," *Federal Probation,* December 1970, pp. 3–9.

9. Annual Chief Justice Earl Warren Conference on Advocacy in the United States, *A Program for Prison Reform* (Cambridge, Mass.: Roscoe Pound-American Trial Lawyers Foundation, 1972), p. 11.

restitution and negotiated settlements as methods for diverting offenders from the criminal justice system.[10]

In addition to these policy statements, a few projects have been developed in the 1970's which involve the explicit use of restitution.

The purpose of this paper is twofold: (1) to review contemporary examples of the use of restitution in pretrial diversionary programs, as a condition of probation, and as part of community-based, residential correctional programs which allegedly provide an alternative to the imprisonment of offenders; (2) to articulate a series of issues which emanate from the use of restitution. The issues relate to the lack of specificity of the concept of restitution, the purpose of restitution, the relation of restitution to other criminal justice sanctions, and the role of the victim in restitution programs.

Restitution is defined to mean a requirement, either imposed by agents of the criminal justice system or undertaken voluntarily by the wrongdoer but with the consent of the criminal justice system, by which the offender engages in acts designed to make reparation for the harm resulting from the criminal offense. This definition has three central components: action by the offender which may be either voluntary or coerced, knowledge and consent of agents of the criminal justice system, and the repairing of damages.

CONTEMPORARY APPLICATIONS

Restitution is applied in pretrial diversion programs, as a condition of probation, and as a part of the program of community correction centers established to provide an alternative to traditional imprisonment.

Pretrial Diversion

While there is little published material, restitution has quite likely been used regularly and informally by police and prosecutors as a pretrial diversionary tactic. Permitting youth to return stolen merchandise or to pay for damage done as a result of vandalism exemplifies this use of restitution. Police and prosecutors may permit check offenders to make good in lieu of prosecution. Unfortunately, as is true of other early diversionary practices, this use of official discretion is informal, out of the public scrutiny, and usually not reported or recorded in any orderly way. An immediate need is information on the nature of restitution requirements imposed as a part of traditional, informal diversion practices.

Restitution components may also be built into new, structured pretrial diversion programs. Both Project de Novo in Minneapolis and Project Remand in St. Paul divert arrested juvenile, misdemeanor, and felony defendants into a work evaluation, training, and job placement

10. Law Reform Commission of Canada, Working Paper No. 3: *The Principal of Sentencing and Dispositions*, pp. 7–10, Working Papers 5 & 6: *Restitution and Compensation Fines*, pp. 5–15 (Ottawa: Information Canada, 1974).

program. In these projects restitution is a frequent condition of diversion, especially for property offenders.[11]

In Tucson, Ariz., the Pima County Attorney's Office administers an Adult Diversion Project for nonserious, first-time defendants who volunteer for the project and whose participation is approved by the victim, the arresting officers, and the prosecutor. If all approve, the victim and the offender meet in face-to-face confrontation to define the restitution obligations which are included along with other treatment obligations that the defendant undertakes as a condition of diversion.[12]

The Community Youth Responsibility Program (CYRP) in East Palo Alto, Calif., provides services to juveniles as an alternative to juvenile court referral. Cases are reviewed by a Community Panel, consisting of neighborhood juveniles and adults, which may require the youth to make restitution to the victim or perform community services. While the orders do not carry legal authority, failure to comply creates the possibility of referral back to the court.[13]

Restitution is also one of the settlement procedures used by the Citizen Dispute Settlement Centers of the American Arbitration Association [14] and the Night Prosecutor Program in Columbus, Ohio.[15] Both of these programs were established to develop dispute-settlement procedures by means other than use of the criminal justice system and to provide noncriminal justice alternatives for handling private criminal complaints. Both involve efforts to bring the victim and the offender together and may utilize some form of restitution as a part of the settlement.

Probation Condition

Statutes in several states permit courts to order payment of restitution as a probation condition, and, in other jurisdictions, courts are making use of this sanction as a part of their general power to establish reasonable probation conditions. There is some case law defining reasonableness of restitution and the beginning of judicial guidelines for courts in utilizing this sanction.[16] Some courts have also been experimenting

11. Conversations with William Henschel, of Operation de Novo, and Kathryn Bleecker, of Project Remand.

12. Herbert Edelhertz, *Restitutive Justice: A General Survey and Analysis* (Seattle, Wash.: Battelle Human Affairs Research Centers, 1975), pp. 57–59.

13. Id., pp. 53–55.

14. Janet Kole, "Arbitration as an Alternative to the Criminal Warrant," *Judicature*, February 1973, pp. 295–97; Carl A. Eklund, "The Problem of Overcriminalizing Human Conduct: A Civil Alternative," paper presented to the

American Society of Criminology Annual Meeting, Chicago, November 1974.

15. John W. Palmer, "Pre-Arrest Diversion," *Crime and Delinquency*, April 1975; U.S. Dept. of Justice, Law Enforcement Assistance Administration, *An Exemplary Project: Citizen Dispute Settlement* (Washington, D.C.: U.S. Govt. Printing Office, 1974).

16. See for example, William P. Jacobson, "Use of Restitution in the Criminal Process: People v. Miller," *UCLA Law Review*, 1969, pp. 456–75; Sol Rubin, *Law of Criminal Correction*, 2nd ed. (St. Paul, Minn.: West, 1973), pp. 229–32.

with use of community service requirements, especially for juvenile and misdemeanant offenders. Unfortunately there is no systematic reporting of these experiences or assessment of the extent of the practices. A research project is presently under way in Minnesota to determine the extent to which restitution has been used and to assess the views of judges, probation officers, offenders, and victims concerning the appropriateness of restitution requirements as a probation condition.[17]

In the Victims Assistance Program of the Pennington County (S. Dak.) Juvenile Court, restitution and work details are perceived as "therapeutic elements in court supervision" and are incorporated into court orders for juvenile probation.[18]

The West German code offers an interesting alternative for dealing with juvenile and young adult offenders. Judges may impose "corrective measures" on juvenile offenders for whom incarceration is thought unnecessary. Corrective measures may consist of a reprimand, imposition of particular requirements, or use of short-term (not to exceed one month), week-end, or intermittent detention. The particular requirements include making good the damage done, personally apologizing to the person injured, or making a financial contribution toward some useful public establishment. The young person can be required to contribute to a useful public establishment only to deprive him of the proceeds of his offense and only if the payment comes out of his own resources. In addition to corrective measures West German courts may make use of educational-welfare measures or youth imprisonment as sanctions for juvenile delinquency or young adult offenses. The money payment is the primary particular requirement imposed.[19]

Under provisions of the Criminal Justice Act of 1972, judges in Great Britain are permitted, in the instance of adult offenders (predominantly in the 18-to-25 age range), to order 40 to 240 hours of unpaid community service work in lieu of imprisonment. The community service order can be issued only with the consent of the offender, after a determination that suitable opportunities exist for the work and after consideration of the probation officer's report. The order must be carried out within one year and the work must be done in the offender's spare time.[20] Additionally the Community Services Volunteers program in Great Britain has been providing opportunities for delinquent youth (both those residing in

17. Minnesota Department of Corrections, "The Assessment of Restitution in the Minnesota Probation Services," Minnesota Governor's Commission on Crime Prevention and Control.

18. Edelhertz, op. cit. supra note 12, pp. 55–57.

19. Unfortunately data provided by the West German Ministry of Justice do not indicate what proportion of money payments went to the actual victims of crime and what proportion went to useful public establishments. Federal Republic of Germany, Ministry of Justice, "The Treatment of Young Offenders in the Federal Republic of Germany" (mimeo. in English; n.d.).

20. Howard Standish Bergman, "Community Service in England: An Alternative to Custodial Sentence," *Federal Probation,* March 1975, pp. 42–46.

Borstals and those in after-care programs) to engage in voluntary community service activities which are beneficial to both the delinquent and the community.[21]

In 1973 Iowa legislation established a public policy of restitution as a condition of probation for all suspended or deferred sentences. Probation officers are expected to prepare and present restitution plans; payments are to be ordered to the extent of the offender's ability to make restitution.[22] Generally restitution payments are made to the clerk of the court, who forwards them to the victim to minimize the opportunity for direct victim-offender contact. The Restitution in Probation Experiment (RIPE), an LEAA-funded project in the Des Moines area, is building upon this policy by altering the practice of discouraging victim-offender contacts and bringing together the victim, the offender, and the probation officer to negotiate a restitution agreement, which is then presented to the court for consideration. The Iowa projection introduces the variable of offender-victim communication into an existing restitution program.[23]

Residential Community-Correction Center

Halfway houses, group homes, and other residential community correction facilities provide an additional setting for restitution. The Minnesota Restitution Center, established in 1972, is probably the prototype of this type of programing.[24] The Center receives adult male property offenders who have been admitted to the Minnesota State Prison and have served four months of their prison sentence. While in prison the offender, with the assistance of a staff member of the Restitution Center, meets with his victim face-to-face to develop a restitution agreement. After the agreement is prepared and the parole board concurs, the offender is released on parole to the Minnesota Restitution Center, where he lives, secures employment, and fulfills the terms of the restitution agreement. The offender resident may receive additional services, including mandatory group therapy, supervision in a community correction center, and assistance with securing employment. Most of the restitution agreements have involved a monetary exchange between the offender and the victim; in situations where the victim could not be located, was unwilling to participate, or had not suffered damage, restitution in the form of community service or a contribution to some community agency has been used. The trend has been away from community service and

21. Clementine L. Kaufman, "Community Service Volunteers: A British Approach to Delinquency Prevention," *Federal Probation*, December 1973, pp. 35–41.

22. Iowa Senate File 26, 65th General Assembly (1973).

23. Polk County (Iowa) Board of Supervisors, "Restitution in Probation Experiment," grant application submitted to

the Kansas City Regional Office of the Law Enforcement Assistance Administration, 1974.

24. Joe Hudson and Burt Galaway, "Undoing the Wrong," *Social Work*, May 1974, Burt Galaway and Joe Hudson, "Issues in the Correctional Implementation of Restitution to Victims of Crime," in Hudson and Galaway, op. cit. supra note 1, pp. 351–60.

toward payment of money to a community organization as the preferred form of symbolic restitution.

Georgia has established four restitution shelters based partially on the Minnesota model. Generally men referred to these shelters come solely from courts and are on probation; in each case a court has ordered restitution as a probation condition. The offender has been ordered to live in the restitution shelter, secure and maintain work, and complete the court-ordered restitution. Georgia's program operates much like work-release shelters: the resident's salary checks are turned over to the shelter business manager, who deducts an appropriate amount for room and board, family support, a living-expenses allowance, and restitution. Victim-offender contacts are not a part of the program; the business manager mails the court-ordered restitution payment to the victim.[25]

ISSUES

Experiences to date with restitution in the criminal justice system suggest a series of issues that require clarification if it is to be more systematically utilized as a correctional tool. The issues can be grouped into four categories: developing a classification of restitution, specifying the purpose of restitution, clarifying the relationship of restitution to other criminal sanctions, and defining the role which victims might play in a restitution program.

Differing Types

Even a cursory observation of existing programs reveals that the term *restitution* is applied to differing phenomena; sometimes adjectives are added, making references to *monetary* restitution, *symbolic* restitution, *community service* restitution, *moral* restitution, *creative* restitution, etc. An immediate need is the development of a conceptual framework that clearly specifies and defines different types of restitution.

A simple typology of restitution (see Figure 1) can be developed by using two variables: (1) the offender makes restitution in money or service and (2) the recipient of the restitution is the actual victim or some substitute victim. Four types of restitution can be identified by using these two variables:

Type I : Monetary-victim restitution refers to payment of money by the offender to the actual victim of the crime. This is probably the most common definition and actual use of restitution.

Type II : Monetary-community restitution involves the payment of money by the offender to some "substitute victim" (a useful public

25. Georgia Department of Corrections and Offender Rehabilitation, "L.E.A.A. National Scope Project for Citizen Action," application for grant to the United States Department of Justice, Law Enforcement Assistance Administration, June 5, 1974. Personal interviews with Bill Read, Manager, and James H. Deal, Director, Rome Restitution Shelter, Georgia Department of Offender Rehabilitation, April 1975.

establishment).   Examples are the Restitution Center and the West German corrective orders for juvenile and young adult offenders.

Type III: Service-victim restitution requires the offender to perform a useful service for the actual victim of the crime.   Contemporary projects do not provide good examples of this type of restitution, although the Citizen Dispute Settlement Programs of the American Arbitration Association and the Night Prosecutor Program in Columbus, Ohio, are likely sources for this type of restitution.   Both of these programs are designed to bring offenders and victims together to effect a noncriminal settlement of private criminal complaints.   Although accounts of the settlements effected have not been published, the nature of the programs is consistent with Type III restitution.

Type IV: Service-community restitution involves the offender in performing some useful community service.   Probation conditions requiring community service, the English program of substituting the community service for imprisonment, and the use of "symbolic" restitution in the first two years of operation of the Minnesota Restitution Center are all examples of Type IV restitution.

Any typology of restitution will become more complex as additional variables, such as victim-offender contacts or victim participation in developing the restitution contract, are considered.   Whether the restitution is undertaken voluntarily or is coerced might be an important variable in a restitution typology.   The Minnesota Restitution Center has developed agreements calling for the offender to make restitution for offenses (such as bad checks) of which, because of plea bargaining or for other reasons, he was not actually found guilty.   The agreement containing such a provision clearly specifies that the restitution is a moral obligation only and that the offender's failure to adhere to it does not constitute a ground for parole revocation.

Figure 1. Typology of Restitution

		Recipient of Restitution	
		Victim	Community Organization
Form of Restitution	Monetary	Type I Monetary-Victim	Type II Monetary-Community
	Service	Type III Service-Victim	Type IV Service-Community

[B6529]

The restitution concept is broad and requires refinement.   Different types of restitution must be clearly defined and distinguished from one another.

Purpose

Who or what is the intended beneficiary of a restitution program? Is it the victim? The offender? The community at large? The criminal justice system?

Promoting restitution to help crime victims is questionable. The vast majority of crimes go unsolved; in many, arrest of the offender does not result in conviction; and in other instances, even where conviction is secured, restitution may not be an appropriate sanction. Thus, a comparatively small number of crime victims will ever receive redress through a restitution program. If protecting the welfare of crime victims is the primary social aim, a public crime-victim compensation program is likely to be more effective than restitution.

Edelhertz notes that, historically, restitution was the mechanism whereby the offender and his kin group made amends to the victim and his kin group and thus avoided a more severe sanction that the victim's kin group could have legitimately imposed—in short, it benefited the offender rather than the victim,[26] as recently illustrated by a reported case in Minnesota.[27] An Ethiopian student who murdered his roommate, also Ethiopian, was found to be insane and was committed to a program for the criminally insane, after which the Immigration Service began deportation proceedings. The defendant requested a delay in his deportation until his family in Ethiopia could arrange a suitable settlement with the family of the victim (custom required that these negotiations could not begin until after a year of mourning had elapsed) so that he could return to Ethiopia without risk of being killed by the family of his victim.

A second purpose of restitution, consistent with its historic intent, is to provide a less severe and more humane sanction for the offender. This purpose is implicit in diversionary programs and is more or less explicit in the Minnesota and Georgia programs. The Minnesota Restitution Center is an alternative to imprisonment for property offenders, and the Georgia Restitution Shelters are part of a package of programs that were funded to reduce the size of the state's prison population.

A third related but conceptually distinct purpose of restitution is aid in the rehabilitation of the offender, as advocated in the 1940's by the chief probation officer in New York City, in the 1950's by psychologist Albert Eglash, and more recently by Stephen Schafer (who sees restitution as an opportunity to integrate the punitive and rehabilitative purposes of the criminal law), O. Hobert Mower, and Galaway and Hudson.[28]

26. Edelhertz, op. cit. supra note 12, pp. 1–20.

27. Minneapolis *Tribune,* Nov. 15, 1974, p. 1.

28. Irving E. Cohen, "The Integration of Restitution in the Probation Services," *Journal of Criminal Law, Criminology, and Police Science,* January-February 1944, pp. 315–21 (also in Hudson and Galaway, op. cit. supra note 1, pp. 322–39); Eglash, supra note 4; Schafer, op. cit. supra note 4; O. Hobert Mower, "Loss and Recovery of Community," in George M. Gazda, ed., *Innovations to Group Psychotherapy* (Springfield, Ill.: Charles C. Thomas, 1968), pp. 130–48 (also in Hudson and Galaway, op. cit. supra note 1, pp. 265–83); Galaway and Hudson, supra note 4.

The rationale for speculating that restitution might be more rehabilitative than other correctional measures includes the notion that restitution is related to the amount of damages done and thus would be perceived as more just by the offender, is specific and allows for a clear sense of accomplishment as the offender completes concrete requirements, requires the offender to be actively involved in the treatment program, and provides a socially appropriate and concrete way of expressing guilt and atonement.   It maintains that the offender who makes restitution is likely to elicit a more positive response from persons around him than the offender who is sent to prison or is subjected to some other correctional sanction.   Restitution is perceived as a sanction that enhances self-respect.

A fourth possible purpose for restitution is to benefit the criminal justice system by providing a fairly easily administered sanction permitting the reduction of demands on the system.   The system can process offenders rather easily at the same time that it avoids a public appearance of doing nothing or being soft.   While not articulated as a purpose, this rationale may be implicit in the use of restitution in informal diversion or as a probation condition.

A fifth purpose of restitution may be reduction of the need for vengeance in the administration of criminal law as offenders are perceived as responsible persons taking active steps to make amends for wrongdoing.

These five possible purposes—redress for the victim, less severe sanction for the offender, rehabilitation of the offender, reduction of demands on the criminal justice system, and reduction of the need for vengeance in a society—are not mutually exclusive.   Individual restitution programs, however, can reasonably be expected to specify the purpose or purposes of their existence.

Relation to Other Sanctions

Is restitution a sufficient sanction for some types of crime?   Does restitution detract from the effectiveness of other sanctions?   Are there situations in which a restitution requirement may impose an injustice on the offender?   These are some of the more troublesome questions in attempting to assess the relationship between restitution and other criminal justice sanctions.

With the possible exception of the community service programs in England, there is considerable reluctance to use restitution as the sole sanction for any identified group of offenders.   (Some of the informal pretrial diversionary strategies, however, may be a *de facto* sole use of restitution as the sanction of wrongdoing.)   The Minnesota Restitution Center imposes additional treatment requirements on residents (including mandatory group counseling) and, because of the comparatively small dollar damages done by residents, limits the monthly amount of repayment to hold residents in a treatment program for a specified period of time.[29] Restitution is generally perceived as one of a series of conditions which may be imposed on the wrongdoer. As experience is gained, perhaps restitution can be used as the only penalty for some specified kinds of offenses or offenders.

The prevailing view of the impact of restitution on other sanctions is that the restitution requirement may inhibit the offender's rehabilitation by weakening his ability to support himself and his family or to meet other financial obligations.[30] Some correctional staff maintain that focusing on restitution would interfere with their work on more important problems. Others have suggested that restitution is simply a bill-collecting procedure requiring little skill on their part and offering questionable help to the offender. When restitution is not the sole penalty, the challenge is to find ways of integrating its use with other correctional services and sanctions. In the 1940's, Irving Cohen suggested that restitution requirements provided a positive focus for the probation officer's work.[31] More recently, Kathleen Smith has proposed that financial restitution (both directly to the victim and also to the society in the form of a court-ordered discretionary fine) become the basis for determining the length of time that an offender would be incarcerated.[32] Essentially, the Smith proposal provides inmates with the opportunity to work at prevailing union rates. The prisoner would be charged a fee for room and board, would be required to contribute to support of his family, and would be discharged from prison upon completion of his restitution obligations.

Under certain circumstances restitution may be perceived as an unjust sanction—for example, when the damage is so extensive that even a lifetime of peak earnings would not be sufficient to make reparation.

The task is to begin specifying the kinds of offenders or the kinds of offenses for which restitution is an appropriate sanction. When is it appropriate as the sole sanction, when should it be used together with other sanctions, and when it is inappropriate?

Victim Involvement

What role, if any, should the victims of crime play in a restitution program? If restitution is being used as a less severe sanction—e. g., as an alternative to imprisonment—what consideration should be given to the wishes of the victim on this question? Some victims refuse to participate in the restitution process. Should this failure to participate be

29. Hudson and Galaway, supra note 24.

30. See, for example, President's Commission on Law Enforcement and Administration of Justice, *Task Force Report: Corrections* (Washington, D.C.: U.S. Govt. Printing Office, 1967), p. 35; Rubin, op. cit. supra note 16, pp. 231–32.

31. Cohen, op. cit. supra note 28.

32. Smith, op. cit. supra note 4.

allowed to veto the use of restitution and, in effect, mandate a severe sanction? The Minnesota Restitution Center has resolved this issue, in the comparatively few times it has arisen, by permitting the substitution of community service or payment of restitution to a community organization for direct involvement of the victim. The Adult Diversion Project of Tucson, however, permits either the victim or the arresting officer to veto the defendant's entry into a pretrial diversionary program using restitution.

Existing programs range from attempts to involve the victim and the offender actively in direct communications to develop a restitution plan and to continue contacts as the plan is implemented (as in the Minnesota Restitution Center, the Iowa Restitution in Probation Experiment, and the Adult Diversion Project) to those in which court-ordered restitution is made through an intermediary to avoid victim-offender contacts (as in the Georgia Restitution Shelters). The Iowa program is an effort to introduce victim-offender involvement into a system in which restitution was already present but was being handled through court officials without victim and offender communication. The Minnesota program has had considerable success in securing the assistance of the victim in negotiating the restitution contract but less success in maintaining offender-victim communication once the contract is drawn up and the offender is actually implementing the agreement.[33]

The impact of victim-offender communication on both the victim and the offender is, at present, unknown. Can they engage in communication that would be beneficial to both? What does such communication do to the offender's perception of victims and the victim's perception of offenders? Would such communication reduce the need for scapegoating and cries for vengeance?

The question of victim involvement raises two further issues—differentiating types of victims and degrees of victim culpability. Victims range from individuals to large organizations. Should the type of victim be a consideration in determining the restitution obligation: How is "victim" to be operationalized in the case of large organizations? Does the type of victim influence the impact which restitution may be presumed to have on the offender? A growing body of evidence suggests that in some situations victims may be partially responsible for their own victimization.[34] What part, if any, should the issue of victim culpability play in imposing restitution requirements?

SUMMARY

Restitution has probably been fairly widely used, both as an informal diversionary strategy by police and prosecutors and as a probation condi-

---

33. Galaway and Hudson, op. cit. supra note 24.

34. Lynn A. Curtis, *Criminal Violence: National Patterns and Behavior* (Lexington, Mass.: D. C. Heath, 1974).

tion by judges. During the last five years it has been employed more systematically in pretrial diversion projects, in specialized probation projects, and as a part of programs of community correction centers serving as an alternative to imprisonment.

A number of issues have evolved from these uses of restitution, including need for a classification scheme to differentiate types of restitution and clarification of the purpose of restitution, the relationship between restitution and other criminal justice sanctions, and the role of the victim in the restitution process.

More adequate reporting of the nature of restitution and the extent of its use is badly needed. The publication of information on the extent of use of restitution in various jurisdictions and of description of restitution projects and how they can resolve the foregoing issues is essential to the orderly development of this concept and the appraisal of its place in the criminal justice system.

TOPICS FOR THOUGHT AND DISCUSSION

1. What is *diversion*? At what points in or before the criminal justice process may diversion be effectively utilized?

2. Robert M. Carter states that our treatment of crime in America reflects the prevailing notions of the origins or causes of crime. Discuss how the evolving understanding of criminal behavior has been reflected in the "punishment/treatment" segment of the process.

3. Some "standards" for diversion must be promulgated in order to eliminate inequities. List and discuss the standards suggested by Carter.

4. Klein predicts a short, inconclusive life for police diversion programs. Upon what basis does this conclusion lie?

5. Pretrial intervention programs are a form of diversion. Roesch has studied the effects of such programs on jail populations. What are his conclusions and recommendations?

6. Will diversion reduce recidivism? Richard Lundman believes it will not. What are the advantages and disadvantages of diversion programs? Do you believe that the disadvantages outweigh the possible benefits? Why or why not?

7. Review and discuss various forms of halfway houses and community treatment centers. If such programs are operating in your community, visit them and try to determine their goals, methods and impact on the client and community.

8. Most experts agree that the halfway house movement must integrate within the totality of the correctional process to succeed and survive. Why?

9. If halfway houses are to be a part of the correctional system, what should be their function in relation to that system?

10. What might be the function of a halfway house in relation to a pretrial release program (ROR)? In other diversion programs?

11. Richard Seiter believes community corrections to be in a state of turmoil. Discuss some major reasons for this condition and means by which it might be corrected.

12. Seiter concludes that halfway houses are no more effective than other community based programs, but more effective than traditional prison-parole methods. Discuss the study upon which these conclusions are based.

13. Cromwell discusses the sociological concept of continuities and discontinuities in cultural conditioning. How does this relate to corrections; particularly to the utilization of halfway houses for released prisoners?

14. Discuss the four phases of adjustment observed and delineated by Cromwell. Of what value to the correctional worker are these observations?

15. As a part of the correctional process, restitution is both ancient and new. How is this true?

16. How may restitution be utilized as an adjunct to other community based correctional programs?

CHAPTER TWO

PROBATION AS COMMUNITY-BASED CORRECTIONS

INTRODUCTION

The basic idea underlying a sentence to probation is very simple. Sentencing is in large part concerned with avoiding future crimes by helping the defendant learn to live productively in the community which he has offended against. Probation proceeds on the theory that the best way to pursue this goal is to orient the criminal sanction toward the community setting in those cases where it is compatible with the other objectives of sentencing. Other things being equal, the odds are that a given defendant will learn how to live successfully in the general community if he is dealt with in that community rather than shipped off to the artificial and atypical environment of an institution of confinement. Banishment from society, in a word, is not the way to integrate someone into society. Yet imprisonment involves just such banishment—albeit for a temporary sojourn in most cases.

This is of course not to say that probation should be used in all cases, or that it will always produce better results. There are many goals of sentencing, some of which in a given case may require the imposition of a sentence to imprisonment even in the face of a conclusion that probation is more likely to assure the public that the particular defendant will not offend again. And there are defendants as to whom forced removal from the environment which may in some part have contributed to their offense may be the best beginning to a constructive and useful life.

By the same token, however, it is to say that probation is a good bit more than the "matter of grace" or "leniency" which characterizes the philosophy of the general public and of many judges and legislatures on the subject. Probation is an affirmative correctional tool, a tool which is used not because it is of maximum benefit to the defendant (though, of course, this is an important side product), but because it is of maximum benefit to the society which is sought to be served by the sentencing of criminals. The automatic response of many in the criminal justice system that imprisonment is the best sentence for crime unless particular reasons exist for "mitigating" the sentence is not a sound starting point in the framing of criminal sanctions. The premise of this report is that quite the opposite ought to be the case—that the automatic response in a sentencing situation ought to be probation, unless particular aggravating factors emerge in the case at hand. At least if such aggravating factors cannot be advanced as the basis for a more repressive sentence, probation

88

offers more hope than a sentence to prison that the defendant will not become part of the depressing cycle which makes the gates of our prisons resemble a revolving door rather than a barrier to crime.

It must of course also be realized that this thesis cannot be practiced in a vacuum. Too often a sentencing judge is faced with the Hobson's choice of a sentence to an overcrowded prison that is almost a guarantee that the defendant will emerge a more dangerous man than when he entered or a sentence to an essentially unsupervised probation that is little more than a release of the defendant without sanction, as well as without incentive to avoid the commission of a new offense. Such a state of affairs represents a failure of the legislative process of the highest order. The criminal justice system has failed in this country for this reason more than any other; not enough attention has been paid to providing adequate correctional choices to those who must operate the system. The thesis of these standards is that an adequate correctional system will place great reliance on appropriately funded and manned probation services. Within such a context, probation can lead to significant improvement in the preventive effects of the criminal law, at much less of a financial burden than the more typical prison sentence. This much has been proven in those jurisdictions where it has had a chance to work. One should not treat lightly an approach to crime control that offers the hope of better results at less cost. This, in a sentence, is the hope of probation.[1]

This chapter presents the student an opportunity to examine probation for its conception in English common law roots through the relative sophistication of probation systems today. Theories of supervision are presented and particular problems are analyzed. The presentence report is discussed in detail and legal aspects of probation grants and revocation are considered. The authors range from distinguished members of the judiciary and scholars to live probation officers and practitioners. The role of the probation officer is discussed as well as such management problems as caseload size, supervision intensity and the use of probation prediction models. Each author brings to bear upon the topic his special and particular expertise to create a chapter which is comprehensive, integrated and above all, informative.

THE ORIGINS OF PROBATION: FROM COMMON LAW ROOTS *

Several attempts have been made to trace back the legal origins of probation to medieval and early modern European law. The precedents

1. The American Bar Association, Project on Minimum Standards and Goals, *Probation.*

* Reprinted in part by permission of the United Nations, Department of Social Affairs, *Probation and Related Measures,* 1951, pp. 16–26. Footnotes are omitted.

found in this period of legal history, however, generally relate to the suspension of punishment subject to good behavior rather than to probation as such, that is, a *combination* of the conditional suspension of punishment and the personal supervision of the released offender during a trial period. There can be little doubt that there has not been any continuous process of historical development linking early Continental instances of the use of the conditional suspension of punishment with contemporary probation. Probation as it is known today has been derived from the practical extension of the English common law, and an analysis of the legal origins of probation must therefore be principally concerned with England and America.

In England and in the United States of America probation developed out of various methods for the conditional suspension of punishment. Generally speaking, the court practices in question were inaugurated, or adopted from previously existing practices, as attempts to avoid the mechanical application of the harsh and cruel precepts of a rigorous repressive criminal law. Among these Anglo-American judicial expedients which have been mentioned as direct precursors of probation, are the so-called benefit of clergy, the judicial reprieve, the release of an offender on his own recognizance, provisional "filing" of a case, and other legal devices for the suspension of either the imposition or the execution of sentence. With a view to a full understanding of the legal origins of probation, it is necessary to review briefly the nature of these practices.

THE BENEFIT OF CLERGY

The so-called benefit of clergy was a special plea of devious origin by virtue of which certain categories of offenders could, after conviction, but before judgment, claim exemption from, or mitigation of, punishment. In practice it was primarily a device to avoid capital punishment. The importance of this plea in the criminal proceedings of the eighteenth and early nineteenth century is beyond any doubt: "according to the common practice in England of working out modern improvements through antiquated forms, this exemption was made the means of modifying the severity of the criminal law." It is, however, extremely doubtful whether this device had any direct influence on the later development of the suspension of sentence or of any other immediate percursor of probation.

THE JUDICIAL REPRIEVE

The judicial reprieve was a temporary suspension by the court of either the imposition or the execution of a sentence. It was used for specific purposes such as to permit a convicted person to apply for a pardon, or under circumstances such as where the judge was not satisfied with the verdict or where the evidence was suspicious. Although this measure involved only a temporary stay of imposition or execution of sentence, it did lead, in some cases, to an abandonment of prosecution. It does not appear, however, that in England this device was ever extended to embrace what is now termed an indefinite suspension of sentence, particularly in cases which presented no peculiar reason, arising out the lack of or limitations on procedure, for withholding execution of sentence. On the other hand, there is, no doubt, more than a modicum of good reason in tracing the later pretensions of American courts to a power of indefinite suspension of sentence back to this early practice of reprieve in the English courts.

THE RECOGNIZANCE

The recognizance is a legal device deeply embedded in English law. It originated as a measure of preventive justice, and as such it consists in obliging those persons, whom there is a probable ground to suspect of future misbehavior, to stipulate with and to give full assurance to the public, that such offense as is apprehended shall not happen. . . . This "assurance to the public" is given by entering into a recognizance or bond (with or without sureties) creating a debt to the State which becomes enforceable, however, only when the specified conditions are not observed. The recognizance is entered into for a specified period of time.

At an early date the use of the principle of the recognizance (or binding-over) was also extended to actual offenders arraigned before the criminal courts. The device came to be used both to ensure the appearance of an offender before the court at a future date when called upon, and as a disposition (or part thereof) in the case of convicted offenders. With the passing of time, the recognizance came to be used almost exclusively with reference to criminal proceedings rather than as a measure of preventive justice. It should be noted, however, that the recognizance, when used in connection with persons arraigned before criminal courts, does not lose its character as a measure of preventive justice but is actually designed to ensure the future lawful behaviour of the offender or, as Blackstone said, "must be understood rather as a caution against the repetition of the offence, than (as) any immediate pain or punishment."

For centuries the courts of England on occasion bound over and released minor offenders on their own recognizance, *with* or *without* *sureties*. Similarly, instances of this practice can be found in the records of the American colonies. During the first half of the nineteenth century this device was adopted with increasing frequency, particularly in the case of youthful and petty offenders, the imprisonment of whom did not appear to be warranted. The practice seems to have been common in New England (particularly Massachusetts) at the time and was to be found also in other jurisdictions of the United States of America.

The device of binding-over was used extensively and imaginatively by Judge Peter Oxenbridge Thacher during his term of office (1823–1843) in the Municipal Court of Boston, and the practices developed by him were of particular significance in the later development of probation in

Massachusetts. The earliest recorded case in this connection is the case of
Commonwealth v. Chase (1830). In Judge Thacher's opinion we find in
this case a clear statement of the nature of the practice of binding-over as
employed by him:

> "The indictment against Jerusha Chase was found at the
> January term of this court, 1830. She pleaded guilty to the
> same, and sentence would have been pronounced at that time,
> but upon the application of her friends, and with the consent of
> the attorney of the commonwealth, she was permitted, upon her
> recognizance for her appearance in this court whenever she
> should be called for, to go at large. It has sometimes been
> practiced in this court, in cases of peculiar interest, and in the
> hope that the party would avoid the commission of any offense
> afterwards, to discharge him on a recognizance of this descrip-
> tion. The effect is, that no sentence will ever be pronounced
> against him, if he shall behave himself well afterwards, and
> avoid any further violation of the law.   .   .   ."

In 1836, the State of Massachusetts, as part of a general revision of
its statutory law, gave legislative recognition to the practice of release
upon recognizance, *with sureties*, at any stage of the proceedings, insofar
as it applied to petty offenders in the lower courts. In the report of the
commissioners charged with the revision of the statutory law of the State,
the commissioners formulated the theoretical basis of this alteration in
the law relating to the punishment of petty offenders, as follows:

> "This alteration consists in the discretionary power proposed
> to be given to the courts and magistrates, before whom this class
> of offenders may be brought, to discharge them, if they have any
> friends who will give satisfactory security for their future good
> behavior, for a reasonable time. When such sureties can be
> obtained, it can hardly fail to operate as powerful check upon the
> conduct of the party, who is thus put upon his good behavior.
> And if his character and habits are such that no one will consent
> to be sponsor for him, it must forcibly impress on his mind the
> value of a good character, while it deprives him of all ground of
> just complaint of the severity of the law, or the magistrate."

It is significant to compare this formulation of the theory underlying
the use of release on recognizance, with a British formulation of the
second half of the nineteenth century. In a book published in 1877,
Edward William Cox, Recorder of Portsmouth, specifically described the
release of offenders on their own recognizance, with sureties, as a
"substitute for punishment," and he noted that, while the conduct of the
released offenders was proper, no further action was taken. In particular, he was strongly motivated by the desire to avoid the demoralizing and
contaminating influence of short terms of imprisonment, especially in the
case of first and juvenile offenders. As for the *rationale* of the use of the
recognizances, with sureties, he says, "The suspension only of the judg-

ment, the knowledge that if he (the offender) offends he may yet be punished—the hold which his bail thus has upon him, to a great extent guarantee that if there is in him an inclination to redeem himself he will return to a life of honesty."

PROVISIONAL RELEASE ON BAIL

It has been noted in the preceding paragraphs that the device of releasing an offender on his own recognizance (binding-over) may be used *with*, or, *without, sureties.* Conversely, the device of sureties (or bail) may be employed with or without simultaneously binding over the defendant on his own recognizance. The significance of the device of sureties, when combined with the recognizance, as a precursor of probation, has already been discussed; it remains to be pointed out, however, that both in England and in the United States of America the device of bail as such (that is, when not used in conjunction with the recognizance) has similarly been of major historical significance in the evolution of probation, namely, as a device for the provisional suspension of punishment in relation to rudimentary probation practices.

BINDING–OVER, BAIL AND THE ORIGINS OF PROBATION

It has been noted above, that the recognizance is essentially a preventive rather than a punitive measure of dealing with actual or potential offenders. In the early nineteenth century the increased use of this device was motivated, no doubt, to a considerable extent by considerations of mercy and in this respect the device was one of the measures employed to reduce the hardships involved in the mechanical application of a rigorous criminal law. The rehabilitative object of the measure—i. e., the prevention of crime by the restoration of the offender as a law-abiding member of society—was, however, always present. Nevertheless, during this era the device came to be applied with an increasing realization of its rehabilitative potentialities, and same to be accompanied by increasingly effective safeguards and aids in the form of the personal supervision of, and assistance to the released offender during the trial period. It should further be noted that the recognizance has always contained the germs of supervision—it involves the conditional suspension of punishment, and some vigilance is required to ascertain whether the conditions concerned are being complied with.

It is clear that the provisional release of offenders in the charge of sureties similarly contained the germs of probationary supervision (irrespective of whether this device was combined with the recognizance or not). In view of their financial interest in the conduct of the provisionally released offender, sureties are bound to try to ensure the good behavior of the offender through personal supervision, assistance or influence. The deliberate use, by the courts, of the salutory influence of sureties on offenders released conditionally, either on their own recognizance or on bail, indeed seems to have been in a very real sense the first, rudimentary stage in the development of probation.

THE PROVISIONAL "FILING" OF CASES

The practice of provisionally "filing" a case seems to have been peculiar to Massachusetts. This device consisted of the suspension of the imposition of sentence when, "after verdict of guilty in a criminal case . . . the Court is satisfied that, by reason of extenuating circumstances, or of the pendency of a question of law in a like case before a higher court, or other sufficient reason, public justice does not require an immediate sentence. . . ." The use of this procedure was subject to the consent of the defendant and of the prosecuting attorney, and the suspension was made subject to such conditions as the court in its discretion might impose. The order that a case be laid on file was not equivalent to a final judgment, but left it within the power of the court to take action on the case at any time, upon motion of either party.

THE SUSPENSION OF SENTENCES AT COMMON LAW

By way of summary, it may be noted that there existed, during the nineteenth century and earlier, several legal devices which enabled the English and the American courts to suspend either the imposition of sentence (recognizance to keep the peace or to be of good behavior and to appear for judgment when called upon, provisional release on bail, the provisional "filing of a case," and the judicial reprieve) or the execution of sentence (also the judicial reprieve). That these devices existed, and allowed *at least* for the temporary suspension of sentence for *specific purposes*, is beyond any doubt. The question whether the English and American courts possess, at common law, an inherent power to suspend sentence *indefinitely* is, however, more problematic.

In analyzing the question of an inherent judicial power to suspend sentence *indefinitely*, it is necessary to distinguish clearly between the use of the special devices of the recognizance and bail, on the one hand, and other devices used for the provisional suspension of punishment, on the other hand. Prior to statutory provisions to this effect, the courts both in England and in the United States of America *did*, in fact, engage in the suspension of the imposition of sentence when releasing offenders on their own recognizances, and took no further action with regard to the infliction of punishment if the condition of good behavior was complied with. Similarly, this procedure was followed, prior to statutory authorization, in at least two of the other countries of the British Commonwealth, viz., New England and Canada. Both in England and in certain jurisdictions of the United States of America (notably Massachusetts), the conditional suspension of the imposition of sentence, with the ultimate release of the offender from all punishment in case of good behavior, was practiced (without statutory authorization) also in relation to the provisional release of offenders on bail.

For all practical purposes it may be said that—beyond the relatively circumscribed practice of suspending the imposition of a sentence by means of releasing an offender on a recognizance and/or bail—the English courts *did not* assume the existence of an inherent common law power to suspend sentence indefinitely. In the United States of America, however, a variety of practices developed, with a tendency to extend the suspension of sentence beyond the employment of the recognizance and/or bail. In particular, this involved the suspension of the imposition or of the execution of sentence on the basis of the common law precedent of the judicial reprieve. With the increasing use of the conditional suspension of punishment, with or without some sort of probationary supervision, courts in different jurisdictions adopted contradictory points of view on the question of the existence, at common law, of an inherent judicial power of indefinite suspension of sentence. While some held that the courts had such a power, others rejected this view arguing either that the conditions justifying the recognition of such a power in England did not obtain in the United States, or that the indefinite suspension of sentence by the court constituted an encroachment on the executive prerogative of pardon and reprieve, and thus infringes upon the doctrine of the separation of powers.

The United States Supreme Court finally expressed itself on the issue in question in the so-called *Killits* case. In his opinion in this case, the late Chief Justice White decided that the English common law did not give the Federal courts the power to suspend sentence indefinitely.

> "It is true that, owing to the want of power in common law courts to grant new trials and to the absence of a right to review convictions in a higher court, it is we think, to be conceded: (a) that both suspensions of sentence and suspensions of the enforcement of sentence, temporary in character, were often resorted to on grounds of error or miscarriage of justice which under our system would be corrected either by new trials or by the exercise of the power to review; (b) that not infrequently, where the suspension either of the imposition of a sentence or of its execution was made for the purpose of enabling a pardon to be sought or bestowed, by a failure to further proceed in the criminal cause in the future, although no pardon had been sought or obtained, the punishment fixed by law was escaped. But neither of these conditions serves to convert the mere exercise of a judicial discretion to temporarily suspend for the accomplishment of a purpose contemplated by law into the existence of an arbitrary judicial power to permanently refuse to enforce the law."

With reference to the decision in the *Killits* case, the Attorney General's Survey concludes as follows:

> "For practical purposes it may be said that this decision served to explode the erroneous belief that had grown up in some states. . . . It may be concluded, therefore, that there is no historical warrant in the English common law for the claim that

American courts have an inherent power to suspend sentence indefinitely. Where this power has been asserted, it has been based on a misconception of English authorities or recognized because it tempered the criminal law with mercy and had grown as a local practice."

It should be noted that the Court's decision in the *Killits* case did not seek to invalidate the practice of releasing offenders on their own recognizances, but referred to "the fact that common law courts possessed the power by recognizances to secure good behavior, that is, to enforce the law. . . ." This fact did not, however, afford support for "the proposition that those courts possessed the arbitrary discretion to permanently decline to enforce the law."

From the point of view of the development of probation as a distinct method for the treatment of offenders, the extent to which the judicial devices in which it had its historical origins, were, in fact, extra-legal and not warranted by the English common law, is of small significance. The important point is that these devices developed, and could in fact only develop, in a system of common law jurisdiction which is flexible enough to allow for the gradual adjustment of existing practices to new needs and new objectives. In England this process of adjustment was more conservative and it is probable that the courts stayed within their common law powers, in any case, the legality of the devices used for the conditional suspension of punishment, in relation to early pre-statutory probation practices, was never challenged in England, in Canada, or in New Zealand. In the United States of America, the courts overstepped their common law powers, and the resulting diversity and confusion of principles and authorities necessitated the authoritative revision of the legal bases of the practices that have developed. Nevertheless, the definitive explosion of the doctrine of an inherent judicial power to suspend any part of the administration of criminal justice, and when public opinion had already been fully prepared for this new method for the treatment of offenders. Consequently, the final rejection by the Supreme Court of the doctrine of a common law judicial power of indefinite suspension of sentence actually served as a stimulus for the enactment of statutes expressly authorizing the suspension of sentence and probation.

PROBATION: STANDARDS AND GOALS *

Extensive use of institutions has been giving way to expanded use of community-based programs during the past decade. This is true not only in corrections, but also in services for the mentally ill, the aging, and dependent and neglected children.

* National Advisory Commission on
Criminal Justice Standards and Goals,
Report on Corrections, 1973.

The movement away from institutionalization has occurred not only because institutions are very costly, but also because they have debilitating effects on inmates, who have great difficulty in reintegrating themselves into the community. Therefore, it is essential that alternatives to institutionalization be expanded in use and enhanced in resources. The most promising process by which this can be accomplished in corrections—probation—is now being used more as a disposition. Even greater use can be projected for the future.

Broad use of probation does not increase risk to the community. Any risk increased by allowing offenders to remain in the community will be more than offset by increased safety due to offenders' increased respect for society and their maintenance of favorable community ties. Results of probation are as good, if not better, than those of incarceration.[1] With increased concern about crime, reduction of recidivism, and allocation of limited tax dollars, more attention should be given to probation, as a system and as a sentencing disposition.

Although probation is viewed as the brightest hope for corrections, its full potential cannot be reached unless consideration is given to two major factors. The first is the development of a system for determining which offenders should receive a sentence of probation. The second is the development of a system that enables offenders to receive the support and services they need so that ultimately they can live independently in a socially acceptable way.

Currently, probation has failed to realize either of these. Probation is not adequately structured, financed, staffed, or equipped with necessary resources. A major shift of money and manpower to community-based corrections is necessary if probation is to be adopted nationally as the preferred disposition, as this Commission recommends. The shift will require strengthening the position of probation in the framework of government, defining goals and objectives for the probation system, and developing an organization that can meet the goals and objectives. In this chapter, consideration will be given to what must be done if probation is to fulfill its potential as a system and as a disposition.

DEFINITIONS

In corrections, the word "probation" is used in four ways. It can refer to a disposition, a status, a system or subsystem, and a process.

Probation as a court disposition was first used as a suspension of sentence. Under probation, a convicted offender's freedom in the community was continued, subject to supervision and certain conditions established by the court. A shift now is occurring, and probation is being used increasingly as a sentence in itself. The American Bar Association Project on Standards for Criminal Justice defines probation as:

1. See National Council on Crime and Delinquency, *Policies and Background*   *Information* (Hackensack, N.J.: NCCD, 1972), pp. 14–15.

A sentence not involving confinement which imposes conditions and retains authority in the sentencing court to modify the
conditions of sentence or to re-sentence the offender if he
violates the conditions. Such a sentence should not involve or
require suspension of the imposition or execution of any other
sentence.   .   .   .

A sentence to probation should be treated as a final judgment for purposes of appeal and similar procedural purposes.[2]

Probation as a status reflects the position of an offender sentenced to
probation. For the offender, probation status has implications different
from the status of either free citizen or confined offender.

Probation is a subsystem of corrections, itself a subsystem of the
criminal and juvenile justice system. Unless otherwise specified, "probation" will be used throughout this chapter to refer to the probation
subsystem. When used in this context, probation refers to the agency or
organization that administers the probation process for juveniles and
adults.

The probation process refers to the set of functions, activities, and
services that characterize the system's transactions with the courts, the
offender, and the community. The process includes preparation of reports for the court, supervision of probationers, and obtaining or providing services for them.

The terms "written report" or "report" will be used to denote both
presentence investigation reports and social studies prepared for the
courts. The term "presentence investigation report" is used for those
dealing with adults and "social study" for those dealing with juveniles.

"Intake" refers to the process of screening cases prior to court
appearance, in order to take or recommend a course of action. It involves
discretion to resolve a matter informally, to arrange court-based diversion
services, or to proceed with a court hearing. It also may include investigative or assessment activities and pretrial release or detention decisions.

EVOLUTION OF PROBATION

Probation's origins go back to English common law and the efforts to
alleviate the severity of criminal sanctions. The earliest probation device
appears to have been "benefit of clergy," which was used originally to
release clergymen from criminal court on the theory that only church
courts had jurisdiction over their personnel. Later, "benefit of the
clergy" was extended to include anyone who could read.

Judicial reprieve, another device used in the Middle Ages, was the
precedent for the practice of suspension of sentence, which was brought

2. American Bar Association Project on   Institute of Judicial Administration,
   Standards for Criminal Justice, *Stan-*   1970), p. 9.
   dards Relating to Probation (New York:

to America from England. Recognizance practice also was developed in England, apparently in the 14th century, involving release with some type of surety or bail to assure good behavior.

John Augustus, a Boston shoemaker, is recognized as the father of probation in this country. As a volunteer, he asked the court to release certain offenders he thought he could assist. Practices he began using in 1841 have stood the test of time: investigation and screening, interviewing, supervision of those released, and services such as employment, relief, and education. His efforts were so successful that legislation formally establishing probation and providing for paid staff was enacted in Massachusetts in 1878. By 1900, six States had enacted probation legislation; four dealt with adult probation and two related only to children.

Probation as a disposition and a system is essentially a development of the 20th century. The first directory of probation officers in the United States, published in 1907, identified 795 probation officers, mostly serving juvenile courts. Some were volunteers, some welfare workers, some attached to courts, and some employed part-time. By 1937 more than 3,800 persons were identified as probation officers, of whom 80 percent worked full-time and the rest had additional duties such as sheriff, welfare worker, minister, attendance officer, or attorney. In 1947, the directories began to include both probation and parole. In 1970, nearly 25,000 persons were identified as probation and parole personnel, and only 2 percent had other duties such as county welfare worker or sheriff.

As probation use increased, growing interest in its effectiveness developed. One demonstration of its effectiveness was the Saginaw Project conducted in Michigan between 1957 and 1962. The project staffed by trained workers with manageable workloads, had three objectives. First, probation should be used for 70 to 75 percent of convicted offenders. Second, there should be no increased risk to community safety. Third, actual tax dollar savings should be achieved by reduced construction and maintenance of institutions. All objectives were accomplished.[3]

Follow-up studies of probation elsewhere indicated that failure rates of persons on probation were relatively low.[4] Although many of these studies were not conducted under controlled conditions, with definitive information about variables such as service rendered and matched groups of offenders, the gross evidence cannot be discounted.

GOVERNMENTAL FRAMEWORK OF PROBATION

The position of probation in the government framework varies among the States. The continuing controversy over the most appropriate

3. National Probation and Parole Association, Michigan Council, *The Saginaw Probation Demonstration Project* (New York: National Council on Crime and Delinquency, 1963).

4. See Robert L. Smith, *A Quiet Revolution* (Washington: U.S. Department of Health, Education, and Welfare, 1972).

placement of probation centers on two main issues: whether it should be a part of the judicial or executive branch of government; and whether it should be administered by State or local government.

In all States, corrections components and subsystems, except probation and some juvenile detention facilities, operate within the executive branch. Probation is found in the executive branch in some States, in the judicial in others, and under mixed arrangements elsewhere.

State governments operate most subsystems of corrections. The exceptions are probation, jails, and some juvenile detention facilities. Juvenile probation usually developed in juvenile courts and thus became a local function. As adult probation services developed, they generally were combined with existing statewide parole services or into a unified corrections department that also included parole and institutions. The exceptions were in major cities that had already created probation organizations for the adult courts and States in which probation responsibilities were divided.

Variations in the way probation has been organized and placed within the government framework have created differences between States as well as within States. Ohio provides an example of the complicated arrangements that have developed. There, juvenile probation is a local function in the judicial branch, but the State aid program is in the executive branch. Adult probation can be either a State or local function. A State agency in the executive branch can provide probation service to local courts, or they may establish their own. Where local probation exists, the control may be shared by both branches in an arrangement under which the county commissioners and judges of the court of common pleas must concur on appointments.

In New York State the State Division of Probation is in the executive branch as are all local probation agencies except those in New York City, which are in the judicial branch.

Such variations appear to have arisen as emphasis was given to one or the other of the two traditional functions of probation officers: to provide presentence reports and other services for the courts; and to supervise and provide services for probationers. These are different tasks with different objectives.

Variations occur within probation itself. There may be one agency for all offenders or separate agencies for juveniles and adults. Adult probation may be divided into one agency for felons and another for misdemeanants.

The question of where probation should be placed in the framework of government becomes more critical as its use expands and staff numbers increase. It is time to take a serious look at where probation could function most effectively, rather than using chance and history to support the status quo.

Judicial vs. Executive Branch

In the debate over the appropriate governmental branch for the probation system, those who favor the judicial branch give the following rationale.

1. Probation would be more responsive to court direction. Throughout the probation process, the court could provide guidance to probation workers and take corrective action when policies were not followed or proved ineffective.

2. This arrangement would provide the judiciary with an automatic feedback mechanism on effectiveness of dispositions through reports filed by probation staff. Judges, it is urged, may place more trust in reports from their own staff than in those from an outside agency.

3. Courts have a greater awareness of needed resources and may become advocates for their staffs in obtaining better services.

4. Increased use of pretrial diversion may be furthered by placing probation in the judicial branch. Courts have not been inclined to transfer authority and therefore may set more stringent limitations on the discretion of nonjudicial personnel to release or divert than on judicial staff.

The arguments for keeping probation in the judicial branch, which center around the direct relationship between the courts and probation, are not persuasive. Subsystems of the criminal justice system in the executive branch are able to work effectively with the courts.

Those who oppose placement of probation within the judiciary argue that:

1. Under this arrangement judges frequently become the administrators of probation in their jurisdictions—a role for which they usually are ill-equipped. The current trend toward use of court administrators reflects the belief that judges cannot be expected to have the time, orientation, or training to perform two such distinct roles.

2. When probation is within the judicial system, the staff is likely to give priority to services for the courts rather than to services to probationers.

3. Probation staff may be assigned functions that serve legal processes of the court and are unrelated to probation, such as issuing summonses, serving subpenas, and running errands for judges.

4. Courts, particularly the criminal courts, are adjudicatory and regulatory rather than service-oriented bodies. Therefore, as long as probation remains part of the court setting, it will be subservient to the court and will not develop an identity of its own.

Another class of arguments supports placement of probation in the executive branch of government, rather than merely opposing placement in the judicial branch.

1. All other subsystems for carrying out court dispositions of offenders are in the executive branch. Closer coordination and functional integration with other corrections personnel could be achieved by a common organizational placement, particularly as community-based corrections programs increase. Furthermore, job mobility would be enhanced if related functions are administratively tied.

2. The executive branch contains the allied human service agencies including social and rehabilitation services, medical services, employment services, education, and housing. Where probation also is in the executive branch, opportunities are increased for coordination, cooperative endeavors, and comprehensive planning.

3. Decisions involving resource allocations and establishment of priorities are made by the executive branch. It initiates requests to the legislative bodies, either local or State, for appropriation of funds, and by so doing sets priorities for allocating limited tax dollars. When probation is included in the total corrections system, more rational decisions about the best distribution of resources can be made.

4. Probation administrators are in position to negotiate and present their case more strongly, if they are in the executive branch. When probation is part of the court system the judge, not the probation administrator, is responsible for presenting the budget request and acting as negotiator. The latter is not a role traditionally undertaken by the judiciary.

On balance, the arguments for placement of probation in the executive branch of government are more persuasive. Such placement would facilitate a more rational allocation of probation staff services, increase interaction and administrative coordination with corrections and allied human services, increase access to the budget process and establishment of priorities, and remove the courts from an inappropriate role.

For these reasons, this report calls for inclusion of probation departments within unified State correctional systems.

This is, in the Commission's view, the proper long-range objective. It would do away with the current duality of roles for probation staff. However, in view of the current variety of local arrangements, it may for the present be appropriate for personnel carrying out services to the courts to be employed by the probation division of a unified State corrections system but detailed to perform court services. It would be essential in such an arrangement that probation staff take direction from the court and the court administration in establishment of policies, procedures, and performance standards for carrying out their tasks and that the probation division be responsive to the needs of the courts. Where such an arrangement appears to be desirable, written agreements setting out and defining the relationship between the court and the corrections system should be developed and agreed to by both.

State vs. Local Administration

Few States in which probation is a local function have provided any leadership or supervision for probation agencies. Tremendous variations are likely to exist within a State in terms of number of staff employed in counties of similar size, qualifications of personnel employed, and relative emphasis on services to courts and probationers. County probation agencies often are small and lack resources for staff training and development, research and program planning, and, more basically, services to the probationers.

State Efforts to Set Standards

Attempts to bring about some degree of uniformity have been limited. In a few States where probation is a local function, standards are set by the State in either the judicial or executive branch. For example, in New Jersey the judicial branch is responsible for setting standards for its local probation systems, while in California the responsibility is placed in the executive branch.

The degree to which local probation systems comply with State standards is dependent upon the rewards and sanctions used. As a reward for meeting specified standards, the State may provide either revenue or manpower. Michigan assigns State-paid probation officers to work alongside local probation officers. The more common practice, however, is direct payment by the State to local governments for part of the costs of probation services. New York State reimburses local communities up to 50 percent of the operating costs for probation programs, provided that local communities meet State staffing standards. This subsidy has nearly doubled in the last 6 years and has resulted in an increase of probation staff in the State from 1,527 in 1965 to 1,956 in 1972.[5]

The States of California and Washington use a different approach in providing revenue to local jurisdictions. These States attempt to resolve a problem that is inherent when probation is a local function; namely, that financing probation is a local responsibility. However, when juveniles or adults are sent to correctional institutions, these are usually administered and financed by the State. A consequence often is the shifting of financial responsibility from the local government to the State government by sentences of incarceration rather than probation.

California and Washington have developed probation subsidy programs in which counties are reimbursed in proportion to the number of individuals that remain in the community rather than being sent to State institutions. The subsidy program in California was developed as a result of a study that indicated that some individuals eligible for commitment to State correctional institutions could safely be retained on probation and that with good probation supervision, they could make a satisfactory

---

5. Information supplied by the New York State Division of Probation.

adjustment. It was estimated that at least 25 percent of the new admissions to State correctional institutions could remain in the community with good probation supervision.

The California Probation Subsidy Program was instituted in 1966 by the State's youth authority. The youth authority was authorized to pay up to $4,000 to each county for every adult and juvenile offender not committed to a State correctional institution. The counties were required to demonstrate a commitment to improved probation services, including employment of additional probation workers and reduction of caseloads. In addition, each county had to demonstrate innovative approaches to probation, such as intensive care probation units for dealing with hardcore adult and juvenile offenders.

California estimates that, even with expanded probation services, the cost of probation runs little more than one-tenth of the cost of incarceration, approximately $600 per person annually for probation, compared to $5,000 annually for institutionalization. In all, the program has resulted in substantial savings to taxpayers. In the six years between 1966 and 1972, California canceled planned construction, closed existing institutions, and abandoned new institutions that had been constructed. Almost $186 million was saved in these ways, while probation subsidy expenditures came to about $60 million. Furthermore, although there has been a general decrease in commitments to State institutions throughout the United States, the decrease is sharper in those counties in California that participate in the subsidy program. The decrease in those counties almost doubles that of California counties not participating in the subsidy program.[6]

The State of Washington has had a similar experience with the probation subsidy program begun in January, 1970. Its purpose was to reduce the number of commitments to institutions from county juvenile courts. In the 2 years the program has been in operation, there has been a marked reduction in the number of children and youth sent to State institutions. To illustrate, in 1971, the State received 55 percent fewer commitments than expected.[7]

Advantages of State Administration

Even in those instances where the State provides financial incentives to local jurisdictions, as in California, participation of counties is discretionary. Uniformity in probation can be achieved only when there is a State-administered probation system, which also has a number of other distinct advantages.

A State-administered system can more easily organize around the needs of a particular locality or region without having to consider local

6. Smith, A Quiet Revolution, gives the background of and experience under California's probation subsidy plan.

7. Information supplied by the Washington State Department of Social and Health Services.

political impediments. It also can recommend new programs and implement them without requiring additional approval by local political bodies.

A State-administered system provides greater assurance that goals and objectives can be met and that uniform policies and procedures can be developed. Also, more efficiency in the disposition of resources is assured because all staff members are State employees and a larger agency can make more flexible use of manpower, funds, and other resources.

When it is simply not possible for a State to administer a probation system, the State, through a designated agency in the executive branch, should be responsible for developing standards for local probation systems that provide for a minimum acceptable level of functioning. State standards have a greater chance of being implemented if the State indicates a willingness to share the costs with local governments when standards are met and maintained.

In addition to setting standards for local jurisdictions, the State agency should be responsible for establishing policies, defining statewide goals, providing staff training, assisting in fiscal planning and implementation, collecting statistics and data to monitor the operations of local probation agencies, and enforcing change when necessary. Through these means, a state-supervised program can bring about some degree of uniformity in operations throughout the State, but not to the same degree as a State-administered program.

PROBATION ADMINISTRATION

The complexities of administering a probation system have been reflected in several studies. A poll conducted for the Joint Commission on Correctional Manpower and Training indicated that administrators felt the need for more training, especially in public administration.[8] Another study revealed support for two different types of education for administrators. One group advocated social work education, apparently representing a concern for substantive practice matters. The others advocated public administration because of a concern about managerial responsibilities.[9]

Need for Administrators to Formulate Goals

The administrator is expected to formulate goals and basic policies that give direction and meaning to the agency. If these goals are not formulated specifically, they are made by default, for staff will create their own framework. Should policies and goals not be developed quickly, or well enough, persons outside the agency may determine policies, with or without consideration of long-range goals.

8. Joint Commission on Correctional Manpower and Training, *Corrections 1968: A Climate for Change* (Washington: JCCMT, 1968), p. 30.

9. Herman Piven and Abraham Alcabes, *The Crisis of Qualified Manpower for*

Criminal Justice: An Analytic Assessment with Guidelines for New Policy (Washington: Government Printing Office, 1969), vol. 1.

Unfortunately, clearly defined objectives for probation systems rarely are set forth. The probation administrator has contributed to variations in philosophy, policy, and practice. Often staff members of the same agency have different perceptions, with top management having one view, middle management another, and line personnel reflecting some of each.

Probation staff members bring to the organization their own backgrounds, and the beliefs they acquired before becoming employees. These in turn are modified by other staff members, judges, law enforcement officials, personnel of other parts of the correctional system, probationers, complainants and witnesses, lawyers, and the news media.

If an administrator has failed to define goals and policies for his organization, dysfunction within the organization must follow. Some dysfunctioning is rooted both in tradition and rapid growth.

Training for Probation Work

Since the 1920's there has been an emphasis on social work education as a prerequisite for entering probation. The preferred educational standard was a master's degree in social work. This emphasis was paralleled by the concept of professionalism. To achieve professionalism, staff members had to be provided opportunities to increase their knowledge and skills. Such a thrust created a staff expectation that they would have opportunity to use the increased knowledge and skills. However, as probation systems grow in size, agencies tend to develop the characteristics of a bureaucracy that increase constraints on staff behavior which result in frustration.

New graduates of schools of social work have been reluctant to enter probation. Newer staff members sent by probation agencies to graduate schools of social work often leave the agency as soon as they fulfill any commitment made to secure the education. Such workers are likely to express their reason for leaving as frustration over the lack of opportunity for using their knowledge and skills.

Dysfunctions in Probation Operation

Training emphasis has been at a staff level, and this too can contribute to dysfunction. More emphasis has been placed on training probation officers than on equipping executives and middle-level managers with skills to administer effectively. Organizational change must begin with the executives and middle management if probation officers are to have an opportunity to use increased knowledge and skills acquired through training.

Another dysfunction may result from the change from one-to-one casework emphasis of the probation officer to the group emphasis needed for an administrator. Many staff members are promoted from the ranks of probation officer to supervisor and administrator. If effective organizations are to be developed, supervisors and administrators should meet and work with staff on a group basis. If the supervisors and administrators do not have the skills to do this effectively, they will revert to the pattern of one-to-one relationship.

Another form of dysfunction may stem from promotion of a probation officer to a supervisory or administrative position. Ideally a supervisor should receive training that enables him to create a supportive atmosphere for the probation officer, both inside and outside the agency. The probation officer who has been promoted but given no training for his new role has a natural tendency to see himself as doing his job well by concentrating on internal matters. Support and supervision of staff may consist of nothing more than shuffling papers, reporting statistics, and giving basic training to probation officers.

SERVICES TO PROBATIONERS

The Current Service System

Many problems have prevented development of a system for providing probationers with needed resources. For one thing, the goal of service delivery to probationers has not been delineated clearly and given the priority required. Services to probationers have not been separated from services to the court. Generally, both services are provided by the same staff members, who place more emphasis on services to the court than to probationers.

Because the goal for service delivery to probationers has not been defined clearly, service needs have not been identified on a systematic and sustained basis. Priorities based on need, resources, and constraints have not been set. Measurable objectives and ways of achieving them for various target groups have not been specified. Moreover, monitoring and evaluation of services have been almost nonexistent.

Another problem is the lack of differentiation between services that should be provided by probation and those that should be delivered by such agencies as mental health, employment, housing, education, and private welfare agencies. Because of community attitudes toward offenders, social agencies other than probation are likely to be unenthusiastic about providing services to the legally identified offender. Probation offices usually lack sufficient influence and funds to procure services from other resources and therefore try to expand their own role and services. This leads to two results, both undesirable: identical services are duplicated by probation and one or more other public service agencies, and probation suffers from stretching already tight resources.

Some probation systems have assumed responsibility for handling matters unrelated to probation such as placement of neglected children in foster homes and operation of shelter facilities, both of which are the responsibilities of the child welfare or other public agencies. Probation also has attempted to deal directly with such problems as alcoholism, drug addiction, and mental illness, which ought to be handled through community mental health and other specialized programs.

These efforts to expand probation's role have not been successful because there is not enough money to provide even the traditional basic probation services.

Overemphasis on Casework

One result of the influence of social work on probation has been an overemphasis on casework. Development of child guidance clinics in the 1920's and 1930's influenced particularly the juvenile courts and their probation staff.

The terms "diagnosis" and "treatment" began to appear in social work literature and not long after in corrections literature. Those terms come from the medical field and imply illness. A further implication is that a good probation practitioner will understand the cause and be able to remedy it, just as the medical practitioner does. Essentially, the medical approach overlooked any connection between crime and such factors as poverty, unemployment, poor housing, poor health, and lack of education.

A review of the literature of the 1930's, 1940's, and 1950's indicates that the casework method became equated with social work, and in turn, casework for probation became equated with a therapeutic relationship with a probationer. A study manual published by the National Probation and Parole Association in 1942 reflects this equation in the table of contents. The titles of three of the chapters are: "Social Casework," "Case Study and Diagnosis," and "Casework as a Means of Treatment." [10]

The literature discussed the development of social work skills in interviewing, creating therapeutic relationships with clients, counseling, providing insight, and modifying behavior. When practitioners began to view themselves as therapists, one consequence was the practice of having offenders come to the office rather than workers going into the homes and the communities.

Although the literature refers to probation officers working with employers, schools, families, and others in the probationer's life, the chief concern is the relationship between probation officer and probationer. Indeed, if probation staff members see casework as their model, it may well be asked how much contact and what kind of contact they should have with persons other than probationers.

Recently a much broader view of social work practice has been developed, a view that social workers in corrections have taken an active role in developing. After a 3-year study of social work curriculum sponsored by the Council on Social Work Education in the 1950's, the

10. Helen D. Pigeon, *Probation and Parole in Theory and Practice* (New York: National Probation and Parole Association, 1942).

report of the project on "Education for Social Workers in the Correctional Field" said:

"The social task in corrections seems to call for social workers rather than for caseworkers or group workers. All social workers in corrections work with individuals, groups and communities, with less emphasis on the use of one method than is characteristic of many social work jobs." [11]

A task force organized in 1963 by the National Association of Social Workers to study the field of social work practice in corrections suggested that the offender's needs and the service system's social goals should determine methodology. The task force stated that social workers should have an array of professional skills—based on knowledge, understanding, attitudes, and values required for professional use of the skills—from which they could draw on appropriate occasions to meet the offender's needs and the goals of the probation system. [12]

When casework was applied to probation, a blurring of roles occurred between the probation officer and the probation agency. When each probation officer is assigned a certain number of cases, it is implied that he has full responsibility for all individuals concerned. He is expected to handle all the problems that the offenders in his caseload present and to have all the necessary knowledge and skills. The role of the agency in this arrangement is unclear.

No one person can possess all the skills needed to deal with the variety of complicated human problems presented by probationers. This situation is complicated by the diversity of qualifications required by jurisdictions throughout the country for appointment to the position of probation officer. The requirements range from high school or less to graduate degrees. Requirements for prior experience may be nonexistent or extensive.

Furthermore, few criteria exist as to what is acceptable performance. This deficiency makes it necessary for individual probation officers to set their own standards and gives them a great deal of latitude in working with probationers. Therefore it is difficult to assess the degree to which any probation officer has been successful in positively influencing a probationer.

The expectation that probation officers must know what their probationers are doing is traditional. If a probationer is arrested, the first question likely to be asked is when the probation officer last saw his client. The probation officer is expected to account for what is known, or more specifically for what is not known, about the probationer's activities. One consequence is that a probation officer quickly learns that he must protect himself. The system demands accountability when probationers

11. Elliot Studt, *Education for Social Workers in the Correctional Field* (New York: Council on Social Work Education, 1959), p. 50.

12. G. W. Carter, *Fields of Practice: Report of a Workshop* (New York: National Association of Social Workers, 1963).

get into the public view through alleged violations or new crimes. Probation staff members recognize that a high level of visibility exists, that they are answerable for their decisions, and that, if the matter comes to the attention of the court, the decisions will have to be justified.

The Caseload Standard

One impact of the casework model has been a standard ratio of probationers to staff. The figure of 50 cases per probation officer first appeared in the literature in 1917. It was the consensus of a group of probation administrators and was never validated. The recommendation later was modified to include investigations.

The caseload standard provides an excuse for officers with large caseloads to explain why they cannot supervise probationers effectively. It also is a valuable reference point at budget time. Probation agencies have been known to attempt to increase their staff and reduce the size of the caseload without making any effort to define what needs to be done and what tasks must be performed. Caseload reduction has become an end unto itself.

When caseloads alone have been reduced, results have been disappointing. In some cases, an increase in probation violations resulted, undoubtedly due to increased surveillance or overreaction of well-meaning probation officers. Some gains were made when staff members were given special training in case management, but this appears to be the exception. The comment has been made that with caseload reduction, probation agencies have been unable to teach staff what to do with the additional time available.

The San Francisco Project described in a subsequent section challenged the assumption of a caseload standard. Four levels of workloads were established: (1) ideal (50 cases); (2) intensive (25, i. e., half the ideal); (3) normal (100, twice the ideal); and (4) minimum supervision (with a ceiling of 250 cases). Persons in minimum supervision caseloads were required only to submit a monthly written report; no contacts occurred except when requested by the probationer. It was found that offenders in minimum caseloads performed as well as those under normal supervision. The minimum and ideal caseloads had almost identical violation rates. In the intensive caseloads, the violation rate did not decline, but technical violations increased.

The study indicated that the number of contacts between probationer and staff appeared to have little relationship to success or failure on probation. The conclusion was that the concept of a caseload is meaningless without some type of classification and matching of offender type, service to be offered, and staff.[13]

13. James Robison et al., *The San Francisco Project*, Research Report No. 14 (Berkeley: University of California School of Criminology, 1969).

But the caseload standard remained unchanged until the President's Commission on Law Enforcement and Administration of Justice (the Crime Commission) recommended in 1967 a significant but sometimes overlooked change by virtue of the phrase "on the basis of average ratio of 35 offenders per officer." [14] The change was to a ratio for staffing, not a formula for a caseload.

Agencies are now considering workloads, not caseloads, to determine staff requirements. Specific tasks are identified, measured for time required to accomplish the task, and translated into numbers of staff members needed.

The Decisionmaking Framework

The framework for making decisions about probationers varies widely from agency to agency and within a single agency. Some decisions about a case, such as recommendations for probation revocation or termination, may be made only by the head of the probation agency, while other decisions about the same case may be made by any of a number of staff workers. Consequently, many probational personnel may not know who can make what decisions and under what circumstances. Part of the difficulty may come from statutes that define the responsibilities of a probation officer more explicitly than those of an agency. In addition, probation administrators often do not establish a clear decisionmaking framework.

The decisionmaking patterns vary not only for staff but for the offender placed on probation. If the system views its task as surveillance of the probationer, he has low status in any decisionmaking. The decisions are made for and about him, but not with him. If the system is oriented toward service, using the social work model, his role in decisions still is likely to be circumvented. This occurs despite the social work concept that the client has the right to be involved in what is happening to him, that is, self-determination.

This paradox exists because the probationer has an assigned status restricting his behavior. Probation conditions, essentially negative in nature although often expressed in a positive fashion, are imposed on him. The probationer may have to obtain permission to purchase a car, to move, to change a job, and this necessity restricts his choices of action. The probationer, therefore, has the task of adapting to an assigned status while seeking to perform the normal roles of a self-sufficient individual in the community: working, being a parent or a family member, paying taxes, obeying the law, meeting financial obligations, etc. Technical violations of probation conditions can result in revocation and commitment to a correctional institution.

14. President's Commission on Law Enforcement and Administration of Justice, *The Challenge of Crime in a Free Society* (Washington: Government Printing Office, 1967), p. 169.

If the client consults a noncorrectional social agency, he has the right to explain his problems and to terminate the relationship with that agency if he chooses. A probation client legally is required to appear but not legally required to ask for help. He may or may not be ready to receive help. He may be encouraged by staff to use resources of other community agencies, but the decision rests with him.

He may, however, be required to utilize some services offered by probation, such as psychiatric examination or testing. He may have some goals, but they are accepted by probation staff only if they are consistent with the conditions of probation or with the notions of the probation system, which usually means the probation officer. In short, the probationer's right to participate in decisionmaking has been limited by probation conditions and the role assigned him by the probation staff or the system.

Although probation staff members may be receptive to the social work concept of self-determination, they are aware that they occupy a position of authority. The very words, "probation officer" signify authority, indicating an assigned role of power over another individual.

Furthermore, probation staff members may not be aware of or sensitive to what it means to be a probationer. A study on the interaction between parole staff and parolees indicated that most staff were relatively unaware of the difficulties of being a parolee. Staff and parolees saw the difficulties of parolees differently. Significantly, the parolees seemed more aware than the staff of what the staff could do and consequently to whom they could turn for expert information and advice when needed.[15]

For the most part, the probation system has tended to view offenders as a homogeneous group. The assumption has been that all require the same kind of service; namely, treatment on a one-to-one basis. Confusion exists about the form of treatment to be used and what it is supposed to accomplish. Discussion with most probation staff members reveals their difficulty in explaining what they do to "treat" a probationer and why. They speak of a relationship with each probationer as an end in itself and the sole means of providing services to individuals. Probation staff members also perceive the periodic contact they must make to account for the probationer's presence in the community as helping, treating, or rehabilitating the probationer.

Probationers are a heterogeneous group. The needs of juveniles differ from those of adults; girls and women have different needs than boys and men. There may be some common needs but one means, casework, will not meet them all. For example, casework is not a satisfactory technique for the probationer who has a drug problem. The

15. Elliot Studt, *People in the Parole Action System: Their Tasks and Dilemmas* (Los Angeles: University of California Institute of Government and Public Affairs, 1971).

problem of a probationer may not be interpersonal but one that should be met through specific help such as a job, employment training or education. Reducing caseloads alone to improve supervision does not necessarily result in better probation services. Research in the past decade provides evidence that other approaches are needed.

The emphasis should be on classification of offenders and development of appropriate service programs, which usually are labeled "treatment." The impetus for this shift has been slowed by lack of research and the ideology of the caseload standard. A recent monograph from the Center for Studies of Crime and Delinquency at the National Institute of Mental Health, provides a good summary of the various models that have been or are being tested.[16] These include specialized supervision programs, guided group interaction programs, and delinquent peer group programs, as well as out-of-home placement and residential treatment. The monograph also covers specialized units in probation and parole such as the California Community Treatment Project and the Community Delinquency Control Project of the California Youth Authority.

Classification of probationers is only one approach to typology. Another is identification and classification of the probationer's needs. To date, this has not been done systematically by any probation agency; what have been identified as basic needs usually are derived from anecdotal reports concerning individual offenders.

A third approach to the typology question involves the question, "Who is to be changed?" To date the primary target for change has been the probationer. A suggestion has been made that the typological approach might be applied to families and to the community.[17]

Future Directions for Service Delivery

To implement an effective system for delivering services to all probationers, it will be necessary to:

1. Develop a goal-oriented service delivery system.
2. Identify service needs of probationers systematically and periodically, and specify measurable objectives based on priorities and needs assessment.
3. Differentiate between those services that the probation system should provide and those that should be provided by other resources.
4. Organize the system to deliver services, including purchase of services for probationers, and organize the staff around workloads.

16. Eleanor Harlow, J. Robert Weber, and Leslie T. Wilkins, *Community-Based Correctional Programs: Models and Practices* (Washington: Government Printing Office, 1971).

17. Seymour Rubenfeld, *Typological Approaches and Delinquency Control: A* *Status Report* (Rockville, Md.: National Institute of Mental Health, Center for Study of Crime and Delinquency, 1967), pp. 21–25.

5. Move probation staff from courthouses to residential areas and develop service centers for probationers.
6. Redefine the role of probation officer from caseworker to community resource manager.
7. Provide services to misdemeanants.

Developing Goals

The probation services system should be goal-oriented, directed toward removing or reducing individual and social barriers that result in recidivism among probationers. To achieve this goal, the probation system should provide a range of services directly and obtain others from existing social institutions or resources. The goal should be to help persons move from supervised care in their own communities to independent living.

The probation system must help create a climate that will enable the probationer to move successfully through transitions from one status to another. The first is from the status of an individual charged with committing an offense to that of a probationer living in the community but not completely independent. The final transition occurs when probation is terminated and the probationer moves from supervised care to an independent life. The goal should be to maintain in the community all persons who, with support, can perform there acceptably and to select for some type of confinement only those who, on the basis of evidence, cannot complete probationer status successfully, even with optimal support.

With this goal in mind, the practice of commitment to an institution for the initial period of probation (variously known as shock probation, split sentence, etc.), as the Federal and some State statutes permit, should be discontinued. This type of sentence defeats the purpose of probation, which is the earliest possible reintegration of the offender into the community. Short-term commitment subjects the probationer to the destructive effects of institutionalization, disrupts his life in the community, and stigmatizes him for having been in jail. Further, it may add to his confusion as to his status.

Identifying Needs of Probationers

To plan for services, a probation system must initiate and maintain an assessment of needs of its target group, the probationers. This assessment must be ongoing because needs change. An inventory of needs should be developed by involving probationers rather than relying solely on probation staff to identify what it believes probationers' problems to be. More specifically, needs assessment requires:

• Knowledge of the target group in terms of such factors as age, race, education, employment, family status, availability of transportation.
• Identification of what services the offender most wants and needs to remove individual and social barriers.

- Identification of services available and conditions under which they can be obtained.
- Determination of which needed and wanted services do not exist or are inadequate.

From an assessment of needs, problem areas can be highlighted and priorities determined. This process makes it possible to specify how the various needs identified are to be met; whether directly through the probation system or through other social institutions; for what number or percentage of the target group; in what period of time; and for what purpose. Specifying objectives provides a means for evaluating whether the system was able to accomplish what it set out to achieve. If an objective is not met, the basis for pinpointing possible reasons is provided.

Differentiating Internal and External Services

Direct probation services should be defined clearly and differentiated from services that should be met by other social institutions. Generally the kinds of services to be provided to probationers directly through the probation system should:

- Relate to the reasons the offender was brought into the probation system.
- Help him adjust to his status as a probationer.
- Provide information and facilitate referrals to needed community resources.
- Help create conditions permitting readjustment and reintegration into the community as an independent individual through full utilization of all available resources.

In addition, probation must account to the court for the presence and actions of the probationer.

Other needs of probationers related to employment, training, housing, health, etc. are the responsibility of other social institutions and should be provided by them. Therefore, most services needed by probationers should be located outside the system itself. These services should be available to probationers just as they are to all citizens, but some social institutions have created artificial barriers that deny ready access by persons identified as offenders.

Employment is an example. Some probation agencies have created positions of job developers and employment finders. Probation systems should not attempt to duplicate services already created by law and supposedly available to all persons. The responsibility of the system and its staff should be to enable the probationer to cut through the barriers and receive assistance from social institutions that may be all too ready to exclude him.

The probation system has a responsibility to assure that probationers receive whatever services they need. To mobilize needed resources for helping probationers, the probation system must have funds to purchase services from an individual vendor, such as a person to provide foster care for a probationer or a psychiatrist to provide treatment or from agencies or social institutions, such as marital counseling, methadone maintenance, education, and training. The potential for purchasing services for groups has been largely untapped. For example, juvenile probationers with reading difficulties may need diagnostic testing and remedial help. If these cannot be provided through local schools, the probation agency may have to locate a resource and purchase the needed testing and remedial help.

For older probationers who are unemployed or underemployed, probation staff may interest a university or college in developing special programs. These might include courses to provide remedial education or vocational training, depending upon the identified need of a given group of probationers.

Many other kinds of services may be purchased. Regardless of the service purchased, it is essential that provision be made for monitoring and evaluation of the services to insure that they are, in fact, being provided and that they meet the specified objective.

Organizing the System to Deliver Services

To meet the needs of the increased number of individuals that will be placed on probation within the next decade, the probation service system must be organized differently than it has been. With the recognition that needs continually change, that the probation system itself will not be able to meet all the needs of the probationers, that many of the needs can be met through existing community resources, that new resources will have to be developed, and that some services will have to be purchased, the system should be organized to accomplish the following work activities:

- Needs assessment—ongoing assessment of probationers' needs and existing community resources.
- Community planning and development—establishing close working relationships with public and private social and economic groups as well as community groups to interpret needs; identifying needs for which community resources do not exist; and, in concert with appropriate groups, developing new resources.
- Purchase of services—entering into agreements and monitoring and evaluating services purchased.
- Direct services—receiving and assessing probationers; obtaining and providing information, referral, and follow-up; counseling; and supervising.

Differentiating work activities permits staff assignments to be organized around a workload rather than a caseload. Tasks directed toward achieving specific objectives should be identified and assigned to staff to be carried out in a specified time. This activity should be coordinated by a manager who makes an assessment of the staff members best able to carry out given tasks. Thus, the manager should know the capacities and capabilities of his workers and their specific areas of competence. He also should be able to help his subordinates work together as a team rather than as individuals.

A trend in modern organizational theory is to use teams of staff members with different backgrounds and responsibilities. Teams of individuals from varying disciplines and with differing skills may be assembled for a given task and project and disbanded when the project is completed. The leadership within the team may change, with a junior person serving as the team leader if there is particular need for his knowledge and skills.

In examining the various functions within the probation service delivery system it becomes apparent that there is a range of jobs requiring different kinds of knowledge and skills. Paraprofessionals and those in other "new career" occupations can provide services complementary to those of the probation officer. The potential for assigning a group of probationers to a team of probation officers, paraprofessionals, and other new careerists, headed by a team leader who does not function in the traditional social work supervisory role, is worth testing.

Location of Services

Probation services should be readily accessible to probationers. Therefore they should be based in that part of the community where offenders reside and near other community services. Staff serving probationers should be removed from courthouses and separated from staff providing services to the courts.

Services to probationers in rural areas may have to be organized on a regional rather than the traditional county basis. Service centers should be located in the more populated areas, with mobile units used for outlying districts. In such areas, where transportation is a problem, it is important that probation and other community services be in the same physical location.

Services to offenders should be provided in the evening hours and on weekends without the usual rigid adherence to the recognized work week. The problems of offenders cannot be met by conventional office hours. Arrangements should be made to have a night telephone answering service available to probationers.

Probation Officers as Community Resource Managers

The responsibility for being the sole treatment agent that has traditionally been assigned to the probation officer no longer meets the needs of the criminal justice system, the probation system, or the offender. While some probation officers still will have to carry out counseling duties, most probation officers can meet the goals of the probation services system more effectively in the role of community resource manager. This means that the probation officer will have primary responsibility for meshing a probationer's identified needs with a range of available services and for supervising the delivery of those services.

To carry out his responsibilities as a community resource manager, the probation officer must perform several functions. In helping a probationer obtain needed services, the probation officer will have to assess the situation, know available resources, contact the appropriate resource, assist the probationer to obtain the services, and follow up on the case. When the probationer encounters difficulty in obtaining a service he needs, the probation officer will have to explore the reasons for the difficulty and take appropriate steps to see that the service is delivered. The probation officer also will have to monitor and evaluate the services to which the probationer is referred.

The probation officer will have a key role in the delivery of services to probationers. The change in responsibility will enable him to have greater impact on probationers. As community resource manager, he will utilize a range of resources rather than be the sole provider of services— his role until now and one impossible to fulfill.

———

EXPOSING THE QUASI-JUDICIAL ROLE OF THE PROBATION OFFICER *

As judges appear to be shedding more and more of their judicial functions, the role of the probation officer is undergoing sympathetic change. While there is a distinction to be made between the judicial tasks of a judge and the judge's administrative tasks, the distinction often becomes blurred in the actual operation of the court. Constitutionally, the judge may delegate his administrative powers but he may not delegate his judicial powers. Under the circumstance where judicial powers and administrative powers are becoming increasingly confused, the probation officer seems to find himself more and more in a quasi-judicial position.

Unquestionably, there is a difference between administrative decision-making and adjudication. Administrative decision-making depends on free, extensive and informal discussions with many interests and informed individuals or groups. Adjudication requires formalized procedures, the building of a record, and the presentation and cross-examination of evidence. In adjudication, the final judgment is based on the record alone. The aforementioned difference is well known and this discussion of the probation officer's quasi-judicial role does not rest on an analysis between judicial process and administrative process. Questions

* Eugene   H.   Czajkoski,   *Federal Probation*, September 1973. Reprinted with permission.

are raised. It rests rather on the analysis of judicial effect. Questions are raised as to the propriety of the probation officer's achieving judicial effect without judicial process.

The case for the quasi-judicial role of the probation officer is made along five lines of functional analysis.

(1) PLEA BARGAINING AND THE ABDICATION OF THE JUDGE FROM SENTENCING

It wasn't too long ago that plea bargaining was curtained off in the courtroom. To insure a valid guilty plea, one which could not later be upset on appeal, judges engaged in a litany with the defendant wherein the question was asked, "Did anyone make you any promises?" [1] Promises made to induce a guilty plea were, in effect, denied in open court. Everyone involved, including the judge, knew about the plea bargaining and the promises made but all, especially the defendant, (lest his deal be upset) denied the negotiated promises in open court. All seemed to have benefited from the charade except that it was unseemly for the court to participate in subterfuge and, certainly, the recipient of justice was often left with a quizzical notion of the basic honesty of the court. Now that plea bargaining is openly acknowledged and has the imprimatur of the United States Supreme Court,[2] the air in the courtroom is a little clearer. Another result is that the pace of plea bargaining, with its new-found legal respectability, has been stepped up.

To even the most casual observer of the court, it is evident that the judge's role in sentencing has shrunk almost to that of a mere announcer. Not unwillingly, it seems, the judge has abdicated a major portion of his sentencing role. It is the prosecutor, the chief plea bargainer, who in reality determines sentence.

Some very large prosecution offices have gone so far as to produce handbooks to guide assistant district attorneys in fixing sentence through bargaining. Completely ignoring the generally accepted correctional philosophy that sentencing should be in accord with the individual characteristics of the offender, the guidelines used by prosecutors are usually based on the crime committed. The prosecutor's influence in sentencing is drawing us further back toward classical concepts of penology (sentencing in accordance with the crime) even while lawyers in other contexts, such as through the Model Penal Code of the American Law Institute and the Model Sentencing Act of the National Council on Crime and Delinquency, espouse sentencing in accordance with the characteristics of the individual offender. It is doubtful that prosecutors are moved by one or

---

1. An example of the detailed questioning pursued by a judge prior to accepting a guilty plea can be found in: Frank J. Remington, et al., *Criminal Justice Administration*, New York: The Bobbs-Merrill Co., 1969, p. 567.

2. In Brady v. U. S., 397 U.S. 742 (1970), the Supreme Court held that plea inducements were generally compatible with the goals of the criminal justice system.

the other of the two philosophical stands. It is more likely that they are motivated by production goals and by bureaucratic standards of efficiency and self-interest.

By permitting plea bargaining, judges have left themselves little to do other than to certify conditions previously agreed to by defendant, prosecutor, and police. Largely relieved of their sentencing role, many judges also appear to be also giving up their role of interpreting the law for trial juries.[3] Many juries find themselves having to decide on the requirements of law as well as decide on facts to be fitted to law. The fitting is less likely to be done by judges these days.

The abdication of sentencing responsibility to the plea bargaining system leaves the probation officer in an even more peculiar position than it leaves the judge. Theoretically, the probation officer is supposed to make sentencing recommendations to the judge on the basis of his professional estimate of the rehabilitation potential of the defendant. Whether or not a defendant is sentenced to probation probably depends more now on his success in plea bargaining than on his promise of reformation. How does the probation officer fit into this new scheme of extensive plea bargaining? What point is there in conducting an elaborate social investigation by way of evaluating rehabilitation potential? In answer to the first question, Professor Blumberg points out that the probation officer serves to "cool the mark" in the production-oriented and confidence game-like-system of expeditiously moving defendants through the court by means of plea bargaining.[4] The probation officer can assure the defendant of how wise it was for him to plead guilty and of how much benefit there is to be derived from the correctional efforts arising out of the sentence. In answer to the second question, social investigations of defendants (presentence reports) are becoming shorter, more factual, and less analytical.

Like the judge's role, the probation officer's role in sentencing is diminishing. If it has become the judicial role of the judge to simply certify the plea bargaining process, then the probation officer's role is quasi-judicial in that he does the same thing. It is admittedly a peculiar argument, but where the probation officer does a perfunctory presentence report and aims his recommendation toward what he already knows will be the plea bargaining sentence, then he is indeed playing out a de facto judicial role.

It has long been argued that the probation officer's role in sentencing has been a quasi-judicial one, especially where the judge more-or-less automatically imposes the sentence recommended by the probation officer. Various empirical studies have shown a very high correlation be-

3. This phenomenon has been reported to the writer by a number of practicing trial lawyers, and it would appear to warrant some empirical investigation before a trend can be agreed upon.

4. Abraham Blumberg, *Criminal Justice.* Chicago: Quadrangle Books, 1967.

tween probation officer recommendation and disposition made by the judge. Carter and Wilkins have pointed out that judges have followed probation officer recommendations in better than 95 percent of the cases.[5] Among the factors which might explain the high level of agreement between recommendations and dispositions, it was postulated that probation officers make their recommendations in anticipation of what the judge desires (second guessing the judge). Nowadays it is more likely that the prosecutor has found a way to communicate the plea bargaining agreement to the probation officer and the probation officer responds with an appropriate recommendation (or no recommendation) in his presentence report.

Insofar as it firmly determines sentence, the plea bargaining process clearly undermines the professional role of the probation officer. It is now probably more appropriate for the probation officer to counsel the prosecutor on rehabilitation potential than the judge. The prosecutor might want to use the probation officer's professional estimate in the plea bargaining. As a matter of fact, probation officers frequently conduct "prepleading investigations" which are used by both judge and prosecutor to decide plea matters.

(2) INTAKE PROCEDURES

Intake service by probation officers in adult courts is practically unknown. At the juvenile court level, however, it is considered good practice to have some form of intake apparatus.

When serving as a functionary in a juvenile court's intake unit the probation officer is asked to decide which cases are appropriate for formal judicial processing. This kind of decision is obviously a judicial one somewhat akin to those made by the judges or magistrates at preliminary hearings. Except for supervision within an administrative hierarchy, the probation officer in intake functions quite independently in his quasi-judicial decision-making. Despite the fact that the intake process does not meet the ordinary requirements for adjudication, there have been few complaints from defendants subjected to the process. Clearly, inasmuch as intake offers the defendant an opportunity for leniency and perhaps a chance for being saved from legal stigmatization, there is little inclination on the part of defendants to challenge the procedure. Indeed, very many of them consent to an informal probation supervision which is carried out in nearly the same way as adjudicated probation. Behavior required of the defendant is almost the same in both cases and there is a "penalty" for failure under both formal and informal supervision. Under informal probation supervision, the penalty becomes referral to the court for formal judicial processing, the threat of conviction and the likelihood of incarceration.

---

5. Robert M. Carter and Leslie T. Wilkins, "Some Factors in Sentencing Policy," *Journal of Criminal Law, Criminology and Police Science*, 58, No. 4 (1967), pp. 503–514.

In terms of controlling input to the court the intake probation officer is very much like the prosecutor. The pattern for both the probation officer and prosecutor usurping judicial prerogatives begins to emerge.[6]

(3) SETTING THE CONDITIONS OF PROBATION

The granting of probation always involves conditions either by specification or by implication. It is usually the court that sets conditions of probation and it has frequently been held in case law that the court may not delegate its power and responsibility to impose conditions. It has also been frequently held that the court may not delegate the setting of conditions to the probation department. It is hard to find an intrinsic legal reason why a probation department cannot be given the responsibility for imposing conditions of probation. In the legal cases which have denied probation departments such authority, there has usually been the background of statutes requiring the courts to set conditions. Where statutes do not specifically state that the court must set the conditions of probation, it appears that the setting of conditions may be left to the probation department. In any case, it is common for the judge to impose a "blanket" condition such as "heed the advice of the probation officer" which in effect gives the probation officer condition-setting power.

Oral or unrecorded conditions have been generally held to be invalid and in order for a defendant to be bound by conditions, they must be definite, clearly stated, and effectively communicated to the defendant. Unfortunately, conditions of probation are notoriously vague and poorly communicated to the defendant. Typical conditions of probation include such ambiguous requirements as: Avoid undesirable associates; stay away from disreputable places; and do not keep late hours. Such conditions are obviously very difficult for the defendant to conscientiously manage. What is "undesirable"? What is "disreputable"? Standards for adhering to such conditions are seldom adequately set down and the enforcement of those conditions, where it is done at all, is left to the personal, and frequently capricious, judgment of the probation officer. The indefinite conditions become a vehicle for maintaining the moral status quo as interpreted by the probation officer. According to surveys made by Arluke, conditions seem slow to change.[7] While a few jurisdic-

---

6. The efforts of defense lawyers to find a role in the intake process is explained in: Margaret K. Rosenheim and Daniel L. Skoler, "The Lawyer's Role at Intake and Detention Stages of Juvenile Court Proceedings," *Crime and Delinquency*, 11, No. 2 (1965), pp. 167–174.

7. Nat R. Arluke, "A Summary of Parole Rules—Thirteen Years Later," *Crime and Delinquency*, 15 No. 2 (1969), pp. 267–274. Although Arluke surveyed parole conditions (dealing with about 50 parole jurisdictions is easier than trying to deal with literally hundreds of probation jurisdictions), his findings are relevant to probation conditions. Probation conditions and parole conditions are very similar and both are frequently administered in unison by a single agency having combined probation and parole functions. For a specific analysis of conditions of probation and for demonstration of their similarity to conditions of parole also see: Judah Best and Paul I. Birzan, "Conditions of Probation: An Analysis," *Georgetown Law Journal*, 51 (1963), pp. 809–836.

tions are turning to brief, streamlined sets of conditions, for the most part, particularly in the juvenile courts, conditions of probation remain moralistic, negativistic, and vague.

Apart from conditions of probation serving as a means for controlling nonlegally proscribed behavior, in other words, behavior which is morally undesirable but not unlawful, conditions of probation intrude upon or become substitutes for certain formal judicial processes. Many conditions of probation involve monetary obligations. Some are the kind that any citizen may have, e.g., support of dependents; and others arise out of criminal conviction, such as fines or restitution. Because of the existence of such monetary conditions of probation, the probationer is deprived of the usual judicial safeguards and is placed in the administrative or quasi-judicial hands of the probation officer.

Consider, for instance, the matter of supporting dependents. Defendants who are on probation as a result of criminal conviction are seldom brought into civil or family court on the issue of supporting dependents. Dependents wishing support from the probationer need only go to the probation officer to obtain satisfaction. The probation officer, using the condition of probation, can compel support payments in amounts determined by the probation officer himself, through his own administrative investigation. Without a court hearing on the question of support payments, the order of the probation officer in enforcing the conditions of probation has significant judicial effect. Were he not on probation for a criminal case, the defendant might easily seek an adjudication process in the appropriate court on the question of support. Instead he is forced to submit to the judicial effect brought about by the probation officer enforcing a standard condition of probation. The defendant makes his case before the probation officer and not before the court which is specially set up to adjudicate the question of family support.

A similar usurpation of civil court process occurs when a restitution condition is imposed on a criminal court probationer. It is usually left to the probation officer to determine the appropriate restitution payment. Too often, victims, particularly corporate victims, seek to gain through restitution conditions that which they would have great difficulty in gaining in civil court. Civil courts are comparatively careful in restoring exactly what has been lost. Relying on adversary proceedings, they analyze and evaluate the loss in fair detail. Civil courts may hold jury trials on matters of restitution. When the criminal court probation officer is given the responsibility of settling the matter of restitution, he does not have the same resources for hearing evidence on the loss as do the civil courts. He usually accepts the victim's flat statement as to what the loss is. The probationer, since he is not arguing the matter in a genuine court setting, can do little to rebut the victim's claim. Victims frequently do far better in gaining restitution through the criminal court probation officer than through a civil court. Because he is operating on the basis of a criminal conviction having occurred, the probation officer is bound to presume in favor of the victim in terms of both the quality and quantity of the restitution claim. Since the criminal court judge rarely conducts a full-dress hearing on the question of restitution, preferring to assign resolution of the matter to the probation officer, the judicial effect of the probation officer's determination of restitution is significant indeed.

(4) PROBATION VIOLATION PROCEDURES

The traditional view of probation has been that it is a privilege rather than a right and as such the probation status does not invoke ordinary due process. While this view has experienced considerable erosion in recent years, the revocation of probation remains highly discretionary. In some jurisdictions, probation violation hearings closely approach the characteristics of a trial. Still a hearing is not a trial and the courts generally retain substantial discretion in revocation of probation proceedings.[8]

While it is the judge who actually revokes probation, it is the probation officer who initiates the revocation action and largely controls it. In a very high proportion of cases, the judge's revocation action is in accord with the probation officer's recommendation. The hegemony of the probation officer in probation violation proceedings is well known and requires little unfolding here. It plainly casts the probation officer in a quasi-judicial role.

In the case of so-called technical violations, the judicial role of the probation officer becomes amplified. Technical violations are those which are somehow covered by the conditions of probation but which are not specified in criminal statutes. Failure to report to the probation officer or failure to avoid undesirable persons might be a type of technical violation. Oftentimes probation officers proceed on the basis of technical violation when new criminal offenses are suspected but cannot be easily proved. Police and prosecutors regularly call upon the probation officer to invoke some technical violation against a probationer who they believe has committed a new crime. It is patently easier to put a defendant behind bars as a result of a probation violation hearing than it is to send him to prison as a result of a full-fledged trial. In consenting to proceed on the basis of a technical violation when the real issue is a new criminal offense, the probation officer is playing a judicial role. In effect, he is deciding that there is sufficient basis to conclude that the defendant is guilty of the new offense and thus deserves to have the technical

---

8. For a very thorough review of legal practices in probation revocation see: Ronald B. Sklar, "Law and Practice in Probation and Parole Revocation Hear- ings," *Journal of Criminal Law, Criminology and Police Science*, 55 (1964), pp. 175–198.

violation placed against him. Given the vague and all-encompassing nature of conditions of probation, it is not difficult for the probation officer to muster a technical violation as needed. Many probationers are in a steady state of probation violation as a result of conditions relating to keeping "decent hours," abstaining from alcohol, and various prohibitions relating to sexual activity. These violations usually go unenforced by the probation officer until such time as he is given reason to believe that a new criminal offense has occurred. Invoking the technical violation thus becomes the result of the probation officer's making the adjudication that a crime has been committed. The probationer has a hearing on the technical violation but is denied a trial on the suspected crime which triggered the technical violation.

(5) PUNISHMENT BY THE PROBATION OFFICER

The legislator sets punishment, the judge imposes it, and the administrator executes it. Under our constitutional scheme, it is the judge who decides when a particular individual is to have legal punishment. While probation is a sentence, it is ideologically not a punishment. Nevertheless, implicit in probation supervision are numerous opportunities for punishment. With his awesome authority over the probationer, the probation officer may in various ways restrict his liberty. It is easily argued that restriction of liberty amounts to punishment. The probation officer, in the name of rehabilitation and under the banner of standard conditions of probation, can demand that the probationer not live in or frequent certain areas, that he not engage in certain employment, and that he refrain from a number of interpersonal associations.

Sometimes probation-officer-decided punishments are more direct than denial of freedom. In some jurisdictions, a probationer may not receive a driver's license without the specific approval of the probation officer. From place to place, various occupational licenses are subject to the approval by the probation officer. If one chooses not to regard the probation officer's withholding of license approval as punishment and therefore not in the nature of a judicial action, it is at least still possible to conceive of the probation officer's approval role in licensing as being quasi-judicial.

In sum, the probation officer's rule is multi-faceted. Many of the facets are not easily recognized and may be dysfunctional to our concepts of justice and due process. It is difficult to say whether the probation officer's quasi-judicial role is increasing. It is very closely tied to the judge, but the judge seems to be giving up more and more of his own judicial role. If the probation officer ties in more with the prosecutor, then the probation officer's quasi-judicial function may paradoxically increase because of the judicial aggrandizement of the prosecutor's office through plea bargaining and other arrangements.

THE PRESENTENCE INVESTIGATION REPORT *

ITS FUNCTIONS AND OBJECTIVES

The presentence investigation report is a basic working document in judicial and correctional administration. It performs five functions: (1) to aid the court in determining the appropriate sentence, (2) to assist Bureau of Prisons institutions in their classification and treatment programs and also in their release planning, (3) to furnish the Board of Parole with information pertinent to its consideration of parole, (4) to aid the probation officer in his rehabilitative efforts during probation and parole supervision,[1] and (5) to serve as a source of pertinent information for systematic research.

The primary objective of the presentence report is to focus light on the character and personality of the defendant, to offer insight into his problems and needs, to help understand the world in which he lives, to learn about his relationships with people, and to discover those salient factors that underlie his specific offense and his conduct in general. It is not the purpose of the report to demonstrate the guilt or the innocence of the defendant.

Authorities in the judicial and correctional fields assert that a presentence investigation should be made in every case. With the aid of a presentence report the court may avoid committing a defendant to an institution who merits probation instead, or may avoid granting probation when confinement is appropriate.

Probation cannot succeed unless care is exercised in selecting those who are to receive its benefits. The presentence report is an essential aid in this selective process.

Where the defendant is committed to the custody of the Attorney General, copies of the presentence report are sent to the institution. The institution relies on the report for pertinent data relating to the kind and degree of custody required by the defendant, needed medical attention, and the needs, capacities, and the problems of the individual. Often it takes more than one interview to establish a cooperative relationship and to give the defendant confidence in the probation officer.[2]

If the investigation discloses information that is substantially different from statements given by the defendant, the probation officer should reinterview the defendant and resolve the conflicting statements. This

* Division of Probation Administrative Offices of the U. S. Courts, A Monograph. Reprinted with permission.

1. The Federal probation officer also supervises persons released from Federal correctional institutions and the U. S. Disciplinary Barracks.

2. See articles on the initial interview, by Henry L. Hartman, M.D., in the September and December 1963 issues of *Federal Probation.*

will assist the probation officer in determining the motivation behind any erroneous statements and will help to explain the defendant's personality and character.

Generally, the probation officer should have 2 to 4 weeks to complete his investigation and write his report. If necessary, he should be given more time.

START WHERE THE DEFENDANT IS

In conducting the investigation and in writing the presentence report, the probation officer should be primarily concerned with how the defendant thinks, feels, and reacts *today*. He starts with the defendant as he finds him—as of this moment—and includes in his report no more from the past than what is believed essential to help the court understand the defendant as he is *today*. This is not to say that early developmental influences have no relevance to current behavior. However, a mere recitation of experiences, relationships, and circumstances, without relating them to the present picture, offers little or no insight in understanding the defendant's present thinking, feeling, and behavior.

THE WORKSHEET

Each probation system has some type of worksheet. In the Federal Probation System it is known as Probation Form No. 1. It is essential that all offices use the latest revision of this form.

The form is not intended to be a presentence investigation report itself but rather a guide for the probation officer in gathering basic factual information. From this information on the worksheet he selects, evaluates, and assembles the data under the major headings of the presentence report.

TANGIBLE FACTS NOT ENOUGH

A presentence report is more than a compilation of tangible facts. Facts about family composition, employment, health, and so on, have relatively little value unless they are interpreted in relation to the defendant and how he thinks, feels, and behaves. Such facts alone do not give an account of a living person—his character and personality in action. People in the report must come to life. Instead of giving an accumulation of cold facts the report should rather present a true, vivid, living picture of the defendant.

Facts are not limited to the tangible. Attitudes, feelings, and emotional responses are facts, too. Knowledge of these more or less intangible elements is essential to really know a person and what makes him behave as he does.

How the defendant feels about those with whom he comes in daily contact, what he thinks about his family, his peers, and his coworkers—and what he believes they think about him—are essential to an understanding of his relationships with people. Also significant are his feelings about baffling problems in his life, including his offense and his reaction to opportunities, accomplishments, disappointments, and frustrations. His moral values, his beliefs and his convictions, his fears, prejudices, and hostilities explain the "whys" and "wherefores" of the more tangible elements in his life history.

Time, patience, and skill are required to undercover these more subjective factors and to develop their relevance, but they are basic in good report writing. Each of them should be interpreted in terms of the defendant's family background, culture, and environment, and in relation to the groups with whom he has associated and is closely identified. Even an untrained investigator can pull together the bare facts required in a presentence report and assemble them in an established outline and format. But the ability to select the pertinent data, to distinguish between factual data and inferences to draw out the subjective elements, and to assess their relative importance in the personality makeup and the needs of the defendant, differentiate the trained and skilled probation officer from the untrained and inexperienced probation officer.

WHEN ANOTHER OFFICE IS CALLED ON TO ASSIST

When another Federal probation office is called on to assist in developing a presentence report, it should be made clear what specific information is desired, when the information is needed, and the probable date of sentence. No more information should be requested than is required.

The same procedure applies when requesting information from cooperating welfare agencies, institutions, and State and local probation and parole offices. The request should include sufficient data to enable the officer of the cooperating district or agency to make an intelligent inquiry.

When a request is made of another Federal probation office for a *complete* investigation report, the following minimum data should be supplied on the form 1 worksheet, if possible, or in a letter: true name; place of residence and exact address (including apartment number); birthdate; sex and race; date of arrest; status of custody; brief summary of the offense; defendant's statement; prior record; names and addresses of parents, brothers, and sisters, and other relatives close to the defendant; and places of employment. Specific directions for locating persons to be interviewed should be supplied wherever possible.

When the cooperating probation office is asked to write the report in presentence form, the office for the court in which sentence is to be pronounced (office of origin) will determine how it wishes to present the report to the court. The report from the second office may be appended to the report prepared by the office of origin or may be incorporated as a part of it. If the report from the second office is to be incorporated in the report of the office of origin, it would be desirable to indicate what information comes from the second office.

INVESTIGATIONS PRIOR TO CONVICTION OR PLEA

Where a court is not continuously in session and the judge sits for only short periods in the various places of holding court a probation officer may find it difficult to complete the presentence reports within the limited time available. In these circumstances some courts request that investigations be conducted prior to conviction or plea. When such a request is made, the probation officer should ask the defendant after having advised him of his right to the advice of counsel, to sign the Probation Division's form authorizing the probation officer to institute the investigation. It is also desirable to have on file a letter from the defense attorney stating that he has no objection to the probation officer beginning the investigation prior to conviction or plea.

As provided by rule 32(c)(1) of the Federal Rules of Criminal Procedure, the presentence investigation report shall not be submitted to the court or its contents disclosed to anyone unless the defendant has pleaded guilty or has been found guilty.

DISCUSSION OF THE REPORT WITH THE JUDGE

It is the practice of most judges to call the investigating officer into chambers to discuss the various aspects of the case as reflected in the presentence report. Where certain information in the report is unfavorable to the defendant, the judge may discuss these points with the probation officer in chambers.

CONFIDENTIAL NATURE OF THE REPORT

The presentence investigation report is a confidential document and should not be available to anyone without the permission of the court. In some instances the court delegates to the probation office the responsibility for determining what information from the report may be disclosed.

The presentence report often contains highly privileged information about the defendant and his family and also confidential data from cooperating public and private welfare agencies, law enforcement officials, employers, and others who know the defendant. This information is frequently given to the probation officer with the understanding that it is to be kept confidential.

The defendant's family, which is the best source of information about him, frequently divulges confidential information which, if disclosed, can impair the relationship between him and his family.

Welfare agencies adhere to the principle of confidentiality. When they share their case file information with the probation office they rely on the probation office to comply with the agencies' standards in the use of this information. They expect that the information will be used solely in the rehabilitation of persons under investigation and supervision by the probation officer.

Probation officers often have access to confidential information in the arrest and investigation reports of law enforcement agencies—Federal, State, and local.

An employer will be reluctant to supply information if he believes what he says will get back to the employee. There may be, for example, such on-the-job problems as drinking, quarrelsomeness, and lack of dependability.

Some defendants have had a close relationship with dangerous associates. If incriminating information about these persons is divulged, there is the risk of retaliation.

The family physician is often the source of information that is privileged as a matter of law.

A probation office will lose the respect and confidence of an informing person or agency if confidential information is disclosed. There will be a reluctance to give further information. Eventually, sources of information will dry up and the value of the report will be seriously impaired. Therefore, the probation officer must be cautious and discreet to avoid divulging confidential information.

No presentence report should be read aloud in open court.

At all times there should be a cooperative relationship between the probation office and those institutions and agencies on which the probation office calls for information and professional assistance. A mutual exchange of information may be helpful not only to the respective agencies, but also to the probation office and the court.

The presentence investigation report eventually becomes a part of the defendant's case folder. The courts generally leave to the judgment of the probation office whether cooperating agencies should be permitted to read the case record—including the presentence report—or whether the desired information should be given by individual interpretation or written summaries.

OUTLINE, CONTENTS, AND FORMAT OF THE REPORT

Identifying Information

The following identifying information is requested on Probation Form No. 2, the first page of all presentence reports (see facsimile on p. 8).

Date. Give the date the presentence report is typed.

Name. Enter the name of the defendant as shown on the court record. Also insert the true name, if different, and any aliases.

Address. Give the present home address.

Legal Residence. Give the legal residence (county and State) if different from the present home address. Otherwise insert "Same."

Age and Date of Birth. Give the age on last birthday and the date of birth. Use the symbol "ver." when verified by an official source.

Sex.

Race. Race is determined by ancestry; e. g., white, Negro, American Indian, etc. It should not be confused with national origin.

Citizenship. Give name of country. Citizenship refers to the country of which the defendant is a subject or citizen.

Education. Give highest grade achieved.

Marital Status. Single, married, widow, widower, divorced, legally separated, common law.

Dependents. List those entirely dependent on the defendant for support; e. g., "Three (wife and two children)."

Social Security No.

FBI No.

Docket No.

Offense. Give a brief statement, including statutory citation; e. g., "Theft of Mail (18 U.S.C. 1708)."

Penalty. Insert statutory penalty for the specific offense. This should be obtained from the U. S. attorney in each instance. The probation officer should not attempt to state the penalty on the basis of his knowledge.

Plea. Nature and date.

Verdict. Date.

Custody. Give status (summons, personal or surety bond, recognizance, jail) and period in jail.

Assistant U. S. Attorney. Give name of the assistant U. S. attorney handling the case.

Defense Counsel. Give name and address. When appointed by court, this should be indicated.

Detainers or Charges Pending. Give the name and address of the office issuing the detainer or preferring the charge. Also give the dates action was taken.

Codefendants. Enter the names of codefendants, if any, and status of their respective cases. If there are no codefendants, insert "None."

The following information, below the double rule on form 2, is inserted after the final disposition of the case:

Disposition. Sentence imposed by the court.

Date. Date of sentence.

Sentencing Judge.

Presentence Report Outline

The presentence report outline adopted by the Judicial Conference Committee on the Administration of the Probation System on February 11, 1965, consists of the following marginal headings and the respective subheadings:

Offense

    Official version

    Statement of codefendants

    Statement of witnesses, complainants, and victims

Defendant's Version of Offense

Prior Record

Family History

    Defendant

    Parents and siblings

Marital History

Home and Neighborhood

Education

Religion

Interests and Leisure-Time Activities

Health

    Physical

    Mental and emotional

Employment

Military Service

Financial Condition

    Assets

    Financial obligations

Evaluative Summary

Recommendation

In each presentence report the probation officer should follow the title and exact sequence of these headings.

The suggested contents for the marginal headings are given starting on this page. The items listed under *Essential Data* are those which should appear in *all* presentence reports. Those listed under *Optional Data* will appear in many reports, depending on their significance in the particular case. Each probation officer will determine which of the optional data are essential for the respective defendants under study and how each is to be treated.

In writing the report the probation officer need not follow the sequence of the *essential* and *optional* items. This may prove awkward, hinder readability, disrupt the trend of thought, and obstruct the logical development of the subject matter in question. He will have to shape the general content of the report according to the requirements of each case.

Offense

Official Version

    Essential Data:

        Nature and date of plea or verdict.

        Brief summary of indictment or information, including number of counts, period covered, and nature, date(s), and place(s) of offense.

        Extent of property or monetary loss.

        Extent of defendant's profit from crime.

        Aggravating and extenuating circumstances.

        Nature and status of other pending charges.

        Days held in jail.

        Reasons for inability to divert (juvenile cases).

    Optional Data:

        Date and place of arrest.

        Circumstances leading to arrest.

        Statement of arresting officers.

        Attitude of defendant toward arresting officers.

        Degree of cooperation.

        Where detained prior to trial or sentence.

        Amount of bond.

        Extent to which offense follows patterns of previous offenses.

        Relation of offense to organized crime or racket.

        Amount of loss recovered.

        Has full or partial restitution been made.

        Other violations involved in addition to those charged.

Statement of Codefendants

    Essential Data:

        Extent of their participation in offense.

        Present status of their case.

    Optional Data:

        Attitude toward offense.

        Attitude toward defendant.

        Their statement of defendant's participation in offense.

        Relative culpability of defendant in relation to codefendants and coconspirators.

Statement of Witnesses, Complainants, and Victims

(Optional.)

Comment. The *official version* of the offense may be obtained from the office of the U. S. attorney. The U. S. attorney's file will give the nature of the charge, details of the offense, statements of arresting officers, statements of codefendants, complainants, witnesses, and victims, and also a summary of the arrest record.

Apprehending and prosecuting officers will give greater emphasis in their reports to the offense, the prior arrest record, and the evidence that is essential to convict a person. They are not necessarily as concerned as probation officers are with the kind of person who commits the crime, the motivations underlying the offense, and his personal and social adjustment. The probation officer is interested in the crime and its details to the extent to which they tell something about the defendant. He knows the offense represents only one facet of the defendant's behavior in general and that there is no need in telling any more about the offense than what light it sheds on the defendant. It is not necessary, for example, to give check numbers, auto serial numbers, etc.

In giving the official version of the offense, involved legal terminology should be avoided.

It is important to have the *codefendant's version* of the offense and the extent to which he may have been a leader or an aggressor. His account can be as significant in interpreting the defendant's part in the offense as the defendant's "own story." The court is generally interested in knowing the relative culpability of the defendant in relation to codefendants or coconspirators.

The report should indicate whether the codefendant has been apprehended and what disposition was made in his case.

Statements of *complainants, witnesses,* and *victims,* in some cases, can also help in understanding the defendant in relation to the offense he has committed. Their firsthand account of the offense and the defendant's attitude and conduct while carrying out the offense also can be helpful. It is important to know whether the victim is a possible contributor to the crime.

In assessing the nature of the offense and the underlying motives, the probation officer should not be carried away by the feelings, attitudes, and plight of the victim and the reactions of an indignant public. However, it must be remembered that the court before it places the defendant on probation, must be "satisfied that the ends of justice and the best interest of the public as well as the defendant will be served thereby." (18 U.S.C. 3651.)

Defendant's Version of Offense

Essential Data:

> Summary of account of offense and arrest as given by defendant if different from official version.

Discrepancies between defendant's version and official version.

Extent to which defendant admits guilt.

Defendant's attitude toward offense (e. g., remorseful, rationalizes, minimizes, experiences anxiety, etc.).

Defendant's explanation of why he became involved in the offense.

Extent to which offense was impulsive or premeditated.

Environmental and situational factors contributing to offense, including stressing situations, experiences, or relationships.

Optional Data:

Defendant's feelings from time of offense until his arrest.

Defendant's reactions after arrest (e. g., defiant, relieved, indifferent, etc.).

Defendant's attitude toward the probation officer and his degree of cooperation.

Defendant's attitudes toward prior convictions and commitments if they contribute to an understanding of the present offense.

Comment. Whatever the defendant says about the offense and his part in it is necessary to understand him. His statements may vary from that of the law enforcement officers and the U. S. attorney, but he is entitled, nevertheless, to make clear his part in the offense and to give his own interpretation of the circumstances and motivations underlying it.

Any extenuating and aggravating circumstances should be reported.

It is important to learn whether the offense was impulsive or carefully planned. The feelings of the defendant prior to the crime, during the commission of the crime, between the time of the crime and arrest, and after arrest are pertinent data in many instances. A person who had a feeling of remorse and concern before he was arrested is likely to be different from one who is neither remorseful nor much concerned until after he is apprehended. A person who carefully devises a plan, carries it out calculatingly and with confidence, and is caught because of some unanticipated circumstance or oversight, is likely to be different from one who commits a crime impulsively or who, with some reluctance, commits a crime in which he most likely will be caught.

The attitude of the defendant toward his offense is significant in determining whether he should be considered for probation. It must be kept in mind that some defendants may attempt to rationalize or justify their crime or even place the blame on someone else.

Prior Record

Essential Data:

Clearance with FBI, social service exchange and police departments and sheriffs' offices in respective localities where defendant lived.

Juvenile court history.

List of previous convictions (date, place, offense, and disposition).

List of arrests subsequent to present offense (date, place, offense, and disposition).

Military arrests and courts martial (date, place, offense, and disposition) not covered in *Military Service* (see text).

Institutional history (dates, report of adjustment, present release status, etc.).

Previous probation and parole history (dates, adjustment, outcome).

Detainers presently lodged against defendant.

Optional Data:

Defendant's explanation why he was involved in previous offenses.

Codefendants in previous offenses.

Comment. The identification record (fingerprint record) of the Federal Bureau of Investigation is the best source of information on the arrest record of a defendant. Through the office of the U. S. Marshal the FBI sends a copy of the fingerprint record to the probation office. Although the FBI record has a fairly complete coverage of arrests and convictions, it is recommended that the probation office also clear with local identification bureaus, police departments, and sheriffs' offices in those cities and communities in which the defendant has resided. Particularly in smaller communities, they may have information about the defendant's reputation and his general attitude and behavior at the time of the offense.

Clearances with social service exchanges will give information regarding juvenile court contacts. Where there are no exchanges, the probation officer should check any case where it seems likely the defendant (or his parents in neglect and dependency cases) may have a juvenile court record.

Where the FBI fingerprint record does not give the disposition of a case, the probation officer should communicate with the law enforcement office which filed the print or the court in which the case was tried.

If the defendant has an institutional record, the date of commitment and release, the institutional adjustment, and the present release status should be determined by writing to the institution.

Petty offenses and misdemeanors, including arrests for drunkenness and disorderly conduct, may be summarized in a single paragraph, giving the period during which the offenses occurred, the nature of the violations, and the dispositions.

A succession of offenses resulting in acquittals, or arrests which do not result in prosecution, may reveal something significant about the defendant and may also be summarized in a single paragraph.

An extended record of traffic violations should be summarized in a single paragraph.

Where the defendant admits arrests which are not reflected in official arrest records, the report should indicate they are by his admission.

Prior convictions should be listed according to (1) *juvenile* and (2) *adult* offenses and in chronological order under each of the two headings. Serious military offenses which resulted in incarceration and also those which have a civil counterpart should be listed under adult offenses. The prior convictions should be set up as follows:

PRIOR RECORD:

Juvenile	Offense	Place	Disposition
7–2–40	Petty theft	Detroit	1 yr. probation
(Age 13)			

IM–280

While in the 9th grade at junior high school the defendant and a classmate, age 15, each took a bicycle from the school's bicycle stand. They were arrested the following day and brought to the Wayne County Juvenile Court. Both were placed on probation for 1 year. According to the Juvenile Court, the defendant completed his probation satisfactorily.

Adult	Offense	Place	Disposition
4–14–55	Conspiracy to	Detroit	3 yrs. probation
(Age 28)	steal and receive		and $150 costs
	stolen property		

IM–281

The defendant was convicted in the Wayne County Recorder's Court of the theft of approximately 3,000 pounds of body solder from the Ford Motor Company (value $614). As a truck driver for a parts manufacturing company, the defendant made frequent trips to the Ford Motor Company. It was through his contacts there that the solder was loaded on his truck. Later, attempts were made to sell it to scrap metal dealers. He was involved with three other men, including a Detroit police sergeant who was the defendant's brother-in-law. On 10–31–55 he was placed on probation for 3 years and ordered to pay $150 costs. He was discharged from probation 10–31–58 "with improvement" (verified by Recorder's Court).

Under each offense include institutional record in a separate paragraph, giving dates of custody, escapes and returns, type of release, and expiration of sentence.

Family History

Defendant

Essential Data:

Date, place of birth, race.

Early developmental influences (physical and emotional) that may have a significant bearing on defendant's present personality and behavior.

Attitudes of the father and the mother toward the defendant in his formative years, including discipline, affection, rejection, etc.

By whom was defendant reared, if other than his parents.

Age left home; reasons for leaving; history of truancy from home.

Relationship of defendant with parents and siblings, including attitudes toward one another.

Extent of family solidarity (family cohesiveness).

Relatives with whom defendant is especially close.

Optional Data:

Naturalization status (country of birth and place and date of entry into United States).

Order of birth among siblings.

Parents and Siblings

Essential Data:

(All information optional.)

Optional Data:

Parents (name, age, address, citizenship, naturalization status, education, marital status, health, religion, economic status, general reputation).

If deceased, also give age at death and cause.

Siblings (same as parents, above).

History of emotional disorders, diseases, and criminal behavior in the family.

Attitude of parents and siblings toward defendant's offense.

Comment. No more of the family background should be included in the report than is necessary to understand the defendant and to help him in his personal and social adjustment. As has already been emphasized, the probation officer should start where the defendant is *now*.

Defendant. Attitudes and relationships between the defendant and his parental family are especially significant if the defendant lives or has regular contact with them. In some instances where there is little or no contact, it may be helpful to determine what relationships exist and what effect it has on the defendant.

Are there interfering relatives?

Include here the defendant's role in the parental family as he sees it, particularly if he is single. Does he feel he is part of the family, that he is wanted, appreciated, understood? Does he feel left out, discriminated against, rejected?

What does he say that is favorable about his parental family? What is unfavorable? What family problems and relationships disturb him and with which ones is he unable to cope? What the defendant thinks about his parental home, family background, and family relations will help the probation officer to understand why he thinks, responds, and behaves as he does.

Parents and siblings. The probation officer should resist the tendency to give in the report too much extraneous information about parents and siblings. Such information as dates and places of birth, residence, health, education, religion, employment, and earnings may, in some instances, have little or no relevance.

What is the cultural background of the family? What family influences are apparent? What stabilizing factors are there in the parental family? To what community agencies is the family known?

As a general rule detailed information about the family is more pertinent in understanding juvenile and youth offenders than it is in the case of the older offender.

Data about each member of the parental family may be presented in the following format, giving the name, age and address in each instance:

Father. Donald Jones, died in 1958 from a heart attack at age 52. For 17 years prior to his death he worked as a cook at various restaurants.

Mother. Violet (nee Thomas) Conrad, 54, lives at 1928 Chestnut Street, Detroit, with her second husband, Noel Conrad, a factory worker. She is employed as a cook at a bar and restaurant.

Brother. William Jones, 35, 423 Elm Street, Ann Arbor, Michigan, is married, has two children, and is employed in his own business as a house painter. He has not been seen by the defendant in 5 years. They are distant in their relationship.

Sister. Mary Louise Jones, 32, 5127 Foster Avenue, Detroit, single, is a saleslady with the Hudson Department Store. The defendant has always maintained close ties with his sister. She visits the defendant's family every other week.

Marital History

Essential Data:

> Present marriage, including common law (date, place, name and age of spouse at time of marriage).
>
> Attitude of defendant toward spouse and children and theirs toward him.
>
> Home atmosphere.
>
> Previous marriage(s) (date, place, name of previous spouse, and outcome; if divorced, give reasons).
>
> Children, including those from previous marriage(s) (name, age, school, custody, support).

Optional Data:

> Significant elements in spouse's background. History of courtship and reason for marriage. Problems in the marriage (religion, sex, economics, etc.).
>
> Attitude of spouse (and older children) toward offense.
>
> Attitude of defendant and spouse toward divorce, separation, remarriage.
>
> Contacts with domestic relations court.
>
> Juvenile court record of children.
>
> Social agencies interested in family.
>
> Divorce data (including grounds, court, date of final decree, special conditions, and to whom granted).

Comment. A disorganized family life can contribute in large measure to unbecoming conduct. The wife can be a contributing factor to the defendant's difficulties with the law. It is just as important to know about the wife's personality and character, and her problems and needs and social adjustment, as it is to have that knowledge about the defendant.

The wife can be a valuable source of information about the family and the marriage relationship. It is not sufficient to have only the defendant's account of the marriage. The wife's statements can be significant, too. She should be interviewed by the probation officer regarding many of the defendant's problems and needs. No presentence report is complete without interviewing her. But it should be kept in mind that the wife can also be a biased informant. She can be against her husband or be protective of him.

Sometimes neighbors and relatives can throw considerable light on the marriage relationship.

The attitudes between husband and wife and their relationship with one another and the children, may have a significant bearing on the emotional responses of the defendant and his behavior in general. It is important to know how both husband and wife assess their marriage and their family life and what their children mean to each of them. It is helpful to know what family problems each finds especially difficult to cope with. The probation officer should know in what ways they are not compatible and what problems each creates in the home. He should know to what extent the marriage has not been successful and what history of discord there may have been in previous marriages.

What stabilizing influence can the wife and children have? To what extent can the wife help resolve his problems and needs and in what ways can he help her? She may need help, too.

It should be known with what welfare agencies the family has had contact.

Home and Neighborhood

Essential Data:

> Description of home (owned or rented, type, size, occupants, adequacy, and general living conditions).
>
> Type of neighborhood, including any desirable or undesirable influences in the community.
>
> Attitude of defendant and family toward home and neighborhood.

Optional Data:

> Date moved to present residence and number of different residences in past 10 years.
>
> How long has defendant lived in present type of neighborhood.
>
> What race, nationality, and culture predominate.
>
> Prior home and neighborhood experiences which have had a substantial influence on the defendant's behavior.

Comment. In commenting on the home the probation officer is interested not only in the type of construction, costs, size, conveniences, and furnishings. He is also interested in what they reflect about the cultural background and the social and economic status of the family. What do they mean to the family in terms of attitudes, feelings, and relationships, and in what ways do they affect the behavior of the family members?

What the defendant and his wife are willing to put up with in the home and neighborhood tells something about them. How do they feel about the home? Are they dissatisfied with what they have? Does the wife feel her husband should have provided a better home? Is he disturbed by the way she keeps their home? Do the conditions of the home suggest any breakdown in the personality of the defendant or his wife?

Are the husband and wife trying to maintain a home above their earning capacity? Is the home a financial burden?

Meaningless "label" terms should be avoided in describing the home. Moreover, the probation officer should not judge the home by his own standards or by the way his wife keeps their home. Rather, it should be judged by what is expected in the general neighborhood. And it should be remembered that a nicely furnished and well-maintained home does not necessarily mean that family life is well organized.

In describing the neighborhood it is not only important to know about neighborhood influences—good and bad—but also to know how the defendant and his family feel about the area and what effect living in the area may have on their feelings, status, and behavior.

Education

Essential Data:

Highest grade achieved.

Age left school and reason for leaving.

Results of psychological tests (IQ, aptitude, achievement, etc.), specify test and date.

Optional Data:

Last school attended (dates, name, address).

Previous schools attended covering 5-year period (dates, name, address).

School adjustment as evidenced by conduct, scholastic standing, truancy, leadership, reliability, courtesy, likes and dislikes, special abilities and disabilities, grades repeated, and relationships with pupils and teachers.

Business and trade training (type, school, dates).

Defendant's attitude toward further education and training.

Ability to read and write English.

Comment. The school is a valuable source of information about the defendant, particularly in juvenile and youth offender cases. Through its teachers, attendance officers, guidance counselors, social workers, and school nurses it has accumulated pertinent information about the family and family relationships.

Only so much of the school record as will help understand the defendant as he responds and behaves *today* should be included in the report. Any significant patterns of behavior which persist from school days should be reported.

Reactions to schools, teachers, and classmates are important in juvenile and youth offender cases.

Religion

Essential Data:

Religious affiliation and frequency of church attendance.

Optional Data:

Church membership (name, address, pastor).

Member of what church organizations.

What has religious experience meant to defendant in the
past and at present.

What are defendant's moral values.

What is the pastor's impression of the defendant.

Comment. Centuries of human experience have given testimony to
the dynamic qualities of religion. Depending on the defendant's past
church experiences, a renewal of interest in church affiliation or religious
expression may be a significant factor in helping him overcome some of
his difficulties. If church participation had meaning for him at one time,
it may be important to know at what point and for what reason he lost
interest in church activities. His clergyman may be in a position to tell
how his church experience in the past may be utilized in his reclamation.
He can also be of assistance in pointing out the defendant's strengths and
weaknesses.

Of what importance is his church participation and religious experience? Where there is no history of church affiliation it would be helpful
to know what guides the defendant follows for his moral and spiritual
values. It may be important to know where there are conflicts in family
relationships because of differences in faith of family members.

Interests and Leisure-Time Activities

Essential Data:

Defendant's interests and leisure-time activities (including
sports, hobbies, creative work, organizations, reading).

What are his talents and accomplishments.

Optional Data:

Who are his associates; what is their reputation.

Extent to which he engages in activities alone.

Extent to which he includes his family.

Extent to which his leisure-time pursuits reflect maturity.

Comment. How a person spends his leisure time may offer leads to
problems the defendant might have in his social adjustment. The character and extent of his recreational pursuits and his special interests help
the probation officer to understand the defendant's sense of values, social
needs, outlook on life, and his goals. Frequently they tell something
about the character of his family life and how they hold the family
together or pull them apart.

Does the defendant have a well-balanced array of interests and
recreational activities? Do physical or emotional handicaps limit him in
his social relationships? With what groups does he identify? Is he a
leader or a follower? What are his hobbies? What are his active sports
interests? In what creative work is he engaged? To what organizations

does he belong? Which of them may be a source of help in his social adjustment?

Health

Physical

Essential Data:

> Identifying information (height, weight, complexion, eyes, hair, scars, tattoos, posture, physical proportions, tone of voice, manner of speech).

> Defendant's general physical condition and health problems based on defendant's estimate of his health, medical reports, probation officer's observations.

> Use of narcotics, barbiturates, marihuana.

> Social implications of defendant's physical health (home, community, employment, associations).

Optional Data:

> History of serious diseases, including venereal disease, tuberculosis, diabetes (nature, date, effects).

> History of major surgery and serious injuries (nature, date, effects).

> Hospital treatment (hospital, dates, nature, outcome).

> Last medical examination (date, place, pertinent findings).

> Current medical treatment (prescribed medicine and dosage).

> Use of alcohol.

> Allergies (especially penicillin).

Mental and Emotional

Essential Data:

> Probation officer's assessment of defendant's operating level of intelligence as demonstrated in social and occupational functions.

> Personality characteristics as given by family members and as observed by probation officer.

> Attitude of defendant about himself and how he feels others feel about him (parents, siblings, spouse, children, associates).

> Social adjustment in general.

> Social implications of mental and emotional health (home, community, employment, associations).

Optional Data:

> IQ (support with test scores).

> Findings of psychological and psychiatric examinations (tests, date, by whom given).

Emotional instability as evidenced by fears, hostilities, obses-
sions, compulsions, depressions, peculiar ideas, dislikes,
sex deviation (include any history of psychiatric treatment).

Defendant's awareness of emotional problems and what he
has done about them.

Comment. The probation officer is concerned with the social implications of the defendant's physical, mental, and emotional health as they
relate to his family life, his relationships with people, and his ability to
earn a living. It is not unusual for a defendant to say he has "good"
health. But on further inquiry, health problems and concerns about
health come into focus. It is important to know how the defendant
actually feels about his health in general and to report what health
conditions need special attention.

Where authorization is required to release medical information, a
copy of a form authorizing release of confidential information should
accompany the request.

Physical. Physical ills can lead to aberrations in behavior. Physical
disabilities and deformities may be related to the offense and the defendant's behavior in general.

No more than is necessary to understand the defendant's present
health condition should be included in the report. A listing of injuries,
diseases, and surgery serves no purpose unless they have a bearing on the
defendant's present health or are connected in some way with the offense.
Ordinary childhood diseases or surgery without serious after effects
would be classed as extraneous information. The test of what to include
in the report should be: Is the disease, injury, or surgery likely to be
related in any way to the defendant's present health and behavior?

Mental and Emotional. The statement of the defendant's mental
health should be supported wherever possible by psychiatric and psychological reports. A mere diagnostic label serves little or no purpose. The
diagnosis should be expressed in understandable terms in relation to the
specific problems and needs of the defendant.

Whether or not an IQ is available, the probation officer should assess
the defendant's operational level of intelligence as demonstrated in social
and occupational functions.

As pointed out earlier it is important to know something about the
attitudes, feelings, and emotions of the defendant and also his relationships with people. How does he feel about himself? In what ways does
his image of himself differ from how others see him?

A description of the defendant's personality may be presented in this
portion of the presentence report. In describing his personality and traits
of character such descriptive labels as high strung, timid, sullen, boastful,
impulsive, suspicious, remorseful, etc., may be used. But each should be
supported by examples to help clearly portray the trait or quality.

Employment

Essential Data:

Employment history for past 10 years (dates, nature of work, earnings, reasons for leaving).

Employer's evaluation of defendant (immediate supervisor, where possible), including attendance, capabilities, reliability, adjustment, honesty, reputation, personality, attitude toward work, and relationships with coworkers and supervisors.

Occupational skills, interests, and ambitions.

Optional Data:

If unemployable, explain.

Means of subsistence during unemployment, including relief and unemployment compensation.

Comment. A job is different things to different people. It is a means of livelihood; to some it is pleasant and to others it is not so pleasant. Others regard it as a necessary evil—a frustrating experience. It can be status-giving. It can provide a feeling of belonging and fellowship with friendly people. Particularly in creative work, or employment requiring special skills, it gives a sense of achievement and a partnership in a worthwhile enterprise. One-third of an adult's life is spent on his job. Hence, a defendant's employment adjustment and his attitude toward his job can be significant factors in his personal and social adjustment.

Wherever possible, the employment history should be verified by each employer. What the employer (particularly the immediate supervisor) says about the defendant's job adjustment is significant. It may differ considerably from the statement of the defendant.

It is not necessary, in most cases, to report on the employment history beyond a 10-year period.

It is important to know in what ways the defendant's personality, physical condition, and appearance may have contributed to his spotty employment record and his inability to get and to hold a job. If he is unemployable, the nature of his limitations or handicaps might be mentioned again. (*Note:* His disabilities and handicaps will have already been covered under *Health.*)

The employment record should be set up in the following format, giving at the start of each paragraph the dates of employment, name of the employer, nature of work, and the salary or wage. This should be followed by the reason for leaving the job, an evaluation of the defendant's job adjustment, and an estimate of the skills achieved.

EMPLOYMENT:

September 1950 to April 1955 (4 years, 7 months). The defendant was employed at the Fitzsimmons Manufacturing

Company, 3775 E. Outer Drive, Detroit, as a semi-truck driver at $2 per hour (verified). Employment was terminated when he was arrested 4–10–55 for involvement in theft of material from the Ford Motor Company (see PRIOR RECORD).

May 1955 to February 1963 (7 years, 7 months). Employed at the Acme Manufacturing Company, 1400 E. Nine Mile Road, Ferndale, Michigan, as a stock handler and crib attendant at $2.94 per hour (verified). The firm's records show that employment was terminated because of the defendant's arrest in the present case, that he had violated a shop rule by leaving the premises during the lunch period, and had failed to punch out or notify his foreman. When he returned to work 2 days later he was notified of his dismissal.

April 1963 to February 1964 (10 months). Employed as a toolmaker's helper at the Broaching Specialities, Inc., 1500 E. Eleven Mile Road, Madison Heights, Michigan, at $2 per hour. According to the company he was a satisfactory employee and left voluntarily to accept a better-paying job.

February 1964 to present (9 months). Employed at the Vulcan Engineering Company, 222 Conner Street, Detroit, as a bench hand helper at $2.49 per hour. His supervisor describes him as a dependable employee and believes he has the potential for advancing to a higher-skilled and better-paying job. His employer knows about his present offense.

The defendant's wife is employed as a saleslady at the Hudson Department Store where the defendant's sister is also employed. Her earnings are $52 a week.

Military Service
Essential Data:
> Branch of service, serial number, and dates of each period of military service.
>
> Highest grade or rank achieved and grade or rank at separation.
>
> Type and date of discharge(s).
>
> Attitude toward military experience.

Optional Data:
> Inducted or enlisted.
>
> Special training received.
>
> Foreign service, combat experience, decorations and citations.
>
> Disciplinary action not covered in *Prior Record* (see text).
>
> Veteran's claim number.
>
> Selective Service status (local board, classification, registration number).

Comment. The military service record of *former* military personnel should be obtained in each instance from the Military Personnel Records Center. Requests for information on *active* personnel should be sent directly to the defendant's commanding officer.

The medical history supplied by the Military Personnel Records Center should be reported under the marginal heading, *Health.* Only minor military offenses should be included here. As already pointed out, serious military offenses which resulted in incarceration and also those which have a civil counterpart should be listed under *Prior Record.*

Financial Condition

Assets

Essential Data:

Statement of financial assets.

General standard of living.

Optional Data:

Net worth statement.

Property (type, location, value, equity).

Insurance (type, amount, company).

Checking and savings account (bank, amount).

Stocks and bonds (type, value).

Personal property (car, furniture, appliances).

Income from pensions, rentals, boarders.

Family income.

Available resources through relatives and friends.

Financial Obligations

Essential Data:

Statement of financial obligations.

Optional Data:

Current obligations, including balance due and monthly payment (home mortgage, rent, utilities, medical, personal property, home repairs, charge accounts, loans, fines, restitution).

Money management and existing financial delinquencies.

Credit rating.

Comment. How a defendant handles his finances sometimes tells a lot about him—the things he buys, the number of items he purchases on time, regularity of payments, the extent to which purchases have been picked up for nonpayment. Knowledge of the defendant's debts and financial obligations helps the probation officer to understand the defendant. To what extent are there money-management problems and current delinquencies in the payment of financial obligations? The defendant's credit rating may offer helpful leads to his financial status.

Evaluative Summary

Essential Data:

Highlights of body of the report.

Analysis of factors contributing to present offense and prior convictions, (motivations and circumstances).

Defendant's attitude toward offense.

Evaluation of the defendant's personality problems and needs, and potential for growth.

Optional Data:

Reputation in the community.

Comment. Writing the evaluative summary is perhaps the most difficult and painstaking task in the entire presentence report. It has a significant bearing on the future course of the defendant's life. It is here that the probation officer calls into play his analytical ability, his diagnostic skills, and his understanding of human behavior. It is here that he brings into focus the kind of person before the court, the basic factors that brought him into trouble, and what special helps the defendant needs to resolve his difficulties.

The opening paragraph of the evaluative summary should give a concise restatement of the pertinent highlights in the body of the report. There should follow in separate paragraphs those factors which contributed in some measure to the defendant's difficulty and also an evaluation of his personality. (*Note:* A fuller description of his personality should appear under *Health—Mental and Emotional.*)

Recommendation

Essential Data:

Recommendation.

Basis for recommendation.

Optional Data:

Suggested plan, including role of parents, spouse, pastor, further education, future employment.

Sentencing alternatives.

Comment. Some judges ask for the probation officer's recommendation regarding probation or commitment. Where recommendations are requested, they should be a part of the presentence report. If the judge does not wish to have the recommendations included as a part of the report, they may be given on a separate sheet which may be detached if the presentence report is later sent to an institution.

If it is recommended that the defendant be placed on probation, the proposed plans for residence, employment, education, and medical and psychiatric treatment, if pertinent, should be given. The part to be played in the social adjustment of the defendant by the parental and immediate family, the pastor, close friends, and others in the community should also be shown. If commitment is recommended, the probation officer should indicate what special problems and needs should receive the attention of the institutional staff.

Where the judge asks for sentencing alternatives, they may be included in this part of the report.

SOME GENERAL SUGGESTIONS

Writing the Report

The presentence report should be dictated at the earliest possible time following the investigation. Notes "grow cold" if they are not dictated relatively soon. Moreover, the longer the delay, the greater is the chance of overlooking significant observations.

Prior to dictating, the worksheet information and other interview notes, together with reports and correspondence regarding the case, should be well organized. This is especially true in dictating directly to the stenographer. Attempting to organize notes during dictation results in a waste of time.

The probation officer who dictated the presentence report should sign the report—not the chief probation officer. It is not necessary to have the names of both the chief probation officer and the investigating officer on the report.

Objectivity and Accuracy

Objectivity is one of the essential attributes of a probation officer. Impartiality in his report writing will depend to a large extent on the degree of objectivity he has achieved. The trained and skilled probation officer will not read into situations what is not there. He recognizes his own prejudices and blindspots and makes allowances and adjustments for each of them. He is careful not to assess the defendant's behavior and actions on the basis of his own standards of conduct and moral values. He does not allow himself to overidentify with the defendant. He guards against the psychological mechanisms of rationalization and projection. He rids himself of any preconceived notions about the defendant, for he knows that premature or snap judgments can be not only embarrassing to the defendant, the probation officer, and the court, but damaging as well. He is never guilty of "slanting" a report.

Facts contribute to objectivity, but it is possible to misrepresent or distort facts. In evaluating or reporting the statements, impressions, and observations of collateral contacts, the reliability of the informant should be made clear in the report. Where there is an element of uncertainty about the informant's statement, this should be made known.

Inferences, impressions, and opinions are important at times and may have a place in the presentence report. But a clear distinction should be made between what is factual and what is inference. Facts are more likely to be presented accurately than inferences, impressions, and interpretations. It is better to say "Mr. Brown impresses one as honest and sincere" than to say "Mr. Brown *is* honest and sincere."

Indicating Sources of Information

Sources of information should be shown in the report, not at the close of the report. In reading about the defendant's employment record, for example, the reader should know whether the statement is given by the defendant himself, his wife, the employer, or some other source. When reporting that the defendant gets along well with his wife it is essential to know whether it is based on his statement only, the wife's, or the statement of each of them.

Ways in which the source may be reported are the following: "According to the defendant's wife   . . ."; "The report from Central High School indicates that   . . ."; "The defendant insisted that   . . ."; "The report of the psychiatrist disclosed   . . ."; "The defendant's pastor states   . . ."

Unverified statements should be clearly shown as "unverified," "rumor," or "unconfirmed report." Immeasurable harm and irreparable injury may result from unverified information presented as fact.

Only in most unusual circumstances should a presentence report be based solely on the defendant's statement. When this is done, it should be made clear in the report, preferably at the beginning.

Selectivity in Writing the Report

The presentence report should not be cluttered with extraneous information which has little or no relation to the personality, character, and behavior of the defendant. Information about the defendant's birth and his early development, for example, may be irrelevant in the case of an adult who appears to have normal intelligence and seems to behave in a relatively normal way. Detailed information about family members with whom an adult defendant has had no contact in many years may be of little significance. A comprehensive school report will be more pertinent in understanding a juvenile or youth offender than a person in his forties and fifties.

A verbatim account of the indictment would seem to have no place in the report. A brief summary should suffice since the judge has before him the indictment or information from the official file of the court. A lengthy recital of every detail in the offense serves no purpose unless it tells something about the defendant, his personality, and his conduct in general.

An extended history of employment instability, family discord, similar types of offenses, inability to tolerate tedium, and the need to be on the go, do, of course, throw light on the defendant.

The average length of the presentence report should generally be six to eight pages of single-space typing on 8- by 10½-inch sheets. This does not include the face sheet (form No. 2), the evaluative summary, and any recapitulation the probation officer may carry at the close of the report.

Brevity

Needless repetition and wordiness should be avoided. Redundancy often occurs when the probation officer has no opportunity to edit a preliminary draft of the report before it is typed in final form. Too many persons tend to waste words.

All data in the report should be concise and to the point, but brevity should not be sought at the expense of completeness. Discriminating selection of relevant material is one means of shortening the report.

Negative statements of no significance should be omitted. The following "irrelevant negatives" contribute nothing to an understanding of the defendant. "This juvenile has had no military experience"; "The defendant had no brothers or sisters"; "There is no history of hospitalization for emotional disorders."

Complete, short sentences and paragraphs confined to a single topic or thought are an aid to clarity and help to sustain the interest of the reader. In general, sentences should be brief. Paragraphs should be held to about 15 typed lines.

Style and Format in Writing the Report

Good report writing adheres to the rules of rhetoric. A good style need not be elaborate. A simple, direct, lucid style is most effective. Time and effort should not be wasted to achieve a dramatic effect. However, the report should be written so that the defendant comes alive. It should present him as a living person. Enlargement of descriptive vocabulary enhances the ability of the probation officer to describe for the court the kind of a person it has before it.

"Subject" should not be used in referring to the defendant; it is much too impersonal. The defendant is a human being to be helped. Some refer to him as "the defendant" and others prefer to call him "Mr. Brown" or by his first name if he is a juvenile or youth offender. An adult should never be referred to by his first name. The usual alternatives of "mother," "father," "sister," "wife" may be used as called for.

The repetitious use of "he said" should be avoided. Some more descriptive variations are: mentioned, asserted, replied, recalled, admitted, suggested, promised, emphasized, disclosed, revealed, divulged. Variations which describe the mood or manner in which the defendant made his statements are especially helpful, for example: objected, confided, argued, mumbled, interrupted, volunteered, contested, denounced, confessed, warned.

The probation officer should avoid the use of "I" in his reports. He should refer to himself as little as possible. Third person makes for readability.

Use of "Label" Terms

The use of generalized terms and unsupported adjectives should be avoided. These so-called "label" or "blanket" terms fail to define sharply the differences between persons, situations, and circumstances. Terms such as "disorderly home," "shocking conduct," "lacking in judgment," "poor disciplinarian," "undependable person," "makes a good living," "heavy drinker" have varied interpretations and meanings to different people. The judge, the probation officer, the defendant, the employer do not give the same evaluation to these vague terms.

"Highly emotional" gives little insight into the personality makeup of the defendant. A "bad" heart does not tell whether the defendant is bedridden or ambulatory, or to what extent he is handicapped or unable to work. Stating that the defendant can do "light work" has little significance because persons interpret "light work" differently. Medical diagnostic terms will have more meaning if the social and physical implications of the disease are spelled out.

If used at all, blanket terms should be supported by meaningful, descriptive information. For example, "irresponsible husband" may be followed by statements such as "fails to bring home the pay check"; "deserted the family 3 days last month"; "overlooks paying rent and utilities."

Clichès and stereotyped terms and phrases have no place in report writing.

Technical Words and Phrases

Technical words and phrases, in general, should be used only if they have wide usage and a common meaning. Such terms as sociopath, schizophrenic, moron, paranoid, sex psychopath, neurotic, psychotic, character disorder—which often are used indiscriminately by the public and the press and sometimes probation officers, too—have a distinctive professional meaning to psychiatrists and psychologists. They should be restricted to these specialists in behavior. The probation officer should not attempt to apply them on his own.

Where psychiatric, medical, or psychological terminology is used in the presentence report, it may be accompanied by an explanation of the diagnostic statements.

Verbatim Reporting

Verbatim reporting may be helpful at times in portraying the feelings, attitudes, and responses of a person. But the direct quotation should be used only if it gives a better picture of the defendant or the situation and circumstances than would a paraphrased statement. Where quotation marks are used, the quoted portion should contain the *exact* words of the person quoted—not an interpolation. Moreover, the language should *not* be taken out of context. Meanings can be distorted or altered if any statement preceding or following, or any part of the quoted portion, is omitted.

Verbatim reporting is helpful for the unbiased picture it presents of the defendant's thinking processes, attitudes, and feelings, and the precise way in which he expressed himself. On the other hand, verbatim reporting is unreliable unless full notes are taken in the presence of the defendant. Recording direct quotations following the interview cannot be reliable. Without shorthand devices, the probation officer will have difficulty in recording word-for-word statements.

Handwritten statements by the defendant on certain aspects of the presentence investigation fall in the category of verbatim reporting and should be carried in quotes.

THE FIVE FACES OF PROBATION *

In seeking to meet the challenge of crime and delinquency, the modern probation officer finds himself caught up in a peculiar double bind. He must serve the needs of his probationers, on one hand, and the needs of the community, on the other. This two-sided facet of the probation officer's function is a result of evolutionary changes in both the conception and scope of probation. It represents corrections' attempt to discover the most effective means of accomplishing humane but realistic treatment of offenders.

The law mandates that probationers should be "helped" to overcome or neutralize their antisocial behaviors. At the same time probation is aimed as "protecting" the community from those same overt behaviors. The dilemma which this poses is well known to probation officers who must put this dual task into some manageable perspective in their work. Too often, the training of correctional personnel shows features of choosing one goal over the other. Depending on whether one's orientation comes from psychology, sociology, criminology, social work, counseling, etc., probation styles tend to treat the dual goals as somewhat mutually exclusive.

Out of this duality here emerges what may be termed the "five faces of probation." This is taken to mean that probation officers manifest certain strategies, approaches, or styles of "probationing" which reflect their degrees of concern for meeting the stated goals of help and protection. Each of these styles "shows its face" to the probationer and starts the interaction which leads to five differential outcomes in probation officer-probationer relationships.

This set of relationships can be examined and clarified where viewed in terms of a Probation Grid. The grid concept stems from Blake and Mouton's [1] well-known "Managerial Grid" used so successfully by them for training managerial personnel. Such a construct has been applied to

---

* Louis Tomaino, *Federal Probation,* December 1975.

1. Robert Blake and Jane Mouton, *The Managerial Grid.* Houston: Gulf Publishing Co., 1964.

other content areas like decisionmaking, change, and leadership. This article proposes to explicate a Probation Grid stemming directly from the probation objectives of helping individuals and protecting the community.

These objectives will be expressed as the probation officer's concern for effective *control* over his client's illegal behaviors, and the probation officer's concern for satisfactory *rehabilitation* of his probationer. These concerns, for analytical purposes, are seen as being independent of each other, though in practice, probation officers may impose a relationship on them which manifests the five faces of probation. Therefore in the grid model, the two dimensions are oriented at right angles to each other. The horizontal axis of the Probation Grid represents the goal of control experienced by officers, and the vertical axis reflects his concern for rehabilitation of the probationer.

This article is interested in the degree to which a probation officer is concerned about the two grid dimensions. Therefore, as in the Blake-Mouton grid, each axis is scaled from 1 to 9 in order to reflect degree of concern. The value 1 denotes low or minimal "concern for" while 9

Figure 1. The Probation Grid

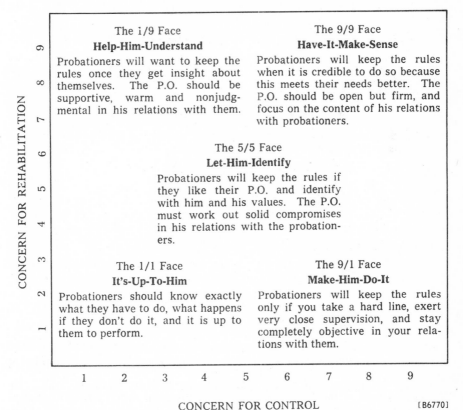

symbolizes high or maximal "concern for." By arranging the concerns at right angles to each other and by providing a scalar arrangement the probation faces of probation officers can be assessed from the frame of reference which they bring to the relationship between the concerns. "Concern for" is not a static term rooted only in the officer's attitude. What is significant is how that officer is concerned about control, or about rehabilitation or about how these concerns fuse.

The Probation Grid is presented in figure 1. Three faces of probation in the grid assume that concerns for control and rehabilitation are in basic conflict with each other and are mutually exclusive. The officer who has this frame of reference finds himself choosing one concern over the other, but not both, as his probation focus. The probation faces which result from this forced choice, reading in grid fashion (right and up) are the 9/1, 1/9, and 1/1. Each of these faces will be evaluated according to its primary characteristics in probation counseling.

Control is defined as a condition in which the probationer is under close behavioral surveillance by his probation officer and is not violating probation rules. Rehabilitation is defined as a condition obtained when the probationer is not violating his probation rules, is not under close surveillance, and apparently has internalized some prosocial behaviors.

The lower right-hand corner of the grid represents a maximal concern for control and a minimal concern for rehabilitation. This frame of reference is based on the assumption that probationers will respond only when they have to, under coercive surveillance with swift penalties when they do not conform. It is not suggested that P.O.'s with a 9/1 face have no interest in their clients but rather that this interest becomes manifested only under rigid control variables. The 9/1 officer sincerely believes that probationers need a strict leader who governs their otherwise hedonistic tendencies.

A 9/1 officer believes that control is rehabilitation and that his most crucial obligation is to protect community interests via strict limits placed on his clients. If the community is properly protected a kind of *fait accompli* effect is produced in the probationer whose illegal behaviors are blocked through control. Such a system of enforced cooperation induces clients to accept probationary conditions without having to internalize them. Interaction between probation officer and probationer tends to be formal, official, and largely a question of "one upsmanship" on the side of the P.O.

This one-dimension probation face may be effective. It could also lead to false security that a client is under control when, in fact, his compliance is only superficial. Kelman[2] has demonstrated that conformity behavior which occurs under conditions of high power remains intact

2. Herbert C. Kelman, "Compliance, Identification, and Internalization: Three Processes of Attitude Change," *Journal of Conflict Resolution.* 1958, 2, pp. 51–60.

only so long as there is surveillance. Removal of close monitoring results in a decrease of conformity behavior and a return to more prepotent modes of acting which may well be antisocial. Combined with the hostility and resentment which a 9/1 probation face often produces in others, this approach represents an unstable form of behavior management.

The P.O.'s 9/1 face says to the probationer, "I expect you to keep these probationary conditions. I'll do what I can to help you but you will have to 'toe the mark' and there is no room for error."

THE 1/9 FACE

The 1/9 face is designated by the upper left hand grid position which indicates high probation officer concern for rehabilitating his probationer and small concern for controlling him. In this approach the P.O.'s overriding motivation is based on the assumption that individuals are basically good and will seek appropriate, legal behaviors once they are helped to understand themselves. This self-knowledge will promote growth, foster prosocial attitudes, and terminate in satisfactory observance of probationary rules.

The 9/1 face is rejected as constituting an effort by the community to impose its own values of correct behavior on the probationer. This is seen as antithetical to the free choice condition needed if the client is to foster his own adaptation to the orders of the court. The face projected to the probationer in this framework is a warm, supportive, and nonjudgmental countenance. The probation officer tends to emerge primarily as a therapist who facilitates insight on the client's part. He learns to form a close relationship with the probationer and refines a repertoire of clinical skills aimed at rehabilitation.

Unlike the 9/1, a 1/9 face produces probationary supervision under conditions of freedom, mutuality, and a high level of client decisionmaking. The psychodynamics of individual probationers emerge as more potent than the social determinants of crime or delinquency. This also poses a dilemma for probation officers. A 1/9 face lends itself to manipulation, a perception that it is permissive and there is some likelihood of being "conned."

The P.O.'s 1/9 face says to the probationer, "I hope that you will understand the need for these probationary conditions. I will support you in every way I can and help you make your own decisions in a way that you will find contentment and not feel threatened by me."

THE 1/1 FACE

The lower-left grid location refers to probation officers who manifest minimal concerns for both control and rehabilitation. In this face, probationers are thought of as autogenous and, therefore, will change or fail to do so as a result of their own motivation. No conscious or systematic probation strategy will be effective because circumstances, spontaneous occurrences, and genetic chance are the important variables. If individual probationer tendencies for illegal behaviors are in conflict with external probationary attempts to alter them, the probation officer must set up a situation to evaluate what happens. His role is to appraise and advise his client about failure to conform, keep the court informed on the probationer's observance of the rules, and operate as an observer of progress rather than initiator of behavioral change.

Considerable energy is invested into the logistics of probation. Records are well-maintained, reports are current, and probationer contacts are regular. However, the limited affective involvement with clients, and a mechanical approach to probation leaves this officer with no dynamic probation face. It should be noted that such an outcome is not necessarily due to the officer's personality. A 1/1 probation program or administration might well promote status quo values which frustrate aggressive probation officers who then revert to "reporting" procedures as a way to fill the role assigned in their work.

The P.O.'s 1/1 face says to his probationer, "I'm sure you understand these conditions of probation. It's up to you to stick to them. No one can do it for you. If you need me be sure to contact me."

THE 5/5 FACE

In the grid center is found the 5/5 probation officer who proceeds on the assumption that both control and rehabilitation are necessary but that full concern cannot be given to both. This face demonstrates a belief that probationers need leadership; they have not benefited from sound identification figures in the past; in fact, their very alignment with deviant models probably induced their earliest extra-legal actions. Individuals have strong needs for positive affiliations with others and probation officers provide this opportunity for probationers.

The 5/5 face must have and display the personal, psychological, social, and culturally valued qualities which probationers can learn to assume. The probation officer works hard at gaining trust and respect by demonstrating a "regular guy" face which can be trusted to understand the "real" problems encountered by probationers.

A positive relationship between P.O. and client has always been central to good probation but not necessarily with the view of maintaining the personal charisma of the officer. In the 5/5 face this likeableness becomes crucial. If the probationer likes his probation officer and attempts, therefore, to please him, then the likelihood of his breaking court orders is less. By implication, this helps to secure some control while also helping the individual probationer to alter some of his antisocial predispositions.

Some work completed in recent years by attraction theory psychologists suggests that a 5/5 face holds promising components for the

P.O.-probationer relationship. Aronson[3], for example, thinks that increasing rewards and punishments from a person have more impact on his attractiveness than constant, invariant rewards and punishments. For the P.O. who must so often "start from scratch" with his probationer, Aronson's mini-theory seems to be significant for developing 5/5 attractiveness in his work.

The P.O.'s 5/5 face suggests to probationers that "you and I will work together in keeping these probation rules. I know how you must be feeling and thinking and if you stick with me you can make it."

THE 9/9 FACE

By orienting the concern for control and the concern for rehabilitation at right angles to each other, it is possible to clarify probation faces reflected to individuals who are on probation. The countenances postulated so far indicate an orientation toward an incompatibility of the dual concerns. This dichotomization has bedeviled corrections for decades.

The 9/9 face seeks to integrate concerns for control and rehabilitation. A 9/9 P.O. brings full concern for both dimensions of the grid at the same time. This means he creates conditions which help a probationer help himself but limited by the reality of probationary conditions. This means that he stresses goals rather than personality traits of his probationer. These traits are treated as important but not necessarily in cause and effect fashion. Instead, the probationer is helped to select from goals calculated to meet his needs more effectively within a legal framework. The 9/9 face organizes legitimate choices and through a collaborative relationship induces the client to act in accord with prosocial expectations.

Underlying a 9/9 face is the notion that probationers are more likely to exert control over themselves and become rehabilitated when they can internalize what is expected of them.

> Internalization can be said to occur when an individual accepts influence because the content of the induced behavior—the ideas and actions of which it is composed—is intrinsically rewarding.[4]

Put another way, it may be said that clients change when it makes sense to do so because there is some kind of "pay off." Their needs are met in better fashion. In the 9/1 face probationers tend to see resentment or fear; in a 1/9 face they are inclined to see chances to manipulate their P.O.; in a 1/1 face, probationers may read apathy; in a 5/5 profile a tenuous balance of charisma shows up. The 9/9 face projects credibility and says to the probationer "let's put our heads together, take a look at what needs to be done, how we may be able to go about doing it and determine the best way of finishing a realistic probation program."

3. Elliot Aronson, "Who Likes Whom   4. Kelman, ibid., p. 54.
and Why," *Psychology Today*, August
1970, pp. 48–50, 74.

It seems reasonable to assert that probation officers reflect all of these faces with various probationers under different circumstances. Each carries with it a different set of probable outcomes. This article suggests that a basic 9/9 face is more likely to give equitable attention to concerns for both control and rehabilitation. If true, we may hypothesize that this set of conditions is most likely to meet the needs of both probationers and community.

PROBATION COUNSELING *

The probation officer, in dealing with his clients in the counseling relationship, confronts a problem inherent to all psychotherapeutic relations—the problem of multiple realities.[1] The term "multiple realities" refers to the array of different *experiential* (versus intellectual) meanings that the individuals participating in a common social relationship use to understand that relationship. This is to say, any human relationship always is made up of as many different perspectives of that situation as there are individual members involved in it. While these participants share some general, common expectations about the significance of their association, these are generally objective, legal, or formal understandings of the situation. They bear little, if any relevance to the subjective, attitudinal, or informal meanings held by the individuals involved. This difference in experiential interpretation, perspective, or assumption about the meaning of any given relationship is the phenomenon of multiple realities.

In probation work this issue of multiple realities is dramatically present. Here we find a situation where two individuals are joined by legal force in a counseling (and supposedly) trusting relationship. From the beginning, the probation officer is confronted with a problem which not only entails communicating meaningfully with an unknown individual (a meeting of two realities, difficult enough under voluntary conditions), but one which, if he is at all flexible, constrains him to pay heed to two different perspectives simultaneously: his obligations as a court-appointed supervisor of probationers, and the idiosyncratic needs of the probationer as client in a counseling relationship. Inherent in the job of a probation officer is this tension of perspectives. It localizes itself between the officer and the court (how closely to abide by its formal rules of supervision), the officer and the client (how many breaks to give an offender), and between the officer and himself (what kind of officer to be).

It is from this general problem that we will examine the nature of probation work. To this end we will (1) try to describe some features

---

* Jose Arcaya, *Federal Probation*, December 1973.

1. Schutz (1971) has spoken very cogently about this theme in a philosophical context.

prevalent in a typical, first-time counseling situation; (2) attempt to highlight the conflicts present there; (3) discuss the way these are often handled; and (4) suggest approaches which might mitigate these conflicts.

A DESCRIPTION OF A MEETING

When a probationer enters a probation office for the first time part of his awareness is occupied by a nagging feeling of apprehension. Viewed from the eyes of the probationer, the office represents a power that can, and does, limit his freedom. It is an institution to which he must submit involuntarily (as a "client," euphemistically put). In the background of this submission is an implicit assumption made by our legal system that a probationer is in need of supervision, rehabilitation, or guidance. Thus, even before the first contact is ever made between officer and client, the client is already led to believe that he is considered less than a responsible human being. It is not surprising, therefore, that the probationer encounters his supervising officer with a mixture of fear, wariness, and defiance. Generally, in the beginning of his introduction to the probation system, the probationer's attitude is to obey the formal rules of probation and maintain a respectful, if distant, relationship with whoever might be assigned to work with him. During this initial contact period the probationer's "sniff out" evaluates his officer, determining to what extent he may be trusted.

At the other pole of this meeting is the officer himself who has little say with regard to who is assigned to his caseload. He, too, meets a stranger for the first time. Like the probationer's experience, fear and apprehension accompany the initial meeting. The officer is fearful because he knows nothing of the individual's capacity to cooperate, follow the rules, or give a hard time. He is apprehensive because he knows that there might come a day when he will have to reprimand, admonish, or even incarcerate his new client. Maybe, from past experience, he feels he has failed to really help many of his probationers. Perhaps the memories of these failures haunt him now. Yet, in spite of these discouragements, he maintains an optimistic hope that the relationship will be worthwhile for the probationer. He desires the probationer's betterment through his experience on probation. With these feelings in mind, the officer chooses one of two broad counseling approaches toward his new ward.[2]

ROLES

First, he may choose to put out of his awareness the ambiguity of his position—that he is both a counselor of the individual and the representative of a legal institution. Instead of integrating the two responsibilities,

2. We draw these distinctions only in a general way. No individual officer completely fits either of the "pure" approaches which will now be described. These characterizations are solely intended to convey overall *tendencies* which, in many cases, are found to be typical in the normal probation counseling situation.

he may dichotomize the functions and choose to act on one more than the other. In doing this he adopts what might be called a "nonthinking" stance, since he eliminates from his considerations the different ways in which he could be helpful. Instead he presents a constant role to each client, well-planned and rehearsed in advance of any actual encounter. This role has few creative or spontaneous elements, and even bores the officer himself. In this stance, two possibilities for behavior are open: To be an "authority figure" or a "nice guy."

The *authority-figure* role is inevitably presented by an officer hoping to cover his own fear of the interpersonal counseling experience. He conveys an image characterized by a determination to show the client "who's boss." He sees probation work to involve the legal surveillance of his cases. To this end, his major occupation centers around keeping paperwork in order, taking appropriate legal action when a clear violation of rules has occurred, and providing the person on probation with clear and strong reminders of the latter's probation responsibilities. Normally this officer "has all the answers" to any predicament. He is an "authority." Because he surrenders his ability to spontaneously react, to make decisions appropriate to the individual situation, he entrusts his thinking to the black and white answers contained in the probation rulebook.

The *nice-guy* officer is as inflexible and thoughtless as the authority figure. This individual chooses the other extreme of the spectrum by giving the probationer power over *him*. He has little consideration for the rights of society as a whole, or, for that matter, the basic welfare of his client. He is an example of someone who believes that any rule broken is unimportant. By his silence, he subtly fosters and condones antisocial behavior on the latter's part. This officer is "bent" on being liked, proving that he is "humanistic," that he is, in short, a "nice guy." Like the authority figure, he fears the intimacy of an open counseling relationship because in it he might have to reveal anger, disagreement, or other negative feelings which he wants to deny. This "type" is perhaps the more difficult to describe of the two because its thoughtlessness leads to what is very socially desired—being liked. However, in this role the officer is out of touch with the full gamut of spontaneous emotions. He would rather repress an unkind or critical word needed by the client than to risk the loss of a potential friend.

AN ALTERNATIVE

The alternative stance is what is here termed a "dwelling" presence.[3] This attitude openly accepts the ambiguity of feelings and responsibilities attached to probation work and uses this ambiguity to bring the client an awareness of the officer's own humanity. Here the officer attempts to share with the person on probation the personal tensions he experiences in

3. Heidegger (1966) speaks of a similar idea when he contrasts "calculative thinking" (spurious, superficial understanding) with "meditative thinking" (dwelling with the ambiguity of thought without dichotomizing it).

counseling within the legal system and discloses his difficulties in accomplishing this feat. The client is not made to feel that he confronts an unerring, larger-than-life, authority who has all the answers or a permissive, easily deceived fool. The officer has no interest in either having power over the probationer or having the probationer have power over him. Rather, in the dwelling stance the officer creates a relationship that encourages both to relate as equals. A respect for the inherent worth of both individuals is presumed in spite of the fact that one is a convicted criminal and the other a court-appointed supervisor. This stance acknowledges that there are no privileged positions in authentic human communication: The lasting benefits of a counseling relationship derive from the mutual trust and lack of power conflicts.

To accomplish this rapport the client and officer must develop a common ground of communication as a result of the experience with each other. This means building a *shared world* of meanings which occurs principally from a willingness to not only talk, but also listen. To truly listen implies to dwell in what the other says. It is not the absence of talk which characterizes listening, but the effort to interpret the other's words from his perspective. Communication proceeds only to the extent the speaker feels that someone is trying to understand him. In the most fundamental sense, listening communicates more than talking. The problem of multiple realities is no more than the challenge of really understanding what the other says.

CONFLICTS CONTAINED IN EVERYDAY LANGUAGE

If we were to overhear a typical client-officer conversation certain words and phrases, such as "cooperation," "honest," "responsibility," "helping yourself," might arise. These probably would be spoken by the officer in the hopes of conveying to the client the need for him to participate openly in their relationship.

Let us suppose the officer's newly designated probationer has had a long history of excessive drinking. He has been placed on probation after causing a near-fatal accident in which he himself was almost killed. The task which the officer sees before him now is how to keep the client from driving after drinking. In accomplishing this goal, the officer might urge the individual to go to an Alcoholics Anonymous chapter, see a psychiatrist or psychologist, maybe even live in a residential treatment center. In explaining his recommendation to the probationer, the officer might state that it was time that the offender "help himself," become "honest about his problems," and take "responsibility for his life." These words he would justify to himself by reasoning that he was helping to rid the public byways of a driving menace as well as helping the individual come to grips with his deep-seated emotional problems.

To the probationer, however, such talk smacks of personal rejection, lack of acceptance, or, simply, unconcerned advice. Perhaps such ethical-sounding terminology has been spoken to him by hypocritical authority figures (teachers, parents, government officials, employers) all his life. Now he lumps the words "responsibility," "honest," "self-help," and their ilk into a highly personal "language-to-make-me-do-something-I-don't-want-to-do" category. From this perspective he answers that he has been helping himself, that he does not drink anymore, and that he is "as honest as anyone else" with his emotions. Yet even as he speaks, the tone in which he makes his reply reveals a mood of anger and defensiveness which is not evident explicitly from the spoken words themselves. Perhaps the officer perceives that the probationer's eyes narrow as he talks, that his hands clench into fists, that his body tightens—all tacit signs that the probationer understood something offensive in what he said. Maybe both will speak for awhile longer and then the client will leave. Later, the officer, in thinking back over the incident, will have a subtle intuition that they really did not communicate, that he did not "reach" the client. The client, on the other hand, will feel that he was reprimanded like a misbehaving child or objectified "like some kind of a nut."

What occurred here? Viewed from the perspective of their *lived* meanings, the words used by the officer were of a different reality than those employed by the probationer. A conflict occurred between the "languages" of the two individuals and their perceived realities of the situation. For the officer, reality demanded that he convince the client to cure his drinking problem, stay off the road, and, in an indirect way, become happier. For the probationer, on the other hand, reality informed him that the officer is "just like all the rest," someone who is "pushing me around," who, in some way, "rejects me." Perhaps, if the probationer had confronted an extreme case of the "authority figure," he would have been right. However, even if the officer had no value-judgments in mind and did not want to exhibit power over the individual, no communication occurred. Permit me to cite a nonprobation example.

Suppose that a husband and wife are continuously bickering to the point that each considers it best that they divorce. However, they do not want to be hasty in their decision so they appear before a marriage counselor to obtain his services before going through with the action. They say to the professional, each in turn, that the other spouse does not "love" him or her. The wife complains that she feels neglected by the husband, that he fails to show her affection or be around when she needs him. Moreover, she suspects that he is really interested in another woman because he seems to be away at his job more than he should be. The husband, on the other hand, fervently denies that he is unfaithful. He asserts that she does not love him because she does not respect his privacy and his solitude. The reason why he stays away at the office, he says, is because he gets engrossed in his work and forgets his other responsibilities. He claims that he does not want to deliberately neglect her.

At the core of their problem seems to be their different understandings of "love." From the wife's perspective love means attention, presents from her husband and, and demonstrative affection. To the husband "love" translates as tolerance and respect for the other, as well as quiet and nondramatic affection. Both seem to have presuppositions about the meaning of "love" which are not only different but actually antagonistic. Basically, their problem reduces to the fact that each cannot see the context of the other's comprehension of that word and notion. They have smugly assumed, each in his own way, that the idea, "love," can only have one possible significance. They have lost sight of the fact that its meaning for them arises from their particular point of view.

The argument which we wish to make, in brief, is that no language in human dialogue is complete without an attempt to concretely ground the meaning of the words used. No fixed definitions of terms exist apart from the significances, explicitly or implicitly, given them by the people who are involved in the speaking relationship. Language, in order to communicate a meaningful reality, must be situated. One can only understand the words of the other when he has taken into account the other's entire speaking context. In turn, one's own words can be understood by the other only if the meanings to one's personal "language" are disclosed, in as complete a way as possible. Dialogue occurs in a rate proportional to the degree that the two individuals risk revealing and reacting, emotionally and intellectually, to the words of the other. Yet, simultaneous with reacting and revealing, it is necessary that one "actively" listen and "responsively" speak.

TOWARDS AN INTEGRATION OF REALITIES

In order for the probationer to feel that the counseling relationship is of benefit, it is necessary that he feel he is understood *as he understands himself*. This is important because no one trusts someone else if he feels that that other is not "with" him. Only when the client experiences the feeling of being understood will he, in turn, listen to what the officer has to say. He cannot be forced to listen. To lead the person on probation to voluntary listening, the officer must be responsive to his words. This means that he has to be a listener who respects the client sufficiently to let the latter's words *count*. This is to say that in a dwelling stance with the probationer, the officer tries to make sense of what his client has to say from the reality of the client's own "words." To meaningfully "be" with the other necessitates entering into his "world," trying, as much as possible, to leave one's own world apart. Let us examine two dimensions of responsiveness: listening and speaking.

Active listening[4] means that the officer actively attempts to put aside his preconceptions of what the client is saying. He tries, instead, to silently remain with the language which the probationer uses as much as

4. Thomas (1970) employs the same term in the context of parent-child communication problems.

possible, allowing him to describe what he means in his own words. The officer does not try to define the reality and experience of the client for him. He accords the individual enough respect to assume that he will relate his story better than the officer could. Nevertheless, it will occur that, as the officer listens with this end in mind, many uncertainties about what is actually said will arise. When this happens, the officer may ask the probationer to clarify what he means. This request, however, must be phrased also in the "language" of the client if the question is to be meaningful to him. Let us illustrate:

In our example of the "highway menace" some ambiguity arose between what the officer meant by "help" and the client's understanding of that word. Moreover, when the probationer stated that he "*was* helping" himself, he emphasized his difference with what appeared to be anger: The tone of his voice seemed harsher, his body tightened, his facial expression changed. The officer, in turn, overlooked the client's response and only later did he suspect that maybe he had not communicated effectively with him. However, if he had been sensitive at that moment to the body-language of the client, to the tone of his words, to the general interpersonal counseling "atmosphere," the officer might have been dismayed and angered at the reception which his well-meant suggestions received. He might have lashed out with a reprimand ("Why you dirty so-and-so I'm only trying to help and look at the way that you treat me!") or, on the other extreme, suppressed any mention of his feeling at all while silently dismissing his client as a "hothead" or as dangerous and disturbed ("some kind of a nut"). None of these actions, however, would have served the purpose of understanding the client's perspective.

Yet if he had been actively listening, trying to make sense of the client as he sees himself, the officer would neither have overlooked his own immediate feelings, reprimanded the client, nor dismissed him privately with demeaning labels ("hothead," "nut"). Instead, he would have attempted to set aside his own wounded pride in order to understand why the client responded as he did. An inquiry to the client about why he reacted as he did to the officer's suggestions would have been made in nonjudgmental, descriptive terms. Thus the officer might have stated: "You appeared disturbed just now. Your hands were clenched into fists, your body was tightened, and the tone of your voice grew harsher as you said 'I *am* helping myself.' You look like you were angry about something. Am I right? If not, then what was the matter, if anything?"

By grounding and contextualizing his question in this manner, the officer lets the probationer perceive himself as the officer perceives him, and permits him to realize the rationale which motivated the question in the first place. Contained in this inquiry are no hidden, evaluative terms ("Why were you being *defensive, hostile, irrational,* etc."). No motives, causes, explanations, or evaluations are ascribed with this concrete, descriptive language. Unlike its opposite, evaluative terminology, it permits a freedom of response to the client without having him feel as though he were admitting to a character flaw in the process. This language is open-ended, allowing the client to explain himself as he thinks he is—"Yes, I am angry at being pushed around" or "No, I'm not mad at you but I don't like myself for being in this fix," etc.

Through this and numerous other clarifications of the probationer's language and behavior, the officer slowly builds up an image of the style and perspective of the probationer. As a result of this type of inquiry, he actively listens to what the other says by having him serve as his own source of "reference." Meanings of words and body gestures are understood not through some independent "dictionary" definition but in terms of the inner "logic" of the client. Thus, the probationer is, for the listening officer, a self-defining being. Success in understanding someone as he understands himself comes only slowly and laboriously. In the above example it could be that the client is surprised or threatened that the officer was so close to his emotional world. Chances are that no breakthrough in communication would be accomplished through one inquiry. This does not matter. What is of greater importance is that the client see that the officer cares enough to consult with *him* about what *he* means without prejudging his experience. Of greater benefit than any discovered "facts" is the feeling conveyed to the probationer that someone is attempting to hear him. Listening requires patience.

Responsive talking has been reserved for the last topic of discussion because meaningful talk only follows as a consequence of meaningful listening. To talk, as understood from this stance, means really to *respond*. One talks as a consequence of having understood the client as he himself allows one to understand him. This means that the officer works together with the client through dialogue to contextualize and situate the latter's world. Any suggestions, recommendations, or, even orders originate from the mutual dialogue. A set of probation goals is not the outgrowth of unverified and unshared prejudices of what *should* be best for the client. The client always serves as his own best advisor to action.[5]

While certainly this does not mean that the officer must capitulate his responsibilities to the courts and not abide by the guidelines of probation, it does mean that any rules enforced or any unpopular decisions made by him must, at the very least, be documented to the probationer in terms of the latter's concrete behavior. Hence in our example of the "highway menace" the recommendation that he seek professional help might be justified by citing the particular offenses which even the client admits to enacting ("yes, I was drunk while driving," "yes, I have drunk a little too much in the past and gotten into trouble," etc.). Even if the client remains unhappy about the officer's

---

5. See Fischer (1969, 1970) for an elaborate discussion of the merits contained in using the client as a source of reference for formulating his own psychological recommendations.

decision, solid ground work would have been established between the officer and client where the latter realizes the the officer effects decisions only from specific instances of behavior and shares his reasoning with the client. Again the client is consulted even if the final decision, after due consideration has been given, is not to his liking.

By way of conclusion, we must emphasize that all of the above suggestions (active listening, responsive talking, contextualization of language) are not intended to be understood as manipulative *techniques* to control the behavior of the probationer. These approaches to counseling cannot replace an original desire on the officer's part to be with and help the client. There is no substitute for simple human concern. Only if the officer respects the humanity of the other can our ideas have lasting benefits.

REFERENCES

Fischer, C. T., "Rapport as Mutual Respect," *Personnel and Guidance Journal*, 1969, 48, pp. 201–204.

"The Testee as Co-Evaluator," *Journal of Counseling Psychology*, 1970, 17 pp. 70–76.

Gordon, Thomas, *Parent Effectiveness Training: The No-Lose Program for Raising Responsible Children*, Wyden Press, 1970.

Heidegger, Martin, *Discourse on Thinking*, New York: Harper Torchbooks, 1966.

Schutz, Alfred, "The Problem of Multiple Realities," *Collected Papers, Vol. I*, The Hague: Martinus Nijoff, 1971, pp. 207–259.

PROBATION SUPERVISION OF THE BLACK OFFENDER *

Any perceptive individual who works in probation for a while quickly comes to realize that many of the problems of the general racial crisis which grips our society are reflected in the problems of the probation caseload. There is an increasing cry from black professionals in psychology and social work that only blacks can work in a helping way with other blacks. This argument may have many merits in the fields of psychology and social work. In the field of probation, however, this proposition breaks down on both theoretical and practical grounds. On the theoretical side there is the fact that although our profession has many social work aspects, it is also involved in the business of social control. This inherently means coercing subcultural groups into at least nominal acceptance of the laws of the dominant white society.

On the practical side there are relatively few black probation officers in relationship to the size of the black caseload. Even if the field were committed to assigning black officers to black probationers there would be insufficient manpower to do so. This situation is not likely to improve

* William M. Breer, *Federal Probation*, March 1972.

in the near future because probation work seems to have little appeal to the black youth now coming out of our colleges. The black officers with whom I have discussed this problem feel very alienated from the black offender and almost as much at a loss for ways of dealing with these offenders as white officers.

We are thus left in the following dilemma. We have a large number of black probationers combined with an overwhelmingly white staff in probation departments. We owe it to ourselves, society, and the black community to develop ways to work as effectively as possible with the black caseload. The focus of this article will be to explore some of the ways in which a white probation officer might strive to work more effectively with the black probationer.

A BLACK SUBCULTURE?

One of the salient features of our age is the chasm which separates black and white. My own academic background has been in anthropology. Applying the insights of this field to probation, I have come to feel that the differences which separate black and white can best be described as cultural differences. The sociologist might insist that they are subcultural, but the hiatus is so great that it seems to me more useful in stressing the magnitude of the difference to characterize white and black America as two separate cultural entities existing side by side. Much of black culture is an adaption to the conditions imposed by the dominant white culture. White culture is almost autistic, existing independently of and usually trying to ignore the very existence of a separate cultural entity within the borders of the Nation.

To prove the assumptions made in the paragraphs above would involve several chapters in an extended discussion of black America. Within the limited scope of this article, the reader is simply asked to question his own assumptions, test them against his own field experience, and if useful, add them to his casework approach.

If the difference between black and white America is indeed cultural, several premises about casework with black Americans seem to follow. Within this framework, the *sine qua non* for working with blacks is at least a rudimentary knowledge of the content of black culture. This discussion is far too limited to present a detailed description of this culture. Only the broadest of its characteristics can be touched on here. The points to be covered are the aspects which I feel are of overwhelming significance in probation casework with black Americans.

Perhaps the most salient trait which blacks derive from their cultural matrix is the black rage syndrome described by Grier and Cobbs in the book of the same title. Blacks are almost universally enraged by the conditions under which they live. They blame white society for holding them in subjugation, limiting their social and economic opportunities, and exposing them to the brutal, dehumanizing process capsulized in the word "nigger." Some blacks will deny their anger, but if you talk deeply and honestly with black Americans some aspect of black rage usually emerges. Sometimes the evidence is only in a psychosomatic channelizing of anger such as high blood pressure. Black rage can shade into a paranoid ego defense which blames every problem a black individual faces on white racism. This is a personal cop out, but at its worst it produces the hardened, violent, revolutionary criminal who may some day become a major problem to parole officers.

A second aspect of black culture relevant to the probation officer is the absolute alienation of blacks from the values and institutions of white society. This will vary among blacks and reaches its absolute level among the criminal variant of black culture with whom probation officers most often deal. Black rage is the emotional and intellectual trigger of black alienation. If "whitey" degrades and confines the black man, what basis is there for loyalty to his institutions or values? Concepts like law and order or the need for law to guarantee the smooth functioning of society are rendered absolutely meaningless when viewed in this cultural framework.

Alienation from the values and institutions of white society enables a black to commit what whites would call a criminal act without guilt or remorse. Blacks may simulate such feelings to avoid the consequences, but with the alienated black this remorse will be real only if the offense involves other blacks or some other value of black culture has been violated. An example from my own caseload is a black mother who for years has shown no concern over her son's involvement in burglary. Now he is charged with attempted murder. She feels murder is a "real" crime and swears she will never see her son again if she becomes convinced he is guilty.

Another characteristic of black culture of concern to the probation officer is that a significant proportion of the ghetto community is dependent upon some version of the illegal hustle for their livelihood. Living by the hustle means that a black develops one or a combination of illegal or semi-legal means of support. Such niches include pimping, drug pushing, prostitution, welfare fraud, theft, and selling stolen property. I do not mean to imply that all or even most blacks support themselves by such activity, but the proportion that does in a ghetto community is always significant. Needless to say, this proportion is particularly prominent in the probation caseload.

Another characteristic of black culture with which the probation officer should be familiar is its group solidarity. This solidarity is best capsulized in blacks' references to each other as brother and sister. Blacks feel alienated from and discriminated against by the larger white society. To compensate they have developed an ingroup feeling of their own. Mutual help is the ideal. This often devolves, however, into simply not calling in outsiders such as the police or probation officers to solve community or family problems. Black cultural values are particularly adamant about not giving information to outsiders which will damage other blacks.

Related to the solidarity of the community is its linkage by a well developed grapevine. Blacks spend a great deal of time talking about what other blacks are doing. News and rumors spread quickly from mouth to mouth. I believe this is much more marked in a black community than in any urban or suburban white community. Rural whites would probably be much the same in this particular respect. This may reflect the recent rural southern roots of most blacks as well as the cohesiveness of the community.

Probation officers will usually find that black probationers know far more about other blacks in their caseload than the probation officer. Trying to elicit any such information, however, would invite suspicion and be met with evasion.

I should also emphasize that black culture is not a monolithic entity. It has several variations in the North alone. Any more than a hint as to these subdivisions is beyond the scope of this article. I would, however, briefly characterize the main subdivisions as the transplanted rural southern type, the black bourgeoisie type, and the poor ghetto type. The poor ghetto variant is of most concern to the probation officer because it is the most criminally inclined. The characteristics of black culture discussed here can be found in all these subdivisions, but they are most marked among the poor ghetto group.

BLACK CULTURE AS AN ADAPTATION

There has been much theorizing within anthropology to the effect that all culture is adaptive. I think this model is very fruitful if it is used to explain the aspects of black culture which we have been discussing. In their roughly 400 years on this continent, black people have had to endure a variety of unfavorable circumstances ranging from slavery to economic and social discrimination. Many of the traits of black culture in this country can be viewed as adaptations to the unfavorable circumstances that blacks have been forced to deal with in their historical odyssey in North America.

In black rage we are harvesting the seeds of injustice sown over these last centuries. It is unlikely that any subservient caste would endure what black people have endured without developing a rage syndrome. Black rage also has adaptive features in the following sense. Blacks have been degraded and held at the bottom of society for so long that many blacks have internalized deep-seated feelings of worthlessness and helplessness. Black rage offers itself as an ego defense against these feelings. Without this defense overwhelming feelings of worthlessness and helplessness might intrude into consciousness and immobilize the personality. I want to emphasize here that I feel that blacks have been treated unjustly in this country and their rage is a predictable and normal

phenomenon given their historical circumstances. As a secondary feature
it is adaptive in that it offers a useful ego defense widely used by
unstable individuals within black culture.

A sense of alienation from white society is also adaptive. In terms of
their historical experience in this country, alienation results from an
accurate perception of social conditions and appropriate action based on
these perceptions. Throughout the history of this country the intent of
the white majority has been to exclude the black from the mainstream of
society. The black should be available for cheap labor. He should not be
allowed to compete for the better jobs, allowed to live next door, or have
a significant role in the political process. Very recently this has started
to break down. Much discrimination still exists and we will be confronted with residues of ill will for a long time even if full equality could be
granted over night.

The firm conviction of his alienation from the mainstream of American society frees the black from what could be an immobilizing conflict.
With all the barriers to full participation in white society, the black until
,ery recently would get nowhere if he tried to internalize the values of
white society. To make realistic survival decisions and to put together
the most satisfying life style possible under the circumstances, the black
American needed to separate himself from any loyalty to the values and
institutions of white society.

Of the hustle, little need to be said to explain its adaptive value.
Blacks have always been excluded from the most lucrative roles in our
society. First this was done by formal institutions such as slavery and
segregation. Now most blacks find themselves across a cultural chasm
from the white. As a result of his different experience, the black
American cannot simulate the middle class mannerisms so useful in
seeking employment. Often his education has been inferior, and he has
been emotionally scarred by a background of poverty. Even today only a
black elite of background and/or intelligence can compete meaningfully
with whites for jobs and power in our society. If you take an individual
of above average talent and ambition who totally lacks the skills to
compete in the white world and add a dash of black rage and alienation,
the product is the ghetto hustler.

Black solidarity is also adaptive. This is a logical development of
alienation and discrimination. Since black skin is white society's basis for
discrimination, it is the black man's rallying point. Black solidarity is
highly adaptive in that it enables the community to pull together and help
each other out against what would otherwise be hopeless odds. It also
prevents whites from using a divide and conquer approach in the ghetto.

I should emphasize that solidarity is an ideal value of black culture,
and that the reality often falls far short of the ideal. This solidarity is
often more of an emotional tie based on identification than a consistent
unity of the community against outsiders. Black people are notorious for

their factiousness and infighting within their own community. Sometimes this infighting reaches the point where blacks inform on each other to outsiders or call in law enforcement as an ally against other blacks. This is generally regarded as a violation of the community's mores, however.

No claim is made that this vignette of black culture as relevant to the probation officer is complete. Anyone who is really serious about working with blacks should pursue this further. One of the best ways is to talk openly with ghetto blacks, if you can ever get their confidence as a probation officer. This is difficult, if not impossible. Fortunately there are a number of good books in this area. The ones with which I am familiar are included in the bibliography.

CULTURALLY ORIENTED CASEWORK

Moving on from aspects of black culture, I would like to examine some of the techniques which a white probation officer can use in working with black probationers. The first area of concern revolves around whether or not to bring up the matter of race where relevant. Many whites seem to feel more comfortable pretending that race does not make any difference any more. They like to talk as if full equality is here now, and all Americans are just the same. This is a fiction that makes black people very uncomfortable. Most black people are acutely aware of their black culture and how it varies from white culture. They are also extremely wary of discrimination and scrutinize whites carefully to find evidence of prejudice.

I feel that race and black culture should be discussed frankly and openly with blacks. If it is not, the probationer is very likely to attribute thoughts to the probation officer which are not in fact his. If a probation officer can handle discussions of racial issues and differences with honesty and empathy, the black probationer is more likely to believe that the officer can give him reasonable advice in other areas where the probationer does not feel so knowledgeable. If an officer starts out by handling racial factors awkwardly, the rest of his counseling is likely to be shelved as irrelevant.

Somewhat related to this last point is the use of the reality principle in casework with blacks. This is probably the best single tool a white caseworker has in working with blacks. Attempts to rebuild the personality structure of the black probationer or really even to try to improve black family life to avoid pressure areas leading to criminal acting out are usually beyond the grasp of the white probation officer.

By use of the reality principle I mean pointing out immovable reality factors which must be dealt with by the probationer. To implement this approach the probationer and officer should agree on a minimal goal which both can accept as desirable. The lowest common denominator of course is keeping the probationer out of an institution. Other areas such as finding a job are feasible if the probationer really wants to find one. Once such mutual goals are set, the probation officer can use his knowledge of the black probationer as a person and his black cultural context to point out traps in his life style and cultural patterns which are going to lead the probationer right into an institution or sabotage his other goals.

In addition to the reality principle, the white officer in dealing with blacks can use some of the built-in structure of black culture in his casework. Black culture itself has a variety of roles some of which are not likely to get individuals into trouble with law enforcement. One of the safest roles from this standpoint is the religious. Black culture has deep religious roots. The old line black Christian churches, however, seem to appeal mostly to older southern blacks. The Muslims, although virulently antiwhite, seem to keep their followers on a puritanical track which might keep them out of trouble with law enforcement.

BLACK IS BEAUTIFUL

What I consider a more positive movement is the drive for black pride and black identity. If carried to their logical developments, these movements should substantially improve the mental health of the black population and cut at many of the roots of crime in the black community. In guiding a black probationer in this direction there is, however, one potential pitfall. Black psychologist Charles W. Thomas in a dialogue published in *Psychology Today* (September 1970) describes a five-step process in the development of black identity. The first stage is "a brother who wastes all his time rapping on whitey." The second stage includes a conflict about "burning down the city or grabbing a gun." Needless to say this could get a probationer in trouble.

If a black probationer is moved in this direction, this risk should be stressed to him. Thoughts are OK; black rage is often justified, but violence will lead only to incarceration. Here again the reality principle dovetails into the casework approach.

The final stage of black psychological evolution is an exciting one for both races ". . . through your unique blackness you lose your hangups about race, age, sex, and social class, and see yourself as part of humanity in all its flavors." Change the word blackness to whiteness and you have a goal that would be a great accomplishment for a white. A person with this kind of intact ego structure is not likely to become involved in criminal behavior. I would regard this as a very desirable goal for a probationer.

This does not mean that such a black man will never get in trouble again. He will most likely become involved in the black struggle and may get into trouble with political overtones. To me, this is far more constructive than violent crime against the person and property of others. Hopefully our courts will allow ample latitude for political protest and reform.

CASEWORK TRAPS

We have touched on some of the positive aspects of casework with black probationers. It might be well now to mention some of the things which a white probation officer would do well to avoid. Two of the worst mistakes have already been touched upon. The first is trying to "rehabilitate" a black probationer into a white mold. The second is to try to pass over and ignore the differences between black and white. There is still discrimination in America. White America now holds most of the material wealth and power positions in our civilization. A black who wants his share has a long uphill fight. To deny these facts of modern America taxes one's credibility with the black probationer.

A third pitfall is of a different nature, but is no less destructive of probation casework. This is to fall into the trap of being a white liberal patsy. Black people tend to be highly realistic and pragmatic. They respect strength and determination. Most West African societies from whence the American Negro came were headed by autocratic chiefs and kings. This tradition has been continued here in the form of the black matriarch who rules her family with an iron hand.

Pragmatism and realistic evaluation of their own world lead blacks to expect interpersonal relationships to be based on some form of self-interest. At its best this might be an enlightened self-interest. At worst blacks expect frank mutual exploitation. Deep-rooted traditions of autocracy and matriarchy lead blacks to expect those with power to use and enjoy it. Most blacks are artists at manipulating whites when they care to do it. The probation officer who falls into the trap of abdicating his inherent authority and trying to "help" the black will most likely be regarded as a fool.

This is not to say that a helping relationship has no place in working with blacks. If this approach is to be used, however, the probation officer should spell out what his motives are, what the limits are, and what he will do if the limits are transgressed. The probation officer who wants to take a helping role needs to examine his own motivations. Often this can be a cover up for underlying hostility. To credibly explain to a black who may hate all whites why you want to help him requires considerable self-awareness. If the probation officer is deceiving himself, this will very likely be picked up intuitively by the probationer.

THE ALTERNATIVES

I realize that much of what I have said here may be unpalatable to many people in the field of probation. Myths such as "Full equality exists now"; "Any black who wants can make it"; and "Black people are no different from whites" are very popular. They are part of the ego defenses of white people and white culture. I am also advocating channeling blacks toward black pride and black identity which may be unacceptable to many probation officers.

Personally, I regard the goals set forth by Thomas in the quest for black identity as very desirable. For those who do not I can only say, what are the alternatives? Law enforcement and probation are not now working effectively with black people. To try to pour blacks into a mold which has no prototype in their culture is very unrealistic. If we could rehabilitate a black into something as white as ourselves, we would thoroughly cut off his roots in his own community. His chances of being accepted in a white community would still be remote. The prognosis for such an approach is dismal indeed. For those who cannot tolerate cultural pluralism, I would suggest that they regard the casework approach outlined here as one with limited goals, but goals which are within our reach, and whose implementation might lead to a successful probation program for a large segment of our caseload.

BIBLIOGRAPHY

William H. Grier and Price M. Cobbs, *Black Rage*. New York: Basic Books, 1968. This is the best treatment of the unique features of black psychology I know of.

Elliot Liebow, *Tally's Corner*. New York: Little, Brown and Co., 1967. This is an excellent study by an anthropologist of black existence in the streets of the big city ghetto.

Charles W. Thomas, and Jo Ann Gardner, "Different Strokes for Different Folks" in *Psychology Today*, September 1971. The main thrust of this article is a dialogue between a black psychologist and a feminist. In the course of this dialogue, however, Thomas makes some excellent remarks about personal development within the framework of blackness.

Richard Wright, *Black Boy*. New York: Harper, 1945. This is an account of black childhood in the Old South. It gives the reader an almost firsthand grasp of the pain and frustration of being black in the heyday of Jim Crow. As such it gives a feeling for the roots of our present racial crisis.

COUNSELING OFFENDERS OF SPANISH HERITAGE *

Throughout my own employment experience, I have seen that it is not a simple matter to help people through counseling. The so-called hard core are victims of psychological and physiological problems which many of us tend to overlook or grossly misinterpret. There are many things which can weaken the motivation of people in the *barrio*: illiteracy, malnutrition, poor health, drug addiction, prison records, and distrust, among others. Notwithstanding, counselors have been encouraged by our progress, though it has been painfully slow. Our success has been dependent in part upon supportive agency resources. The key, however,

* Felix J. Chaves, *Federal Probation*, March 1976.

is the personalized attention given to the client who is encouraged to come to the agencies. It is not enough merely to provide information about the probation process. There must be a wholesome personal interaction between the offender and the probation officer. The probation officer must maintain and convey an attitude that reduces barriers of suspicion and distrust instead of creating them. In working with a population which is basically feeling-oriented, the concept of *relationship* looms as possibly the *most important* factor in counseling.

ESTABLISHING RAPPORT WITH THE SPANISH–HERITAGE OFFENDER

In attempting to establish rapport and to communicate with offenders of Spanish heritage, the probation officer should be aware of the traditional patterns of etiquette followed by this group of people. While the use of first names and discussion of personal matters may establish rapport between "Anglo" probation officer and "Anglo" offender, this approach can have the opposite effect on a person of Spanish heritage. In his society, formal address indicates respect for the dignity of the other person. The probation officer should, therefore, always address the Spanish-heritage offender Mr., Mrs., or Miss.

Even if the offender seems to communicate satisfactorily in English, he may be mentally translating from English to Spanish and vice versa. The probation officer should make sure that the offender fully understands any verbal exchange.

A probation officer who has studied Spanish may try to use it to communicate with a Spanish-speaking offender. Unless the probation officer is both fluent and familiar with the offender's colloquialisms and idioms, his efforts to speak Spanish may actually establish a barrier. There are many variations in dialect and expression between Mexican, Spanish, and Puerto Rican Spanish, and within these categories there are even more variations. In addition, the Spanish taught in American colleges is usually a form of so-called Castellano or Castilian Spanish, which is not the language used by any of these groups. It would be like speaking Shakespearean English to an English-speaking offender.

In ascertaining the interests of the Spanish-heritage offender, the probation officer must be aware that such a person's values may differ in many ways from those of the dominant culture. Even though there is a definite professional hierarchy in the Spanish-heritage culture—e. g., doctor-lawyer-teacher versus menial occupations—there is not as much emphasis given to the amount of income. Under certain circumstances a profession enjoying high prestige in the Spanish-heritage community may be more appealing than a lesser-prestige vocation with more pay. In certain isolated cases another factor may have a bearing on the vocational and social preference: The Spanish-heritage male offender may be uninterested in occupations that do not require physical strength, e. g., librarian, office clerk. Generally speaking, this attitude is disappearing.

COUNSELING THE SPANISH–HERITAGE OFFENDER

Traditionally, the person of Spanish heritage has been relegated almost exclusively to low-skill occupations, e. g., seasonal farm laborer, material handler. The probation officer may find the offender reluctant to consider entering a profession or field higher than that which has traditionally been assigned to members of his ethnic group. The offender must be told that it is possible to break out of traditional occupations and to function successfully in high-level jobs. Every effort should be made by the probation officer to develop self-confidence in the individual and encourage him to raise his vocational and social sights. One method is to enlist the aid of a member of the offender's ethnic group who has risen above the limitations of traditional employment.

The person of Spanish heritage usually has a very strong basic orientation toward the importance of his immediate as well as his extended family. Thus, the probation officer may in effect be counseling the whole extended family. Success or failure of the probation officer to attain a positive goal in working with the offender may, in this manner, be transmitted to the entire family group.

In addition to the formality appropriate in communicating with the Spanish-heritage offender, the probation officer should be aware of other important factors which would not enter into the Anglo-Anglo relationship. In his society, the Spanish-heritage male is accorded higher status than the female. The term "machismo" which describes this concept is not limited to sexual superiority. Both male and female are assigned definite roles in the traditional Spanish society. This factor is of special importance in the relationship between a female probation officer of other than Spanish heritage and a male Spanish-heritage offender. However, this should present no problem if the female probation officer can strike the right tone of respectful courtesy.

Another factor which may appear minor to the probation officer is the Spanish surname. When an offender exhibiting none of the stereotyped "Mexican" physical characteristics has been discriminated against merely on the basis of his Spanish surname, it might occur to a probation officer to suggest that he anglicize his name, e. g., change it from "Martinez" to "Martin." With very few exceptions, the individual will resent this suggestion because of traditionally intense pride in his family and name. The probation officer should also exercise care in pronouncing names. There is a tendency among non-Spanish-speaking persons to mispronounce Spanish names. For example, in the name "Martinez" emphasis is sometimes erroneously placed on the last syllable; it should be placed on the second syllable. The probation officer should listen attentively to the individual's pronunciation of his own name.

Great pride in the family name is usually only one manifestation of the Spanish-heritage individual's desire to maintain his particular culture, traditions, and language. Like the new generation of American Indians and Blacks, the young person of Spanish heritage is beginning to strive for a full revival of his cultural traditions. Where he may formerly have spoken only English outside the home, he now openly and proudly speaks Spanish. In this way, he not only establishes solidarity with other individuals of similar background but uses his language as a device to separate himself from the "assimilated" Mexican, Cuban, etc., who avoids speaking Spanish.

Regardless of how friendly the non-Spanish-heritage probation officer may feel toward the offender, he should keep in mind the latter's preconditioned negative opinion and reaction to the dominant culture. Although such negative attitudes vary in intensity, they have a definite bearing on the effectiveness of counseling and casework. Past experiences may have taught the Spanish-heritage offender to expect no benefits or acceptance from individuals of other ethnic groups. This attitude may be intensified in his contacts with the "establishment," e. g., Federal and State agencies, police, social workers, probation officers.

As mentioned above, traditional patterns may tend to limit the offender's concept of his own vocational and social interests and goals. Because of the historical and economic turbulence in which many generations of Spanish-heritage people have had to live, they tend to be oriented toward immediate gratification of desires rather than toward planning for the future. The offender might choose immediately remunerative work instead of a prolonged period of training which would lead to employment security and a higher income. The advantage of careful planning for his employment future should be pointed out to him in terms of the ultimate benefits to be derived by him and his family. The probation officer must make sure that his suggestion of training and the offender's agreement are not misinterpreted as a guarantee of placement in a particular training course. The offender must also understand that referral to a job opening does not guarantee placement. It is far better for the probation officer to candidly explain the difficulties in placement than for him to raise false hopes which will only confirm the offender's belief that he will receive no assistance from the employment service.

The probation officer should attempt to familiarize himself with the differences between and within the various groups of Spanish-heritage persons. Among Mexicans in the United States, for example, some proudly claim to be of "pure" Spanish descent to distinguish themselves from persons of Spanish-Indian mixture.

The differences in education and experience between the American-born person of Spanish heritage and the immigrant should be carefully considered. Also, the offender of Spanish-heritage should not be automatically labeled "Mexican," for instance; he might be of Cuban or Puerto Rican descent. The probation officer should guard against inadvertently reflecting some of the popular stereotypes and misconceptions about the person of Spanish heritage. As in all other human relationships, respect for the individual as a person with pride and dignity should be paramount.

Suggestions for Working With the Spanish-Heritage Offender

The following suggestions for working with Spanish-heritage offenders are an outgrowth of a study of the cultural backgrounds of Spanish-heritage persons that stemmed from dissatisfaction with the results of casework efforts in this field. Although they grew out of a concern for a particular type of offender in a particular casework situation, these suggestions may have implications for any probation officer-offender relationship.

UNDERSTAND THE CULTURAL DETERMINANTS OF THE OFFENDER'S BEHAVIOR

The Anglo probation officer should be keenly aware of the possible cultural differences between himself and the Spanish-heritage offender. A failure to demonstrate an understanding of the cultural determinants of the offender's behavior may signify to the offender that the probation officer is unwilling or unable to understand him. The Spanish-heritage offender may demonstrate attitudes toward dependency, work, money, ambition, time, and sex which are quite different from what might be expected from an Anglo offender. Some Anglo probation officers may tend to undervalue or be critical of the cultural traits and attitudes of the Spanish-heritage person. Other probation officers may have a need to deny that there are differences between groups of people or that it is possible to generalize about cultural groups. The democratic-minded probation officer might be reluctant to generalize about groups lest he be accused of using stereotypes associated with prejudice. However, social scientists have made it clear that groups of people do think and act differently from other groups, and that to ignore this fact is to deprive ourselves of useful knowledge. To make cultural generalizations is not to deny that individual variations exist. One can be enriched by the understanding of a group of which the individual is part.

BE SURE THE OFFENDER UNDERSTANDS YOU

Communications problems rate high in the group of obstacles encountered with Spanish-heritage offenders. Frequently, the offender has been expected to speak Spanish in his home and neighborhood, and English at school or work. Many professionally trained probation officers habitually use vocabulary that has little meaning to the Spanish-heritage person. At the time the offender may not understand the probation officer, but may be hesitant to reveal his lack of understanding. The breakdown in communication is often the precursor of a breakdown in the whole process. The probation officer should therefore use language that is clear, concise, and simple; he should be constantly alert for indications that he is not getting his meaning across.

BE WARM AND PERSONAL

The culture of the Spanish-heritage offender places a high value on close, warm personal relationships. One of the most frightening things about an Anglo medical, correctional, or social agency is the cool, crisp, efficient and impersonal way in which offenders are often handled. The probation officer, therefore should make an effort to be less formal and more warm and personal in his dealings with Spanish-heritage people. However, an overly friendly, effusive approach should be avoided; it will only make the offender more suspicious. It is difficult to be more specific about this recommendation, since warmth and a personal quality are so intangible.

UNDERSTAND CULTURALLY DETERMINED DEPENDENCY

The Anglo culture places a high value on independence, strength and initiative. The Anglo probation officer is likely to place a high value on self-determination. These values, however, are not necessarily shared by the Spanish-heritage offender, whose culture is more tolerant of dependency and less concerned with initiative and self-determination. Many times, the Anglo is for getting the offender out of the agency or hospital and on his own as quickly as possible. The Spanish-heritage person may perceive this as rejection or as grudging assistance. He may tend to view his dependency as natural and acceptable, while the Anglo may consider it as socially and psychologically unhealthy.

It should be recalled that while Spanish-heritage offenders accept the idea of being taken care of in times of personal need, they just as readily step into the role of taking care of others. It is a rare probation officer who hasn't seen a Spanish-heritage family with limited resources displaying generosity and self-sacrifice in taking care of relatives in even worse circumstances. To state that culturally determined dependency should be understood and accepted is not to say, however, that permanent dependency should be fostered.

ASK QUESTIONS AND MAKE SUGGESTIONS

Often we find the Spanish-heritage person fearful, suspicious, and reserved. He is apt to be considerably less articulate than the Anglo offender. Where this is true, the probation officer must be prepared to participate more actively in the interaction process. A nondirective approach which throws the burden of the interview on a fearful and inarticulate offender can be anxiety-producing and may leave the offender with the feeling that the probation officer is not prepared to offer much help. This often increases the passive negativism so frequently seen in Spanish-heritage offenders. Long silences may make anyone uncomfortable and heighten resistance. Therefore, the probation officer should be prepared to assume a major share of the responsibility for the interview by asking questions (thus demonstrating interest in the offender) and offering information and suggestions (thus demonstrating that he is willing to give).

REMIND THE OFFENDER ABOUT APPOINTMENTS

The Spanish-heritage offender may be less time-conscious than the Anglo; therefore, the probation officer would do well to schedule appointments more carefully. Appointments made far in advance are often forgotten. The probation officer would probably get better results if he took the trouble to send a reminder a day or two before the appointment. If the offender is late for an appointment, it should not necessarily be interpreted as resistance or unwillingness to cooperate—the Spanish-heritage offender simply may not be a clock-watcher.

OFFER SERVICES

Because of his dependency and his suspicion of the Anglo, the Spanish-heritage offender may, by way of testing the sincere interest of the probation officer, request many tangible services. When such services can realistically be offered, the relationship may be facilitated. For example, too often a probation officer or caseworker works very hard to prepare a Spanish-heritage mother for a visit to a well-baby clinic and then is disappointed and annoyed to learn that the mother did not take her baby to the clinic. Perhaps if the probation officer or caseworker had recognized the mother's reluctance to travel alone outside her neighborhood, her uncertainties about asking for and understanding directions in a language she may not have completely mastered, and her fear of encountering strange Anglo doctors and nurses in an imposing and impersonal medical setting, the probation officer or caseworker might have had better success. If the probation officer or caseworker had introduced her to a doctor or nurse so that she would feel less strange and fearful, the results probably would have been even more gratifying.

CONCLUSION

"Sal si puedes"—get out if you can—has been the cry of parents and their children in the *barrios* for many years. However, the tools of education and meaningful employment, which provide the real basis of opportunity, have been ineffective for those who are now in need. There can be no justification for this imbalance. No one individual or organization is responsible, but everyone, including local leadership, shares the responsibility.

We must view each person as an individual with not only unique problems but also unique ways of making positive contributions. The typical Spanish-heritage offender has experienced many failures and is trying to hold on to his cultural values in order to maintain his integrity. If the probation officer attempts to take away these basic values and instill his own "correct" values, he will meet with great resistance. If, however, the Spanish-heritage offender feels that his background is acknowledged and accepted, he will usually allow himself to accept help. In other words, if the help is an additive process whereby the individual is not asked to give anything up, but rather to accept additional positive values—e. g., appropriate responses to supervision, relating well with probation officer—then the process is seen as positive and effective. The meaningful product of this process is communication, which is vitally important in providing assistance.

Thus, social and emotional support need not and cannot be a feature of the role of the nonindigenous professional in the counseling process. But then, it does become part of the probation officer's role to work effectively with the indigenous workers in other agencies, so that he is in a position to receive the transferred rapport which such workers can develop. Probation officers, who are generally now seen as frustrated semiprofessionals who have little opportunity to actualize the existing prestigious models of counseling as defined by the graduate schools, will thus move from such a disvalued status to a unique professional identity, whose validity rests on its relevance to the needs of the Spanish-heritage offender, and on its unique knowledge, skills, and functions.

THE VOLUNTEER IN PROBATION *

Probation began with volunteers; some believe it will end with them, with volunteer probation counselors, tutors, foster parents, office workers, and the like. However, that is taken, the early volunteers were honorably discharged as soon as we could pay people, and the pendulum swung hard toward paid professionals in the first five decades of this century. Today the pendulum swings back toward volunteers—but with a difference. Where first probation was all volunteer and later virtually all paid professional, today it is both, and both are here to stay.

Probation will never again be all volunteer. But neither will it ever again be all paid professional. Therefore, the problem of *modern* volunteerism differs crucially from the problem of early volunteerism in corrections, for it becomes an issue of *relationship* between volunteer and paid professional, a problem of defining optimum roles for each in a productive probation partnership. John Augustus, as probation's founding father, incorporated "volunteer" and "probation officer" in one body; just so, we must learn to incorporate in the body of probation, both volunteer and paid professional. As in any new marriage, we will have to work at it, and we may still have to be satisfied with something less than perfect integration; but we cannot afford to be content with as little as coexistence. Divorce is impossible. Whatever the secret hopes of some, the modern court volunteer is not going to go away.

* Ivan H. Scheier, *Federal Probation*. June, 1970. Reprinted with permission.

THE VOLUNTEER RETURNS TO THE COURT

The ghost of John Augustus rose again in 1960, looking somewhat different, when Royal Oak, Michigan, began easing into the use of volunteers with misdemeanants. Juvenile courts at Lawrence, Kansas, and Eugene, Oregon, had experimented with this kind of volunteer usage, since the mid-fifties. Judge Horace B. Holmes began using volunteers at the Boulder, Colorado, Juvenile Court in 1961. But not until 1967 did the court volunteer movement really take hold. Today, some 50,000 citizens contribute several million hours of service a year, in 1,000 court probation departments, and at least one new court a day is estimated to be launching its venture into volunteerism. These figures would be approximately doubled if one included parole and detention volunteer programs, as well as probation.

Even in this infancy of the movement, there are more volunteers than paid people in probation and they may soon be contributing a larger total of service hours as well. Moreover, the explosive acceleration in current growth rate extrapolates to a near future in which one-quarter of all courts will have volunteers working in probation programs, for better or for worse, in, say, 1972.

A similar sign of the times is the recent interest in planning and implementation of court volunteer programs on a *statewide* basis. Florida and Washington are already doing so, and 20 other states have indicated to the National Information Center, serious interest at this level. This immediately raises the question whether court volunteer programs are adaptable to the variety of local court and community conditions.

ADAPTABILITY TO LOCAL COMMUNITIES AND COURTS

There are good reasons for approaching court volunteer programs with care and caution. Not among these is saying: "It works in your town because your town is unique." In the first place, 500 communities wear out the word "unique" and, on the evidence, the volunteer penetration into probation is broad as well as deep. Thus, what was said 2 years ago is more true today:

> The court volunteer movement is already too large for the "hothouse flower" label. It is also too hardy in surviving various types of environment. One of the clearest conclusions thus far is that a volunteer probation program is not restricted to any one unique set of court or community conditions. Volunteer programs now flourish in every size and shape of American community and court. They span rural areas, small towns, large cities and suburbia. Some volunteer courts are in communities with colleges and depend heavily on them; others do not.[1]

1. H. B. Holmes, et al., "The Volunteer Returns to the Court," *Juvenile Court*   *Judges Journal*, Volume 18, Number 4, Winter 1968.

To be sure, very small and very large communities have been relatively slow on the uptake (the latter, probably related to the skepticism of established professionals). But the broad weight of dissemination evidence simply will not permit the "unique" shrug-off.

As for type of courts, volunteer programs tend to take root in courts with a rehabilitation rather than a purely retributive philosophy. Other than that, they are not peculiar to any particular type of court. As noted recently:

> All levels of jurisdiction are represented: municipal, county, district or superior. About half are juvenile courts with a core of professional probation officers who preceded the advent of volunteers. The remainder are misdemeanant courts which would have had no probation department at all, except for volunteers.[2]

As of today, add that a few courts are even beginning to experiment with volunteers assigned to *felons* on probation. For American service volunteerism—where too many college graduates have licked too many stamps, too long—entrusting volunteers with any kind of probationer was itself something of a pioneer venture into elevated responsibility and meaningfulness. The extension to *felon* probationers is surely on the growing edge of *serious* service volunteerism.

THE VOLUNTEER ENCOUNTER WITH PROFESSIONALS

Increasingly we realize this difference in court setting is important. This is not so much because of the age of volunteers assigned probationers. They tend to be younger probationers in adult courts, averaging 18 to 20 years of age, which is not too far from the juvenile court average. Rather, the crucial difference is that in most juvenile courts, volunteer programs have to be grafted onto a pre-existing paid professional structure. But misdemeanant courts, the forgotten area of probation, rarely had probation departments of any sort prior to volunteers. Accordingly, this pre-existing staff "limitation" on the activities and attitudes of volunteers does not usually exist in misdemeanant courts. By the same token, volunteer programs in previously unprofessionalized courts lack the potentialities for growth of volunteer programs through professional leadership. Or, at any rate, they do at first. For volunteer programs actually have *created* paid leadership positions in corrections where none existed before. The evidence on this point is overwhelming and, on the other side of the ledger, there is not one authenticated instance of a corrections professional losing his job because of volunteers.

Thus, in both juvenile court and misdemeanant systems, paid professionals come to be involved with volunteers. But the volunteer-produced type of professional is a different kind of fellow. He is committed to

2. Ibid.

volunteers by choice, and if it comes to that, he owes his job to them. His relationship to volunteers is central and natural, if not entirely without friction, as he concentrates on supervising or facilitating their work. If he locks horns with anyone, it is far more likely to be the traditional professional (whose stake is in supervising probationers, not volunteers). Let us hope this does not happen, but it could, as the "new professional" becomes more numerous. In that sad case, the traditional professional could have a relationship problem, not only with the volunteer, but also with the volunteer-created "new professional." Indeed, while our attention has been riveted on the emerging court volunteer, we have neglected an area of equal personnel significance: the concurrent emergence of the volunteer-created new professional.

Visibility of this "new professional" in corrections has been somewhat obscured because, especially in the early days of the movement, he was called by traditional titles such as chief probation officer or director of probation services, even though that is not what he was actually doing in the *traditional* sense. Also, one person might perform quite successfully in both job dimensions at once. More and more, however, the new professional is being advertised for and called what he actually is: "Volunteer Coordinator (Corrections)," "Director of Probation Volunteer Services," "Volunteer Specialist," or even "Community Organization Specialist."

THE INSPIRATION ISSUE

All the above may seem to invent fanciful problems for a profession already supplied plentifully with real ones. Let me therefore reiterate: probation volunteer programs are suddenly past the oddity stage. Present figures, and close-in projections show them upon us in ever more significant numbers, giving little quarter to leisurely reflection. In fact, they have already changed the question before the house. The question no longer is, "will it be done?"; the only question is, "will it be done well?"

It must be said that, to some, it is virtually the same question. They feel the idea is intrinsically so good it will work itself. Some mystic quality in the volunteer has only to be permitted a chance and it will succeed. That is, volunteerism is placed in the Judeo-Christian tradition rather than the more secular democratic citizen-participation tradition. Indeed, this emphasis on spiritual values frequently reaches the point where to good people who hold this view seem to be proposing that probation become an arm of Christianity (as it is actually said to be in at least one European country). In any event, the position is that you need not concern yourself overly with managerial procedures where inspiration is concerned; in fact, the idea is so good, you can scarcely "procedure yourself out of it."

To others, procedure is just about everything. Running volunteer programs is a complex, professionally demanding body of specialized *knowledge.* You *can* fail at it, and on the record, quite a few courts have. Yes, inspiration is one of the important things volunteers offer, but you'd better have a good organization behind that inspiration, if you want it to work massively in program-level interventions. Indeed, why do we feel we can show our faith in spirit only by being disorganized? Why must we suffocate goodwill in chaos, when we have applied organizational genius to just about everything else in this country? Surely, we can no longer suffer misguided sentiment to waste precious human resources. We must let hard heads help soft hearts.

EVIDENCE OF THE IMPACT OF COURT VOLUNTEERS

But there is a prior question: Why invest time, intelligence, and effort in the organization of volunteers if they are not, in the first place, demonstrated to be effective agents of positive probation change? To a certain extent, the present inadequacies of probation justify trying anything that even looks hopeful, not so much because it is proved better, as that it can hardly be worse. But in the long run, we need more than desperation as justification, and we already have some evidence. Courts using volunteers consistently report reductions in institutionalization rates, as more and more, they are able to work with the offender in his home community. At the same time, striking reductions in repeat offense percentage are also claimed (although this can be a somewhat elusive statistic). Perhaps the most impressive research finding is one which has been independently confirmed in three separate courts: one juvenile, one misdemeanant-suburb, and one misdemeanant-metropolis. As recently summarized,[3] all three researches agreed in finding that a group of probationers assigned volunteers one to one showed lessening of antisocial attitudes when tested before and after probation. By contrast, groups of probationers not assigned volunteers showed actual *increase* in antisocial attitudes—a damning indictment of "empty probation."

This does not clinch the case, by any means. First of all, these positive results were produced by relatively *well-run* volunteer programs. Other programs are poorly run and, presumably, show poorer results. A second complication is the multi-dimensional impact of court volunteer programs. In addition to probationers, they have important influences on the court, the community, and the volunteers themselves.

Thus, anecdotal observation and evidential analysis in process at the National Information Center concur strongly that court volunteer programs are popular and well received in the community. Volunteers function effectively as the court's ambassadors and educators in the community. Even other social control and social service agencies in town—from whom "jealously" might conceivably be expected—tended to approve the Boulder Court's venture into volunteerism.

---

3. I. H. Scheier, "Court Volunteer Impact on Probationers: Attitudes and Personality," reprint from Volume 1, Number 18 (1969) of *The Volunteer* *Courts Newsletter*, published at the National Information Center on Volunteers in Courts, Hall of Justice, Division C, Boulder, Colorado 80302.

Impact on the volunteers themselves is less well known. There is the traditional assumption that volunteers find their work satisfying—generally they do—but anecdotal observation of volunteers in action also suggests that at least some volunteers will hang on in a poorly run program, though unhappy, just because they think the ultimate objectives of probation so worthy. As for statistics, Denver County Court has reported a very favorable re-volunteer rate, well over 80 percent, but this number reflects volunteers who have already survived the test of a year's service during which the first 3 to 6 months appear to be the "volunteer death" period of greatest dropout. When one is talking about court volunteer turnover rate for a 1-year period, the figure is not much better than 50 percent.

Finally, the volunteer's impact on professional roles and structures in the court is a profound and complex one which we shall touch on later in this article. But clearly, court volunteer programs are not a one-edged sword, or even a two-edged sword. They cut many ways in the court and the community. Put otherwise, anyone who sees only black and white misses much in this chiaroscuro world. And too many people see volunteers in this all-or-nothing way; either anathema or panacea, with nothing in between; either not in the ball park or the only game in town.

THE RANGE OF COURT VOLUNTEER CONTRIBUTIONS

Either extreme is unrealistic. Court volunteer programs are actually a complex mix of advantage and disadvantage. Therefore, planning and evaluation must carefully balance expected yield against necessary inconvenience, adjustment, and stress on the court. We must be as clear as possible on the nature of this expected yield. What precisely may a probation department expect to get out of volunteers? Generally, the answers are: (1) amplification of services and, (2) diversification of services.

(1) *Amplification of services.*—As for amplification, consider the case of the probation officer who, after paperwork chores, has an hour a month left to spend with each probationer in his caseload. He can spend it directly (a) supervising the probationer, in which case his 1 hour input of time results in 1 hour output of attention received by the probationer. Alternatively, he can spend this hour directly (b) supervising a *volunteer* who then spends much more time supervising the probationer as his "caseload of one." The 1 hour input of time by the probation officer may thus result in 15 hours output of attention received by the probationer ("amplied" via the volunteer).

Combinations of the two systems are possible, too, of course, where the probation officer spends part of this time supervising the volunteer and part of his time keeping some direct contact with the probationer with whom the volunteer works.

In the second system in which probation officers supervise probationers indirectly by the use of volunteers, the same probation officer input of time eventually delivers 15 hours' attention to the probationer instead of one—15 times as much time. The case is a great deal more complex than that, of course, but our calculations have indicated generally an "amplication factor" averaging between 10 and 20 for court volunteer programs. That is, for each hour of staff supervisory or facilitatory time invested (and this investment is necessary) 10 to 20 hours of volunteer service are outputted into the probation service system.

(2) *Diversification of services.*—Potentially, the probation treatment plan can now tap any skill that exists in the community, a mind-stretching prospect we have scarcely begun to absorb. Do you need a cobbler, a carpenter, a marriage counselor, cosmetologist, a psychiatrist, a guitar player, a stock market expert? They are there. The report of the Joint Commission on Correctional Manpower and Training indicates that almost 50 percent of the community would probably or certainly volunteer for juvenile corrections work if asked (see "Readings" section at the close of this article). Indeed, we know of at least 50 different types of skills that have been volunteered to courts the past few years. The breathtaking possibility for the probation officer is: Your staff *is* the community, a reservoir of skills which can be orchestrated to probation planning. Volunteers are *not* a rigid format, take it or leave it. They are a *medium with which you can work*, the bricks and stones which you select and place in order to build your own house of probation. They are not a house already built.

The facts support this variegated view of volunteers. No less than 155 distinct court volunteer job descriptions have been catalogued as actually filled by volunteers in one court or another, in 20 major categories of contribution, and several major program areas. The volunteer as a range of options, rather than a restriction, is further suggested by the types of roles volunteers can and have filled in courts (one volunteer can fill several at once, of course):

Thus, in the area of direct contact with probationers, volunteers can offer services such as: (1) support-friendship, sincere warmth; (2) "meditation," facilitation of social-physical environment (get jobs, intercede with teacher, etc.); (3) behavior model, good example; (4) limit-setting, social control, conscience; (5) teacher-tutor of skills, academic, vocational or social; (6) observation-information-diagnosis-understanding [extra eyes and ears (a) on the probationer (b) on the community, or even (c) on court operations]; and (7) advisory or decision-making participation in formulation or modification of probation plan.

Volunteers can also do many things not primarily involving direct contact with probationers. Among these are: (8) administrative, office work, and related facilitation; (9) help recruit, train, advise, and supervise other volunteers; (10) expert consultant to regular staff; (11) advisor to court, participation in policy-making, formally or informally, the volunteer as a source of ideas; (12) public relations, public education, and related impact on the community; and (13) contributions of money, materials, facilities, or help in securing them from others (e. g., fund raisers).

As late as 1962, I remember reading an eloquent plea for citizen participation which culminated in a suggestion to this effect: "Now, why don't you folks get together and *discuss* delinquency." By contrast, the list above announces citizen participation at a new pitch. And as citizens assume these new levels of responsibility, so does the court, for if citizens can do so many different and real things, the court must take explicit responsibility for articulating and directing the efforts of this powerful instrumentality.

MANAGEMENT OF COURT VOLUNTEER PROGRAMS

The supervision of such a range of effort demands real skill in a director of court volunteer programs. Books and big manuals barely scratch the surface of this subject and the introductory guidelines below are merely a shorthand for formidable complexities. They are certainly not meant to encourage the dangerous myth that "anyone can do it." Nor do they mean to impute a tidy consensus to that special body of knowledge concerning the purpose and conduct of court volunteer programs, which is only now beginning to emerge from the writings of pioneers.[4]

Recruiting.—The early fear is that you will not get enough good people, but the danger is almost exactly opposite. Premature, broadcast recruiting will get you more people than you are ready to use (and they will likely resent overlong waiting). Quantity of volunteers is rarely a problem—Boulder typically has a waiting list. Talks at local groups, word-of-mouth, even "help wanted" ads, all bring their human yield.

As for volunteer quality, the ancient unconscious prejudice—what you don't pay for can't be worth much—is at last being laid to rest. Overwhelming experience and actual statistics show that today's court volunteer is well educated, successful, mature—the kind of person you would be glad to pay for if you had the money. Not incidentally, you would need quite a bit of money. Nationally, 10 to 15 percent of court volunteers are professionals contributing as professionals, without charge. Overall, in a modest-sized community such as Boulder, the purchase price of volunteer services would be $50,000 a year, at a conservative estimate. Boulder does not have that kind of money, of course, but we do have that kind of service.

Within the middle-class predominance of court volunteers (poor people usually cannot afford to volunteer) all races and religions are propor-

---

4. See "Readings" section at the end of this paper, and especially a summarizing work entitled, *Using Volunteers in*   *Court Settings: A Manual for Volunteer Probation Programs.*

tionally represented. All have a great deal more sophistication on social matters than their parents had, and anyone who thinks of them in terms of sweet, naive "Lady Bountiful," is simply whipping a dead volunteer.

There are misfits, of course, but so far as The National Information Center has been able to ascertain, the percentage is no higher among volunteers than among paid people in corrections.

Screening and selection.—The second secret nightmare of those who sleep on volunteer program planning is: "We're going to get all these kooky people and since they're volunteers we're going to have to accept them." Wrong on both counts! Begin your screening back in recruiting, by keeping your focus sharp. Recruit only where you are most likely to find the kind of people you want, e. g., church groups, colleges, labor unions, your personal friends, etc. Do not use "come one-come all" newspaper releases, especially in the early stages of the program.

After focussed recruiting, do not be afraid to screen hard. Begin by being clear in your own mind as to exactly what you want in the job and in the volunteer's qualifications. Be honest with yourself and the volunteer about it, rather than apologetic. Indeed, you will do just about everything right if you act as if you're offering the volunteer a $10,000-a-year job: application form, character references, police checks, replicated interviews, good motivation, etc. Actually, volunteers seem to appreciate it more when they are taken seriously in this way.

True, you will occasionally—not often—have to reject a nice person who is just not suitable. More often, however, they will screen themselves out if you give them a chance to do so, via honest realism in describing the job, during training, and even in trial jobs. Or there may be other less sensitive jobs to offer such a person, in the court or elsewhere in town (e. g., via a local volunteer bureau). Moreover, people come increasingly to respect your high standards. It becomes a privilege to be a volunteer at your court, and citizens understand if they do not quite make it. We know of only one case in which a rejected volunteer took his case to the Governor, won it, and did a good job. The Governor's wife is a volunteer too!

Orientation and training.—Auslander's recent M.S.W. study (see "Readings" section) confirmed that currently, what the average court is doing about training volunteers is essentially very little. Some reject it almost entirely on the grounds, plausible in themselves, that the volunteer is not supposed to be just another watered-down professional. True enough, but orientation can do other needed things.

For example, it can *familiarize* the volunteer (1) with the job and its boundaries, (2) with what probationers are like, (3) with typical problems and solutions of volunteers working with probationers, (4) with the court, the "who, what, where" of staff, procedures, laws, facilities, and (5) the same for community resources available for helping probationers.

Secondly, volunteer orientation and training has an important *morale* function. Training says to the volunteer: the court takes your work seriously. Also, the volunteer looks around and sees that he's not alone (loneliness being a real morale problem for volunteers). Nor should *staff* morale implications be overlooked. When staff have a hand in the planning and conduct of training, they have a chance and a channel for saying: This is how we would like the job done. This relieves their "loss of program control" nightmare about volunteers. Staff also can catch here, some of the enthusiasm and concern of good volunteers.

For these reasons volunteer orientation is viewed as a critical area of the court volunteer movement at this juncture, and the National Information Center will be spending the year 1970 reviewing and developing practical resources in this domain, under a grant from the Office of Juvenile Delinquency and Youth Development, U. S. Department of Health, Education, and Welfare.

Other managerial areas.—We have no space to cover entire areas of volunteer program managerial expertise, each of which would merit a chapter in any book, e. g., public relations, financing volunteer programs, volunteer incentive and support, communications and record-keeping, evaluation of individual and program performance, etc.

CHANGES IN THE ROLE OF THE PROFESSIONAL

Space permits mention of only one more matter—but a tremendously important one: the profound changes in professional roles produced by the introduction of volunteers into a court system. But this role change is not role *degradation*; far from it. First of all, the probation professional can do nothing but profit from enhanced interaction with the additional professionals brought in as volunteers. Secondly, leadership of the high-quality court volunteers we are getting, challenges the probation officer *professionally* as never before. Thirdly, the ability of the profession to attract and retain high quality people depends directly on improved pay scales. On the record, local volunteers have been effective allies of professionals here, in various courts around the country. All in all, the claim that volunteers deprofessionalize corrections proves on examination to be precisely contrary to fact. Volunteers will professionalize corrections as never before, and one may suspect that some old-liners who claim volunteers demand too little professionally are really afraid they will demand too much.

The really sobering role-change impact of court volunteerism is that it appears to deprive the probation officer of one of his chief satisfactions professionally: direct contact with probationers. But this is not necessarily so, or, at least, the matter is more involved than this simple statement indicates.

Let us make three assumptions about probation caseloads and from these deduce three role models for the professional of a future in which volunteers are a substantial factor in probation programming. The assumptions are: (1) Certain types of probationers can be rehabilitated primarily by what a "caseload of one" volunteer can offer, e. g., warmth, a behavior model, individualized mediation in the environment, etc.; (2) certain other cases cannot, and require the attention of a professional probation officer (or associated professional); and (3) diagnosis will increasingly develop precision in discriminating among these two types of probationer.

Given these reasonable assumptions, three professional role-types can be discerned: (1) the volunteer specialist, the "new professional" who works primarily with and through volunteers, rather than directly with probationers, (2) the traditional professional who continues to work directly with a caseload of probationers, (3) the two-way professional who derives satisfaction both from contact with volunteers and contact with probationers. Part of his caseload is carried via supervision of volunteers, while the other involves direct contact with probationers.

The professional of types two and three not only retains the satisfaction of direct work with probationers; he probably enjoys it in enhanced form. For with volunteers taking over a number of cases which do not require his attention, he now has a chance for direct work with probationers which is ideal in two senses. First, having been relieved of part of his caseload by volunteers, he can concentrate better on the fewer probationers remaining as his direct responsibility. Secondly, this reduced caseload may be composed largely of the probationers he deliberately selects to work with, as those who are most likely to benefit from his professional attention. Thus, where formerly the probation officer was something like the football coach at a school so small he had to teach flower arrangement for the girls and lacrosse for the alumni, now others take on the chores peripheral to his interest and capacity, and he can concentrate on football. This, of course, is better for the football players, and the flower arrangers too.

These new professional roles in probation are exciting and promising, yet little is being done to prepare for the dislocation and retraining the next few years will require in adjusting to them. The National Information Center's publications and institutes need to be amplified tenfold, and soon, or we shall never get the best out of our new and growing army of volunteer assistants. Instead, we will join our cousins in 30 other major areas of service volunteerism, where 60 million volunteers constitute the largest leaderless army in the world, and the most tragic, because not enough people are being trained well enough to lead them and develop their immense potential. Volunteerism has no West Points in or out of corrections, now or on the horizon, and this may be the most stupendous oversight of the century.

SERVICES TO PROBATIONERS

[Editor's Note. The following chapter is excerpted from *State and County Probation: Systems in Crisis,* a Report to the Congress by the Comptroller General of the United States, May 27, 1976.

[The *Report* attempted to determine if probation activities—sentencing, planning, diagnosis and treatment and delivery of services—were being effectively managed. Adult felon probation services were studied in Maricopa County, Arizona; Multnomah County, Oregon; Philadelphia County, Pennsylvania; and King County, Washington, to determine:

—Whether the Law Enforcement Assistance Administration (LEAA), the States, and the county probation departments were addressing the problems of developing probation systems that insure the public's safety and enable offenders to remain in the community and receive rehabilitation services.

—How much the services received by probationers increased their chances of successfully completing probation.

—Whether systems existed to identify individuals with good chances of completing probation and remaining out of contact with the criminal justice system and how such systems could be used to improve probation operations.

About 77 percent of the adult criminal offenders in the four counties were sentenced to probation in 1974.]

Important influences on whether probationers are rehabilitated are the extent and effectiveness of services they receive. To assess these services, we reviewed the closed cases in Maricopa, Multnomah, and Philadelphia counties and sent questionnaires to probation officers who supervised or were familiar with the cases.

Although some offenders benefited from services provided during probation, many did not receive needed services.

—Only 23 percent completed programs designed to address their needs.

—About 59 percent of court-ordered conditions of sentence and rehabilitative services were not enforced by probation departments.

—There was a highly significant statistical relationship between the extent to which probationers received needed services and success on probation, that is, as the probationer received more of the services he needed, he was more likely to complete probation successfully.

Probationers can receive services from community organizations and from the probation departments which supervise them. Probation officers should provide a number of direct services to offenders, such as

—arranging for necessary job training, education, drug or alcohol treatment, health care, and counseling,

—providing personal and family counseling, and

—providing direct assistance in changing housing or obtaining specific benefits like unemployment insurance, welfare, or food stamps.

Some probation officers also perform investigations before writing presentence reports.   Probation officers also are required to carry out investigations and write revocation recommendations when offenders on probation either violate conditions of probation or commit new crimes.

The following charts show information about the 900 probationers we sampled to assess service delivery and effect.   More complete information can be found in appendix IV.   Having such information makes it easier to understand some of the probationers' problems and needs.

These key facts show that:

—At least 61 percent had not completed high school.

—40 percent were unemployed at arrest.   Another 16 percent were employed in unskilled or manual labor.

—59 percent of the offenses committed were property offenses, 19 percent were against persons, and 18 percent were drug offenses.

—At least 63 percent were not first-time offenders.

—57 percent of the major treatment needs were related to employment and vocational and academic education.

KEY FACTS ABOUT PROBATIONERS

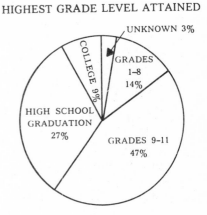

MARITAL STATUS

HIGHEST GRADE LEVEL ATTAINED

SEPARATED 8%   UNKNOWN 1%
WIDOWED 1%
DIVORCED 8%
SINGLE 49%
MARRIED 31%
COHABITING 3%

UNKNOWN 3%
COLLEGE 9%
GRADES 1-8 14%
HIGH SCHOOL GRADUATION 27%
GRADES 9-11 47%

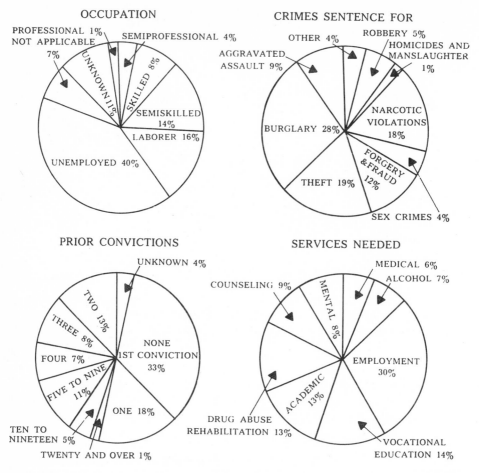

OCCUPATION

PROFESSIONAL 1%
NOT APPLICABLE
7%
SEMIPROFESSIONAL 4%
UNKNOWN 11%
SKILLED 8%
SEMISKILLED 14%
LABORER 16%
UNEMPLOYED 40%

CRIMES SENTENCE FOR

OTHER 4%
ROBBERY 5%
HOMICIDES AND MANSLAUGHTER 1%
AGGRAVATED ASSAULT 9%
NARCOTIC VIOLATIONS 18%
BURGLARY 28%
FORGERY &FRAUD 12%
THEFT 19%
SEX CRIMES 4%

PRIOR CONVICTIONS

UNKNOWN 4%
TWO 13%
THREE 8%
FOUR 7%
FIVE TO NINE 11%
NONE 1ST CONVICTION 33%
ONE 18%
TEN TO NINETEEN 5%
TWENTY AND OVER 1%

SERVICES NEEDED

MEDICAL 6%
ALCOHOL 7%
COUNSELING 9%
MENTAL 8%
EMPLOYMENT 30%
ACADEMIC 13%
DRUG ABUSE REHABILITATION 13%
VOCATIONAL EDUCATION 14%

[B6533]

SERVICES CAN HELP

The results of our statistical tests indicated a positive association between receiving services and succeeding on probation.

The following table summarizes the results of statistical tests for individual services which we considered rehabilitative in nature. (See app. II for details.) In many cases, no tests were made because of the small number of probationers whose success or failure and amount of service received were both known.

As indicated above, receiving vocational education and employment services were associated with successful completion of probation in all three counties. So were drug abuse rehabilitation in Multnomah and Maricopa counties and academic education in Multnomah County.

The fact that the statistical tests for some services did not show a relationship to probationary success does not necessarily mean that these services were ineffective. For example, the fact that alcoholism treat-

Statistical Relationship Between
Services and Probation Success

Relationship [a]

Rehabilitative service	Multnomah County, Oregon	Maricopa County, Arizona	Philadelphia County, Pennsylvania
Medical evaluation and treatment	No	—	—
Mental health treatment	No	—	No
Academic education	Yes	—	—
Vocational training	Yes	Yes	Yes
Employment services	Yes	Yes	Yes
Alcoholism treatment	No	—	No
Drug abuse rehabilitation	Yes	Yes	No
Individual or group counseling	—	—	No

a. Association established at the 95 percent confidence level.

IM-282

ment could not be shown to be statistically associated with successful probation could be explained if a large number of probationers who received such treatment also had other problems which were untreated.

To avoid the problems associated with testing each service, we looked at the extent to which a probationer received the *range* of services listed on the previous page. We determined that there was a highly significant association in each of the three counties between the extent to which a probationer received needed services and success in probation.

A recent study by Robert Martinson, an expert in criminal rehabilitation, concluded that rehabilitation has generally been unsuccessful and its role in the criminal justice system needed reexamining.[1] Our test results do not negate his conclusions. But we have shown that in certain circumstances rehabilitative services can help reduce offenders' tendency to commit additional crimes.

Our findings could have important implications for decisionmakers interested in improving probation operations. If probation departments could allocate their scare resources more effectively, they could begin to more adequately rehabilitate offenders.

Following is an example of an individual who was helped because his probation officer found the type of service needed and arranged for the probationer to participate. A 30-year-old offender was sentenced to 3 years probation for illegal possession of narcotics. A special condition of sentence required him to take part in the State rehabilitation program. The probation officer found the probationer at his parents' home under

1. "What Works?—Questions and Answers About Prison Reform," *Public Interest*, No. 35, Spring 1974.

the influence of drugs, several months after the probation began. Instead of sending the client to the State hospital, the probation officer arranged for him to enter a self-help rehabilitation program. The probation officer in this case was so impressed with his client's progress in removing himself from the drug scene and becoming involved in helping others with drug problems, that he recommended early end to probation, which was granted. A followup of this case after 19 months showed no further arrests or convictions.

PROBATIONERS' NEEDS WERE INADEQUATELY IDENTIFIED AND ADDRESSED

To plan for services, a probation system should assess probationers' needs. Problem areas can thus be highlighted and priorities determined. This process makes it possible to specify how, for whom, when, and why the various needs are to be met. Specifying objectives in this manner makes it easier to evaluate the system's success in identifying and providing services.

In reviewing case files, we found (1) lack of rehabilitation plans, (2) failure to comply with court conditions, and (3) inadequate delivery of service for such needs as unemployment, drug and alcohol problems, and academic and vocational training deficiencies.

Lack of a rehabilitation plan

Corrections experts generally agree that an effective rehabilitation program should include a plan for each individual which recognizes what services that person needs to become a useful member of society. Interim evaluations are also needed to assess the plan's effectiveness and to change when necessary.

The extent of probationers' needs, such as education, drug abuse treatment, and employment are shown in the charts on page 27. Most probationers, however, did not have a written rehabilitative plan that identified their needs because such plans were not required by probation departments. Probation officers stated that an offender's plan is usually an unwritten composite of court-ordered conditions, probation-officer-analyzed conditions, and probationer-requested services. Responses to our questionnaires by 74 percent of the probation officers who supervised the

County	Total closed cases	Cases for which information was available on plans	Cases having plans	
			Number	Percent
Maricopa	300	159	77	48
Multnomah	300	289	79	27
Philadelphia	300	220	99	45
Total	900	668	255	38

IM–283

900 closed cases showed that written plans were prepared for only 38 percent of the probationers under their supervision.

Oregon's new client case management system provides for a full analysis of needs and a written rehabilitation plan. Probation officers and probationers agree on a written plan and then carry it out. Oregon State probation officials said probation officers have resisted the new system because of already excessive caseloads and the amount of added work required. We were told by State Corrections Department officials that an increase in the number of probation officers, needed to reduce caseloads, has been denied by the State legislature.

Each county required progress reports to the court on every case supervised. Such a report, although not a formal rehabilitation plan, at least provides some indication of an offender's progress. The problem is that these reports usually cannot measure progress against specific goals because rehabilitation plans including such goals were not prepared. Maricopa and King county officers prepared progress reports every 120 days. Philadelphia County officers prepared reports about every 3 months. Multnomah County required progress reports semiannually, unless restitution or child-support payments were a condition of the offender's sentence. In such a case, or when the probation officer and his supervisor agreed that the case needed closer supervision, a quarterly report was submitted.

Most judges noted the need for formal rehabilitation plans. Of 101 judges responding to questionnaires in the 4 counties, 75 said a written, detailed rehabilitation plan is necessary to help assure treatment of diagnosed needs. In addition, 63 judges believed the plans should be approved by judges after the probation officers develop them.

Court-imposed conditions not met

At the time of sentence the court normally assigns certain standard conditions of probation, violation of which could cause probation to be revoked. Examples of standard conditions are

—remaining law-abiding,

—not leaving the State without the probation officer's approval,

—refraining from excessive use of intoxicating liquors, and

—not possessing or using drugs in violation of any law.

Judges may also require a probationer to fulfill special conditions, such as maintaining employment while on probation, paying restitution, or enrolling in rehabilitative programs.

We found that probationary conditions ordered by judges generally were not being met. The following table shows the extent of compliance with court-ordered conditions for the cases sampled in the three counties.

Court-ordered conditions	Number of cases	Compliance Number	Compliance Percent
Restitution	145	89	61
Court costs	74	41	55
Mental health treatment	43	18	42
Medical evaluation	20	8	40
Alcoholism treatment	42	12	29
Drug abuse rehabilitation	79	17	22
Academic education	12	4	33
Vocational training	13	3	23
Employment (securing and keeping)	60	14	23
Counseling	19	3	16
Total	a 507	209	41

a. There were an additional 75 cases which had court-ordered conditions, but we could not determine compliance. Therefore, we did not include them in the analysis.

IM-284

The average compliance with court-ordered conditions of probation in each county was as follows.

County	Percentage
Maricopa	46
Multnomah	33
Philadelphia	51

IM-285

Because only 41 percent of court-ordered conditions were met before probation ended and courts generally did not monitor compliance, all States should have an information system which would indicate probationers' compliance with conditions of sentence. The percentage of court conditions met also indicates a need for better probation department management.

Some improvements were being made to insure that court conditions were met. For example, Multnomah County recently initiated a computerized listing of the account status of those probationers sentenced to pay fines and restitution. Judges receive a monthly report which shows how well probationers whom they sentenced are meeting their obligations.

A similar tracking system has not been developed for monitoring the services that probationers are sentenced to receive. About 78 percent of the Multnomah County judges believed that probationers' compliance with conditions of probation has been only fair or poor, but neither the courts nor the probation department knew the extent of noncompliance with conditions. Information on fines and restitution payments should help probation departments make such determinations.

King County recently began requiring probation officers to write violation reports on all clients who do not comply with court conditions and commit technical violations. The judge then decides what action will be taken.

Following is an example of court conditions not enforced. In August 1973, an offender was sentenced to 5 years probation for burglary and larceny. The court recognized that the offender was a drug addict, and as a condition of probation, directed that the offender be placed in a drug rehabilitation unit and periodic urinalysis reports be provided to the court.

Our review of the case file shows the subject was assigned to the drug unit. The file contained no indication that urinalysis reports were ever provided the court. One year after being placed on probation, the probation officer notified the offender that an appointment had been made for a urinalysis test to comply with the court condition. The subject failed to appear for the scheduled test. In November 1974, the subject was arrested for robbery, theft, unlawful taking, receiving stolen property, criminal conspiracy, possession of a weapon, and violation of the Uniform Firearms Act. He was held for trial, and at the time of our review, a detainer was in force pending disposition of the new charges.

Allowing probationers to continue or complete probation once they have violated the basic conditions of probation seriously interferes with rehabilitation. Under these conditions, repeat offenders do not take conditions of probation seriously.

Service delivery inadequate

Probationers needed various services, but those that needed rehabilitation did not participate in relevant programs which might have helped meet those needs. Each county supplied a different amount of services.

We determined probationers' needs, participation in programs, and reception of services, by analyzing such information in case files as pre-sentence reports, court-imposed conditions, psychiatric diagnoses, and

TOTAL IDENTIFIED NEEDS SATISFIED

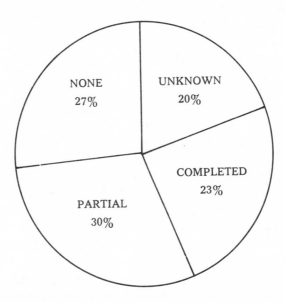

[B6532]

probation officer progress summaries. However, we cannot be sure that we identified all needs; for example, as noted on page 21, only about 14 percent of closed cases received a formal diagnosis. We did not determine the quality of the services provided.

The following graph shows the percentage of the major needs (medical, mental, academic, vocational, employment, alcohol and drug abuse rehabilitation, and counseling) that were satisfied for the 900 probationers sampled.

Only about 23 percent of identified needs were satisfied in that an offender completed a treatment program.

The average percentage of services completed in each of the counties is shown below.

County	Percentage
Maricopa	19%
Multnomah	21
Philadelphia	26

IM–336

The following table shows how many probationers had specific service needs and how many completed participation.

Services Provided to Probationers

| Service | Cases of identified need | Number participating | | | Percent of participation [a] |
		Unknown	Partial or none	Complete	
Medical evaluation and treatment	103	27	34	47	58
Mental health service	142	28	77	37	32
Academic education	225	44	153	28	15
Vocational training	250	59	144	47	25
Employment (securing and keeping)	520	89	288	143	33
Alcohol programs	124	24	78	22	22
Drug programs	226	37	142	47	25
Counseling (group and individual)	156	46	85	25	23
Total	1,751	354	1,001	396	28

a. Considers only known cases. Probation officials attributed the low participation (complete for only 28 percent of known cases) to probationers' lack of motivation and probation officers' excessive caseloads. Although services were not always delivered nor programs always attended, probation officers did make referrals to service agencies. For example, probationers had been referred to service agencies for treatment of at least 602 of their 1,751 identified needs (34 percent).

IM–337

Detailed analysis of the sampled cases shows that probationers generally had problems in the following areas—employment, academic education, vocational training, drugs, alcohol, and mental health.

Lack of employment opportunities

Of the 900 probationers, at the time of arrest,

—363, or 40 percent, were unemployed.

—377, or 42 percent, were employed.

—65, or 7 percent, were not considered employable.

—For 95, or 11 percent, employment was unknown.

At the completion or termination of probation:

—329, or 37 percent, were unemployed.

—417, or 46 percent, were employed.

—22, or 2 percent, were not considered employable.

—For 132, or 15 percent, employment was unknown.

The lack of job opportunities in most locations we reviewed limited the effectiveness of employment services. Unemployment rates were high and the types of jobs available to probationers were limited. For example, the seasonally adjusted unemployment rate for January 1975 was 9.6 percent in Maricopa County.

In the four States we visited, the unemployment rate for offenders was higher than the seasonally adjusted unemployment rate for the area. For example, while the unemployment rate for the Portland metropolitan area was 6.3 percent in December 1974, the unemployment rate for all offenders supervised by the Portland corrections division was 21 percent.

Many probationers were employed as waitresses, farmhands, and general laborers. While jobs were available for clerks, professionals, salespersons and manufacturing and construction workers, most of these require particular skill, professional training, or education to qualify.

Limited academic education and vocational training

The lack of marketable skills has limited probationers' ability to obtain employment. However, most probationers do not complete academic education or vocational training programs.

Of the 250 probationers we identified as needing vocational training, 37 percent were referred to service agencies by probation officers and 8 percent received services from probation officers without further referral. The other 55 percent were either not referred to programs or went on their own. The extent to which the 250 probationers participated in vocational training programs follows:

—34 percent did not participate.

—24 percent participated partially.

—19 percent completed programs.

—Participation of 23 percent could not be determined.

In addition, 225 probationers needed academic education. Probation officers referred only 20 percent of these to service agencies and provided services to only 6 percent. Of the 225 probationers,

—47 percent did not participate in any program,

—22 percent participated partially,

—12 percent completed programs, and

—could not determine the extent to which the remaining 19 percent participated.

The high unemployment among the sample probationers, along with their low incomes, indicates that probationers need special assistance to obtain and compete for available job openings. Educational or remedial programs should help these probationers get jobs.

Drug, alcohol, and mental health problems

Many of the probationers included in our sample of 900 closed cases had drug, alcohol, or mental health problems that were not adequately treated. The following table shows the extent to which the 492 identified needs were treated.

Service	Cases of identified need	Referrals		Service completions	
		Number	*Percent*	*Number*	*Percent*
Drug program	226	116	51.3	47	20.8
Alcohol program	124	54	43.6	22	17.7
Mental health service	142	68	47.9	37	26.1
Total	492	238	48.4	106	21.5

IM–338

The reasons why probationers failed show the importance of addressing these needs. Analysis of 350 probationers who failed in 3 counties showed that many had drug, alcohol, or mental health problems that were insufficiently treated. While 273 treatment needs were identified among the 350 offenders who failed on probation, overall only 15 percent (41) of the needs were completely met. Service needs were adequately handled for 13 percent of drug problems, 11 percent of alcohol problems, and 22 percent of mental health problems.

CURRENT PROBATIONERS ALSO NOT RECEIVING SERVICES

To determine if probation services had improved since the closed cases were sampled, we also examined 200 active cases. About 65 percent of these active cases were not first-time offenders, compared with 63 percent of the 900 closed cases for which we obtained information. Service delivery has improved somewhat; however, a systematic assessment of all probationers' needs is still lacking, as is sufficient probationer participation in available rehabilitative programs.

Employment

When arrested, 50 percent of the 200 probationers were unemployed; 39 percent were unemployed at the time of our analysis.

One reason for these high unemployment rates is the probationers' lack of marketable skills. Only about 25 percent of the active probationers who were employed when arrested had jobs which could be classed as professional, semiprcfessional, skilled labor, or semiskilled labor. This rate is similar to the 26 percent for closed cases. Although 57 percent of the active probationers and 56 percent of the closed cases were either unemployed or held common labor jobs when arrested, only 12 percent in both cases had learned a job skill.

Academic and vocational

Although many probationers needed academic education or vocational training to successfully complete probation, few had completed services to satisfy these needs at the time of our review. Overall 37 percent (73) of the active cases needed vocational training and 31 percent (61) needed academic education. However, at the time of our analysis, 52 percent and 41 percent, respectively, of those needing services had participated in vocational training and academic education. Only 18 percent and 11 percent, respectively, had completed vocational training and academic education. The participation of 11 probationers is not known.

Drugs, alcohol, and mental health

The majority of closed cases sampled failed probation. Many of these had drug, alcohol, or mental health problems that were inadequately handled. Many of the active probationers had similar needs that were not being sufficiently met. For example, the table shows how many were referred for treatment.

Service	Cases of identified need	Referrals	
		Number	*Percent*
Drug	62	33	53
Alcohol	27	18	67
Mental health	43	28	65
Total	132	79	60

IM–296

The extent to which those referred will complete their treatment is unknown because they are still on probation and receiving services.

CONCLUSIONS

Our study showed that services provided do lead to success on probation. Therefore, probation departments should try to provide probationers with as many of the needed services as possible. At the same time, probation depends on the probationer's being positively motivated to (1) cooperate with his probation officer and (2) avail himself of the various supportive services.

Federal, State, and local probation officials stressed the importance of probation and supportive services to the corrections system. The following chapter discusses problems which limit the delivery of services.

THE SAN FRANCISCO PROJECT: A CRITIQUE *

It has not been established that the rise in reported crime reflects basic changes in American people. It is apparent, however, that seldom in the history of our country has such a majority of law-abiding citizens been so acutely aware of crime and so concerned with its remediation. It is a concern that embraces our political system, increasing our interest in the effectiveness of crime control approaches. In view of heightened public concern, research in probation and parole can no longer be regarded as a luxury; it is essential to improve program effectiveness and to increase public confidence in these processes.

Research is costly and funds for research in probation and parole have been limited. It is important, therefore, that we make our research investments wisely. In 1964 a major research effort, the *San Francisco Project*[1] was undertaken. Because the final project report revealed methodological uncertainties and equivocal results, a critique might reveal some valuable lessons for guidance in future research investments.

---

* William P. Adams, Paul M. Chandler and M. G. Neithercutt, *Federal Probation,* December, 1971. Reprinted with permission.

1. Joseph V. Lohman, G. Albert Wahl and Robert M. Carter, *The San Francisco Project*, Berkeley: University of California, April 1965.

On June 1, 1964, the National Institute of Mental Health awarded a $275,000 grant to the School of Criminology, University of California, Berkeley for research in probation and parole. Funded for four years, the project began September 1, 1964. As then conceived, the main goals of the project were:

1. Develop discriminating criteria for the classification of federal offenders.

2. Study the effects of varied intensities and types of supervision and caseload sizes.

3. Develop a prediction table for supervision adjustment.

4. Examine decision making in presentence recommendations.

Despite its unique aspects, the San Francisco Project was more replicative than innovative. As early as 1952, for example, the California Department of Corrections commenced research with variations in caseload size and supervision.

The San Francisco Project was carried out in the U.S. probation office of the Northern District of California with headquarters in San Francisco and offices in Sacramento and Oakland. Study population problems arose during the research when the Eastern District of California was created, removing a large number of cases from the original project.

During Phase I of the research, data were gathered on almost all offenders received for presentence investigation and released for supervision from federal institutions. Data collection forms were key punched for machine tabulating. While data gathering was proceeding, extensive changes were made in caseload assignments. Based on the 50-unit workload concept,[2] four levels of supervision were established.

There were two *Ideal* caseloads, each containing about 40 supervision cases and two presentence investigations per month, approximating the 50-unit concept. The *Intensive* caseload represented half that standard, with two officers assigned to it, each having a supervision load of 20 and one presentence investigation per month. The *Ideal* cases were to receive supervision on the basis of at least two contacts per individual per month while the *Intensive* caseloads required contacts once weekly.

The *Normal* caseloads consisted of the usual workload in the Northern District of California which had been averaging about 100 work units per month. Since some cases were syphoned off to the other caseloads, and one *Minimum* supervision load was established (consisting of approxi-

---

2. See *Manual of Correctional Standards*, New York: The American Correctional Association, 1962, p. 510. For a different standard consult *The Challenge of Crime in a Free Society.*

mately 350 cases and no presentence investigations), the *Normal* caseloads were diminished in size.[3]

In Phase I of the project, clients for the various caseloads were chosen from the existing loads and from newly received probationers and parolees randomly. These random assignments to all caseloads were made from September 1964 to June 1967 with a few exceptions representing special problems.[4]

In Phase II, beginning June 1, 1967, the policy on case assignment was changed from randomness to selection based on four factors.

PROBATION SUPERVISION

A variety of activities is included in "probation supervision," ranging from surveillance through group counseling to psychoanalysis. In the San Francisco Project reference is made, interchangeably, to *types, kinds,* and *intensities* of supervision. At no point, however, were the characteristics of differing types of supervision identified. During the period of research no extraordinary treatment programs were in progress. Types or kinds of supervision remained dependent upon the styles of individual officers. With one exception, to be discussed later, no qualitative distinction was made among the styles of individual officers. To the contrary, anonymity was ensured and an effort was limited to measurement of different intensities of supervision.

In dealing with these different intensities the number of contacts the officer had with each client was approximately[5] documented. The quality of these contacts was ignored. In keeping with the methodological components of the research, an officer maintaining *Intensive* supervision might see a person four times each month, for 10 minutes per contact. An officer providing *Ideal* supervision might see the individual twice each month, for an hour each time. The measurement used, therefore, not only failed to deal with quality but provided a poor "measure" of quantity (simple time exposure to supervision).[6]

THE SELECTION PHASE

As the shift was made from the random phase to the selection phase of the research, individuals were assigned on the basis of a four-factor

Washington: U. S. Government Printing Office, 1967, p. 167.

3. Normal caseload sizes were quite variable. For instance, during the study one of the authors determined the range to be 70 to 130 supervision cases plus an unknown number of investigations.

4. No substantive estimate of the number and characteristics of these cases appears to be available.

5. The word "approximately" is used here because this documentation depended on entries in records maintained by several different persons. No reliability checks, audits, etc., were used so the data depended almost exclusively on officer attention to detail.

6. Note that time exposure to an officer is an illusive index too. For instance, some officers spend half the time a client is in the office talking to someone else on the telephone.

profile to the four levels of supervision—*Intensive, Ideal, Normal,* and *Minimum.* Because data from the earlier phase of the project were not definitive, selection of the four factors was based upon knowledge derived from other sources.

Individual offenders were given profile numbers of 1, 2, or 3, in each of the categories *type of offense, age,* and *prior record,* and 1 or 3 on the basis of the Socialization Scale (CPI–SO) from the *California Psychological Inventory.* There were 54 possible profiles ranging from 1–1–1–1 to 3–3–3–3, the higher numbers representing those believed to have a higher recidivism probability.

In deciding which of the profile groups should be assigned to the various levels of supervision the "expert-judge" technique was employed. This technique is accepted in social science research, but loss of precision is inherent in its use. Generally the "expert-judge" technique employs a minimum of three "judges" making independent choices and some method to integrate their decisions. In the San Francisco Project only one such "judge" was used. One can speculate endlessly on what characteristics such a judge should have—long, successful, and recent field experience, finely tuned administrative skills, extensive familiarity with correctional research practices, etc. The point is: No one man is likely to be an adequate "judge."

To explore what losses might be experienced because of the application of the "expert-judge" technique, consider for a moment, a familiar federal offender, the postal employee embezzler. If over 40 years of age and scoring within an arbitrary range on the CPI–SO, this offender would have a profile of 1–1–1–1, the lowest recidivism probability.

Such offenders frequently fall into the "ritualist" category in Merton's classification of deviant behavior.[7] On the basis of the "expert-judge" decision, and with conformity as a singular measure, such offenders were placed on minimum supervision. True, in most instances they continued to conform and complete probation "successfully." Not known, however, is how many of these offenders returned to tight patterns of conformity with no increased realization of personal freedom. How many became mental health casualties? With existing criteria they were regarded simply as probation successes.

MINIMUM SUPERVISION: RANDOM PHASE

Minimum supervision has, de facto, been the rule in probation for years, a byproduct of limited appropriations. The San Francisco Project established minimum supervision caseloads by design and much of its evaluative effort focused on this caseload.

During the random phase a representative group of clients were assigned to a single, large caseload. They were not told the nature of the

7. Robert K. Merton, "Social Structure   New York: Harcourt, Brace and Company, 1949, p. 775.
   and Anomie," *Sociological Analysis.*   pany, 1949, p. 775.

supervision they were to have, but were encouraged to contact the probation office if they wished assistance. During an initial interview they received instructions regarding travel limitations and required written monthly reports. Following the initial interview no contact was initiated by the probation office unless monthly reports were absent or certain events, such as an arrest, came to the attention of the probation office. In such cases contacts were assigned to a staff probation officer on the basis of availability. If assistance with a specific problem was sought, that matter was assigned to a staff officer in like manner. Many persons on minimum supervision did take the initiative in making contact.

Excluding technical violations, the violation rate for the minimum supervision caseload was reported as not significantly different from that of other caseloads. The inherent weaknesses of the violation index as a measure of probation success preclude any conclusions, however. Whether this group did or did not do any better than the others is unknown, but an inference worthy of closer attention emerges from the data.

The probability that the talents and time of probation officers might be more efficiently trained on specific needs, as opposed to making routine contacts, awaits verification or rejection through future research efforts. If, at the outset of supervision, a climate of trust and confidence is established, it seems more likely that clients will seek the assistance of a probation officer before permitting their personal adjustment to deteriorate to the point of probation or parole violation. No available evidence documents that routine contacts without goals will increase such a possibility. Clearly needed is closer attention to understanding and measuring the quality, not the quantity, of supervision.

MINIMUM SUPERVISION: SELECT PHASE

During the select phase of research a large minimum supervision caseload was formed with individuals having a low violation probability. The four-factor profile was used. This caseload was assigned to an officer who developed his own management techniques. After the select phase commenced, individuals with other than low profile scores were transferred to this caseload as a result of judgments made by officers who, until such transfers, provided them with other levels of attention.[8]

Considerable information was lost during the evaluation of the select phase of minimum supervision, due, in part, to the fact that much of the collected data had not been stored properly. It appears that the loss of such documentation led, to some extent, to fantasy levels of evaluation

8. Separating these persons to control for possible contaminating effect evidently is not possible. The type of outcome distortion likely through this transfer procedure is obvious; clients transferred to minimum supervision likely would be a highly selected (for

such as reference to the "Superman"[9] qualities needed in an officer handling such a caseload.

If the violation index were valid and reliable, the reported 11.5 percent rate of violation for this group, compared to higher rates of violation for other groups, would, nevertheless, be meaningless because no control group of comparable selectivity receiving other levels of attention existed. The possibility remains that a group with a high recidivism probability might do best under minimum supervision or that persons with low recidivism probability might have even lower violation rates with closer attention.

The violation rate reported for the select group under minimum supervision becomes further suspect when it is noted, in the final report, that the officer periodically reviewed the individual cases, moving for early termination of supervision when he deemed appropriate. No criteria are provided to show under what circumstances early termination was considered appropriate. It is obvious that violation rates can be reduced to nil by terminating cases soon enough. They can also be influenced by computation techniques.[10]

In contrast to the effort made to avoid identification of individual supervision techniques in other aspects of the research project, attention was given to the approach developed by "Mr. X," the officer handling select phase minimum supervision. He attempted to establish clearly the "ground rules" for supervision. His intent was to create a "contract" detailing appropriate performance for the individual under supervision and reciprocal assistance from the probation officer. One purpose was to eliminate a sense of manipulation and shift some responsibility to the client. This could be important because it emphasizes one of the essential ingredients in a reintegration process—that of experiencing responsibility. In reviewing reports on this phase of the research one wonders, however, how consistent intent and practice were when "Mr. X" refers to knowledge not shared by the probationer/parolee as his "hole card," and says "I'll use every bloody tool I have available to get them to meet the contract."

It remains a distinct possibility, as suggested by the San Francisco Project design, that probation supervision caseloads can be organized to improve the use by well trained and highly educated probation officers of

"success") group compared to the general population.

9. James L. Robison, Leslie T. Wilkins, Robert M. Carter, and G. Albert Wahl, *The San Francisco Project Final Report*. Berkeley: University of California, April 1969, p. 60.

10. An example of this is apparent on page 63 of the *Final Report* (Robison, loc. cit.). There the "11½ percent" violation rate is computed by dividing number of cases permanently removed from minimum supervision as successes (124) into number of cases in which warrants were issued or where the closing was "by violation" (14). However 17 of the permanent removals were by transfer, so these were neither success nor failure cases. A transfer is not a termination. This makes the "violation rate" 13.1 percent without any change in client performance.

their effort and concern. In the process it might be determined that through appropriate selectivity many persons can safely be assigned to large, minimally supervised caseloads, and benefit from infrequent attention. One cannot infer, however, that meaningful selection can be made upon age, type of offense, prior record, or results from a psychological test that were not delivered to the computer for evaluation.

VIOLATION INDEX AS A MEASURE OF SUCCESS

To become definitive, social research, like research in the physical sciences, requires criteria for measurement. The complex processes of probation and parole are so poorly understood that methods for evaluation often are illusive. The tendency is to focus upon the obvious, the believed level of subsequent law violations, as a measure of success.

A violation index was developed for the San Francisco Project relating the number of persons with unfavorable terminations to the number of persons with favorable terminations and during the second phase of the research, lumping all persons still active on supervision and having completed 24 months of supervision, with the favorable termination group. Therefore, completion of 24 months on supervision became equivalent to success. No information provided indicated the 24-month period has a relationship to successful community adjustment. It is an arbitrary figure, probably determined more by sample size needs than by the social phenomena.

Use of the violation index established conformity as a measure of success. Probation and parole embrace many complexities; they span human personality interacting with society. If the rate of subsequent law violations were a valid measure of these complex processes, controlled, scientific application of such an index would be essential for the development of reliable information. With the application of the outcome rate, several variables came into play without sufficient control, interfering seriously with the credibility of the findings.

During the random phase of research, with the technical violations excluded, the violation rates reported for the *Minimum* and *Ideal* caseloads were 22.2 percent and for the *Intensive* caseload, 20.0 percent. This represented no significant difference.[11] Including technical violations the violation rate for the *Intensive* group was 37.5 percent, for the *Minimum* group, 22.2 percent and *Ideal* group, 24.3 percent. Persons under supervision at the time of this evaluation had been exposed to the possibility of unfavorable terminations for significantly different periods of time. The project evaluation approach was supported with the statement, "It is believed that the first six to twelve months of supervision are generally the most critical in terms of violation rates." That appears a potentially hazardous assumption, especially since it is not tested in the project.[12]

11. Robison, loc. cit., p. 6.

12. For an assessment of by-month violation rates during the first year of pa-

The first 6, or the first 12 months of supervision might be the most critical in terms of violations but the use of a generalized assumption, without clearer statistical distinctions, to include in the computations persons with significantly different periods of time under supervision, and the failure to deal statistically with the violation potentials beyond a 12-month period for those persons, causes a loss of confidence in the results of those computations.

The various caseloads, during the random selections phase, were comparable initially in some respect such as *age, prior record,* and *type of offense* but significantly different in other areas, such as *family criminality, occupational skills, sex,* and *education.* The implication here is that violation rates were compared across groups dissimilar in some characteristics which may have substantial impact upon community adjustment. The existence of some of the differences has been acknowledged in report form but these differences are described as unsystematic. In fact, if one scrutinizes the six variables in which the three caseloads differ significantly, four of them indicate the intensive caseloads to be disadvantaged and on only one is the minimum caseload prejudiced.

Two important factors affecting violation rates were *early terminations,* representing success, and *termination by warrant,* representing failure. Successful termination is usually the product of agency machinery, whereas unsuccessful termination is likely the result of specific behavior on the part of individuals under supervision. Had the violation index been applied to groups with comparable percentages of favorable terminations (holding number of violators constant), the adjusted violation rates would have been 10.5 percent for the *Minimum* group and 20.9 percent for the *Ideal* group compared to 37.5 percent for the *Intensive* group. Apparently, then, during the random phase the caseloads differed significantly on outcome, albeit not in the direction that might have been anticipated.[13] This difference devolves mainly from the fact that the various modes of supervision differed very significantly on number of cases terminated successfully as well as unsuccessfully.

Termination by issuance of a warrant occurs most often from the commission of new offenses. The second most frequent cause is failure to meet the conditions of probation or parole. Since probation officers differ significantly in recommendations on judgments and the courts are influenced by officer recommendations, decisions concerning the issuance of warrants may be influenced by a variety of supervision philosophies.[14] Deliberate effort to avoid identification of particular officer styles in the research fostered loss of control over this potentially important variable.

role supervision in a heterogeneous parole population. See *Uniform Parole Reports Newsletter*: Davis, California. National Council on Crime and Delinquency Research Center, April 1970, pp. 2–4.

13. The reader is cautioned to take these analyses cautiously. The comparisons on outcome are based on a total of 87 cases (18 from the minimum group, 37 from the ideal, and 32 from the intensive).

14. See "The Decision Making Process" which follows.

Early termination of supervision results largely from an officer's awareness and evaluation of an individual's community adjustment. Except in cases with special conditions, no criteria have been established for early termination so such actions depend largely upon the initiative of the individual officer. Two clients making similar adjustments might have had substantially different chances to be terminated from supervision early, particularly if one had close attention under *Intensive* supervision, and the other had little attention under *Minimum* supervision. Again, inadequate accounting of an important variable raises serious questions about the reliability of the violation index.

The final report, perhaps the most useful of the series, suggested that the high rate of technical violations for persons under *Intensive* supervision probably resulted from officer awareness of activities. Further investigation might unearth some entirely different reasons. Consider at least another possibility. Traditionally in America, imposition of authority is not assimilated easily, even by the essentially law-abiding. Understanding this, entertain the possibility that the higher number of technical violations for persons under *Intensive* supervision resulted as expressions of defiance in response to the frequent authoritative intrusions into their lives. Such a possibility applies to all violations, not technical violations alone.

Emile Durkheim, the 19th century sociologist, suggested that crime serves a social function. If this is so, perhaps by encouraging new violations our correctional processes have assured society of a criminal population. This might appear preposterous, but the efficiency with which our institutional programs have functioned in that direction remains. The "revolving door" jail treatment of skid row alcoholics intensifies rather than interrupts losses of self-respect. Such "treatment" has virtually guaranteed a supply of drunks for our city streets. Many persons are employed revolving the doors and, by offering objects for comparison, these inebriates have given many persons reason to feel better about themselves.

THE DECISION–MAKING PROCESS

Probation officers make decisions affecting clients and communities. A goal of the San Francisco Project was to examine the practice of officers making sentencing recommendations to the court. In the Northern District of California, probation officers recommend criminal case disposition and the courts "follow" these suggestions in about nine of 10 cases.

The "decision game" described by Wilkins [15] was used with 14 United States probation officers stationed in San Francisco. Five cases in which presentence reports had been prepared were analyzed and classified under 24 subject headings. The information was typed on 4" by 6" cards with a

15. Leslie T. Wilkins, *Social Deviance: Social Policy, Action and Research.* Englewood Clifts, N. J.: Prentice Hall, 1965, pp. 294–304.

title on the lower edge, the cards being arranged in a binder for each case so that only the title showed. Each officer was asked to "conduct" the presentence investigation by selecting the information he wished to use. After each selection the officer was asked if he could make a recommendation. The researcher encouraged an early decision and recorded the selections and recommendations. After a decision was made the officer was asked to select three more cards and state whether he wanted to change his recommendation.

On the average, these probation officers selected 4.7 cards prior to decision. *Offense* and *Prior Record* were selected in every case. Six other categories, *Psychological/Psychiatric, Defendant's Statement, Defendant's Attitude, Employment History, Age,* and *Family History* being selected more than half of the time.[16] Decisions, therefore, were based on but few of the 24 factors contained in the presentence report and the additional information seldom changed recommendations. The researchers concluded that much of the information gathered in the investigation was not used in arriving at a recommendation.

The research failed to recognize that the eight categories most often chosen were likely to include information which the investigators indicated was little used. For example, the three separate categories of drug use, homosexuality, and alcoholic involvement were chosen by the officers less than 20 percent of the time, but these are items which are usually found, if present, in the psychological/psychiatric section which was chosen in the 80 percent range. The *Family History* category, chosen more than half the time, could conceivably contain almost all of the pertinent data about the offender. Nearly one-third of the 24 items were selected in the less than 10 percent range but included are such facts as race, religion, and place of birth. While these may be important for identification, or for other reasons, it is hoped and expected that they would have little or no relevance to sentencing. Thus even a casual inspection of the distribution of the information items indicates that the suggestion that a small amount of information is used in decision making is misleading.

There are other uses of the presentence report besides determination of the sentence barely acknowledged in the research reports. Presentence reports may be used both as a guide for supervision and a basis for classification and treatment by institutions. For example, the Bureau of Prisons would perhaps find an evaluation of the individual's educational adjustment very significant in its attempts to develop a meaningful treatment program, although this item was rated, according to the study, at about the midpoint in decision making for sentencing. Obviously the importance of the data relates to the use to which it is to be put. While some of the data collected and recorded by the probation officer may not

16. Joseph D. Lohman, G. Albert Wahl, and Robert M. Carter, *Decision Making and the Probation Officer.* Berkeley: University of California, June 1966, pp. 7, 10.

have significant immediate use in sentencing, he is usually in the best position to glean that information which may be of significance in the correctional process.

Two of the five cases were chosen as being clear-cut, one leading to probation, the other to confinement. In these cases there was perfect agreement among all 14 officers. The other three cases generated a wide range of opinion. In case four, for example, five officers recommended imprisonment, two probation, four split-sentence, and two county jail terms.[17] Given the evidence that there is substantial agreement among probation officers' recommendations and the actual sentence imposed, these data were interpreted as suggesting that disparity in sentencing, usually attributed to judges, may be influenced considerably by probation officers.

Because two of the cases were of the "open and shut" variety, decisions using limited categories of information were invited. To generalize about levels of information usage on the basis of five cases from a universe of thousands is indefensible; to do so when two of the five have been chosen to drive information usage down is worse. Further, officers were instructed to make decisions on as little information as possible; this constraint being the opposite of working conditions.

Minimum documentation needed here is a separate tabulation of the number of factors considered in cases really requiring a decision. Also, it is not wise to imply that because, on the average, only a few factors are used in making most decisions, no data beyond those are needed.[18] Rather, one is better advised to look at the most demanding cases decision-wise and see what they require. This would mean looking at the top of the range of factors. Here that number is 13, suggesting that the "efficiency level" may be rather high.

The statement, ". . . it appears certain that the data most significant (for decision) are the items of information most often initially collected by probation officers . . . as well as being information which serves as the basis for presentence report recommendations,"[19] is unrealistic. Those items initially collected depend on what is in the case folder at assignment. The referral sheet has the name, address, offense, possible sentence, names of codefendants, custody status, sentencing judge, plea, date of plea, date of judgment, court officer's initials, and miscellaneous comments. Sometimes there is an arrest record; often there is not. These items initially collected mostly seem to have little or no bearing on judgment. Also, because the fact gathering process is fairly routinized at referral, what an officer asks for first or second may be more a matter of habit than anything else. The fact that "confinement status," though highly correlated with sentence, is seldom asked for

17. Ibid., p. 14. The total is less than 14,   18. Ibid., p. 16.
    for one officer who recognized his own
    work was excluded.   19. Ibid., pp. 18–19.

in the decision game setting suggests pitfalls inherent in this sort of analysis.

While the authors of the San Francisco Project intimate that these findings document inefficiency in the presentence process, the data presented hardly support a dogmatic stance. The relationship between playing at decision making and actually confronting problems in the field remains a mystery. For example, "Research Report Number Seven" notes that in the decision game officers ". . . did not have to go into the field to verify information such as employment . . .."[20] Apparent is the potential value of such verification, though, because official employment reports are notoriously misleading. That report also states ". . . participants were allowed to 'gather' information or 'conduct' the presentence investigation in any way they desired . . .."[21] As the report unfolds, however, it becomes apparent that the only latitude in the decision game was freedom to choose cards in any preferred order.

What does one do when two pieces of information conflict? What happens when the official version of the offense and the defendant's version are not reconcilable? There are no victims in the cards to be contacted and cryptic paper entries give few clues to their veracity. Who judges the "defendant's attitude"? Is he truly hostile or terribly frightened?

If the implications of this research are correct, presentence investigations could be conducted by case aides and computers at greatly reduced cost and with increased efficiency. If that be true, though, what of the vital relationships—often established between probation officer and offender during the presentence process—that are difficult to establish afterward? What if efforts to get the offender moving in a positive direction at the time when he seems susceptible to change are delayed? The "evidence" presented suggesting that probation decision making is a simple mechanical process is less than overwhelming. It fails to account for the personal "chemistry" between client and officer, the intuitive process that each officer uses to evaluate his cases, and the fitting of pieces together in understanding the offender.

IMPACT OF SUPERVISION

A valuable contribution to the San Francisco Project has been provided by Arthur E. Elliot, then supervisor of social work students training at the San Francisco probation office. Mr. Elliot wished to sample the effects of the project from the clients' point of view. His work on supervision impact was primarily intuitive and interpretive, but employed a systematic approach.

---

20. Ibid., p. 5.   **21.** Ibid., p. 5.

The aims of the study included:

1. Ascertaining the offender's view of probation or parole.

2. Determining the probation officer's concept of his role in supervision.

3. Obtaining information about supervision from persons close to offenders.

Standardized interviews were held in cases terminated successfully between September 1, 1966, and June 1, 1967. The sample contained 100 offenders, 71 of them probationers.[22]

While attitudes and experiences of successful cases may differ from those of failures, other characteristics of the sample generally paralleled the project population. It should be noted, however, that more than 40 percent of Mr. Elliot's sample had no prior record, a circumstance suggesting the group had fewer negative experiences with law enforcement than a general sample of offenders. An earlier report in the project series indicated that 26.6 percent of a sample of 500 had no prior records.[23]

There are some highly suggestive findings in Mr. Elliot's work which may be of use to the probation officer. First, there was a high degree of consensus between offender and officer regarding offender problems and available pertinent resources. This would seem a good omen for a favorable counseling relationship. The study indicated, however, that seldom was there a long-range, well-developed plan of supervision. Counseling generally focused on specific assistance requested by the client and was, of course, limited by the time and skill of the officer. In addition, much time was spent in general contact which was of questionable use to the client. Perhaps these factors explain why only 10 percent of the offenders said probation officers contributed significantly to their supervision success.

Of those who received *Intensive* treatment, not one named the probation officer as important in his adjustment. To the offenders the most important aspect of successful adjustment was assistance from family or friends, followed by having a basically non-criminal orientation. Employment and emotional growth also received priority consideration. Fear of further legal action was considered less important by the study group in preventing further criminal activity.

The results were in close agreement with the probation officer's analysis of his own work. Here is a clue, it appears, to explain why intensive supervision did not seem to reduce the rate of violation. Perhaps it is not the number of contacts but rather the *quality* of work that is vital.

22. Joseph D. Lohman, G. Albert Wahl, Robert M. Carter, and Arthur E. Elliot, *The Impact of Supervision: Officer and Offender Assessment.* Berkeley: University of California, September 1967, pp. 7 & 10.

23. Ibid., p. 27.

Despite pessimistic evaluations of the supervision process, most offenders and their families agreed that positive changes occurred during supervision. However, 15 percent felt there were no changes while another 10 percent believed they had more problems than before. Some improvements were noted in the fields of emotional maturity, family relationships, and employment.

Despite the low regard offenders voiced for their probation officers' contributions to their success, it is interesting to note that 60 percent of the clients rated supervision as "helpful." Some reported specific activity of the probation officer which was helpful while others saw the probation structure itself as assisting in their good adjustment.

Among those who indicated they had not benefited from supervision there was a tendency to claim competence to manage one's own affairs and to see probation as interference. There was a general feeling that the shock of apprehension and court appearances was a specific deterrent.

Of particular interest to line officers is the relationship between the offender and the probation officer. Many social caseworkers feel positive relationships in corrections are difficult or impossible to attain because of the authoritarian setting. In this study more than two-thirds of the offenders had negative ideas about the probation officers prior to contact with the agency. Officers were assumed to be harsh, punitive, critical, moralistic, and enforcement minded. Sixty-seven of the 70 offenders (96 percent) with this view, however, changed their minds after actual contact with their supervising officers. Most offenders reported forming a satisfactory relationship.

It is unfortunate that this part of the research was not extended to persons receiving minimum supervision. Views of the supervision experience from those persons compared to individuals receiving other levels of attention might provide clues to meaningful changes in the administration of probation. Offenders are capable of insights into correctional processes, and, by virtue of their experiences, can teach much with their observations and evaluations.

A THEORETICAL FRAMEWORK NEEDED

Review of the San Francisco Project reveals that method and direction were sought after the research was initiated. In the final report it is suggested that the original design was too ambitious. The absence of a well-developed theoretical framework resulted in lack of orientation and loss of efficiency.

There is yet no integrated theory of corrections.[24] Lacking such, difficulty in evaluating correctional processes, including the process of probation and parole, continues. Corrections embraces many complexi-

24. T. C. Esselstyn, "The Social System of Correctional Workers," *Crime and Delinquency*, April 1966, p. 117.

ties, yet in the San Francisco Project, a relatively simple concept of conformity, never clearly defined, is the focal measure of supervision outcome.[25]

The San Francisco Project found early inspiration from some provocative questions posed by the late sociologist and lawyer Paul Tappan, who asked, "What part of our probation caseloads could have done as well merely on a suspended sentence without any supervision?"[26] He suggested the need for developing discriminating criteria for classifying offenders into categories: those who do not require probation, those who require differing degrees of supervision, and those who require highly professionalized services.[27]

Robert K. Merton, a contemporary sociologist noted for having attained an unusual balance between theory construction and empirical research, recalls that a 17th century columnist, John Aubrey, reported "Dr. Pell was wont to say that in the Solution of Questions, the Main Matter was the well-stating of them; which requires mother-witt and logic . . . for let the question be but well-stated, it will work almost of itself."[28] In responding to the questions posed by Professor Tappan, the San Francisco Project moved too rapidly from speculation to attempted experimentation, and failed to state well the problems to be solved. There was insufficient clarity in exploring doing "as well." No definition was given to the "requirements" which might be met through differing types and degrees of supervision. In future probation research we must endeavor to identify and state well the problems to be solved; this will require a good measure of mother wit and logic.

PROBATION PREDICTION MODELS

[Editor's Note. The following chapter is excerpted from *State and County Probation: Systems in Crisis,* a Report to the Congress by the Comptroller General of the United States, May 27, 1976.

[The *Report* attempted to determine if probation activities—sentencing, planning, diagnosis and treatment and delivery of services—were being effectively managed. Adult felon probation services were studied

25. Items on which the alleged randomly assigned cases differed significantly by supervision level have been enumerated. Outcome factors on which they were significantly different include prior convictions, persons returned to federal custody as violators, time under supervision and monthly earnings under supervision. Any (or all) of these serves as an alternate outcome index. The clear tendency here, too, is for the intensive cases to fare poorly consistently.

26. Paul W. Tappan, *Crime, Justice and Correction*, New York: McGraw-Hill, 1960, p. 584.

27. Ibid.

28. Robert K. Merton, "Notes on Problem-Finding in Sociology," *Sociology Today*. New York: Basic Books, Inc., 1959, p. IX.

in Maricopa County, Arizona; Multnomah County, Oregon; Philadelphia County, Pennsylvania; and King County, Washington, to determine:

—Whether the Law Enforcement Assistance Administration (LEAA), the States, and the county probation departments were addressing the problems of developing probation systems that insure the public's safety and enable offenders to remain in the community and receive rehabilitation services.

—How much the services received by probationers increased their chances of successfully completing probation.

—Whether systems existed to identify individuals with good chances of completing probation and remaining out of contact with the criminal justice system and how such systems could be used to improve probation operations.

About 77 percent of the adult criminal offenders in the four counties were sentenced to probation in 1974.]

To focus services and attention on the probationers who need the most help and supervision, better decisionmaking tools are needed. One such tool is the predictive model.

Much criminological research has been focused on estimating the danger to society posed by offenders under the various rehabilitation options. Probation officials must recommend type of sentence, level of supervision, and length of probation. Although a good deal has been written on possible use of statistically based prediction tables as aids or guides, probation administrators and practitioners continue to rely almost solely on personal experience and subjective judgment to make these decisions. The failure to use statistical models appears to stem from doubts about

—validity, that is, whether a model developed in one location for one group of people would be valid in a different location for a different group of people, and

—predictive power, that is, the extent to which probationers' predicted outcomes correspond to their actual outcomes.

We tested the validity and predictive powers of existing models by applying them to the 900 closed cases in Maricopa, Multnomah, and Philadelphia counties.

We determined that:

—The models were transferable between locations. For example, three of the models were valid in each of the locations. Also, each of the other five models was valid or probably valid in at least one of the locations.

—Existing models may be useful in probation decisionmaking even though their predictive powers are less than might be desired. In one county, probationers with high model scores (indicating high potential for success) were 93 percent successful whereas those with low model scores were only 17 percent successful.

—Probation prediction models could improve probation systems operations by allocating resources to offenders who most need help. For example, model scores appeared to be useful in determining supervision levels for probationers. The actual failure rate of probationers receiving minimum supervision in one location was 35 percent, but only 15 percent of those selected by a model for minimum supervision failed. Models more successfully selected probationers for early release.

WHAT ARE PROBATION PREDICTION MODELS?

A probation prediction model is developed by using statistical methods to summarize the characteristics and outcomes of many probationers in such a way that a decisionmaker can forecast probation results for offenders on the basis of their characteristics. When statistical methods are used to predict success of probation, data is analysed objectively, rather than subjectively.

The actual form of a model will vary. The following table shows how a typical model might look. (This model is for illustrative purposes and is not an actual model.)

Illustrative Predictive Model
Individual risk score calculation

Significant characteristics	Value	Score
No history of opiate use	9	9
Family has no criminal record	6	6
Not an alcoholic	6	6
Is married	4	0
No prior arrests	4	4
Total possible score for probationer	29	25

IM–339

Summary risk table

Score	Success rate
23–29	90%
10–22	70
0–9	10

IM–340

To develop such a model, information about the personal and criminal history of a large number of probationers would be obtained. A statistical technique, such as regression analysis, could then be used to identify the characteristics which seem to differentiate the most between successful and unsuccessful probationers. These characteristics become the basis for the model. The weight or importance given to a particular characteristic is also determined statistically.

To use the model, the decisionmaker would obtain information about an individual either through an interview (while preparing a pre-sentence report) or from existing records (prior probation records or criminal records). On the basis of this information, the individual's score would be computed. In the above example, if the individual did not have a history of opiate use, he would receive nine points, if he had such a history, no points for that item. The individual's total score is interpreted in light of past experience with probationers having similar scores, to estimate the likelihood that he will succeed on probation.

In the sample model, an individual who scored 25 points would be considered a very good risk for probation. This information, along with other factors, could be used to decide whether the individual should be recommended for probation, subjected to only minimum supervision, or be released from probation early.

VALIDATING MODELS

One reason usually given for the limited use of models is the need to validate a model, that is, determine its validity. For example, due to differences in group characteristics and experiences, a model that was developed using *parolees* in Arizona may not be predictive of the success or failure of *probationers* in Pennsylvania. We attempted to validate eight existing models—the "Oregon Form," the "Newark, New Jersey Form" developed by Professor Daniel Glaser of the University of Southern California, four models developed by California correction agencies using data on California parolees, and the "Salient Factors Form" developed for use by the Federal Board of Parole.

These eight models were chosen, after a review of many existing models, because they were the only models for which we believed that

data required for testing validity would be readily available from probation case files and criminal records. Of the eight models used, five were
developed for parolees and three for probationers.

How models were validated

After collecting the necessary data for our sampled cases, we computed a score (or category) for each probationer. Additionally, we
classified each case as a success or a failure using our definition of
recidivism.

We then used statistical tests to determine whether the probationer's
model score (or category) correlated significantly with his actual outcome.
The tests (see app. III) indicated that each of the eight models reviewed
was valid in each of the three counties for all probationers whose model
scores and outcomes could be determined. (Some of the 300 probationers
sampled in each county could not be included in our tests because of
incomplete information in case files and criminal records.)

The following table summarizes our conclusions on the validity of the
models for the probation populations reviewed. (The results of our
statistical tests are contained below)

Results of Model Validation

Model	Based on	Multnomah	Maricopa	Philadelphia
I	Oregon Form	Probably	No conclusion	No conclusion
II	Newark Form	Probably	No conclusion	No conclusion
III–A	Glaser Model	Yes	Probably	Probably
IV	California Form 61A	Probably	No conclusion	No conclusion
V–A	California Form 61B	Yes	Yes	Yes
VI–A	California Form 65A	Yes	Yes	Yes
VII–A	Association Analysis	Yes	Yes	Yes
VIII–A	Salient Factors	Yes	Probably	Probably

IM–341

If at least two-thirds of the cases sampled were included in the
statistical test, we concluded that the model tested was valid for the
entire probation population under review (not just those probationers
whose model scores and outcomes could have been determined). If at
least half of the cases sampled were included in the statistical test, we
concluded that the model was probably valid for the entire population. If
less than half the cases sampled could be in the statistical tests, we
reached no conclusion as to the model's validity for the entire population,
even though the model was valid for the subpopulation for whom both
model score and outcome could have been determined.

As shown above, three models were valid in each of the counties reviewed. If more complete information had been available, we would likely have found many of the other models to be valid in each location.

That we were able to validate three of the models in each location visited indicates that many of these models could be validated by local governments if need be. This contention is further supported by our overall results—of 24 possible validations (8 models at 3 locations), we obtained positive results in 46 percent and probable results in 29 percent.

PREDICTIVE POWERS OF MODELS

Even after a valid model is found for a given probation population, decisionmakers hesitate to use it, partly because the models developed to date do not have extremely high predictive powers. However, several studies, including ours, indicate that existing models are sufficiently predictive to be useful in deciding who should be recommended for probation, what level of supervision is needed, and who might be considered for early release.

While we did not make an exhaustive search of the successful users of models, we found three examples that we thought typified how models might be used.

In one use intended to reduce prison confinement costs, a large inmate population was screened, first by a parole model and then by prison personnel. A group of screened inmates were considered for parole at an earlier date than originally scheduled. This resulted in substantial savings in prison costs with no increase in parole violations.

In another prison, giving minimum parole supervision to those predicted by a model to be good risks enabled parole officers to spend more time with other cases without increasing the failure rate.

In a third application, inmates were initially classified using model scores. Inmates in various classifications were provided with varying institutional treatment, some receiving earlier parole consideration. As a result, the prison population was reduced and money was saved.

These three examples relate to parolees rather than probationers; however, the fact that some parole models proved valid in predicting probation outcomes indicates that they might be used for that purpose.

HOW MODELS CAN IMPROVE PROBATION MANAGEMENT

To suggest possible applications by probation offices, we developed examples using model scores to decide who should be recommended for probation, what level of supervision is needed, and who might be released early from probation.

These examples of applications were developed using Model VI–A, one of the three models found to be valid in all of the counties reviewed. Model VI–A is based on California Base Expectancy Form 65A and is shown in the following table.

Model VI–A
California Base Expectancy Form 65A

To obtain raw scores, add

11	for all persons	11
19	if no more than two prior arrests [a]	___
15	if not arrested for 5 years previously	___
14	if no known prior incarceration	___
8	if offense was not check fraud or burglary	___
0.6	times age of offender	___
	Base expectancy 65A score	===

a. Based on adult information if juvenile record unknown.

IM–342

Given the scoring system for Model VI–A, one would expect people with high model scores to be better risks on probation than people with low scores. This expectation is borne out by the table below, which shows the actual success rates of probationers in our samples whose Model VI–A scores fell within three ranges.

	Percent successful in county [a]		
Model score	*Multnomah*	*Maricopa*	*Philadelphia*
80.7 and above	89	93	93
41.3–80.6	68	65	52
41.2 and below	47	37	17

a. This analysis and all that which follows is based on only those probationers for whom both model score and probation outcome are known.

IM–343

Usefulness of models in recommending sentencing

Probation models can assist probation and court officials in recommending sentencing alternatives (prison, jail, or probation) for individual offenders. While recognizing that models used in this manner should be more broadly based and should include characteristics of those persons not placed on probation, we believe Model VI–A demonstrated predictive ability.

In our test we computed scores for probationers in each of the three counties and considered the 10 percent with the lowest scores as ineligible for probation. We found that had the model been used for decisionmaking, the success rates in all three counties would have improved. The original rates and the rates projected if the model had been used to make the decision were as follows:

	Percent success	
County	Without model	With model
Multnomah	66	68
Maricopa	56	61
Philadelphia	44	49

IM–344

Usefulness of models in deciding level of supervision

Because of caseload sizes and other considerations, probation officers must decide the level of supervision a probationer should receive. By giving only minimum (rather than medium or maximum) supervision to those who are most likely to succeed, probation officers have more time to spend with other probationers who are expected to need close supervision.

To determine the usefulness of the probation model in deciding who requires minimum supervision, we assessed our sample of probationers with complete records, using the model to select some for minimum supervision. We found that when model scores were used to select probationers for minimum supervision in each of the three counties:

—Probationers selected had lower failure rates than did the group actually selected by the probation offices.

—Those probationers selected by both the model and the probation offices had lower failure rates.

Our sample of 186 probationers from Maricopa County contained 57 probationers who had been placed on minimum supervision. Of these, 14 did not successfully complete probation. When 57 probationers were selected for minimum supervision from the 186 using model scores alone, only 11 of the 57 were found to have failed. The following table shows the results of the selection process in terms of groups selected by the probation office, by the model, and by both.

		Selected by	
	Model	Probation office	Both
Number of people	33	33	24
Number of failures	9	12	2
Failure rate	27%	36%	8%

IM–345

In Philadelphia County, Pennsylvania, 20 of 227 probationers in our sample were placed on minimum supervision. Of this group, 7 failed on probation. When the model was used to select 20 probationers for minimum supervision, we found that only 3 failed.

	Selected by		
	Model	Probation office	Both
Number of people	16	16	4
Number of failures	3	7	0
Failure rate	19%	44%	0%

IM–346

In our sample of 251 probationers from Multnomah County, Oregon, 10 of the probationers were placed on minimum supervision. Of these probationers, three did not successfully complete their period of probation. Of the 10 probationers the model would have assigned to minimum supervision, only one was considered a failure. In this county none of the people selected by the probation office were also selected by the model.

In each of the three counties, the group of probationers selected by model scores for minimum supervision had a lower failure rate than the group actually selected by the probation office. Part of the lower failure rate of model selections might be attributable to the fact that some of them received more than minimum supervision. More importantly, in each of the counties the groups selected for minimum supervision by both the probation office and model had lower failure rates than the groups selected by the probation office. This implies that basing selection on model score in conjunction with the probation officer's evaluation would improve results.

Usefulness of models in selecting probationers for early release

Two of the counties we visited evaluated probationers during the course of their probation with a view toward terminating probation early. We attempted to evaluate the model's usefulness in making such decisions.

A total of 124 probationers in Multnomah County and 148 in Maricopa County were granted early releases. When the same number of people were selected using model scores alone, probationers selected by model score had slightly lower failure rates than the group selected by the probation office, and probationers selected for early release by both the model and the probation office had about the same or a lower failure rate.

The Multnomah County probation office selected 124 probationers for early release. Of these, 16 (13 percent) failed to complete probation successfully. When 124 probationers were selected using model scores, 12 (10 percent) were found to be failures.

	Selected by		
	Model	Probation office	Both
Number of people	45	45	79
Number of failures	4	8	8
Failure rate	9%	18%	10%

IM–347

As can be seen above, the group selected by both as well as the model-selected group had lower failure rates than did the group selected only by the probation office.

In Maricopa County, 148 probationers were selected for early release and 25 (17 percent) were considered failures. When the same number of probationers were selected for early release using model scores, 22 (15 percent) were found to be failures.

		Selected by	
	Model	*Probation office*	*Both*
Number of people	30	30	118
Number of failures	9	12	13
Failure rate	30%	40%	11%

IM–348

Again, the group selected by both as well as the model-selected group had a lower failure rate than the group selected by the probation office only.

We recognize that part of the reason probationers selected for early release by the model had a lower failure rate than those selected by the probation office might be that some of these probationers were not released early. This extra time on probation might have helped them become successful. But can the entire difference in failure rates be attributed to this fact? If not, the model would appear to be useful in selecting people for early release. More importantly, as indicated by our results, better results might well be achieved if selection were based on both model score and the clinical evaluation of probation officials.

CONCLUSIONS

Probation models do nothing more than statistically summarize and weigh the experience and characteristics of probationers. In this way they function much like experienced probation officials—based on past experience, they attempt to predict the outcome of a probationer. The actual outcomes of probationers are then compared to those predicted and this new information helps make decisions on the next group of probationers.

The major advantages of models are their objectivity and efficiency as well as the fact that they provide a method to transfer past experience systematically. The advantages of human judgment relate to such factors as compassion and intuition.

We tried to validate existing models at locations other than those at which they had been developed and to establish their utility. Some of the existing models could be validated, three of them in all the locations visited. While the predictive powers of these models were far from perfect, they seem to be greater than those of probation officials. More importantly, even better accuracy could be obtained if both model score and human evaluations were used to make probation decisions. Although existing models have some utility, the full benefits of models for purposes of probation can only be obtained through additional use and research. This research should include:

—Systematically collecting data (1) on characteristics which might have predictive power, including those found to be predictive in other models, and (2) necessary to test hypotheses found in criminal behavior theory.

—Developing models for specific subgroups of the probation population, such as by type or number of offenses, age, etc.

—Evaluating the many mathematical techniques used to combine predictive characteristics.

TOPICS FOR THOUGHT AND DISCUSSION

1. Probation derives from several sources in medieval and early European law. Discuss some of the practices which appear to be early forerunners of modern probation practices such as Benefit of Clergy, Judicial Reprieve and The Recognizance.

2. Discuss provisional filing, early bail practices and suspension of sentence at common law. How do these practices relate to probation as we know it today?

3. What is the *Killits* case? What is its importance to modern criminal justice?

4. Although probation is viewed as the brightest hope for corrections, its full potential cannot be reached unless consideration is given to two major factors. The report of the National Advisory Commission on Criminal Justice Standards and Goals (1973) discusses these factors. What are they and why must they be realized for probation to realize its potential?

5. In corrections, the word "probation" is used in four ways. It can refer to a disposition, a status, a system or subsystem, and a process. Define probation in each of these terms and discuss.

6. Who was John Augustus? What is his importance to corrections today?

7. Discuss pros and cons of probation existing within the executive branch as opposed to the judicial branch of government.

8. Discuss the various points of view in the controversy regarding state vs. local administration of probation services. What is the situation in your state? Is this effective? Why or why not?

9. Discuss the question of caseload size. Compare the National Advisory Commissions' conclusions with the conclusions of the San Francisco Project in Sec. 11 of this chapter.

10. Eugene Czajkoski discusses the quasi-judicial role of the probation officer. In what ways does the probation officer appear to be increasingly involved in what has traditionally been the province of the judge?

11. How may the probation officers' role be viewed as quasi-judicial?

12. What are the five major functions of the presentence investigation report? Discuss each.

13. Professor Louis Tomaino discusses the "probation grid". Of what value is this information and how may the probation officer use it to improve his performance or analyze his particular philosophical position with reference to probation supervision?

14. Which "Face" do you believe is most conducive to proper probation supervision? Why? What are the disadvantages of this "face"?

15. Jose Arcaya discusses the problem of "multiple realities" inherent to all psychotherapeutic relations. What are some of these multiple realities?

16. What are some problems unique to the supervision of black offenders; offenders of Spanish origin?

17. What are some ways in which volunteers may be valuable in the supervision of probationers?

18. The utilization of volunteers can have a profound change on the role of the professional officer. What are some of the role changes and how may they impact on the probation system as a whole?

19. The Comptroller General's study revealed a significant association between the extent to which a probationer received needed services and success on probation. Discuss this finding.

20. The San Francisco Project, a major research study begun in 1964, reached numerous conclusions regarding types, kinds and intensities of probation supervision. What were some of the rather surprising conclusions in these areas?

21. What is a "prediction model"? Give some examples and discuss the pros and cons of the use of these models in probation decisionmaking.

CHAPTER THREE

PAROLE AS COMMUNITY-BASED CORRECTIONS.

INTRODUCTION

At the present time all states and the Federal Government have some form of parole statutes and procedures for the discretionary release of most adult felony offenders from prisons and correctional institutions.

All jurisdictions have at least nominal methods of supervision of offenders released to the community and procedures for their return to incarceration should they fail in community adjustment.

The actual structure of the paroling process, including the composition and selection of the parole board, caseloads, training and authority of field staff and procedures used for the parole grant or revocation varies considerably from jurisdiction to jurisdiction. So does the comparative use of parole. Some states parole virtually all adult prisoners while in others fewer than ten percent of inmates are released on parole.

These variations in the structure and use of the parole process as well as accompanying variations in sentencing structures from one jurisdiction to another, account in good part for the lack of agreement about the legal status of parole across the country. Where parole is the common, almost universal, method of release from prison, it comes to be viewed as a right—where it is granted reluctantly and rarely, and in jurisdictions with long statutory sentences, and no other alternatives to mitigation of sentences, parole becomes crucially important to inmates.

In its origins, release to the conditional freedom of parole was viewed as an act of grace, a discretionary mitigation of long prison terms which offered hope of early release, albeit under conditions of supervision, rules and possible revocation, to most prison inmates if they conformed in penal institutions and showed promise of making a successful adjustment in free society.

The motives for the development and spread of parole were mixed: partly humanitarian, offering some mitigation of lengthy sentences; partly to control in-prison behavior by holding out the possibility of early release; and partly rehabilitative for supervised reintegration into the community is more effective and safer than simply opening the gates.

This section focuses upon parole as a sub-system of the entire field of criminal justice. The history and philosophy of parole are discussed in detail, as well as current practices and legal issues and attempts to clarify the contemporary issues of controversy involving parole and other forms of early release from incarceration. Parole is viewed in its relationship to sentencing, imprisonment and other aspects of the correctional continuum.

————

THE HISTORY AND CONCEPT OF PAROLE *

The procedure known as parole was first tried in the United States one hundred years ago. During the years which have intervened since its first official sanction at Elmira Reformatory in 1876, its use has been expanded into all parts of the country until today it has become the major device by which offenders are released from prisons and correctional institutions. Even after a century of use, there is much misapprehension and misunderstanding about parole and much of this arises from a confusion in terminology. The general public often considers parole to be based on clemency or leniency and seldom distinguishes parole from probation and pardon. These three terms are used indiscriminately not only by the public, but even by officials and judges as well as in some state statutes. Because of the confusion in terminology and administration, parole is often charged with all the shortcomings of other release procedures, for which it is in no way responsible. It is evident, therefore, that the prerequisite for an analysis of parole is a clear definition of the term. Parole is the conditional release of an individual from a prison or correctional institution after he has served part of the sentence imposed upon him.

Probation as Distinguished from Parole. Probation and parole are two different methods of dealing with offenders, although the two terms are often used interchangeably. While parole is a form of release granted to a prisoner who has served a portion of his sentence in a correctional institution, probation is granted an offender without requiring incarceration. Parole is an administrative act of the Executive or an executive agency while probation is a judicial act of the Court. Therefore, so-called bench parole, which is nothing more than a suspension of sentence without supervision is not parole at all, but a form of probation; and the use of the word parole in this connection is improper and misleading and should be eliminated.

Parole as Distinguished from Pardon. Wilcox distinguished between pardon and parole as follows:

Pardon involves forgiveness. Parole does not. Pardon is a remission of punishment. Parole is an extension of punishment. Pardoned prisoners are free. Parolees may be arrested and

* Paul Cromwell, George Killinger & Hazel Kerper, *Probation and Parole in the* *Criminal Justice System*, West Publishing Company, 1976.

reimprisoned without a trial.   Pardon is an executive act of
grace; parole is an administrative expedient.[1]

The distinction between parole and pardon was clearly drawn in an
address before the American Prison Association in 1916: [2]

> The whole question of parole is one of administration. A parole
> does not release the parolee from custody; it does not discharge
> or absolve him from the penal consequences of his act; it does
> not mitigate his punishment; it does not wash away the stain or
> remit the penalty; it does not reverse the judgment of the Court
> or declare him to have been innocent or affect the record against
> him.   Unlike a pardon, it is not an act of grace or of mercy, of
> clemency or leniency.   The granting of parole is merely permis-
> sion to a prisoner to serve a portion of his sentence outside the
> walls of the prison.   He continues to be in the custody of the
> authorities, both legally and actually, and is still under restraint.
> The sentence is in full force and at any time he does not comply
> with the conditions upon which he is released, or does not want
> to conduct himself properly, he may be returned, for his own
> good and in the public interest.

It has been pointed out that there is no similarity between pardon
and parole except that in both cases the person has been released from an
institution: [3]

> In all other respects—the theory upon which he is released, the
> method used in selecting him for release, the treatment of him
> after his release, his return if he violates his parole—are all
> different than those which exist in the case of pardon.   Some of
> these considerations are entirely foreign to the very idea of
> pardon.   The idea involved in the granting of pardon is that
> society is taking the blame for what it has done to a man by
> sending him to prison.   He is sent out on his own without any
> conditions of supervision being imposed.

Release on parole is not based upon any concept of clemency.   Nor is
it regarded as a lenient treatment of prisoners even though they are
released prior to the expiration of their sentence.   Parole, as it functions
today, is an integral part of the total correctional process.   As such, it is a
method of selectively releasing offenders from the institution, under
supervision in the community, whereby the community is afforded continuing protection while the offender is making his adjustment and beginning his contribution to society.

1. Wilcox, Theory of Parole (1927) p. 20,
    quoted in Attn'y. Gen'l. Survey of Re-
    lease Procedures, Parole, Vol. IV.

2. Spaulding (1916) Proceedings Ameri-
    can Prison Association, 548.

3. Miller, "Evils of Confusion Between
    Pardon & Parole" (1932), Proceedings
    American Prison Association.

The Origins of Parole. The word is derived from the French *parole* and is used in the sense of "word of honor" *parole d'honneur.* The choice of word was a very unfortunate one, inasmuch as most people distrust a "word of honor" given by a released prisoner. It is not surprising, therefore, that the French prefer the term "conditional liberation" to the one borrowed from them.

In penal philosophy, parole is a part of the reformatory idea in the general trend in 19th Century criminology in which the emphasis shifted from punishment to reformation. In 1791, during the French Revolution, Mirabeau anticipated modern penal theories by publishing a report based upon the idea of reformation and founded on the principles of labor, segregation, rewards under a mark system, conditional liberation, and aid on discharge.[4] A Frenchman, de Marsangy, in 1847 published a book in which he discussed the pardoning power, conditional liberation, police supervision of discharged convicts, aid upon discharge, and rehabilitation. This book was distributed by the Government to the members of both chambers of Parliament. In 1864, in a further work on this subject, he used the following simile in his argument for what is now called parole: [5]

> As a skillful physician gives or withholds remedial treatment according as the patient is or is not cured, so ought the expatiory treatment imposed by law upon the criminal to cease when his amendment is complete; further his detention is inoperative for good, an act of inhumanity, and a needless burden to the state. Society should say to the prisoner "Whenever you give satisfactory evidence of your genuine reformation, you will be tested, under the operation of a ticket of leave; thus the opportunity to abridge the term of your imprisonment is placed in your own hands."

Parole, as a practice, originated almost simultaneously with three European prison administrators: a Spaniard, Montesinos, a German, Obermaier, and an Englishman, Maconochie.

In 1835, Col. Montesinos was appointed governor of the prison at Valencia, containing about 1500 convicts. He organized the institution on the basis of semi-military discipline and encouraged vocational training and primary education of the prisoners. The novelty of his plan consisted in the fact that there were practically no guards to watch the prisoners, who, nevertheless made few, if any, attempts to escape. The main reason for this probably was that each could earn a one-third reduction from the term of his sentence by good behavior and positive accomplishments. The number of recommitments while Montesinos was governor fell from 35 percent to "a figure which it would be imprudent to name, lest it should not be believed."

---

4. Attn'y Gen'l Survey, Vol. IV, Parole, p. 6.

5. Quoted in Wines, Punishment and Reformation (1895) 219.

The law which allowed this program was subsequently repealed and the system collapsed. Montesinos resigned, and in a pamphlet published in 1846 drew the following conclusions from his experiment: [6]

> What neither severity of punishment nor constancy in inflicting them can secure, the slightest personal interest will obtain. In different ways, therefore, during my command, I have applied this powerful stimulant; and the excellent results it has always yielded, and the powerful germs of reform which are constantly developed under its influence, have at length fully convinced me that the most inefficacious methods in the prison, the most pernicious and fatal to every chance of reform, are punishments carried to the length of harshness. The maxim should be constant and of universal application in such places, not to degrade further those who come to them already degraded by their crimes. Self respect is one of the most powerful sentiments of the human mind, since it is the most personal; and he who will not condescend, in some degree, according to circumstances, to flattery of it, will never attain his object by any amount of chastisement; the effect of ill treatment being to irritate rather than to correct, and thus turns from reform instead of attracting to it. The moral object of penal establishments should not be so much to inflict punishment as to correct, to receive men idle and ill-intentioned and return them to society, if possible, honest and industrious citizens.

The German, Obermaier, became governor of a prison in Munich in 1842.[7] He found approximately 700 prisoners in a state of rebellion kept in order by over 100 soldiers. In a short time he had gained the confidence of the men, taken off their chains, discharged nearly all the guards, and appointed a convict superintendent of each of the industrial shops. His succession in reforming prisoners was so great that only a reported ten percent relapsed into crime after their discharge. He was aided by two favoring circumstances of which the first was that many of the men were sentenced to simple imprisonment with no fixed term; and the second that there was a thorough supervision of discharged inmates through the labors of numerous prison aid societies.

Chief credit for developing an early parole system, however, is due to Alexander Maconochie, in charge of the English penal colony at Norfolk Island in New South Wales and to Sir Walter Crofton, who as director of the Irish Convict Prisons, further developed the scheme originated by Maconochie and known today as the ticket of leave, or Irish system. Inasmuch as the earliest plan of conditional liberation is found in the Australian convict colonies, and since present day parole is closely linked to these experiments, their tragic history is worthy of consideration.

---

6. Id., at 194.   7. Id., at 195.

Transportation to America. The transportation of English criminals to the American colonies began in the early 17th Century. The system evolved from a 1597 law that provides for the banishment of those who appeared to be dangerous. As early as 1617, reprieves and stays of execution were granted to persons convicted of robbery who were strong enough to be employed in the colonies. The government devised a plan to transport convicted felons to the American colonies as a partial solution to the acute economic conditions and widespread unemployment in England, and the shortage of labor in the colonies. The London, Virginia and Massachusetts companies and similar organizations supported the plan. The king approved the proposal to grant reprieves and stays of execution to the convicted felons who were physically able to be employed in the colonies.

Initially no specific conditions were imposed upon those receiving pardons. Consequently, many of them evaded transportation and returned to England prior to the expiration of their terms, and it became necessary to impose certain restrictions upon the individuals to whom pardons were granted. About 1655, the form of pardon was amended to include specific conditions and to provide for the nullification of the pardon if the recipient failed to abide by the conditions.

Until 1717, the government paid a fee to the contractor for each prisoner transported. However, during that year a new procedure was adopted. Under the new procedure, the contractor was given "property in service" and the government took no interest in the welfare or behavior of the offender unless he violated the conditions of his pardon by returning to England prior to the expiration of his sentence. Upon arrival in the colonies, the "services" of the prisoner were sold to the highest bidder and thereafter the prisoner was an indentured servant.

The system of indenture dates to 1512 and originally had no relation to persons convicted of crimes. It applied usually to apprentices who were indentured to their masters for a number of years. The indenture consisted of a contract that stipulated the conditions of indenture. The conditions bore some similarity to the parole agreement of today.

Transportation to Australia and Ticket-of-Leave. The Revolutionary War brought an end to the system of transporting criminals to America; however, the transportation law was not repealed. Detention facilities became overcrowded, resulting in the more liberal granting of pardons. During a serious crime wave, the English public demanded enforcement of the transportation law and Australia was designated for use as a convict settlement, with the first load arriving there in January, 1788. Transportation to Australia differed from transportation to the colonies in that the government incurred all expenses of transportation and maintenance, and the prisoners remainder under government control instead of being indentured. The governor was given "the property and service" for the prisoners, and he assigned them to the free settlers who assumed the "property and service" agreement. As early as 1790, the governor of New South Wales had been given the right of conditional pardon. He could set the convicts free and give them grants of land, afterward even assigning newcoming convict laborers to them. Such was the original ticket-of-leave system which was regulated by statute in 1834.[8] Originally there were no provisions for governmental supervision of those on ticket-of-leave.

In 1811, a policy was adopted requiring that prisoners serve specific periods of time before being eligible to receive ticket-of-leave. Strict enforcement of this policy was not seen until 1921, when a regular scale was formulated. Those prisoners serving a sentence of seven years became eligible for the ticket-of-leave after serving four years; those serving sentences of 14 years, after serving 6 years; and those serving life sentences, after 8 years. In 1837, Alexander Maconochie devised a system whereby the duration of the sentence would be determined by the industry and good conduct of the prisoner. He made his proposal to the House of Commons. Marks were to be accredited to the prisoner daily in accordance with the amount of labor performed and the type of conduct exemplified. His system saw the prisoners passing through a series of stages from strict imprisonment through conditional release to final and complete restoration of liberty, with promotions being based upon marks accredited. In 1840, Maconochie was appointed Governor of the Norfolk Penal Colony, but remained there only four years. While his ideas were progressive and his experiments successful, there were no revolutionary effects due to the short duration of his tenure and the limitation of his experiences to Norfolk.

As the free settlers in Australia increased their numbers, they protested the use of the country as a dumping ground for prisoners. In response to the protest, England initiated a selection system whereby prisoners would undergo an 18 month training process prior to transportation to Australia. The selection experiment failed, but it saw the beginning of the utilization of trained, experienced individuals who were made responsible for the selection of prisoners who had profited by the training program. Three prison commissioners were appointed to make the selections and the membership of the group may well have been the precedent to three member parole boards later established by prison reformers in America. In 1867, transportation of prisoners to Australia terminated.

England's Experience with Ticket-of-Leave. Although England did not terminate the transportation of prisoners to Australia until 1867, the English Penal Servitude Act of 1853, governing English and Irish prisoners substituted imprisonment for transportation. In accordance with the Act, prisoners sentenced to 14 years or less were committed to prison, but the judge was given the option of ordering transportation or imprisonment for prisoners with sentences in excess of 14 years. The law also specified the length of time prisoners were required to remain incarcerat-

8. Archibald, The Parole System (1907)
6 Can.L.Rev. 222.

ed before becoming eligible for conditional release on ticket-of-leave. The Act of 1853 related to conditional release and gave legal status to the system of ticket-of-leave.

Prisoners released on a ticket-of-leave in England were released under three general conditions:

1. The power of revoking or altering the license of a convict will most certainly be exercised in the case of misconduct.

2. If, therefore, he wishes to retain the privilege, which by his good behavior under penal discipline he has obtained, he must prove by his subsequent conduct that he is really worthy of Her Majesty's clemency.

3. To produce a forfeiture of the license, it is by no means necessary that the holder should be convicted of a new offense. If he associates with notoriously bad characters, leads an idle or dissolute life, or has no visible means of obtaining an honest livelihood, etc., it will be assumed that he is about to relapse into crime, and he will at once be apprehended and recommitted to prison under his original sentence.[9]

The British policy falsely assumed that the prison program would be reformative; that the prisoners released on ticket-of-leave would have indicated positive response to prison training programs; and that those released would be adequately supervised. Such was not the case. The three years following the enactment of the Servitude Act saw an outbreak of serious crime which was attributed to a lack of supervision of the ticket-of-leave men. The British public thus believed the ticket-of-leave system to be a menace to public safety and an absolute failure.

A series of prison riots in 1862, accompanied by another serious crime wave, again focused attention on prison administration and the ticket-of-leave system. A Royal Commission was appointed to investigate both areas. The final report rendered stressed the poor programs and gave the opinion that prisoners were released on ticket-of-leave without having been given reliable proof of their reformation.

The report of the Royal Commission resulted in policemen providing supervision of the released prisoners. Later, a number of prisoners aid societies, supported in part by the Government, were established. These agencies aligned their methods of supervision with the method that had proven effective in Ireland.

The Irish System of Ticket-of-Leave. Sir William Crofton became the administrator of the Irish Prison System in 1854, one year after the Penal Servitude Act was passed. He believed that the intent of the law was to make the penal institution something more than houses of incarceration. Crofton felt that the prison program should be designed more

---

9. Parker, Parole—Origins, Development, Current Practices and Statutes, American Correctional Association, Corrections—Parole-MDT-Project, Resource Document No. 1, 1972.

toward reformation and that tickets-of-leave should be awarded only to prisoners who had shown definite achievement and had exemplified positive attitude changes.

Under Crofton's administration, the Irish system became renowned for its three stages of penal servitude—especially the second stage, where the prisoner's classification was determined by marks awarded for good conduct and achievement in industry and education, a concept borrowed from Maconochie's experience on Norfolk Island. So-called indeterminate sentences were employed, and institutional conditions were made as near to normal as possible. The restraint exercised over the prisoner was no more than that required to maintain order. The ticket-of-leave in Ireland was different than the one in England. The written conditions of the Irish ticket were supplemented with instructions designed for closer supervision and control and very much resembled the conditions of parole presently used in the United States.

Ticket-of-leave men residing in rural areas were under police supervision, but those living in Dublin were supervised by a civilian employee called the Inspector of Released Prisoners. He had the responsibility of securing employment for the ticket-of-leave man, visiting the residence, and verifying employment. It was the Inspector of Released Prisoners to whom the ticket-of-leave man periodically reported. The Irish system of ticket-of-leave had the confidence and support of the public and the convicted criminal.

Development in the United States. Three concepts underlie the development of parole in the United States: (1) a reduction in the length of incarceration as a reward for good conduct; (2) supervision of the parolee; and (3) imposition of the indeterminate sentence.

Release as a result of a reduction in the time of imprisonment was always accompanied by an agreement between the prisoner and the authority authorizing the release or what would be considered now as a parole agreement. The agreement normally stipulated that any violation of the conditions would result in a return to the institution. The first legal recognition of shortening the term of imprisonment as a reward for good conduct was the 1817 "Good Time" Law in New York.

Supervision of those released from prison was originally accomplished by volunteers. Masters of indentured children from houses of refuge undertook guardianship and supervision at their own volition. Members of prison societies were also among the first volunteer supervisors of adult offenders. The Philadelphia Society for Alleviating the Miseries of Public Prisons recognized the importance of caring for released prisoners as early as 1822. In 1851, the society appointed two agents to assist those prisoners discharged from the Philadelphia County Prison and the penitentiary. The first public employees paid to assist released prisoners are believed to have been appointed by the State of Massachusetts in 1845.

By 1865, American penal reformers were well aware of the successful achievements in the European systems of prison reformation followed by conditional release, particularly the Irish system. As a result, the first indeterminate sentence law was passed in Michigan in 1869 at the instigation of Z. E. Brockway. However, the Michigan law was subsequently declared unconstitutional. After becoming superintendent of the newly constructed Elmira Reformatory in New York, Brockway succeeded in having an indeterminate sentence law adopted in that state and the first parole system had come into being.

The system established at Elmira included grading inmates on conduct and achievement, compulsory education, and careful selection for parole. Volunteer citizens, known as guardians, supervised the parolees. A condition of the parole required the parolee to report to the guardian on the first of each month. Written reports became required and were submitted to the institution after being signed by the employer and the guardian.

Parole legislation spread much more rapidly than did indeterminate sentence legislation. By 1901, twenty states had parole statutes, but only eleven states had indeterminate sentence laws. Today, every state and the federal government has a parole law, but several states are without indeterminate sentence laws.[10]

PAROLE: A SURVEY *

Almost every offender who enters a correctional institution is eventually released. The only relevant questions are: When? Under what conditions?

Most offenders released from a correctional institution re-enter the community on parole. In 1970, the latest year for which complete data are available, almost 83,000 felons left prison; 72 percent of them were released by parole. Nineteen percent were released by discharge and 9 percent by other forms of conditional release.[1] Parole is the predominant mode of release for prison inmates today, and it is likely to become even more so. This trend can be highlighted by comparing the figures for 1970 stated above with those from 1966, when 88,000 felons left prison; 61

10. The foregoing historical material relied heavily upon two documents: the Attn'y Gen'ls Survey of Release Procedures, Vol. IV, Parole (1939) and on an unpublished M.A. thesis, Adult Parole in Texas, Charles L. Whitehead, Sam Houston State University, Huntsville, Texas, May 1975.

* The National Advisory Commission on Criminal Justice Standards and Goals, Report on Corrections, 1973.

1. National Prisoner Statistics: Prisoners in State and Federal Institutions for Adult Felons, 1970 (Washington: Federal Bureau of Prisons, 1970), p. 43.

percent were released by parole, 34 percent by discharge, and 5 percent by other forms of conditional release.[2]

A 1965 study by the President's Commission on Law Enforcement and Administration of Justice (the Crime Commission) showed that slightly more than 112,000 offenders were then under parole supervision. By 1975, the Commission estimated, this number would be more than 142,000.[3]

These figures include only those offenders sentenced to State prisons. They do not include youth committed to juvenile institutions, virtually all of whom are released under some form of supervision at the rate of about 60,000 a year.

None of these figures include persons sentenced to jail, workhouses, and local institutions. More than one million persons were released from such facilities in 1965, according to the Crime Commission. It is in these facilities that some of the most significant gaps in parole services exist.

The National Survey of Corrections made for the Crime Commission found that almost all misdemeanants were released from local institutions and jails without parole. Of a sample of 212 local jails, the survey found, 62 percent had no parole programs at all. In the 81 jails that offered parole, only 8 percent of the inmates actually were released through this procedure.[4] There is little reason to believe the situation has changed radically since 1965, although efforts have been made in several jurisdictions to extend parole services to jail populations. The need for parole services is acute at the misdemeanant level.

Parole has been attacked as leniency, but its proponents argue that it is both humanitarian and designed to protect the public. They advance these arguments on two grounds. First, virtually everyone convicted and sent to a correctional institution will return to the community. He can be turned loose by discharge with no continuing responsibility on his part or the State's, or he can be released under supervision at what appears to be an optimal time and be assisted in reintegration into the community. From this perspective, parole is simply a form of graduated return to the community, a sensible release procedure.

A second major argument is that the sentencing judge cannot anticipate what new information may be available to a parole board or what circumstances might arise to indicate the optimum release date. Unlike the judge, a paroling agency has the advantage of being able to observe the offender's behavior. Furthermore, decisions on release made at the time of sentencing may be more angry than rational. Greater objectivity

2. *National Prisoner Statistics: Prisoners in State and Federal Institutions for Adult Felons, 1966* (Washington: Federal Bureau of Prisons, 1968), p. 43.

3. President's Commission on Law Enforcement and Administration on Justice, *Task Force Report: Corrections* (Washington: Government Printing Office, 1967), pp. 6–8. Publication referred to hereinafter by title.

4. *Task Force Report: Corrections*, p. 61.

in appraising the offender may be achieved by a parole board when the passions that may have been aroused by an individual's offense have cooled.

Available evidence supports the view that parole does not lead necessarily to a lessening of the amount of time inmates actually serve in prison. In fact, one major criticism of present parole laws is that their administration tends to result in more severe penalties in a criminal justice system that already imposes extensive State control.

Inmates released on parole in the United States in 1964, the last time national data of this kind were available, actually served slightly *more* time than those released through unconditional discharge (Table 12.1). The table does not show the additional time served by offenders returned to prison as parole violators, a hazard to which those discharged unconditionally are not subject. In the major proportion of parole revocation cases, violation of parole rules rather than new felony offenses cause the offender's return to prison to serve more of his sentence. Thus arguments are made that the sentencing structures supporting extensive parole use should be severely modified because of their capacity to inflict additional and unwarranted "punishment."

Table 12.1   **Number and Types of Releases in 1964 and Median Time Served**

Type of release	Number	Median time served
Discharge	22,883	20.1 months
Parole	42,538	21.1 months

Source: *National Prisoner Statistics, State Prisoners: Admissions and Releases, 1964* (Washington: Federal Bureau of Prisons, 1967.)

IM–349

DEFINITION IN HISTORY

The classic definition of parole was provided in the Attorney General's Survey of Release Procedures in 1939 as "release of an offender from a penal or correctional institution, after he has served a portion of his sentence, under the continued custody of the state and under conditions that permit his reincarceration in the event of misbehavior."[5] Though some jurisdictions impose limitations on parole use, offenders generally can be released on parole and repeatedly returned to confinement for parole violation until the term of their original commitment has expired.

Yet to many, parole is still seen as "leniency" for offenders. Others contend that, in well-operated systems, different types of offenders should serve differing periods of time, and the more dangerous and violence-prone should serve more time. This is seen as a proper use of

5. *Attorney General's Survey of Release Procedures* (Washington: Government Printing Office, 1939), vol. IV, p. 4.

sentencing and parole flexibility. To actually understand parole and to make it a more effective instrument of public policy requires sophisticated knowledge of all its processes, procedures, and objectives. Understanding is obscured by the use of such value-laden terms as leniency, harshness, punishment, or coddling. All of them oversimplify what is a complex administrative, legal, and political issue.

Parole resembles probation in a number of respects. In both, information about an offender is gathered and presented to a decisionmaking authority with power to release him to community supervision under specific conditions. If he violates those conditions, the offender may be placed in, or returned to, a correctional institution. Parole, however, differs from probation in a significant way. Parole implies that the offender has been incarcerated in a correctional institution before he is released, while probation usually is granted by a judge in lieu of any kind of confinement.

Recent development of informal institutions (halfway houses, etc.) used by both courts and parole boards make the distinction between probation and parole increasingly difficult to sustain. To add further confusion, some jurisdictions use the term "bench parole" to refer to a form of minimally supervised probation.

Parole and probation also differ significantly in terms of who makes the decision. Parole is almost always an administrative decision; the granting of probation, a court function.

The power to determine when an offender may be released from an institution, to fix the conditions of his supervision, and to order parole revocation almost always passes from the court to an agency within the executive branch. In the case of adults this agency is usually a parole board; in the case of juveniles, an institutional official. As a condition of probation, a sentencing judge may require an offender to spend some time in an institution before he is released under community supervision, as in the "split sentence" in Federal jurisdictions. In this situation, authority to fix conditions and powers of revocation and discharge continue with the court after the offender is released from confinement. Therefore, the case almost always is classified as probation.

Parole also needs to be distinguished from one other kind of release. In a number of jurisdictions—New York, Wisconsin, the Federal system—adult offenders are automatically released under supervision when they have served a portion of their sentence and have earned a specified amount of time off for good behavior. Legislation specifies the calculation of "good time," and the parole authority exercises no discretion in the matter. The procedure is called "mandatory" or "conditional" release and is used to provide supervision for those offenders who have been denied parole, are ineligible for it, or have previously refused it. Although released automatically, such offenders may be returned to serve the remainder of their terms if they violate any of the release conditions.

The advantage of mandatory release is that supervision is provided for those not paroled. Its main disadvantages are that time under supervision usually is short, and inmates are released simply because they have earned time off for good behavior, with little regard for their readiness to return to the community.

The beginning of parole in the United States generally is identified with the Elmira Reformatory in New York, which opened in 1876. In the Elmira system, sentences were indeterminate, dependent on "marks" earned by good behavior. Release was for a six-month parole term, during which the parolee had to report regularly to a volunteer guardian or sponsor.

Elmira drew wide attention by its new approach to imprisonment, which was markedly different from the tradition of incarceration for a term fixed at the time of sentence. The designation of certain institutions for youthful felons as "reformatories," and the accompanying practice of permitting indeterminate sentences and parole, spread rapidly through the United States in the last quarter of the 19th century and the beginning of the 20th. This sentencing system, including its provisions for parole, soon was extended to prisoners of all ages. By 1922, parole laws had been passed by 45 States, and in 1945 Mississippi became the last State to develop parole legislation.

This does not imply, however, that either parole laws or practices have developed uniformly. States still vary widely in the proportion of inmates released under parole supervision. In 1968, for example, the National Prisoner Statistics of the Federal Bureau of Prisons showed that among offenders released in the States of Washington, New Hampshire, and California, more than 95 percent were released under parole supervision. During the same period, less than 10 percent of inmates released in Oklahoma were released on parole. In Nebraska the comparable figure was 20 percent. Nationwide, releases to parole supervision were approximately 60 percent of all releases.

The history of parole for juvenile offenders is different from that for adults. For juveniles, parole usually is traced to the houses of refuge for children in the latter part of the 19th century. From these settings, children were released to work for several years in private homes. Total control of the child was vested in the family to whom he was released. It was the family's responsibility to determine when he had earned his freedom.

The child protection programs developed later assumed many of these activities. Although in recent years juvenile programs have become more correctional, they have continued to be involved closely with child welfare activities.[6] In many States, juvenile aftercare services are the

---

6. See Anthony Platt, "The Rise of the Child-Saving Movement: A Study in Social Policy and Correctional Re- form," *Annals of the American Academy of Political and Social Sciences,* 381:21 (January 1969).

responsibility of the welfare department or a similar agency containing a broad range of services. In these settings, delinquency is seen as merely a symptom of a young person's need for State services. Labels such as "delinquent," "dependent," or "neglected" are de-emphasized. The general thrust is to treat these children within the context of child welfare.

Juvenile parole authorities usually are more than willing to distinguish their services from those for adults. Juvenile officials typically use the term "aftercare" as a synonym for parole, but in many ways the difference is more than semantic. The problems presented by the young releasee are different from those of the adult offender. School attendance and vocational training programs are much more likely to be a central feature of programs for juveniles, while employment is the major concern for adult offenders.[7] The two concerns might be cursorily equated. But no one may be legally required to work, while school attendance is compulsory for juveniles. In fact, chronic truancy is a juvenile "crime."

Juvenile and adult parole services usually are not organized similarly. The National Survey of Corrections showed that in 1965 parole boards decided on the release of juveniles in only two States, although such boards released adults almost everywhere in the country.

SENTENCING STRUCTURES

Any parole system and set of standards designed to improve its functioning can be understood and evaluated only in terms of the structure in which it exists. All parole systems, no matter how autonomous, are part of a larger process—not only of corrections generally, but also of a complex sentencing structure involving trial courts and legislative mandates. The structure and functions of parole systems and their relative importance in the jurisdiction's total criminal justice picture all depend largely on the sources of sentencing authority and limits on sentencing alternatives and lengths.[8] In most jurisdictions, for most offense categories, the sentences that can be imposed and the proportion of sentences actually served are determined by a balance of decision-making powers among legislatures, trial courts, and parole authorities. As noted in Chapter 5, there is no sentencing structure common to all jurisdictions. The relative importance and power of parole determinations vary markedly from one jurisdiction to another and within jurisdictions from one offense category to another.

Variations in Structure

Throughout the history of American criminal justice, there have been various models of "ideal" sentencing structures proposed in different

7. See William Arnold, *Juveniles on Parole* (Random House, 1970).

8. See Chapter 5 of this report. See also Daniel Glaser, Fred Cohen, and Vincent O'Leary, *The Sentencing and Parole Process* (Washington: U. S. Department of Health, Education, and Welfare, 1966).

jurisdictions. Some have been tried, all have been debated, most have been modified. But there is still no uniform sentencing structure. The Model Penal Code of the American Law Institute, the Model Sentencing Act proposed by the National Council on Crime and Delinquency, suggestions of the Crime Commission, and the American Bar Association's Minimum Standards for Sentencing are recent attempts to propose sentencing structures suitable for all offenders in all jurisdictions. Because there have been no common standards for sentencing structures and processes, establishing standards for parole functions is extremely complex.

It might be possible to reach agreement on matters such as structure and composition of parole boards, appropriate workloads, staff training and development, and proper procedures for granting and revoking. But it must be remembered that the meaning and importance of the paroling function vary from one postconviction system to another. For example, in jurisdictions where legislatures set long maximum terms that trial judges cannot modify where good-time laws are stringent, or where pardon is almost unheard of, parole becomes not only an important method of release but virtually the *only* method. Furthermore, where sentences are long, it may mean that parolees must be supervised for decades.

The situation is different in systems that have relatively short legislative limits on sentences, with judges empowered to fix upper terms less than statutory maxima, and with liberal good-time allowances or frequent use of pardon. In such cases parole determinations may play a relatively minor part in overall release processes. In short-sentence jurisdictions, parolees terminate supervision fairly quickly. In jurisdictions in which minimum sentences are not required by either legislation or court determination, parole authorities have wide discretion to release inmates at any time.

Variations also exist among jurisdictions in regard to institutionalized juvenile delinquents, but they are not nearly as disparate as in the case of adults. The extent of control by the State over juvenile offenders generally is fixed by age rather than by offense. In most jurisdictions juvenile commitments do not have fixed minimum terms, so that release authorities have wide discretion.

But laws relating to juveniles are by no means uniform in all jurisdictions. For example, the National Survey of Corrections reported that in five States juveniles can be paroled from State training schools only with the committing judge's approval. In three States, the time a juvenile must serve before release is fixed in advance by the court. In effect, these are minimum sentences.

The sentencing system finally adopted is crucial to the parole function because it fixes the amount and the character of discretion a parole system can exercise. Seeking to eliminate the abuses that lurk in discretion, some persons would eliminate any form of discretionary release after sentencing by the trial judge.[9] However, most authorities hold that discretion is inevitable; the task is to limit and control it. From this view, many more problems arise when the entire releasing decision is placed in the hands of the trial judge or made dependent on a system of totally fixed sentences set by the legislature than if the decision is shared with a parole authority.[10]

On the other hand, most parole officials do not want the amount of power implicitly delegated by completely indeterminate sentencing. They feel that the awesome task of determining sentence limits should be left to judicial and legislative branches.

Sentencing Consistent with Parole Objectives

The sentencing system that seems most consistent with parole objectives has the following characteristics:

1. Sentence limits set by legislation, with the sentencing judge having discretion to fix the maximum sentence, up to legislative limits.

2. No minimum sentences, either by mandate or by judicial sentencing authority.

3. Comparatively short sentences for most offenses, with a legislative maximum not to exceed five years for most offenders.

4. Mandatory release with supervision for offenders ineligible for parole, so that they are not held in an institution until their absolute discharge date.

5. All parole conditions set by the paroling authority, but with opportunity for a sentencing judge to suggest special conditions.

6. Legislative prohibition of offenders' accumulating consecutive sentences if it interferes with minimum parole eligibility.

7. Legislative provisions for alternatives to reimprisonment upon parole revocation.

8. No offenses for which parole is denied by legislation.

In general, the intent of such a system is to give to the legislature and sentencing judges the authority to set outer limits of sentence but not to restrict parole authorities by setting minimum terms. At the same time, the sentencing structure provides supervised release for those offenders whom parole authorities cannot conscientiously release under regular parole criteria. The sentencing structure may provide for extended terms for dangerous offenders, though parole eligibility requirements should remain roughly the same in these cases.

9. See *Struggle for Justice: A Report on Crime and Punishment in America*, Prepared for the American Friends Service Committee (Hill and Wang, 1971), ch. 8.

10. See American Bar Association Project on Minimum Standards for Criminal Justice, *Sentencing Alternatives and Procedures* (Institute for Judi-

A system of this kind would give parole authorities discretion over the release of offenders whom trial courts decided need incarceration. Yet it would be a limited discretion. Parolees would not be under supervision for excessive time periods nor, if parole were denied, would they be incarcerated for unnecessarily long terms.

PURPOSES OF PAROLE

The objectives of parole systems vary widely. Without clearly stated and understood objectives, the administrator cannot make the most basic decisions regarding effective resource allocation. Even a casual attempt to clarify the purposes of parole will reveal that objectives frequently are in conflict. One of the parole administrator's chief tasks is to minimize this conflict.

A Basic Purpose: Reduction of Recidivism

Few things about parole evoke consensus, but there is some agreement that one objective and measure of success is reduction of recidivism. Even this consensus quickly becomes less firm when two specific functions are examined: (1) provision of supervision and control to reduce the likelihood of criminal acts while the offender is serving his sentence in the community (the "surveillance" function), and (2) provision of assistance and services to the parolee, so that noncriminal behavior becomes possible (the "helping" function).[11]

To the extent that these concerns can be integrated, conflicts are minimized, but in the day-to-day activity of parole administration they frequently clash. Decisions constantly must be made between the relative risk of a law violation at the present time and the probable long-term gain if a parolee is allowed freedom and opportunity to develop a legally approved life style. Resources are needed to clarify the choices and risks involved. Key requirements for this kind of assistance are development of clear definitions of recidivism and creation of information systems that make data available about the probabilities of various types of parole outcome associated with alternative decisions. (These requirements are discussed in some detail in Chapter 15.)

Varied Concerns of Parole Boards

Reducing the risk of further criminality is not the sole concern. In fact, it actually may be secondary in some instances. A wider variety of concerns was expressed in a questionnaire completed by nearly half the parole board members in the United States in 1965, who were asked to indicate what they considered the five most important factors to be weighed in deciding on parole. Table 12.2 shows the items selected by at

cial Administration, 1967), Sec. 3, pp. 129–199.

11. American Correctional Association, *Manual of Correctional Standards* (Washington: ACA, 1966), p. 114.

least 20 percent of those responding as being among the five most important considerations. The first three items selected as being the most important were related to the risk of violation. However, the next four related to three other concerns: equitable punishment, impact on the system, and reactions of persons outside the correctional organization.

Table 12.2 Items Considered by Parole Board Members to
be Most Important in Parole Decisions

Item	Percent Including Item as One of Five Most Important
1. My estimate of the chances that the prisoner would or would not commit a serious crime if paroled.	92.8
2. My judgment that the prisoner would benefit from further experience in the institution program or, at any rate, would become a better risk if confined longer.	87.1
3. My judgment that the prisoner would become a worse risk if confined longer.	71.9
4. My judgment that the prisoner had already been punished enough to "pay" for his crime.	43.2
5. The probability that the prisoner would be a misdemeanant and a burden to his parole supervisors, even if he did not commit any serious offenses on parole.	35.3
6. My feelings about how my decision in this case would affect the feelings or welfare of the prisoner's relatives or dependents.	33.8
7. What I thought the reaction of the judge might be if the prisoner were granted parole.	20.9

Source: National Parole Institutes, *Selection for Parole* (New York: National Council on Crime and Delinquency, 1966).

A number of other studies have noted the same phenomenon.[12] Most parole board members consider risk a paramount concern, but other factors assume such importance in certain cases that risk becomes secondary. A well-known inmate convicted and sentenced for violation of a public trust may be denied parole repeatedly because of strong public feelings, even though he might be an excellent risk. In another type of case, an offender convicted of a relatively minor crime may be paroled even though a poor risk, because in the opinion of the board he has simply served enough time for the offense committed. To some analysts these other-than-risk considerations are viewed simply as contingencies that arise from time to time; to others they involve objectives central to parole decisionmaking. In either case, considerations other than risk assessment figure prominently in parole decisionmaking and must be accounted for in any discussion of objectives. To judge from questionnaires returned by parole board members and from studies in the field, there seem to be at least three core sets of concern other than reducing

12. See Robert Dawson, *Sentencing: The Decision as to Type, Length, and* *Conditions of Sentence* (Little, Brown, 1969).

recidivism,[13] which significantly and regularly impinge upon most parole decisionmakers.

Fairness and Propriety

Parole programs are part of larger systems of criminal justice. They are governed by concepts of propriety and modes of conduct arising from American culture and law. Especially in recent years, parole systems have been expected to conform with practices that enhance the ideals of fairness and reflect hallmarks of American justice such as procedural regularity, precedent, and proof.

Most recently these issues have been reflected in increased sensitivity to inmates' or revokees' rights to counsel, the right of a hearing on parole grant and revocation, and disclosure of information used in decisionmaking. Reflecting this emphasis, some parole board members may even refuse to consider at a parole violation hearing evidence that might have been secured by questionable search procedure. Comparable issues also arise in establishing conditions for parole supervision, which are expected to meet the tests of relevance, reasonableness, and fairness.

Appropriate Sanctions and Public Expectations

Though it seldom is stated openly, parole boards often are concerned with supporting a system of appropriate and equitable sanctions. This concern is reflected in several ways, depending upon a jurisdiction's sentencing system. One of the most common is through decisions seeking to equalize penalties for offenders who have similar backgrounds and have committed the same offense but who have received different sentences.

Alternatively, decisions to grant or deny parole, particularly in well-known cases, often may hinge on the question, "Has this person served enough time for the act he committed?" Considerable differences in these matters exist from one system to another, as well as among individuals in the same system. Such concerns usually are less apparent in, and perhaps less relevant to, juvenile agencies. However, in many parole systems, maintaining an appropriate system of sanctions directly or indirectly underlies most decisionmaking. How significant these considerations are depends on the kind of sentencing framework in which the parole system is operating.

In addition to issues of equity, parole decisionmakers sometimes respond to actual or anticipated public attitudes. Such concerns for public acceptance of parole generally, and case decisions specifically, govern the kinds of risks that are acceptable and the actions considered feasible by parole decisionmakers. This public reaction issue is particularly acute in cases affecting society's core beliefs. Criteria having little to do with the question of risk may be used by parole officials in dealing

---

13. Keith Hawkins, "Parole Selection: The American Experience," unpub- lished doctoral dissertation, Cambridge University, 1971.

with certain cases, particularly those involving crimes seen as "heinous." The concern is more for meeting general social norms and responding according to public expectations.

Maintenance of the Justice System

A third set of concerns that influences parole decisionmaking relates to support of other criminal justice operations. Parole boards play a crucial role as a kind of system regulator, influencing other parts of the justice system, from police to prisons. For example, in some systems where a parole board has extensive control over the amount of time a large proportion of inmates will serve, institutional populations can change dramatically depending on board policy. Not only do parole board decisions influence institutional size, but they also reinforce behavior that can have profound effects on the kinds of programs sustained. Inmates are more likely to participate in a program the parole board explicitly values than in one to which the board pays no attention.

Institutional staff members have an obvious stake in the programs in which inmates are involved. Hence they too are affected by parole decisions. Various parole officials are sensitive to the correctional impact of their decisions and some take this factor into account in their decisions.[14] In some instances, boards will be reminded forcefully of their effect on inmates and institutions. For example, it is not uncommon during times of high prison tension (as after riots), when parole policy is under attack by inmates and sympathizers, for boards to become more "liberal." In such instances, the degree of risk acceptable for parole, conditioned by pressures within the institutions, shifts perceptibly. Parole boards directly affect parole supervision staff by the kind of offenders they release and revoke, and by the policies surrounding these actions.

System maintenance and other basic concerns cited clearly influence parole decisionmaking. However, questions of risk, fairness, public expectation, and system maintenance are not the only considerations affecting parole authorities. Of great importance as well are the beliefs they hold concerning the sources of criminality, strategies for changing offenders, and the nature of the relationship between the correctional system and the offender.

ORGANIZATION OF PAROLING AUTHORITIES

Most persons concerned with parole decisionmaking for juveniles are full-time institutional personnel. Only a few juvenile jurisdictions have noninstitutional personnel determining parole releases.

Different circumstances prevail in the adult area. For example, adult boards tend to carry many more direct State-level administrative responsibilities than do releasing authorities for juveniles. Table 12.3

14. Keith Hawkins, "Some Conse- *Future of Parole* (London: Gerald quences of a Parole System for Prison Duckworth, 1972). Management," in D. F. West, ed., *The*

shows that in 1965, 14 adult parole boards supervised probation services for the courts of the State. Few parole decisionmaking groups for juvenile offenders had a similar responsibility. The table also shows the historical link in many States between parole and the clemency or pardon authority of the governor. Many boards carried out advisory functions for the governor in executive clemency matters and in one State, Alabama, the board granting paroles also had the power to pardon.

Table 12.3　Responsibilities of Adult Paroling Agencies Other Than Parole, 1965

Additional Responsibility	Number of Boards
Holds clemency hearings	28
Commutes sentences	24
Appoints parole supervision staff	24
Administers parole service	20
Paroles from local institutions	19
Grants or withholds "good time"	17
Supervises probation service	14
Grants pardons, restorations, and remissions	1
Fixes maximum sentence after 6 months	1
May discharge prior to sentence expiration	1
Sets standards for "good time"	1
Acts as advisory board on pardons	1
None	5

Source: National Council on Crime and Delinquency, *Correction in the United States* (New York: NCCD, 1967), p. 215.

IM–351

Although there is considerable variety in the organizational settings in which parole decisionmakers work, at least two dominant organizational strains can be identified—the institutional model, which largely predominates in the juvenile field, and the independent model, the most common in the adult field. Considerable controversy has arisen around these two models.[15]

The Institutional Model

In general, the institutional model perceives parole as being bound closely to institutional programs. It places the release decision with the correctional facility's staff. Parole is simply one more of a series of decisions affecting the offender. The persons most familiar with the cases make the releasing decision; and this makes it possible to develop a rational and consistent set of decisions that affect the inmate. The Crime Commission reported that 34 of 50 States used this form of organization in the juvenile field.

The major arguments raised against the institutional model is that too often institutional considerations, rather than individual or community needs, influence the decisions. Overcrowding in the institution, desire

15. *Task Force Report: Corrections*, pp. 65–66.

to be rid of a problem case or to enforce relatively petty rules, or other concerns of institution management easily become the basis of decision-making. Institutional decisionmaking also lends itself to such informal procedures and lack of visibility as to raise questions about its capacity for fairness or, what may be as important, the appearance of fairness.

The Independent Authority

In the adult field, a good deal of reform was associated with removing parole decisionmaking from institutional control to an independent authority. Undoubtedly much of the basis for this reform came from the view that paroling authorities were being swayed too easily by institutional considerations or were not being objective enough.[16] The change was so complete that today no adult parole releasing authority is controlled directly by the operating staff of a penal institution.

Whatever its merits in fostering objectivity, the independent parole board also has been criticized on several counts. First, the claim is made that such boards tend to be insensitive to institutional programs and fail to give them the support they require. Second, independent boards are accused of basing their decisions on inappropriate considerations, such as the feelings of a local police chief. Third, their remoteness from the institutional program gives independent boards little appreciation of the dynamics in a given case; their work tends to be cursory, with the result that too often persons who should be paroled are not, and those who should not be paroled are released. Fourth, the argument is made that independent systems tend to place on parole boards persons who have little training or experience in corrections.

Lack of knowledge about corrections, combined with the distance of the parole board from institutional programs, builds unnecessary conflicts into the system. The rapid growth of part-way release programs and halfway houses has increased the probability of those conflicts. In short, critics of the independent model assert that important decisions are being made concerning the correctional system, its programs, and the offenders in it by persons far removed from the system who have little appreciation of its true nature.

The Consolidation Model

While these arguments and their rebuttals continue, an alternate system has gained considerable support in recent years, tending to cut the ground away from both major models. This system is linked with a general move toward consolidation of all types of correctional services into distinctive departments of corrections that subsume both institution and field programs. The consolidation model, emerging from the drive toward centralized administration, typically results in parole decisions being made by a central decisionmaking authority organizationally situat-

16. *Attorney General's Survey of Release Procedures* (1939), vol. IV, p. 49.

ed in an overall department of corrections but possessing independent powers. The director of corrections may serve on such a releasing authority, or he may designate a staff member to do so. In the youth field, the centralized board may have policy responsibilities for institutions as well as parole decisionmaking.

Proponents of the consolidation model argue that there is increased concern for the whole correctional system in departments where parole releasing authority is part of a centralized system. They claim that sensitivity to institutional programs seems more pronounced in consolidated systems than in completely autonomous ones. They also contend that removal of parole decisionmaking from the immediate control of specific correctional institutions tends to give greater weight to a broader set of considerations, a number of which are outside direct institutional concerns.

Although variations in organizational or administrative arrangements may be required to meet special circumstances, certain general organizational requirements seem clear. Among the most essential requisites is that the organizational structure of parole authorities should foster close coordination between parole decisionmakers and the increasingly complex set of programs throughout the correctional network. Yet sufficient autonomy should be preserved to permit parole boards to act as a check on the system.

The trend in this country clearly is in the direction of consolidation. More than 60 percent of the State parole boards responsible for release of adult offenders now function in common administrative structures with other agencies for offenders.[17] This trend enhances integration of correctional operations. If parole boards are to function as useful and sophisticated decisionmaking units that balance a wide set of concerns, they also must achieve and maintain some degree of autonomy from the systems with which they interface. This issue involves appointment and tenure methods, as well as the tasks and functions for which parole authorities take responsibility.

Articulation of Criteria for Decisions

Articulation of criteria for making decisions and development of basic policies is one of the chief tasks that parole decisionmakers need to undertake. While discretion is a necessary feature of parole board operations, the central issue is how to contain and control it appropriately. Few parole boards have articulated their decision criteria in much detail or in writing even though research has shown that criteria exist. Parole

17. National Probation and Parole Institutes. *The Organization of Parole Systems for Felony Offenders in the United States.* 2d ed. Hackensack, N. J.: National Council on Crime and Delinquency, 1972. Unless otherwise stated, factual data on State parole systems

board members tend to display, with slight variations, a consistent response to case situations of which they may be only marginally aware.[18]

Articulating the basis of decision systems is crucial to improving parole decisions, because criteria must be specified before they can be validated. For example, 75 percent of 150 board members queried in 1965 by the National Probation and Parole Institute asserted that rapists generally were poor parole risks. Research data have shown such an assumption to be wrong.

Articulation of criteria is crucial to staff and inmates alike. The notion of an inmate's participation in a program of change depends on an open information system. His sense of just treatment is inextricably bound with it. As one parole board member put it:

> It is an essential element of justice that the role and processes for measuring parole readiness be made known to the inmate. This knowledge can greatly facilitate the earnest inmate toward his own rehabilitation. It is just as important for an inmate to know the rules and basis of the judgment upon which he will be granted or denied parole as it was important for him to know the basis of the charge against him and the evidence upon which he was convicted. One can imagine nothing more cruel, inhuman, and frustrating than serving a prison term without knowledge of what will be measured and the rules determining whether one is ready for release. . . . Justice can never be a product of unreasoned judgment.[19]

And without valid information on the basis of parole decisions, correctional staffs hardly can be expected to deal realistically with offenders or to shape meaningful programs with them.

In most parole systems, board members are so heavily committed to case-by-case decisions that these additional tasks, and those to be suggested subsequently, will require a substantial alteration in work style. Smaller States will need to shift from part-time to full-time parole boards. Other States will require additional personnel at the parole decisionmaking level.

Need for Appeal Procedures

Besides the pressure for clearly articulated policies, there also is a rapidly developing demand for mechanisms by which correctional, and specifically parole, decisions can be appealed. The upsurge of cases being

given in this chapter are from this publication.

18. Don Gottfredson and Kelly Ballard, "Differences in Parole Decisions Associated with Decision Makers," *Journal of Research in Crime and Delinquency,* 3 (1966), 112.

19. Everette M. Porter, "Criteria for Parole Selection" in *Proceedings of the American Correctional Association* (New York: ACA, 1958) p. 227.

considered by the courts documents this need.[20] The courts can and will
test at least certain aspects of parole decisions. Yet if parole authorities
are to develop correctional policy consistent with correctional needs and
judicial standards, they need to establish self-regulation systems, including internal appeal procedures.[21]

Where the volume of cases warrants it, a parole board should
concentrate its major attention on policy development and appeals. The
bulk of case-by-case decisionmaking should be done by hearing examiners
responsible to the board and familiar with its policies and knowledgeable
as to correctional programs.

Hearing examiners should have statutory power to grant, deny, or
revoke parole, subject to parole board rules and policies. In cases of
offenders serving long sentences, those involved in cases of high public
interest, or others designated by the parole board, two or more parole
members personally should conduct the hearings and make decisions.
Hearing examiners operating in teams of two should handle the large
part of day-to-day interviewing and decisionmaking for the board. Inmates and parolees should be entitled to appeal decisions to the parole
board, which could hear cases in panels or en banc. As action is taken on
these cases and the system of appeals refined, the board should further
articulate its policies against which unwarranted uses of discretion could
be checked.

Instead of spending his time routinely traveling from institution to
institution hearing every type of case, the board member should be
deciding appeals and hearing cases of special concern. He should be
developing written policies and using monitoring systems by which decision outcomes could be observed and strategies for improvement developed. The use of the board for all types of appeals from correctional
decisions (loss of good time, denial of privileges) also should be considered.

In smaller systems, many of these activities would have to be carried
out by the same persons. However, procedures can and should be
developed to assure attention to each separate function—policy development, hearings, and appeals. Only a few of these crucial activities now
are carried out by the average parole board. They are critically needed,
and the kind of system described here would greatly facilitate their
attainment. Parts of such a system have been used successfully by the
California and Federal parole boards and other governmental agencies.

An advisory group, broadly representative of the community and
specifically including ex-offenders, should be established to assist the
parole board by reviewing policies and helping shape and implement
improvement strategies developed. This kind of link to the public is

20. For examples of this growth in interest by the courts, see Comment, "The
Parole System," *Pennsylvania Law Review,* 120 (1971), 282.

21. Edward Kimball and Donald New-
man, "Judicial Intervention in Correctional Decisions: Threat and Re-

critically needed if sensible policies are to be developed and support for their adoption achieved.

PAROLE AUTHORITY PERSONNEL

The most recent data available on members of juvenile parole releasing authorities indicate that by far the largest number are full-time staff of juvenile correctional institutions.[22] In several States, such as California and Minnesota, youth commissions parole juveniles. In others, such as Wisconsin and Illinois, the same board is responsible for release of both juveniles and adults.[23] The issues of appointment, qualifications, and training raise precisely the same questions for juvenile release authority members as they do for board members responsible for adult release.

In 41 States, adult parole board members are appointed by the governor. In seven jurisdictions, they are appointed in whole or in part by the department of corrections.

A similar problem exists with any part-time member of a paroling authority. In 18 States, parole board members responsible for the parole of adult males are part-time employees. In six others only the chairman is a full-time employee. Part-time board members tend to be located in the smallest States, but there are exceptions. Tennessee and South Carolina, for example, with part-time boards, have larger populations than several other smaller States that have full-time boards. If parole services were extended to local jails and one board was made responsible for jails, training schools for delinquents, and adult prisons, a full-time board would be needed in virtually every State.

For larger States, the relevant question is, What is the optimum size of the parole decisionmaking authority? Almost half of parole boards for adult offenders consist of three members; 18 jurisdictions have five members; six have seven members; and one parole board, New York's, consists of 12 members. Some parole authorities argue that boards could grow indefinitely. But with a shift in emphasis toward policy articulation and appeals, it would seem prudent to hold the size to a manageable level. Few, if any, State boards should exceed five members. As the workload expands beyond the capacity of these members, hearing examiners should be appointed. The largest States might need 20 hearing examiners or more.

Qualifications of Board Members

Two dilemmas that are common to most appointive public offices are also seen in deciding on the best method of selecting parole board members: first, how to secure appointees with expertise and willingness to challenge the system when necessary rather than merely preserving it;

sponse," *Crime and Delinquency*, 14 (1968), 1.

22. National Council on Crime and Delinquency, *Correction in the United*

States (New York: NCCD, 1967), p. 104.

23. *Correction in the United States*, p. 86.

second, how to select parole board members who will be responsive to public concern, as expressed through elected officials, without making politics rather than competence the basis for appointment.

Parole decisionmakers too frequently have shown the negative possibilities of both dilemmas. In many instances they have become so coopted by a correctional system that there is no independent check against abuses of public or offender interests. Too many times appointments have been governed by patronage considerations, a dangerous criterion when human freedom is at stake and the most difficult moral, legal, and scientific issues are involved.

If parole authorities are to have the competence required for their tasks, specific statutory qualifications for board members must be developed. In 24 States there are no statutory requirements for parole members responsible for the release of adult offenders. In one State generalized references to character are made. In another 21 only the broadest references to experience or training are enunciated.

According to the findings of the first National Parole Conference in 1939, board members "should be selected on the basis of their integrity and competence to deal with human and social problems, without reference to political affiliations." [24] More recently the standards proposed by the American Correctional Association required that parole board members should "command respect and public confidence," be "appointed without reference to creed, color or political affiliation," possess "academic training which has qualified the board member for professional practice in a field such as criminology, education, psychiatry, psychology, law, social work and sociology," and "have intimate knowledge of common situations and problems confronting offenders." [25]

No single professional group or discipline can be recommended as ideal for all parole board members. A variety of goals are to be served by parole board members, and a variety of skills are required. Knowledge of at least three basic fields should be represented on a parole board: the law, the behavioral sciences, and corrections. Furthermore, as a board assumes responsibility for policy articulation, monitoring and review, the tasks involved require persons who are able to use a wide range of decisionmaking tools, such as statistical materials, reports from professional personnel, and a variety of other technical information. In general, persons with sophisticated training and experience are required. In this context, the standards suggested by the American Correctional Association should be statutorily required for each jurisdiction.

Hearing examiners require less specialized education and training. More critical in these roles are persons with educational and experiential qualifications that allow them to understand programs, to relate to

24. *Proceedings, National Parole Conference, 1939* (Leavenworth, Kan.: Federal Prison Industries, Inc., 1970), p. 113.

25. American Correctional Association, *Manual of Correctional Standards*, p. 119.

people, and to make sound and reasonable decisions. These roles should offer particular opportunities for ex-offenders and for those persons most sensitive to the implications of offenders' lifestyles.

Making the Appointment

A critical question concerns who should make the actual appointment to the parole board. Two basic choices are the governor or the head of the department of corrections. Appointment by the governor provides the board increased autonomy and greater responsiveness to public influence. But it increases the likelihood of lack of coordination with the corrections agency, oversensitivity to public reactions, and appointment of unqualified personnel. Selection by the director of corrections, who is himself selected on the basis of professional qualifications, is more likely to secure appointment of knowledgeable persons, protection from political influence, and some shielding from an undue concern for public criticism. The major disadvantage is the possible appointment of a "rubber stamp" decisionmaking body.

Some type of device must be employed if competent board personnel are to be selected. Each State should require by law that nominees for parole board positions first be screened by a committee broadly representative of the community. Representatives of groups such as the State bar and mental health associations should be included, as well as representatives of various ethnic and socioeconomic groups. The law should require that appointments be made only from the approved list of nominees.

Terms of Office, Salary

A number of other suggestions to improve parole board appointments have been made and should be adopted. One of these is to provide parole board members with substantial terms of office, as long as 12 years, during which they cannot be removed except for good cause.[26]

A matter of particular importance in attracting well-qualified persons to parole positions is the compensation. According to the most recent data available, the median salary for full-time parole board members is $19,000 a year. This is not a salary which in 1972 can attract the type of personnel needed for parole decisionmaking posts. The salary for such positions should be equivalent to that of a judge of a court of general jurisdiction.

Training for Board Members

Improvement in the performance of parole members depends heavily on the availability of a training program. The National Probation and Parole Institutes have undertaken to provide biennial training sessions for new members. But much more needs to be done in this area. Ongoing training is needed by both new and experienced board members.

---

26. Phillip E. Johnson, *Federal Parole Procedures* (Washington: Administra- tive Conference of the United States, 1972).

An effective ongoing program should inform board members of recent legal decisions and advances in technology and acquaint them with current correctional practices and trends. Because of the relatively small number of parole board members in each State, such a program would have to be national in scope. An exchange program of parole board members and hearing officers also should receive support. Recent experiments carried out by the National Probation and Parole Institutes, in which parole board members had the opportunity to visit other States, proved to be valuable experience for participants.

THE PAROLE GRANT HEARING

The parole hearing is a critical moment for inmates. At this point they are legally "eligible" for release, their case is studied, they are interviewed, and the decision is made. In all States except Texas, Georgia, and Hawaii, adult felony offenders are present at hearings at the time of parole consideration. Four States screen files and grant interviews only to eligible inmates who seem to merit parole consideration. All other States hear every offender at least once, even those unlikely to be released. Many parole authorities see an inmate several times during the course of his sentence. In fact, a number of States provide for at least annual review of each case, no matter how remote release may be.

Formal hearing procedures are much less common with juveniles. More often, primary emphasis is placed on written reports or staff conferences at which the youth may or may not be present.

Procedures followed at parole hearings for adult offenders are extremely diverse. In some States, each parole applicant is heard by the full parole board. In others, especially those with many correctional institutions, boards are split into smaller working panels, each of which conducts hearings. In several jurisdictions, a single parole board member may conduct a hearing unless the case is regarded as unusually important, when a larger subcommittee or the entire board conducts the hearing. In the Federal system and in California, the parole boards appoint "hearing officers" to assist in some hearings. The number of cases considered in a single day by boards or panels for adult offenders ranges from 15 to 60.

Information Base

Information available to the parole board at the time of a hearing typically is prepared by institutional staff. It is usually based on reports on the offender's adjustment to prison life. Some parole boards request special investigations of release plans for all inmates, while others prefer to wait until they make a tentative decision that parole is indicated. A few States have reports prepared by professional clinical personnel. Since these professionals are scarce, most reports prepared for parole boards are written by caseworkers who actually have relatively little opportunity to observe inmates.

Glaser has suggested use of revised reporting systems, wherein staff members who have the most contact with inmates would be involved most directly in providing data for the board's decisions.[27] With the increasing stress on reintegration, most parole board members need a great deal more information about community services available to released offenders, as well as on feasible programs that might be undertaken. This lack is not solely an information gap; unfortunately, the basic problem is that community resources are meager.

Right to a Hearing

In most jurisdictions the offender has no statutory rights in the parole consideration process, except in some instances the right to a personal appearance before the parole board. Yet at these hearings, the traditional stance has been that the inmate and his record must make an affirmative case for parole. The Model Penal Code represents a turn-around in the traditional assumption that the burden of proof (however evaluated) rests on the inmate. It proposes that an inmate is to be released on parole when he is first eligible unless one of the following four conditions exists:

1. There is a substantial indication that he will not conform to conditions of parole.
2. His release at that time would depreciate the seriousness of the crime or promote disrespect for the law.
3. His release would have substantially adverse effects on institutional discipline.
4. His continued correctional treatment, medical care, or vocational or other training in the institution will substantially enhance his capacity to lead a law-abiding life when released at a later date.[28]

Recently the National Commission on Reform of Federal Criminal Laws substantially endorsed the presumption and the four considerations of the Model Penal Code. It offered in addition the proviso that, once an inmate has served the longer of five years or two-thirds of his sentence, he should be paroled unless the board is "of the opinion that his release should be deferred because there is a high likelihood that he would engage in further criminal conduct." [29]

Procedural Guidelines

In the past few years there has been a noticeable increase in complexity of procedural requirements for parole hearings. Of those jurisdictions holding personal interviews, for example, 21 now permit the "assistance" of attorneys in behalf of the inmate. Seventeen allow the

27. Daniel Glaser, *The Effectiveness of a Prison and Parole System* (Bobbs-Merrill, 1964), ch. 9.

28. American Law Institute, *Model Penal Code,* (Philadelphia: ALI, 1962).

29. National Commission on Reform of Federal Criminal Laws, *Final Report* (Washington: Government Printing Office, 1971), p. 300.

inmate to be represented at the hearing by persons other than counsel whom he feels will help him present his case for granting parole. A verbatim record of proceedings is made in 11 jurisdictions.

Development of guidelines for desirable parole hearings should attend to several concerns simultaneously. First, such hearings should provide parole authorities with as much relevant and reliable information about each case as possible. Second, the hearing process itself should carry the hallmark of fairness. Not only should it be a fair determination in substance, but to the extent possible it also should be perceived by the inmate as fair. Third, as far as practicable the hearing should enhance the prospects for an inmate's successful completion of his parole.

To these ends the hearing can make a number of contributions. The manner in which the inmate is interviewed and notified of decisions affecting him can support or undermine respect for the system of justice. Any opportunity for the offender's active participation in decisions can greatly affect his commitment to the plans made. In the final analysis, *his* commitment is the crucial factor in whether or not these plans will be carried out.

In keeping with the reintegration emphasis, a modern corrections system should embrace a wide variety of alternative programs, not only for institutions, but also for release or partway release. Except in rare cases it will probably be too cumbersome for a parole board to approve specific actions in detail. With community corrections, halfway houses, prerelease centers, split sentences, and similar developments, the line between parole and prison already is becoming blurred. It therefore appears necessary that the parole board increasingly test the appropriateness of programs and match individuals with them by criteria fixed in advance, rather than try to make clinical decisions on an individual's readiness for release.

The Automatic First Hearing

A number of practical steps for parole hearings flow from these changes in overall correctional processing. Every inmate should routinely be seen by a parole authority during the first year of incarceration. This review should be automatic and no application by the inmate should be required. Such a hearing might result in consideration of early parole. More often, it would be devoted to a review of the particular objectives and programs developed by the inmate and staff. Any program involving release for long periods should involve the parole board hearing staff.

The important element of this first, automatic hearing is that the board approves program objectives and program categories for offenders rather than attempting to make detailed clinical judgments about each case. The objective of the hearing, however, should not be to coerce the inmate to subject himself to specific institutional treatment programs. The traditional ineffectiveness of such programs does not make participation a good basis for a parole decision.

A particularly critical determination during this initial interview is scheduling another interview or hearing, if one is necessary before the inmate's release. It should be increasingly common to approve an inmate's program, including a full-time parole release date, as far as a year in advance without requiring another hearing or further interviews by the parole board. If the objectives of the program are met, administration of the parole board's plan would be left to the offender and institutional and field staffs. Should substantial variations occur or important new information develop, the board could be notified and a new hearing scheduled. On the other hand, not all release dates can be predetermined at an initial interview. Additional hearings may be required either because of the length of the inmate's sentence or by the circumstances of a particular case. In such instances, a new hearing date would be fixed after the initial interview. In no case should more than a year transpire between hearings.

Under this plan, the parole board would function more to monitor the decisions of others than to make detailed judgments in individual cases. The plan should also reduce the number of individual release hearings conducted by board representatives. This is particularly important since there is a practical limit on the number that can be conducted in a day. An effective hearing requires close attention of board representatives, institutional staff, offenders, and other persons involved in tailoring programs and releases to individual cases. It also requires careful recording of plans and decisions. With a system of this kind, no more than 20 cases should be heard in a day.

Prompt Decision and Notification

If this system is to work, it requires involvement of at least two representatives of the parole authority who are empowered to grant parole in all but the most exceptional cases. A current problem in a number of parole jurisdictions is that only a single representative of the parole authority actually hears offenders' cases. He is not able to take final action on any case until he returns to a central point where other board officials can join him in making a decision. Hence there is often inordinate delay, while the inmate and others involved must simply mark time. Not only does such delayed decisionmaking lower morale, but also available parole resources may deteriorate and no longer be open to the inmate when the parole finally is granted. The job that was waiting is lost; the chance to participate in vocational education programs is gone.

Delay in making parole decisions should be eliminated. The key lies in sufficient decisionmaking power being allocated at the point of hearing. In almost all cases two examiners can perform the necessary hearing functions if they can agree.

Allied to prompt decisionmaking is the manner in which an inmate is notified of determinations affecting him. About half of the State jurisdictions now inform inmates of the decision and the reasons for it as soon as it is made, at the hearing itself. This practice is relatively new. Formerly, the almost universal practice was to send word of release or deferral to the inmate through a board representative or an institutional official. Such officials have no way of clarifying the meaning of the decision or its implications to the inmate. This task can and should be done only by parole decisionmakers, not by others trying to represent them. Parole authorities should explain the reasons for their decisions directly to the inmate and answer any questions he has.

Written Decisions

Also critical in this respect is the necessity for parole decisionmakers to spell out in writing the reasons for their decision and to specify the behavioral objectives they have in mind. Currently only about 12 parole boards dealing with adult offenders document the reasons for their decisions. It should be a universal practice. It is important for future hearing representatives to have available the reasoning of prior hearing officials.

Likewise, it is important for institutional officials to have the written parole opinion to assist them in shaping future programs for offenders denied parole. It also is important for board self-evaluation; research should be able to measure the relationship between reasons for actions and subsequent events and decisions. Board documents provide a basis for checking the reasons for decisions against the criteria used. This is particularly crucial in a two-tiered system of decision and review in which appeals can be made.

Due Process Requirements

Provisions for sharing the bases of decisions with offenders, making a written record of proceedings, requiring written reasons for decisions, and allowing a two-tiered appeal process not only are good administrative practice but also are consistent with legal requirements of procedural due process. They may come to be viewed as legally necessary. So far, however, courts have been restrained in requiring elaborate procedural safeguards during parole consideration. For example, the Federal Second Circuit Court of Appeals in the recent case of Menechino v. Oswald, 430 F.2d 403 (2d Cir. 1970), in referring to the parole board's function said:

> It must make the broad determination of whether rehabilitation of the prisoner and the interest of society generally would best be served by permitting him to serve his sentence beyond the confines of the prison walls rather than by being continued in physical confinement. In making that determination, the Board is not restricted by rules of evidence or procedures developed for the purpose of determining legal or factual issues.

However, the Supreme Court, in a recent case involving parole revocation hearings, laid down strict procedural requirements to safeguard due process. (See subsequent section on revocation.) It may well be that such requirements will be deemed necessary for the grant hearing as well.

Trends in court decisions are difficult to predict. Certainly in the last few years appellate courts have ordered changes in parole proceedings, particularly those surrounding revocation. There is sound basis in correctional terms alone for elements in the parole hearing that embrace some characteristics of administrative hearings occurring at other points in the criminal justice process. The value of information disclosure, for example, does not rest simply upon legal precedent. Parole boards have as much stake in the accuracy of records as other criminal justice officials. Evidence indicates that decisions are much more likely to be documented carefully and fully when information is disclosed and when those whose interests are at stake have a chance to examine and test it. Rather than resulting in an adversary battle, disclosure more often than not provides information not contained in the report. This is an important addition for decisionmakers.

Information sharing underlies much of the emphasis in modern corrections that is moving toward an open, reality-testing base. From this perspective, it is expected that offenders will be given available evidence and facts. In the average parole file little material is so sensitive that it cannot be reviewed with the inmate. Of course, if there is a need to treat with caution professional material such as certain types of psychiatric reports, it can be held back.

The suggested procedures of the American Bar Association for disclosure of presentence investigation material seem eminently suitable for the parole hearing stage. Materials could be withdrawn when deemed necessary, with a notation made of this fact in the file. In case of appeal, the full parole board would be notified as to what material had been withheld from the inmate and could take this into consideration.

Representation

The issue of inmate representation by lawyers or other spokesmen causes difficulty for many parole board members because it seems to create an unnecessarily adversarial system out of essentially a "clinical" decision process. However, several arguments for representation can be advanced. The offender's representative has the freedom to pursue information, develop resources, and raise questions that are difficult for an inmate in a helpless position. To the extent that the information base can be enlarged by representatives and issues sharpened and tested more directly, there is likely to be improvement in the whole process of parole board decision-making. Equally important, however, is the impression of fairness given to the inmate who is represented. Indeed in many cases it is more than simply a feeling of fairness. It is clear that, in too many situations, the lack of ability to communicate well, to participate fully in the hearing, and to have a sense of full and careful consideration, is extremely detrimental.

Representation also can contribute to opening the correctional system, particularly the parole process, to public scrutiny. It is important that more people become personally involved in the correctional process, since the reintegration movement rests on the involvement of community resources and representatives. Involvement of persons from the outside also provides opportunity for remedy of any abuses in parole processes.

Ultimately the credibility of a parole system will rest on its openness to public scrutiny. For these reasons, a system of providing, or at least allowing, representation for the offender at parole hearings should be sponsored by parole officials. Because of the diversity in parole eligibility and program administration among parole systems, the precise interviews with inmates at which representation is appropriate or feasible will vary. But the principle of allowing representation when crucial decisions regarding the offender's freedom are made should guide the board in fixing policies. Lawyers are only one possible kind of representative; citizen volunteers also could serve as offender representatives.

The idea of representation at hearings may be annoying to parole officials. Implementation may increase costs. On balance, these inconveniences seem a small price for the prospective gains. Assuming representation, the board should be able to prevent abuses in the conduct of hearings. It is crucial for parole boards to develop appropriate policies for information disclosure, forms and methods of representation, and procedural rules to be followed at the hearings.

Model for the Parole Grant Hearing

The hearing examiner model can be easily adapted to parole systems from administrative law. Hearing examiners play a central role in an administrative agency's treatment of controversy. Matters are scheduled before the examiner who conducts a full hearing and then prepares a report which contains findings of fact, conclusions of law, and recommended order. This report, the transcript, and the evidence introduced constitute the exclusive basis for decision. The hearing examiner makes the initial decision which, unless appealed to the full Board or Commission, becomes the decision of the agency.

A party dissatisfied with the recommendations or findings of the hearing examiner can appeal his decision to the full agency board which, being charged with the responsibility for decision, may overturn the findings of the examiner. The full board does not hear the matter de novo, but on briefs and arguments. The final order of the board can then be appealed to court by a dissatisfied party. Court review would determine whether there is substantial evidence on the record as a whole to support the agency decision, or whether it is erroneous as a matter of law.

Adaptation of the administrative law model for use of hearing examiners in parole grant hearings is represented in Figure 12.1.

Figure 12.1. Hearing Examiner Model

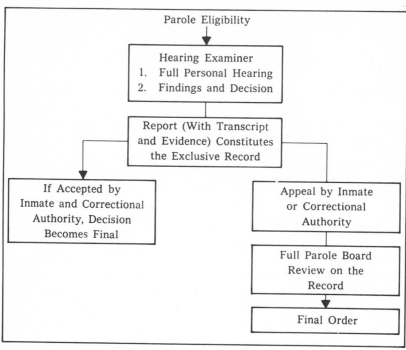

[B6530]

When a parole grant hearing is scheduled, a hearing examiner should conduct a full personal hearing with the inmate, his representative, and appropriate institutional staff members. Contents of any written reports supplied to the hearing examiner should be openly disclosed and become a part of the record, except that the parole board may establish guidelines under which certain sensitive information could be withheld from the inmate with notation of this fact included in the record.

A verbatim transcript of the proceedings should be made. The hearing examiner should make his decision on the basis of criteria and policies established by the parole board and specify his findings in writing. He should personally inform the inmate of his decision and provide him a copy of the full report. The hearing examiner's report, with the transcript and evidence, should constitute the exclusive record.

If the decision of the hearing examiner is not appealed by the inmate or the correctional authority within five days after the hearing, the decision of the hearing examiner should be final. If the decision is not accepted by the inmate or the correctional authority, appeal should be made to the parole board. The full parole board should review the case on the record to see if there is substantial evidence to support the finding or if it is erroneous as a matter of law. The order of the parole board should be final.

REVOCATION HEARINGS

Until the late 1960's, procedures in many jurisdictions for the return of parole violators to prison were so informal that the term "hearing" would be a misnomer. In many instances revocation involved no more than the parole board's pro forma approval of the request of the parole officer or his field staff supervisor. In many jurisdictions the revocation decision represented almost unfettered discretion of parole authorities. In addition to minimal procedural formality, the grounds for revocation also were non-specific, involving such assessments as "generally poor attitude" or allegations of "failure to cooperate," rather than specific breaches of conditions or commission of new offenses.

This was particularly true in revocation of the aftercare of juveniles, where the decision to revoke was viewed primarily as a casework determination. Ostensibly, it did not involve a breach of conditions but was simply an action for the youth's welfare.

This general stance of casual and quick return of both adults and juveniles rested primarily on the "privilege" or "grace" doctrine of the parole grant. To many parole officials, revocation did not warrant much concern with due process, procedural regularity, or matters of proof, hearing, and review.

In 1964 a study of parole board revocations showed that there was no hearing at all in at least seven States. In those States providing a hearing, the alleged violator frequently was returned to prison directly from the field on allegation of the field agent or on a warrant issued by the board. An actual hearing or review of this return by the parole board did not take place until weeks, sometimes months, after the parolee had been returned to the institution.[30] In most cases, then, revocation was a fait accompli by the time the board's representative next visited the institution to review the revocation order and officially declare the parolee a violator.

In a small minority of cases, board members canceled the warrant or field complaint and permitted the prisoner again to resume parole. However, since the parolee had been moved to the institution, employment and family relationships already were disturbed. In effect a canceled revocation order meant that the parolee once again had to be transported to his local community and begin the readjustment process all over again. Counsel rarely was permitted to represent the alleged violator at such hearings. Any witnesses to the alleged violation almost always were seen outside the hearing at the parole board offices, rarely subject to confrontation or cross-examination by the parolee. While at the time of the survey some States allowed parolees to have "assistance" of lawyers, no jurisdiction assigned counsel to indigent parolees.

---

30. Ronald Sklar, "Law and Practice in Probation and Parole Revocation Hear- ings," *Journal of Criminal Law and Criminology*, 55 (1964), 75.

Intervention by Appellate Courts

Since the 1960's there has been considerable appellate court intervention in the parole process generally and in revocation procedures specifically. The new vigor is consistent with a general distinction in administrative law between granting a privilege (as in parole) and taking it away once it has been given (as in revocation). Courts generally have held that initial granting or denial of a privilege can be done much more casually and with fewer procedural safeguards than taking away a privilege once granted.

Development of court-imposed requirements for procedural due process in parole revocation has been somewhat erratic. One of the important leading cases in the Federal jurisdiction was Hyser v. Reed, decided in the D.C. Circuit in 1963 (318 F.2d 225, 235). The decision in this case generally supported the common position that revocation was strictly a discretionary withdrawal of a privilege not requiring adversarial hearings at which inmates are represented by counsel and so forth. This part of the decision was consistent with both the law and the general sentiment of most parole authorities at the time. What *Hyser* did do, however, was to deal with the venue question of where the revocation hearing should take place.

The court supported the U.S. Parole Board practice of conducting a fact-finding hearing on the site of the alleged offense or violation of condition, with review at the institution only if the first hearing determined the offender should be returned. This decision was sensible, particularly in those cases involving a mistake or failure to find any infraction. If in fact the parolee did not commit the alleged infraction he could continue his parole uninterrupted.

Subsequent to the *Hyser* decision, however, courts in some Federal and State jurisdictions reversed the first part of the decision; namely, the lack of any right, constitutional or otherwise, for due process to be applied at revocation proceedings. Most courts that departed from *Hyser* in this regard did so on the basis of the Supreme Court decision in a case involving "deferred sentencing" or probation revocation. In Mempa v. Rhay, 389 U.S. 128 (1967), the Supreme Court held in 1967 that a State probationer had a right to a hearing and to counsel upon allegation of violations of probation. A number of courts interpreted the principle of *Mempa* to apply to parole as well.

The extension of *Mempa* procedural requirements to parole revocation was fairly common in both State jurisdictions and in various Federal circuits. In almost all cases, conformity with *Mempa* requirements meant a reversal of former legal positions, and a major change in administrative practices. For example, the New York Court of Appeals, resting its decision on the *Mempa* case, reversed its former position and required the New York Parole Board to permit inmates to be represented by counsel at revocation hearings, People ex rel. v. Warden Greenhaven, 318 N.Y.S.2d 449 (1971). The rationale most often used as a basis for the requirement of procedural due process at parole revocation was expressed in another Federal Circuit Court case, Murray v. Page, 429 F.2d 1359 (10th Cir. 1970):

> Therefore, while a prisoner does not have a constitutional right to parole, once paroled he cannot be deprived of his freedom by means inconsistent with due process. The minimal right of the parolee to be informed of the charges and the nature of the evidence against him and to appear to be heard at the revocation hearing is inviolate. Statutory deprivation of this right is manifestly inconsistent with due process and is unconstitutional; nor can such right be lost by the subjective determination of the executive that the case for revocation is "clear".

By and large parole officials have resisted attempts by courts, or others, to introduce procedural due process requirements into parole revocation and at other stages of parole. Resistance has rested not simply on encroachment of authority but also on the possible negative effects of stringent procedural requirements on parole generally and on administrative costs. Some parole officials argue that elaborate revocation hearings would create demands on the parole board's time grossly incommensurate with personnel and budget. Other opponents of procedural elaborateness have argued its negative effects on the purpose and use of revocation.

Resistance to increased procedural requirements in revocation apparently is diminishing, whether by persuasion or court order. As of 1972, 37 jurisdictions allow counsel for adult inmates at the time of parole revocation. Nineteen permit disclosure of the record to the offender or his lawyer. Thirty-two States provide for the right to hear witnesses. In some places due process procedures have been extended even to the operation of juvenile aftercare revocation. For example, in Illinois a juvenile parolee is notified in writing of the alleged parole violation and of the fact that he has a right to a hearing.

The State of Washington has developed perhaps the most elaborate system for handling adult parolees accused of violation. It affords them the following rights and procedures: the right to a hearing before parole board members in the community where the violation allegedly occurred; the right to cross-examine witnesses; the right to subpena witnesses; the right to assistance of counsel, including lawyers provided at State expense for indigent parolees; and the right to access to all pertinent records.

Supreme Court Decision

The Supreme Court on June 29, 1972 dealt with several crucial issues relating to parole revocation in the case of Morrissey v. Brewer, 408 U.S. 471 (1972). Two parolees appealed an appellate court's decision on the ground that their paroles were revoked without a hearing and that they were thereby deprived of due process. The appellate court, in affirming the district court's denial of relief, had reasoned that parole is only "a correctional device authorizing service of sentence outside a penitentiary" and concluded that a parolee, who is thus still "in custody," is not entitled to a full adversary hearing, as would be mandated in a criminal proceeding.

In reversing the Court of Appeals decision, the Supreme Court held that:

> . . . the liberty of a parolee, although indeterminate, includes many of the core values of unqualified liberty and its termination inflicts a "grievous loss" on the parolee and often on others. It is hardly useful any longer to try to deal with this problem in terms of whether the parolee's liberty is a "right" or a "privilege." By whatever name the liberty is valuable and must be seen as within the protection of the Fourteenth Amendment. Its termination calls for some orderly process, however informal.

In considering the question of the nature of the process that is due, the Court delineated two important stages in the typical process of parole revocation: the arrest of the parolee and preliminary hearing; and the revocation hearing.

While the Court stated it had no intention of creating an inflexible structure for parole revocation procedures, making a distinction between a preliminary and a revocation hearing was an important decision, since many of the jurisdictions that do grant hearings grant only one. The Court also laid out a number of important points or steps for each of the above two stages which will undoubtedly apply to future parole actions.

In regard to the arrest of the parolee and a preliminary hearing, the Court indicated that due process would seem to require some minimal prompt inquiry at or reasonably near the place of the alleged parole violation or arrest. Such an inquiry, which the Court likened to a preliminary hearing, must be conducted to determine whether there is probable cause or reasonable grounds to believe that the arrested parolee has committed acts that would constitute a violation of parole conditions. It specified that the hearing should be conducted by someone not directly involved in the case.

In interpreting the rights of the parolee in this process, the Court held that the parolee should be given notice of when and why the hearing will take place, and the nature of the alleged violation(s). At the hearing, the parolee may appear and speak in his own behalf. He may bring letters, documents, or individuals who can give relevant information to the hearing officer. On request of the parolee, persons who have given adverse information on which parole revocation is to be based are made available for questioning in his presence unless the hearing officer determines that the informant would be subjected to risk of harm if his identity were disclosed.

The Court also specified that the hearing officer should have the duty of making a summary or digest of what transpires at the hearing and of the substance of evidence introduced. On the basis of the information before him, the officer should determine whether there is probable cause to hold the parolee for the final decision of the parole board on revocation.

The Court said there must also be an opportunity for a hearing, if it is desired by the parolee, prior to the final decision on revocation by the parole authority. This hearing must be the basis for more than determining probable cause; it must lead to a final evaluation of any contested relevant facts as determined to warrant revocation. The parolee must have an opportunity to be heard and to show, if he can, that he did not violate the conditions, or, if he did, that circumstances in mitigation suggest the violation does not warrant revocation. The revocation hearing must be tendered within a reasonable time after the parolee is taken into custody.

The minimum requirements of due process for such a revocation hearing, as set by the Court, include (a) written notice of the claimed violations of parole; (b) disclosure to the parolee of evidence against him; (c) opportunity to be heard in person and to present witnesses and documentary evidence; (d) the right to confront and cross-examine adverse witnesses (unless the hearing officer specifically finds good cause for not allowing confrontation); (e) a "neutral and detached" hearing body such as a traditional parole board, members of which need not be judicial officers or lawyers; and (f) a written statement by the factfinders as to the evidence relied on and reasons for revoking parole.

Issues Still Unresolved

The Court left several questions unresolved. The extent to which evidence obtained by a parole officer in an unauthorized search can be used at a revocation hearing was not considered. Nor did it reach or decide the question whether the parolee is entitled to the assistance of retained counsel or to appointed counsel if the parolee is indigent.

While the Court did address certain features of the parole revocation process prior to a formal revocation hearing, it did not specify requirements for the process by which offenders are taken and held in custody. Present law and practice in many jurisdictions empower individual paroles officers to cause the arrest of parolees for an alleged violation and to hold them in custody for extensive periods.

It is a power that needs careful control because it is easy to abuse, especially in those cases in which the arrest does not lead to a hearing, in which there is no review, and in which the parolee simply is held for a while in jail and then released back to parole status. This is a practice called "jail therapy" by which the parole officer "punishes" the parolee briefly (if he is a drunk, for example, he may be held in "protective custody" over New Year's Eve), then releases him back to community status. While this short-term confinement may not be undesirable in all cases, the lack of administrative control over its use is.

The use of all arrest and hold powers should be carefully narrowed. Parole field agents should be able to arrest and hold only when a warrant has been secured from a representative of the parole board on sufficient evidence. The warrant or similar document requiring parole commissioner approval of administrative arrest should be universally used. At present, only about half the State jurisdictions require such a warrant; in the remainder the parole agent can pick up an alleged violator on his own initiative and have him detained by signing a "hold" order. Initial two-step review of administrative arrest should be established, with appropriate provisions for emergency situations but with no application to law enforcement officer arrests for new offenses.

It must be remembered that taking no action and returning the parolee to the institution are not the only two courses open. The work of the California community treatment programs shows that the availability of alternative measures—short-term confinement or special restrictions—can be extremely useful in dealing with parolees instead of causing them a long-term return to an institution. Likewise, the Model Penal Code suggests that jurisdictions develop alternatives to the no action vs. full revocation dilemma. Such alternative modes need to be developed and formalized and used much more extensively.

ORGANIZATION OF FIELD SERVICES

Transfer of Adult Parole to Correctional Departments

One of the clearest trends in parole organization in the last few years is consolidation of formerly autonomous agencies or functionally related units into expanding departments of corrections. Some of these departments have been made part of still larger units of State government, such as human resources agencies, which embrace a wide range of programs and services. One clear indication of this trend is the number of States that have shifted administrative responsibility for parole officers from independent parole departments to centralized correctional agencies.

Most recently the States of Oregon, New York, and Georgia have made such transfers. A number of smaller States still have parole supervision staffs responsible to an independent parole board. Practically every large State now has adult parole field staff reporting to the same administrative authority as the personnel of the State penal institutions. Today, the majority of parole officers at the State level work for unified departments of correction.

The emergence of strong and autonomous correctional agencies represents an important step toward removal of a major block to needed correctional reform—fragmented and poorly coordinated programs and services. It is important that such consolidations continue, particularly among the services available for misdemeanants, where the more serious program gaps now exist. How quickly and effectively consolidation will take place depends largely on development of coordinated corrections units in large urbanized regions or absorption of these facilities and services into State programs.

Juvenile Parole Organization

The problems in parole services for juvenile delinquents had some of the same characteristics. The National Survey of Corrections found tremendous shortcomings in juvenile aftercare programs. In some States young persons released from training schools were supervised by institutional staff. In others they were made the responsibility of local child welfare workers, who simply included these youngsters in their caseloads of dependent or neglected children. In some States no organized program of juvenile parole supervision existed. Whether distinct juvenile correctional agencies should exist or whether such services should be carried out as a regular part of welfare services has been a matter of controversy for years.[31]

The events of the last years have virtually ended that argument. Distinct divisions and departments of juvenile correctional services are emerging. There is less agreement about whether such departments should be combined with agencies serving adult offenders. Yet it is widely agreed that separate program units should be maintained, even if adult and juvenile programs are combined in a single agency. Statewide juvenile correctional services embracing both institutions and field aftercare represent an established trend that should be supported.

Consolidation is not simply a matter of administrative efficiency; it facilitates important parole objectives as well. From the reintegration perspective, the task of parole staff is to intervene between the offender and his world and, if needed, to work with him to find satisfying and legal modes of behavior.

Confinement is minimized and made to serve as much as possible the goal of dealing with problems in the community. Pre-release activities and community-based correctional facilities, through which offenders can participate increasingly in community life, are central. To be effective, both of these programs require extensive involvement of field staff. It is no longer sufficient to wait for the "transfer" of a case from an institution to a parole staff. The system now must work in such a way that heavy expenditures of field staff energy in the community and with the offender are made for many months prior to his "release" on parole. This requires a close interrelationship between institution and field staffs.

Linking Institutional and Field Staffs

The lack of continuity and consistency of services between institutional and field services has been a severe problem to many jurisdictions.

31. See, for example, State of New York, Governor's Special Committee on Criminal Offenders, *Preliminary Report* (1968), pp. 61–66.

It often is further complicated by what could be described as rural vs. urban perspective. Institutions generally are located miles from population centers. The manpower they tend to recruit is drawn largely from small town and rural areas. The result is that institutional staff may have little understanding of city and especially ghetto life. In contrast, most field workers live in or near the large population centers in which most offenders reside, and more field workers than institutional workers are from minority groups. This cultural difference contributes to feelings of mistrust, hostility, and incredulity that handicap communication between institutional and field staffs.

A number of steps are needed to overcome this communication breakdown. An ongoing series of joint training sessions involving field workers and institutional counselors can be helpful in achieving mutual understanding. Promotions from institutional services to field services and vice versa also can have some effect in building communication channels.

Most important is that institution and field staff be under common administrative direction. It is not enough that they be simply linked administratively at the top; linking must be at the program level as well. This can be done in several ways. One is to provide that both institutional and field services be regionalized and placed under common administrators in each area. Obviously, in States where there are only one or two institutions, problems are compounded for the whole community-based thrust. But even here some program consolidations are possible by devices such as placing all institutional programming responsibilities under full control of the head of parole field services for the last months of the inmate's confinement.

The stress on linking institutional and community supervision also has implications for systems that combine probation and parole services in a common administrative unit. Although this combination is infrequent among juvenile services, in 38 States the same State agency carries responsibility for the supervision of adult parolees and probationers. Having these services in a single agency has great economic advantages and provides an even quality of service to all areas of a State. There also are significant advantages in being able to influence staff toward more consistent programs for offenders. Tying staff to locally based institutional resources can work well for both probationers and parolees. However, in urban areas where case volume is sufficient, specialized staff who work with specific institutions are needed. Such tasks demand considerable time and require field staff to become intimately familiar with institutional personnel and participate actively in their programs.

Caseload vs. Team Assignments

The caseload—the assignment of individual offenders to individual officers—is the almost universal device for organizing the work of parole officers. This concept is being modified importantly in a number of offices through development of team supervision. A group of parole officers, sometimes augmented with volunteers and paraprofessionals, takes collective responsibility for a parolee group as large as their combined former caseloads. The group's resources are used differentially, depending upon individual case needs. Decisions are group decisions and generally involve parolees, including the parolee affected by the decision. Tasks are assigned by group assessment of workers' skills and parolees' objectives and perceptions.

Under the reintegration model, for example, various groups or organizations such as employers, schools, or welfare agencies may become someone's "caseload" and the major targets of his activities. Community representatives are dealt with directly, are directly involved, and help to shape programs. The parole office, instead of being located in a State office building, shifts to the community. The staff becomes expert in knowing both the formal and informal power structure of the community in which it operates and works closely with police, schools, employers, and probation officers. Such functions have a significant impact on the kind of manpower and training required for field staff. For example, there is a heavy involvement of volunteers as tutors and job finders that requires a staff able to use and work with such personnel.

The emphasis in a traditional parole agency is directed toward the proper administration of the specific caseload assigned to each individual officer. It is an administrative style familiar to most large bureaucracies. Front-line workers have responsibility for specific and clearly defined tasks and are checked by their supervisors to see that those tasks are carried out. The supervisors are under the command of middle managers who in turn report to someone above them.

Although the rhetoric of the organization is couched in such phrases as "helping the offender" and "developing a positive relationship," organizational controls tend to be attached to activities designed largely to foster the surveillance work of the agency or protect it from outside criticism. Parole officer performance most often is judged by the number of contacts that have been made with parolees, often with little regard for the quality of events that transpired during these contacts. Complete and prompt reports showing compliance with agency policies, such as written travel permits for parolees, are valued highly and require a major investment of parole officer time.

The result of this kind of administration is a rigid chain of command that is regimented, standardized, and predictable and that allocates power to persons on the basis of their position in the hierarchy. The parolee, being the lowest, is the least powerful.

Flexibility in Organizational Structure

A correctional policy that assumes parolees are capable of making a major contribution toward setting their own objectives and sees the parole agency's main task as helping the parolee realistically test and attain those objectives also must place a premium on developing an organizational structure that promotes flexibility. This means that managers must learn how to administer a decentralized organization that must adhere to broad policies and yet allow for a high degree of individual autonomy.

The dilemmas that arise when a manager tries this style of administration are many. Their resolution requires a sophisticated knowledge of administration and organizational techniques. One of the highest priorities for effective development of community-based services lies in providing managers with precisely this kind of skill.

Nelson and Lovell summarize the issues well:

> The correctional field must develop more collaborative, less hierarchical administrative regimes in order to implement its reintegration programs. The hierarchical format was developed to achieve the goal of production and orderly task performance. When individual change is the prime purpose of the organization, this format is inappropriate for people cannot be *ordered* to change strongly patterned attitudes and behavior. Nor is change apt to come about through the ritual performance of a series of tasks. . . . Power must be shared rather than hoarded. Communication must be open rather than restricted. Thus the managers of reintegration programs will need the skills of cooperation, communication, and collaboration.[32]

Resistance to reintegration-style programs can be widespread. Take for example a job function that has been interpreted traditionally as one of surveillance, head-counting, and maintenance of order. Management says the job is best accomplished by a new set of techniques—including relaxed, open end free communication, and decisionmaking involving parolees. Staff members should perceive themselves less as policemen than as counselors. It is highly likely in such a case that some staff will resist the changes.

Persons who see themselves as professionals also can be major obstacles to change. The trend toward a reintegration model and away from a rehabilitation model has been frustrating to several traditional professional groups who perceive their "expertise" as being challenged or, at worst, rejected. Meetings are held to organize opposition to "nonprofessional practices" and to changes that are "untested" and that have strayed from the "tried and true." It is not surprising that administrators sometimes capitulate. But "let's not rock the boat" or "let's wait till next year" are the cliches of timid leadership that lead to stagnant bureaucracies. It takes great skill and perseverance to change an agency. There is no substitute for intelligence, skill, and above all, courage.

32. Elmer K. Nelson and Catherine H. Lovell, *Developing Correctional Administrators* (Washington: Joint Commission on Correctional Manpower and Training, 1969), p. 14.

COMMUNITY SERVICES FOR PAROLEES

A significant number of parolees can do very well without much official supervision, according to repeatedly validated research.[33] Many offenders can be handled in relatively large caseloads simply by maintaining minimum contact with them and attending to their needs as they arise. Most of these parolees probably should be released from any form of supervision at all. Outright discharge from the institution would be an appropriate disposition and should be used much more frequently than it is. Failing that, minimum supervision can and should be employed for a significant group.

For those parolees requiring more intensive help, the emphasis in recent years, and one worthy of support, has been toward effecting as many needed services as possible through community resources available to the general population. To the extent that offenders can gain access to these opportunities on the same basis as other citizens, the additional blocks that arise when parolees attempt to move into the mainstream of community life are reduced.

Moreover, more resources usually are available to programs designed to deal with a broad public spectrum. For example, vocational training programs operated by correctional agencies cannot begin to offer the range of services offered by government agencies to economically deprive groups in general. Skills developed in programs for these groups are usually much more marketable. Job placement is also more likely to be operating effectively.

Finally, using such services allows flexibility and speed in adapting to needs. It avoids creation of additional specialized bureaucracies on State payrolls that respond more readily to their own survival needs than to changing needs of offenders. Provision of funds to parole agencies to purchase resources in the community represents an important new approach to the problems of securing needed services.

From this perspective, a major task of parole officers is to make certain that opportunities in community services and programs actually exist for parolees and to prepare and support parolees as they undertake these programs. Offenders often are locked out of services for which they apparently qualify according to the criteria established by the agency, not because of any official policy barring them but because of covert resistance to dealing with persons thought to be troublesome. Mental health agencies deny assistance to offenders on grounds that such persons cannot benefit from their programs. Public employment offices often are reluctant to refer to an employer a person viewed as unreliable. Public housing resources may be restricted because of biases against persons with records.

---

33. See Joseph D. Lohman, Albert Wahl, and Robert Carter, *The San Francisco Project: The Minimum Supervision* *Caseload,* Research Report No. 8 (Berkeley: University of California, 1966).

Considering these reactions and the discrimination that too often exists against minority group members, who constitute a significant portion of the offender population in many areas of the country, the need for a parole staff that is willing and able to play the role of broker or resource manager for parolees is clear. This need involves more than skills at persuasion or aggressive argument. It also requires a knowledge of the sources of power in a community and the ability to enlist those sources in changing agency behavior.[34]

Undoubtedly, the trend toward creating new ways of delivering services to meet human needs—mental health, family counseling, physical rehabilitation, employment, and financial assistance—will modify the parole officer's tasks in several important respects. Human service centers designed to deliver a wide range of programs will develop.[35] Part of the task of parole staff will be to support such efforts and play an appropriate role in a coordinated human-services delivery system. Increasingly, the parole officer's unique responsibility will be to make certain that offenders obtain the benefit of available resources, to counsel parolees about the conditions of their parole, and to help them meet those conditions.

Financial Assistance

Perhaps the most common problem immediately confronting offenders released from adult correctional institutions is the need for money for the most basic needs—shelter, food, and transportation. Most States provide new releasees with transportation, some clothes, and modest gate money totaling perhaps $50. Inmates fortunate enough to have been assigned to programs in which money can be earned in prison frequently are much better off financially than those who were not. Those who have participated in work-release programs usually will have saved a portion of their salary for the time of their release.

Data that show parole failure rates clearly related to the amount of money an offender has during the first months of release can be explained in a number of ways.[36] Nevertheless, it is a consistent finding and, in the day-by-day existence of parolees, lack of funds is a critical problem.

A number of solutions to this problem have been tried over the years, the most common being a loan fund arrangement. Although there are several difficulties in administering such a fund, it is a practical necessity in every parole system until arrangements for sufficient "gate money" or other subvention can be provided.

34. John M. Martin and Gerald M. Shattuck, "Community Intervention and the Correctional Mandate," consultant paper prepared for the President's Commission on Law Enforcement and Administration of Justice, 1966.

35. U. S. Department of Health, Education, and Welfare, Community Service Administration, *Toward a Comprehensive Service Delivery System through Building the Community Service Center* (1970).

36. Glaser, *The Effectiveness of a Prison and Parole System,* pp. 333–348.

The most practical and direct way to meet the problem is to provide offenders with opportunities to earn funds while they are incarcerated. For those who are unemployed, funds should be provided, much in the manner of unemployment compensation, when they are first released until they are gainfully employed. The State of Washington recently has adopted precisely such legislation. It should be adopted in every jurisdiction.

Employment

Closely related to the problem of finances is that of getting and holding a decent job. While it is difficult to demonstrate experimentally a precise relationship between unemployment and recidivism, the gross picture does show a fairly consistent link between unemployment and crime.[37] Hence every parole system should maintain its own measures of unemployment rates among its populations.

For the offender already on the street, the most critical skill required of a parole officer is directing him to a wide variety of services available in the community. A prime resource is the State employment service. Almost everywhere such services have commitments at the policy level to extend special assistance in the placement of parolees.

However, the test of these programs is found in the day-by-day working relationships between local employment personnel and parole officers. How well they cooperate is colored by the attitudes of local employment department staff but more importantly by the skill of the parole staff in maintaining relationships. A wide variety of other programs exist; for example, those sponsored by the Office of Economic Opportunity, the Office of Vocational Rehabilitation, and the large number sponsored by the Department of Labor. The key issue in using these programs is good communication at the local operational level.

The most acute employment problems are those associated with persons about to be released on parole. It is a time of great strain on the parolee. The difficulty of finding employment often is an additional source of anxiety because the most common reason why offenders are held beyond the date fixed for their release is that they have no job to go to.

Many States have developed systems of "reasonable assurance," under which a definite job is not required before an inmate is released, provided some means can be found to sustain him until one can be found. This generally is a far better practice than holding him until a job is promised. Parolees find it much easier to get a job if they can personally interview employers. Research consistently has shown offenders do as well, if not better, if they can find their own job.[38]

37. Glaser, The Effectiveness of a Prison and Parole System, ch. 14.

38. John M. Stanton, "Is It Safe to Parole Inmates Without a Job?" Crime and Delinquency, 12 (1966), 149.

Partial release programs in the community go a long way toward eliminating many of these problems. While the offender still is confined, he has the chance to make contacts in the community, be interviewed by employers, work directly with a parole officer, or actually begin an employment program through work release. In terms of a broad correctional strategy aimed at coping with employment problems, prerelease programs are of pivotal importance.

Another activity that has grown in recent years, under sponsorship of both private and public sources, is job training programs in institutions that are connected to specific job possibilities on the outside. The Office of Vocational Rehabilitation has programs in a number of institutions. The Department of Labor has made numerous efforts in this area. Such programs need to be supported because of the large-scale resources and expertise they represent and the network of relationships they possess in the free community.

Residential Facilities

Another major need of many newly released offenders is a place to live. For some, the small, community-based residential facility is extremely useful in a time of crisis.

Young persons particularly need to have a place to go when events begin to overwhelm them. Such centers also can be useful for dealing with offenders who may have violated their parole and require some control for a short period, but for whom return to an institution is unnecessary.

To the extent that such facilities can be obtained on a contract basis, the flexibility and, most probably, the program quality increase. For young offenders especially, bed space in small group facilities can be secured through many private sources. This is less true for adults, and development of State operated centers may be required.

Differential Handling

Making all programs work requires a wide variety of resources, differential programming for offenders, and a staff representing a diversity of backgrounds and skills. Some offenders may be better handled by specialized teams. Drug users of certain types may be dealt with by staff who have considerable familiarity with the drug culture and close connections with various community drug treatment programs. Other offenders may require intensive supervision by officers skilled at maintaining close controls and surveillance over their charges. While the latter may be assigned to a specialized caseload, assignments to specialized treatment caseloads in general should involve a great deal of self-selection by the offender. Arbitrary assignments to "treatment" groups easily can result in the offender's subversion of program objectives. An ongoing program of assessment and evaluation by staff and parolees is needed to make certain that offenders are receiving the kind of program most appropriate for them.

MEASURES OF CONTROL

There is an increasing tendency to minimize use of coercive measures and find ways by which offenders' goals and aspirations can be made congruent, if not identical, with agency goals. These trends can be seen in the shifting emphasis of parole rules, the clearest manifestation of the coercive power of parole.

Until the 1950's parole rules heavily emphasized conformity to community values and lifestyles with little or no relationship to the reason why a person originally committed a crime. One State's rules, only recently amended, give the flavor of such conditions. They provided in part that:

> The person paroled shall in all respects conduct himself honestly, avoid evil associations, obey the law, and abstain from gambling and the use of intoxicating liquors. He shall not visit pool halls, or places of bad repute, and shall avoid the company and association of vicious people and shall at least once each Sunday attend some religious service or institution of moral training.

In the 1950's many rules of this type were replaced by more specific conditions such as requiring the parolee to obtain permission to purchase a car. Until the late 1960's almost every State had a long list of parole conditions.[39] As "tools of the parole officer," these conditions gave reason to expect that violations would occur often although official action would not be taken unless the parole officer felt the case warranted it. Problems of differential enforcement were bound to occur, and did. A great deal of ambiguity developed for both parolees and parole officers as to which rules really were to be enforced and which ignored. Studies have demonstrated that officers tend to develop their own norms of behavior that should result in return to prison. These norms among parole officers became very powerful forces in shaping revocation policies.[40]

The recent trend has been toward reducing rules and making them more relevant to the facts in a specific parole case. Part of this move undoubtedly has been stimulated by the interest of the courts in parole conditions. Conditions have been struck down by the courts as unreasonable, impossible of performance, or unfair. Additional principles constantly are being developed, as when a Federal court recently restrained the State of California from prohibiting a parolee from making public speeches. Hyland v. Procunier, 311 F.Supp. 749, 750 (N.D.Calif.1970).

Several States have reduced the number of parole conditions considerably. In 1969, 45 jurisdictions prohibited contact with undesirable

39. Nat Arluke, "A Summary of Parole Rules," *Journal of the National Probation and Parole Association*, 218 (January 1956), 2–9.

40. James Robinson and Paul Takagi, "The Parole Violator as an Organiza-tion Reject" in Robert Carter and Leslie Wilkins, eds., *Probation and Parole: Selected Readings* (Wiley, 1970).

associates; today 35 do so. Ten States removed the requirement of permission to marry or file for divorce. Oregon, as a specific example, has removed nine discernible general conditions, including the requirement of permission to change residence or employment, to operate a motor vehicle, or to marry; the proscription of liquor or narcotics and contacts with undesirables; and dictates that the parolee maintain employment, support his dependents, and incur no debts. Idaho has removed seven such rules from its agreement of release.

Perhaps the most substantial change in procedure occurred in the State of Washington, where the standard parole conditions imposed on all inmates were reduced to four. They required the parolee to (1) obey all laws, (2) secure the permission of a parole office before leaving the State, (3) report to the officer, and (4) obey any written instructions issued by him. The State parole board imposes additional conditions in individual cases as seems appropriate. Conditions also may be added during the course of parole on the parole officer's application.

The advantage of this system is that both the parolee and parole officer know which conditions are to be enforced, although obviously violations of the remaining rules are judged individually and may not result in a return to prison. The other advantage is that much unnecessary anxiety is avoided over rules that rarely, if ever, would result in a return to prison. More such candor should be encouraged in parole supervision practice.

The removal of unnecessary rules also helps to shape the activity of the parole officer more positively. When unclear or unnecessary rules exist, the effect is twofold: a great deal of busy work by a parole officer; and a corruption of his relationship with the parolee. The trust of the reintegration approach is toward an open problem solving relationship between the parole officer and the parolee in which the parolee's objectives are clarified and tested against the limits under which both he and the parole officer must live. The fewer the limits required by the parole system, the greater the opportunity of locating alternative behavior styles that are satisfying and meet the tests of legality. This is not to say that rules should not be enforced, but that there should be as much honesty in the enforcement process as possible.

Some parolees do require fairly intensive and directive supervision. In such cases, parole officers with the skill and aptitude for this kind of case should be assigned. Some intensive supervision caseloads (12 to 20 parolees) can be differentiated as caseloads for surveillance rather than for counseling and support. The parolee may not be in a position to see the relevance of any services offered, but he can respond positively to the knowledge that his daily whereabouts and activities are under careful scrutiny. In the eyes of the parolee, the efficacy of intensive surveillance caseloads resides in the credibility of the counselor and those he recruits to assist.

The need for high surveillance and intensive supervision for some offenders raises directly the question of the extent to which parole officers should assume police functions, such as arresting parolees, and the associated question as to whether they should be armed. A 1963 survey of parole authority members in the United States revealed that only 27 percent believed that parole officers should be asked to arrest parole violators. Only 13 percent believed that parole officers should be allowed to carry weapons.[41] In general, most parole officers accept the proposition that arrests by parole officers may be necessary on occasion but strong liaison with police departments should be depended on in the majority of instances when arrests are needed.

Guns are antithetical to the character of a parole officer's job. Much concern among some parole officers as to the need to be armed arises from their anxiety in working in areas of cities in which they feel alienated and estranged. This anxiety can be allayed by assigning to such districts persons who live in them. The RODEO project in Los Angeles, where probation officers are assigned two community assistants drawn from the neighborhood, is an excellent example. Because of their intimate knowledge of the community, such workers are able to keep well informed of the activities of their charges without the necessity of using tactics normally associated with police agencies.

MANPOWER

Problems of manpower for corrections as a whole are discussed throughout this text. Here the discussion will be limited to special manpower problems of parole systems.

Recruitment and Personnel Practices

Nothing indicates more starkly the relatively low priority that parole programs have received in governmental services than parole officers' salaries. The National Survey of Corrections indicated that in 1965 the median starting parole officer salary in the United States was approximately $6,000 a year. Although the studies of the Joint Commission on Correctional Manpower and Training three years later showed this salary base had risen, most of the gain could be accounted for by a national upswing in salary levels. It did not represent a substantial gain compared to other positions in government and industry.

The essence of an effective parole service lies in the caliber of person it recruits. Until salaries are made attractive enough to recruit and hold competent personnel, parole programs will be sorely handicapped. Almost half of the State agencies responsible for parole services surveyed

41. National Parole Institutes, *Description of Backgrounds and Some Attitudes of Parole Authority Members of* *the United States* (New York: National Council on Crime and Delinquency, 1963).

by the Joint Commission reported serious difficulties in recruiting new officers.[42]

Though merit system procedures have significantly dampened political patronage influences in staff selection and promotion, they have brought a series of built-in restrictions. These must be overcome if a reintegration style for parole agencies is to be effected. The great difficulties attached to removing incompetent employees and the lack of opportunities for lateral entry are two examples. The most acute problems are those surrounding the criteria for staff selection and promotion. The issue bears most specifically on the employment and advancement of minority group members. For example, in 1969, while blacks made up 12 percent of the general population, only 8 percent of correctional employees were black, and they held only 3 percent of all top and middle level administrative positions.[43]

Some reforms are beginning, but merit systems are traditionally suspicious of new job titles and slow to establish them. When a new program is initiated, existing job titles frequently do not fit. The red tape and delays encountered in hiring staff often seriously damage programs. A sense of the frustration felt by administrators who are trying to modernize their programs is captured in the statement of one State parole system head, who asserts that merit systems can be and frequently are the single largest obstacle to program development in community-based corrections.

Manpower Requirements

The problems of trying to determine staffing needed to carry out an effective parole supervision program is complicated tremendously by lack of agreement on objectives and knowledge of how to reach them. Within any correctional policy, a number of alternative styles are needed, ranging from no treatment at all to a variety of specific and carefully controlled programs. Perhaps the most discouraging experiments in parole supervision were those that sought to test the thesis that reducing caseloads to provide more intensive services would reduce recidivism.

The project that broke most completely from this notion was the Community Treatment Project of the California Youth Authority. The program involved classification of offenders by an elaborate measure of interpersonal maturity or "I-level" and use of treatment techniques specifically designed for each "I-level" type. Treatments ranged from firm, controlling programs for manipulative youths to supportive and relatively permissive approaches for those assigned to a category that included neurotic and anxious youngsters. With certain exclusions, offenders were assigned randomly to 10-man caseloads in the community,

---

42. Joint Commission on Correctional Manpower and Training, *A Time to Act.* Washington: (JCCMT, 1969), p. 13.

43. *A Time to Act,* p. 14.

each of which was designed to carry out treatments consistent with a particular classification, or to a term in a training school followed by regular parole supervision.[44]

The results of the project were impressive. After 24 months, those assigned to special caseloads had a violation level of 39 percent. Those assigned to a regular program had a 61 percent failure rate. Of interest also was the variation in success rates among "I-level" types. Some researchers argue that some of the research results should be attributed to differences in official reaction to the behavior of those in special caseloads as opposed to those in regular ones,[45] rather than improvements in the offenders. Yet results in the context of other research efforts described by Stuart Adams make the argument for a differential treatment approach fairly strong.[46]

The Work Unit Parole program in effect in the California Department of Corrections since 1964 divides parolees into several classifications (based in part on their prior record and actuarial expectancy of parole success). It requires certain activities from the parole officer for each classification of parolee and thereby is able to control the work demands placed on an individual officer.

In this system, the ratio of officers to parolees is approximately 1 to 35.[47] Two facts about the program should be noted.

1. The ratio of 1 to 35 does not express a caseload. Officers are assigned to a variety of tasks that are quantifiable. These task related workloads are the basis for staff allocation.

2. The workload ratios for a specific agency would depend on the kinds of offenders they have to supervise and the administrative requirements of that agency.

The important point is that the concept of a caseload as a measure of workload is outmoded, especially in an era stressing a variety of skills and team supervision. The task is to spell out the goals to be accomplished and the activities associated with their attainment, and to assign staff on that basis. Research information must continuously inform the judgment by which these allocations are made.

Education and Training Needs

Both the Corrections Task Force in 1967 and the Joint Commission in 1969 agreed that a baccalaureate degree should be the basic education requirement for a parole officer, and persons with graduate study might

44. Marguerite Q. Warren, "The Case for Differential Treatment of Delinquents," *Annals of the American Academy of Political and Social Science*, 381 (1969), 46.

45. Paul Lerman, "Evaluating the Outcomes of Institutions for Delinquents," *Social Work*, 13 (1968), 3.

46. Stuart Adams, "Some Findings from Correctional Caseload Research," *Federal Probation*, 31 (1967), 148.

47. California Department of Corrections, *Work Unit Program, 1971* (Sacramento, 1971).

be used for specialized functions. Both also stressed the need to create opportunities for greater use of persons with less than college-level study. Many tasks carried out by a parole officer can be executed just as easily by persons with much less training, and many skills needed in a parole agency are possessed by those with limited education. As observed earlier, persons drawn from the areas to be served are good examples of staff with needed specialized skills. Ex-offenders also are an example of a manpower resource needed in parole agencies. A growing number of agencies have found such persons to be an immensely useful addition to their staffs.[48]

Ways of recruiting, training, and supervising these relatively untapped sources of manpower for parole and other elements of corrections are discussed in Chapter 14.

STATISTICAL ASSISTANCE

Proper organization, selection, and training of personnel are necessary for improved parole services, but in themselves they are insufficient. The crucial task of making the "right" decision remains for whoever must make it, whatever his position in the organization. Although the typical parole board member deals with a variety of concerns in decisionmaking, his basic objective is to lessen as much as possible the risk that an offender will commit another crime. This criterion remains paramount, but it is so variably interpreted and measured that severe handicaps impede its attainment.

To begin with, the measures of recidivism currently used in individual jurisdictions vary so much that useful comparisons across systems, and indeed within systems, are virtually impossible. In one jurisdiction, only those parolees who return to prison are counted as failures, no matter what may have transpired among those parolees not returned. In another, everyone who has been charged with a violation as measured by the number of parole board warrants issued is treated as a failure.

The length of time under parole supervision confounds other comparisons. Thus recidivism variously includes the rest of the parolee's life, the span of the parole period only, or the time immediately following discharge.

The computational methods used in developing success or failure ratios also can do more to confuse than to assist understanding. In one State, recidivism is measured by the proportion of offenders returned to prison compared with the number released in the same period. In another, a much lower rate is shown for exactly the same number of failures because it is arrived at by computing the number of persons returned to prison in a given period compared with the total number of

48. Vincent O'Leary, "Some Directions for Citizen Involvement in Corrections," *Annals of the American Academy of* *Political and Social Science*, 381 (1969), 99.

persons supervised during the same period. Until uniform measures are developed, vitally needed comparisons are not possible. Nor will meaningful participation in policy decisions be possible for agencies and persons outside the parole system.

Uniform Parole Reports System

A major effort to help solve the problem of uniform measures of recidivism was development of the National Uniform Parole Reports System, a cooperative effort sponsored by the National Parole Institutes. This program enlisted the voluntary cooperation of all State and Federal parole authorities having responsibility for felony offenders in developing some common terms to describe parolees—their age, sex and prior record—and some common definitions to describe parole performance. Parole agencies for the last several years have been sending this information routinely to the Uniform Parole Report Center, where it is compiled. The results are fed back to the contributing States. Comparisons across the States thus are beginning to be possible. This effort represents a long step in developing a common language among parole systems.

Although this national system has made great strides, many additional steps need to be taken to develop its capacity fully. The Uniform Parole Report System needs to tie into a larger network that includes data from correctional institutions, so that information collected on the offender can be linked to parole outcome and crucially needed comparative data on discharged offenders can be obtained.

Important also is the need to tie in, on a national basis, to crime record data systems so that followup studies extending beyond parole periods can be carried out. The Uniform Parole Report System should have access to national criminal history information so that the experiences of parolees who have been classified according to a set of reliable factors can be checked. Attempts to use the usual criminal identification record alone to describe the results of parolee performance inevitably suffer from such gross inadequacies as to be almost completely useless. The careful definitions built into the Uniform Parole Report System should be combined with access to criminal data. This would enable tracing of subsequent parolee histories and could be a powerful tool for policy development and research.

A comparable system for releases from juvenile institutions also is needed. Information on misdemeanants released on parole is almost nonexistent. Development of statewide statistical services in corrections is the key for such misdemeanant recordkeeping.

Uses and Limitations of Statistics in Parole

Thus far the stress on statistical development has been on its utility as a national reporting system. But equally needed is a basic statistical system in each parole jurisdiction to help it address a variety of concerns in sufficient detail for practical day-to-day decisionmaking. There are a number of ways such data can be used.

Since the 1920's a number of researchers have concerned themselves with developing statistical techniques for increasing the precision of recidivism probability forecasting, as noted in Chapter 15. Although the methods may vary in detail, the basic aim of the studies has been to identify factors that can be shown to be related statistically to parole outcome and, by combining them, to ascertain recidivism probability for certain parolee classes. These statements usually have been labeled "parole predictions."

Typically, the probability statements produced by statistical techniques are more accurate in estimating the likely outcome of parole than are traditional case methods. There has been relatively little use of these devices in the parole field, although some experimentation has been carried on in several jurisdictions.

A major source of resistance to the use of prediction methods is found in the nature of the parole decision itself.[49] Parole board members argue, for example, that simply knowing the narrow probability of success or failures is not nearly as helpful as knowing what type of risk would be involved. For example, they are more likely to tolerate higher risks if an offender is likely to commit a forgery than if he is prone to commit a crime against a person. Most prediction systems depend largely on prior events, such as criminal age and criminal record. This does not help a parole board that must deal with the offender as he is today within the realities of the decisions and time constraints available to them.

Technology is capable of dealing with a number of the additional concerns of parole authorities and probably will continue to make statistical information increasingly valuable. Currently a major research project is under way with the U.S. Parole Board seeking ways in which statistical material can assist the parole board member in his decisionmaking. Significant help lies in this direction, and each jurisdiction should be made fully aware of the possibility of using statistical information in parole decisionmaking.

With computer technology and the possibility it offers of instant feedback, the usefulness of this kind of system should increase. It seems doubtful, however, that statistical methods in the foreseeable future can substitute entirely for the judgments of parole board members and examiners. The impact and the variety of elements other than the estimation of risks are profound. The intricacies that arise in the individual case make total dependence on any statistical system highly risky at best.

Statistical predictions can be helpful in giving guidelines to parole board members as to general categories into which particular inmates fit, how other inmates similarly situated were treated earlier, and what the trends are in broad decisions. This information is important for parole

---

49. Norma S. Hayner, "Why Do Parole Board Members Lag in the Use of Pre-diction Scores?" *Pacific Sociological Review*, (Fall 1958), 73.

decisionmakers. But most experts are convinced that the optimum system is one in which both statistical and individual case methods are used in making decisions about individuals.

Daniel Glaser sums up the issue as follows:

> I know of no instance where an established academic criminologist, judge or correctional administrator has advocated the replacement of case studies and subjective evaluation by statistical tables for sentencing, parole or other major decisions on the fate of an offender. The many reasons for insisting upon case data may be grouped into two categories. First of all, these officials must make moral decisions for the state as a whole in determining what risks would justify withholding from or granting freedom to a man. . . . Secondly, there always is some information on a case too special to be readily taken into account by any conceivable table in estimating what risks are involved in a specific official action. Thirdly, there are many types of predictions besides the overall prospect of violations which judges and parole board members must consider. These include the type of violation, and the consequences of certain types of violations for community treatment of other parolees.[50]

PAROLE IN CRISIS: A REPORT ON NEW YORK PAROLE *

Parole is generally viewed as an idealistic concept.[1] Its announced purposes seek simultaneously to protect the public and to give the criminal offender a new chance. These noble purposes have not been realized, and the most basic finding of the study reported here is that when parole is combined with other elements of the criminal justice system—unnecessary pretrial detention, overlong and indeterminate sentences, oppressive prison conditions—it renders American treatment of those who break society's rules irrational and arbitrary.

This paper summarizes a 300-page study of the New York State parole system that was conducted by the Citizens' Inquiry on Parole and Criminal Justice.[2] Research for the study included observing 200 parole

50. *The Effectiveness of a Prison and Parole System*, p. 304.

* Citizens Inquiry on Parole and Criminal Justice, Inc., *Criminal Law Bulletin*, Vol. 11, No. 3, May-June 1975.

1. Revisionist historians, like David Rothman, author of *The Discovery of an Asylum*, are beginning to suggest that the growth of parole in this country was stimulated by a realization that it would be an effective plea bargaining and prison-control device. While the

social work-welfare community was allowed to speak publicly of parole's ameliorative effects, the prosecutor-warden community supported the extension of parole as a management-sentence control device.

2. The Citizens' Inquiry is a private, nonprofit organization, founded in the wake of the Attica rebellion to engage in research and public education on postconviction criminal justice issues. Its chairman is former Attorney General Ramsey Clark; its executive vice-

release hearings, interviewing thirty parole officials and over 100 parolees, reviewing all the statutes relating to parole enacted since 1877,
reading all the annual reports of the Division of Parole since 1930,
checking all *New York Times* references to parole in the last forty years,
and studying the relevant legal and sociological scholarship. This, however, does not mean that the viewpoint is value-free. While the Report
strives for objectivity in reporting its findings, it is also informed by a set
of strongly held beliefs about the use of the criminal sanction in a free
society.

VALUE ASSUMPTIONS AND CONCLUSIONS

The Citizens' Inquiry study was premised, in part, on the following
values:

(1) Individual freedom is basic to a democratic society, and the
    occasions for its legitimate deprivation must rest on incontrovert-
    ible evidence that the actions of offenders have caused or threat-
    en substantial harm to the legitimate and legally protected rights
    of others.

(2) Prisons are expensive and brutalizing institutions that too often
    create crime, rather than correct offenders.

(3) When confinement appears necessary to accomplish the aims of
    the criminal sanction, the distance between the offender and his
    community should be reduced to an absolute minimum.

(4) Coercion that extends beyond basic confinement should be re-
    duced to a minimum since the confinement itself is the primary
    sanction for those few offenders who must be separated from
    their community. Inmates should not be deprived of additional
    rights except to the extent made necessary by the fact of their
    incarceration. Neither inmates nor parolees should have to sub-
    mit to correctional efforts that are designed to shape them into a
    homogeneous model of good citizenship.

Reform efforts generally—and certainly in criminal justice—challenge the practices of the institution under fire, while accepting the
validity of its concept and theory. The Citizens' Inquiry study repudiates
both the concept and theory, as well as the practice associated with
parole. It finds that the New York parole authorities do not abide by
their own standards, and that even if they did, the invalidity of basic
parole theory would prevent the realization of its self-professed goals. It
would appear to be desirable for a parole board to be well-prepared and to
conduct careful release interviews based on full information about inmates; but even this would not result in rational and equitable decision-

chairman is Professor Herman
Schwartz of S.U.N.Y. Buffalo Law
School. David Rudenstine was director
at the time of the parole study; its
current director is Diana R. Gordon.

The full version of this report has been
published by Praeger Publishers Inc.
(Special Studies Division) under the title *Prison Without Walls: Report on
New York Parole*, in February 1975.

making. Parole boards would continue to reach arbitrary results because, for the time being at least, future human conduct cannot be predicted with certainty.

Without standards to measure the fact-finding operations of the parole board or the substantive outcomes of the parole process, due process protections are meaningless. When rehabilitation is urged as the overriding objective of parole and is then supported with vague and subjective notions of moral character, personality development, and future conduct, the net effect is to give parole authorities discretion to measure the unmeasurable.

It is important to place parole in the context of a process that begins with arrest and proceeds through the pretrial stage (where a defendant may be held in detention or released), the trial, sentencing, and the period of imprisonment. Long-range and interim recommendations for parole depend on the future direction of pretrial detention, sentencing, and prisons. To abolish parole because of its demonstrated failure and leave the rest of the criminal process as it presently exists would cause even more harm. With all of its faults, parole is not as destructive as imprisonment, and the possibility of release is preferable to the certainty of confinement.

Although the Citizens' Inquiry did not specifically focus on the related institutions that would have to change with the abolition of parole, the study inevitably involved some examination of them.[3] Those changes that are most intimately related to parole and that must be coordinated with its abolition are outlined in the final section on recommendations.[4]

This summary describes the theory of parole in New York and shows how current practices diverge from it. The invalidity of the theory itself is demonstrated, and long-term and transitional recommendations are made. The study reaches the following general findings and conclusions:

(1) The discretionary release and community supervision functions of parole in New York have failed dramatically and are beyond reform. However, since parole is part of the present indeterminate sentencing structure, it cannot be safely abolished without simultaneous, extensive changes in that structure.

(2) Parole in New York rests on faulty theory and has unrealistic goals. The supposed humanitarian goal of treatment and rehabilitation of the offender has been used to justify unnecessarily

3. Several task force members have had considerable experience with the total criminal justice system and their experience and recommendations form an important part of the total package of recommendations presented here.

4. In addition, other criminal justice reforms are also necessary, including the decriminalization of victimless crimes; the elimination of most pretrial detention; abolition of large, remote prisons; and the development of small neighborhood facilities. Continuing careful study should precede and accompany the institution and use of these reforms.

lengthy incarceration and parole supervision. With no agreement on the meaning or the attainment of rehabilitation, decisions as to length of sentence and timing of release are irrational and cruel.

(3) The parole system is often unnecessarily abusive and unfair, giving rise to many serious and legitimate grievances by offenders. Much of the daily oppressiveness flows from the enormous amount of unstructured and invisible discretion that is exercised by the parole board and the parole service.

(4) Parole allows many actors in the criminal justice system to disguise the real nature of their actions and thereby escape responsibility for them. For example, district attorneys may call for, and judges may impose, excessively long sentences in the name of law and order, knowing that the deferred sentencing process of parole will mitigate their harshness. On the other hand, a plea-bargaining arrangement may hold out a promise of early release that is broken by later parole decisions. The parole board's extensive and invisible discretion thus makes it possible to mislead both the public and individual offenders.

(5) Parole authorities continually refuse to adopt or consider widely accepted reforms that are proposed by responsible professional groups. Resistance to proposed legal reforms is pervasive and debilitating, not only for offenders but also for well-intentioned parole functionaries.

RACISM AND PAROLE

The racial consequences of our society's use of the criminal sanction are evident in the disproportionately high percentage of black prisoners and in the imbalance of racial backgrounds between the jailers and the jailed.[5] National commission reports and scholarly studies alike have pointed out the pervasiveness of racism in virtually all operations of the criminal justice system.[6] In order to eliminate discrimination, independent groups and the institutions of the system must first understand its nature and causes. Only sensitivity to the problem, combined with careful data collection and interpretation at every step of the process, can ensure that understanding.

The Citizens' Inquiry, in conducting this study, requested information about racial issues from state officials. The Division of Parole, however,

---

5. At Attica at the time of the rebellion (September 1971), for example, 63 percent of the inmates were black or Puerto Rican, while the correctional staff of 398 had no blacks and only one Puerto Rican. *The Official Report of the New York State Special Commission on Attica*, pp. 24, 28.

6. See *The Official Report of the New York State Special Commission on Attica* (Bantam Books, 1972); President's Commission on Law Enforcement and Administration of Justice, *The Challenge of Crime in a Free Society* (Washington: U.S. Gov't Printing Office, 1967); and *National Advisory Commis-*

as a matter of policy, does not collate statistical data that would reveal the extent to which parole operates in a racially discriminatory manner. As a result, a well-documented judgment concerning the practices and effect of racism in the parole system is not possible. We do know that inmates and parolees are largely members of poor minority groups, while parole board members are generally comparatively affluent and well-educated white males.[7]

Informal inquiries reveal that the proportion of black and Puerto Rican parole officers is considerably lower than that of inmates and parolees. Racial differences between the parole officials and parolee population are representative of both the fact and appearance of racial bias. Parole officials surely are derelict in not systematically collecting facts relating to racial issues and maintaining a vigilance over any discrimination they reveal. Not until blacks and other minorities participate equally with whites in shaping the criminal justice system—as corrections officers, parole officers, administrators, judges—will our society even begin to provide equal justice to its citizens.

THE IMAGE OF PAROLE

Most often, parole is represented as a liberal, humane way to mitigate the agonies of incarceration. Those who administer it today see it in this light. New York parole officials are proud of what they conceive to be a fair and effective institution. This section sets forth a brief history of parole, a description of its place in New York's criminal justice system, and a picture of the way in which the parole system sees itself—its goals, policies, and practices.

Background

Until the nineteenth century, prisons were used mainly to house detainees who awaited trials at which they were sentenced to such punishments as whipping, maiming, or execution. Long-term incarceration became the preferred practice when it was seen as a means whereby deviants could be reformed into productive citizens. Within the first fifty years of their existence, the fundamental defects of prisons became apparent. Beyond any other problems, they did not rehabilitate their inmates. An 1867 report to the New York State legislature said of state prisons around the country, "There is not one, we feel convinced . . . which seeks the reformation of its subjects as a primary object. . ." The late 1800s witnessed the birth of parole, accompanied by the rhetoric of an attempt to extend the theoretically rehabilitative benefits of prison

sion Report on Civil Disorders (Bantam Books, 1968).

7. Of the thirty-nine persons appointed to the board since 1930, there have been three black males, one black female, one Hispanic male, and thirty-four white males. Board members make over $36,000 a year.

life into the community while simultaneously reducing the likelihood that prison would have detrimental effects.[8]

New York, the first state to do so, adopted parole at the Elmira Reformatory nearly 100 years ago. In 1899, it spread to some adult institutions, and during the early years of the twentieth century, sentencing laws were changed to make a large number of inmates eligible for parole.[9] From the basic framework of the present parole system, which was established in 1930, parole has grown from an obscure agency, with a three-member board and a budget of less than $350,000, into a substantial bureaucracy (617 professionals in 1969, the last year for which figures were available), with a twelve-member parole board, a budget of close to $15 million, and nine offices around the state. In 1972, 4,412 inmates were released from state institutions on parole, and at the end of the year there were approximately 10,000 people under parole supervision in the state.

Parole Today

The basic components of parole are the same now as a century ago. Parole is granted to inmates after they have served a portion of their sentence, but before completion of the maximum term. Parolees, in theory, are supervised while in the community by parole officers and are expected to abide by special rules or suffer the penalty of reincarceration.

All states and the federal government now have parole systems. Parole is an integral part of the criminal justice system: Sentencing schemes are built around it, prosecutors take it into account in charging defendants and participating in plea bargaining, and the judicial role in sentencing has been diminished as the jurisdiction of parole boards over release has increased. Perhaps most significant is the role of parole in the operation of prisons. In New York, nearly two-thirds of all inmates leaving state prisons annually are released by the parole board; and the one-fifth released through a mechanism other than parole are subject, like parolees, to community supervision. Prison programs may be well or poorly attended, depending on whether inmates believe that their participation will improve their chances for parole.

While parole is often viewed by prison officials as a way of maintaining prison order and discipline, it may also be a cause of catastrophic prison uprisings. After a thorough investigation of the uprising at Attica prison in September 1971, in which forty-three inmates and guards died, the Official Report of the New York State Special Commission on Attica concluded:

8. For the history of American prisons, see D. J. Rothman, *The Discovery of the Asylum: Social Order in the New Republic,* Chapters 4 & 10 (Boston: Little, Brown & Co., 1971); and O. F. Lewis, *The Development of American* *Prisons and Prison Customs* 1776–1845 (Albany, N.Y., 1922).

9. For the theory and history of parole in New York, see IV *Attorney General's Survey of Release Procedures* (1939).

"Inmates' criticisms were echoed by many parole officers and corrections personnel, who agreed that the operation of the parole system was a primary source of tension and bitterness within the walls." [10]

While parole in New York has become an increasingly important part of the postconviction criminal justice system, it continues to function behind a veil of secrecy. The New York board is the largest, best-salaried state parole board in the country, yet few people could name or identify a single member. The public has only the slightest notion of parole's functions, goals, modes of operation, and its degree of success or failure. As a quasijudicial, antonomous body, the board is uniquely removed from the scrutiny of the courts, the legislature, the media, and the public.

How Parole Is Supposed to Work

Parole is seen by most corrections officials, legislators, judges, and citizens as a sensible device to ease the transition from incarceration to freedom, to shorten sentences, and to provide individual consideration of offenders' problems. To this end, the parole board theoretically tries to release an inmate when he has reached that optimal moment when he can lead a crime-free life "on the street." At this point, the community supervision program claims to aid his reintegration into society by offering him services and guidance beyond the prison walls. That parole officers are to act simultaneously as counselors, brokers of services, and policemen does not seem impossible to those who direct the system.

For the past 100 years, corrections professionals have embraced an undefined goal of rehabilitation of offenders as the aim of incarceration. One report sets forth the theory as follows:

"(1) There are certain personal characteristics that impede an individual's ability to function at a generally acceptable level in one or more basic social areas.

"(2) The difficulty of performing at a generally acceptable level in such areas significantly contributes to criminal conduct.

"(3) Treatment should be directed at overcoming the aforesaid personal characteristics.

"Thus, the aim of rehabilitation is to treat characteristics of the offender which are inconsistent with the basic characteristics needed to function acceptably. It is felt that, if the treatment has a positive impact, the offender will be more likely to satisfy his needs through socially acceptable conduct and the likelihood of his return to crime will be reduced." [11]

10. *Official Report of the New York State Special Commission on Attica*, p. 93.

11. Preliminary Report of the Governor's Special Committee on Criminal Offenders (New York State, 1968) p. 55.

Neither the parole board nor the parole service attempts to articulate the "certain personal characteristics that impede an individual's ability to function at a generally acceptable level."

Parole officials see the parole decision-making process as expert and fair, guided only by determinations of an inmate's degree of rehabilitation. The parole board is supposed to be an independent body of exemplary citizens with a range of experience to insure their impartiality. They are theoretically enabled to make highly individualized decisions because they are supposed to receive careful, official reports on each inmate and conduct an interview with him designed to reveal the likelihood that he will be a successful parolee. Preparation for parole is to be started in the prison with the skilled assistance of institutional parole officers.

All aspects of parole supervision are intended to further its two principal aims: the protection of the public and the assistance of the parolee in becoming reintegrated into nonprison life. The community supervision parole officer is to be a well-educated, sensitive person, able to maintain a helping relationship with the parolee, while at the same time enforcing the terms of the parole agreement. Parole officers are to be equally concerned about finding jobs for parolees and checking up to make sure that parolees live and work where they say they do. The parole service considers it important to invest these officers with a broad discretion in enforcing the less important parole conditions, but it also attempts to provide effective guidance and regulation through a detailed manual. A good parole officer must be able to anticipate when a parolee is beginning to stray and return him to prison, through initiating revocation proceedings, before a new offense is committed.

The parole system subscribes to the view that the combination of expertise, broad discretion, and concern for the offender and the community leads to equitable treatment. How well this is achieved is examined in the next section.

THE REALITY OF PAROLE

New York corrections officials believe that the goals of parole are sound and that its operation reflects professional competence and even-handed performance. The Citizens' Inquiry study, however, uncovered an enormous gap between what the parole system professes to do and what it actually does. Indeed, the dichotomy between objective and achievement, between philosophy and practice, is so great as to erode the very basis for parole.

The Parole Release Decision

The New York Board of Parole is an autonomous body within the State Department of Correctional Services. Its twelve members serve

full time and are appointed to six-year renewable terms by the governor. The formal autonomy of the board does not guarantee its independence since board memberships are often given out as political reward or favor. The range of relevant experience among board members is not wide; most are white males, over fifty, and from outside New York City. Many have come to the board from corrections and law enforcement.[12] People who have made careers of arresting and confining are now asked to wield the power of release.

The parole board's jurisdiction is very broad. It decides

—When most inmates will become eligible for parole;

—Who shall or shall not be paroled;

—What conditions parolees must obey while in the community;

—Who shall or shall not have his parole revoked;

—Who shall or shall not be discharged from community supervision prior to completing the normal term; and

—Who shall or shall not be granted a certificate partially restoring his civil and employment rights.[13]

Its jurisdiction extends to all inmates serving sentences of more than ninety days—a total well in excess of 20,000—and to all former inmates under parole supervision. As a result, the board's work load is enormous. In 1971, for example, the board reported that it was responsible for 17,628 hearings or decisions.

The parole board, operating in panels of three, is to set a parole eligibility date which, in the main, reflects its judgment as to when an inmate may be sufficiently rehabilitated to be seriously considered for release on parole. To this end, the board is endowed with broad discretion in establishing the date. In practice, however, parole eligibility dates are reflections of arbitrary rules, rather than judgments about the individual character of each inmate. For most inmates serving an indeterminate sentence, parole eligibility will be set as a matter of course at one-third of the maximum term or three years, whichever is less. This practice not only ignores the board's stated objectives, but abrogates its responsibilities under New York law.

Institutional parole officers prepare a case file on each inmate for parole board members. But this file does not ensure a truly individual-

12. Of the twelve board members in 1973, five came from New York State or City parole, three had been sheriffs, one had been a deputy director of the State Division for Youth, one had been an Assistant U.S. Attorney, one had been a lawyer and official of the Buffalo Urban League, and one had been assistant appointments officer to Governor Rockefeller.

13. N.Y.Correc.Law §§ 6, 210–216.

ized decision-making process. Although crammed with reports from a variety of sources—from prison officials to probation officers—the often bulky file is not very useful. Since board members receive it only at the moment they are ready to hold an inmate's release interview, there is no opportunity to examine the reports closely. Except for the "parole summary," which is prepared by an institutional parole officer, usually a few months before an inmate's hearing, only one board member actually scrutinizes the case file; duplicates are not provided to other members. Beyond this practice of hasty, one-member review, the quality of the file is not sufficiently high to be very helpful in any event.[14] With only one institutional parole officer for every 241 inmates, contacts with inmates are necessarily infrequent and superficial. Also, inmates and institutional parole officers do not meet in circumstances likely to elicit candid information for reports. In 1967, a study by the National Council on Crime and Delinquency found that New York case files contained inadequate depth as to the causes and manifestations of inmates' problems.[15]

The parole board makes its release decisions in panels of three during monthly visits to each state prison. The actual conduct of release interviews makes a mockery of the board's claim that it considers each individual inmate's case carefully. If only because of the board's work load, the interviews are generally very short. Those observed by the Citizens' Inquiry generally lasted less than twelve minutes, with some as short as five minutes; the longest release interview observed lasted twenty-five minutes. Although New York law requires that the release interview be conducted by three members of the parole board, in practice only the member who reads the file usually questions an inmate, while the other two panel members examine the files of the inmates who will come next. Most of the questions asked are predictable and general. Inmates are tense and usually try to say what they think will most favorably impress the parole board members.

The release process is manifestly unfair. The inmate is not permitted to have an attorney or other representative appear with him at his interview. He is not permitted to present his own witnesses or to confront those against him. He may not see any of his case file. New York officials claim that to provide the inmate with these basic due

14. This conclusion has been drawn from a very limited sample, since the parole board would not make case files available to Citizens' Inquiry researchers.

15. This study, prepared for the Department of Correctional Services (Field Services for Offenders in New York State: An Evaluation), asserts that

(1) The Board of Parole is not getting the quality of records needed to as-

sist them in the decision-making process;

(2) corrective treatment, if any, prior to the parole hearing is unplanned, not geared to the needs and problems of the individual, and not systematically evaluated; and

(3) institutional and field staff involved in the diagnostic and treatment process are either overloaded, unskilled, or lacking proper direction and supervision.

process rights at the setting of the parole eligibility date or at the release interview is unnecessary and undesirable.

Inmates are not informed of the decisions—how long they must serve before they are eligible for parole, or whether they have been granted or denied parole—until after the parole panel leaves the prison for the month. The inmate is then given only a form stating the decision without any explanation. In nearly all cases, there is no review of the parole panel's decision by either the entire parole board or the courts.[16]

Although the parole board professes to make release decisions on the basis of whether or not an inmate has been rehabilitated, the applicable statute offers no guidance in reaching that decision.[17] The statute stipulates that an inmate shall be released only if there is a "reasonable probability that . . . he will live and remain at liberty without violating the law and that his release is not incompatible with the welfare of society." Another provision requires that the inmate be "suitably employed in self-sustaining employment if so released."[18]

This statute is not the product of carefully designed and evaluated experiments over the years, but rather a collection of phrases that appeared in different statutes from 1877 to 1928 and that were simply pasted together. The parole board has not supplemented the statutory provisions by developing any formalized precedent to guide a panel in reaching a decision, nor does it rely on any of the available prediction tables. The absence of prescribed release criteria is reflected in the usual lack of discussion among panel members after an inmate leaves his interview. When discussion does take place, it is usually about when the unsuccessful inmate should appear before the parole board again or to what kind of community supervision unit the successful inmate should be assigned.

The board, in trying to apply the general legislative standards for release decisions, seems to rely informally on five criteria.[19] They are: (1) the inmate's psychological condition—whether his state of mind appears to have changed since he entered the institution, particularly whether he seems remorseful about his criminal ways and sincere in wishing to change them; (2) the inmate's past criminal record and present offense—how serious his offenses have been and how often repeated; (3) the inmate's adjustment to prison life, particularly his discipline record and his participation in programs, which the board think shows a desire to improve; (4) any record of previous community supervi-

---

16. See Berry v. Attica Prison Board, 59 Misc.2d 392, 299 N.Y.S.2d (1969).

17. The Citizens' Inquiry report asserts that no criteria exist; but if the parole board considers a determination of rehabilitation to be possible, it ought at least to have developed means that it thinks could aid it in making that determination.

18. New York Correc.Law § 213.

19. This conclusion is based on discussions with parole board members and on 210 parole release hearings observed by the Citizens' Inquiry chairman and staff director.

sion under probation or parole; and (5) the inmate's parole plans for work, family life, therapy, and housing. There is no empirical evidence that any of these criteria are reliable indicators concerning whether an inmate will commit another crime or how serious a crime he might commit. Instead, the criteria appear to reflect the subjective value patterns and paternalistic attitudes of the parole board.

Despite its legislative mandate, the board is sometimes as much influenced by bureaucratic and political considerations as by the reasonable probability "that an inmate will live and remain at liberty without violating the law." For example, an individual may be granted parole because he has cooperated with law enforcement personnel investigating a case, or denied parole because he has a poor prison discipline record. Occasionally, the board denies parole to an inmate because his original crime generated a lot of publicity and the board would be subject to public criticism if it released him.

The New York parole decision-making process is basically lawless. The absence of specified criteria and procedures is an unqualified invitation to inconsistent and unfair decisions based on unreasonable and illegal grounds.[20]

The lack of review and low visibility which accompanies the extensive discretion of the parole board ensures that the lawlessness will continue without being corrected or reduced.

Released and Returned as Violator—Same Year, By Method of Release *

	1968		1969		1970		1971	
	Parole Release	Condtnl Release	Parole Release	Condtnl Release	Parole Release	Condtnl Release	Parole Release	Condtn! Release
Released to Community Supervision	4623	1703	4086	1633	3860	1795	4051	1793
Returned as Violators	475	191	414	189	393	250	325	194
%	10.3	11.2	10.1	11.6	10.2	13.9	8.0	10.8

* **Notes:** (1) Source: Annual Report of the Division of Parole 1968–1971, Tables 25, 25A, 28, 28A.

(2) This chart does not purport to reflect general recidivism rates, even for a one-year period, because it shows only the return rates of inmates released and returned within the same year. Inmates released in November or December of one year are included as well as those released in January or February, although their return rates will clearly be much lower.

(3) Prisoners released by the parole board and on conditional release are subject to the same community supervision program.

(4) There is one unmeasured factor that might affect the validity of this comparison. A parole violator has the time remaining on his sentence credited with the time he spent in the community, whereas a conditional release violator does not.

IM–352

20. Citizens' Inquiry staff observed numerous cases of release decisions that were made on the basis of personal moral standards and that were applied unevenly to inmates convicted of similar offenses. This is not to suggest that the presence of criteria would address the underlying defects of the process, which rest on the invalidity of the notion that any human group can now assess changes in an inmate's character and predict his future behavior.

The ultimate test of a program, after all, is its results. Parole decision-making is simply ineffective. The following chart demonstrates that the percentage of parolees who return to prison during the same calendar year they are released is not significantly lower than the return rate of inmates denied parole and released only at the expiration of their maximum sentence, minus "good time" (conditional releasees).

The fact that parolees do no better in the community than other releasees suggests that the parole board does not assess the changes in an inmate or accurately predict the likelihood of his recidivism.

It is possible to argue that the chart shows the effectiveness of parole decisions rather than the opposite. Perhaps the return rate of those not released on parole would have been higher than that of parolees if the former had not been kept in prison for the extra period. But that view is substantially impaired in light of what is known about the effect of incarceration on recidivism rates. First, there is no evidence that any programs sponsored in prison affect the inmate's behavior after release from prison.[21] Second, even if prison programs were proven to be effective, most inmates are not offered participation in them. Third, scholars and ex-offenders alike believe that the prison experience is injurious to inmates, and instead of decreasing the likelihood of criminal behavior upon release, it increases it.

Community Supervision

The gap between the image and the reality of parole is evident in the inadequate provisions that are made for the material assistance of a parolee.[22] The personal and material problems of a parolee are staggering when he first comes out of prison. Nevertheless, he is given only a suit, $40, the name and address of a community supervision parole officer to whom he must report within 24 hours, and a list of rules that he must follow on pain of losing his freedom. He is generally qualified only for unskilled or semi-skilled work, and faces other major problems in getting and keeping a job. Although the parole service recognizes employment as a major goal of each parolee, the parole officers provide little assistance in finding jobs. In 1970, New York parole officers helped obtain only 506 jobs, although over 16,000 people were on parole at some time during the year, with 5,680 of them employed full time. Similarly, the Department of Correctional Services does next to nothing to help the penniless parolee with financial problems. "Gate money" of $40 is inadequate, the parole

21. See Martinson, "What Works?— Questions and Answers about Prison Reform," The Public Interest 22 (Spring 1974).

22. The term "parolee" as used here generally refers both to inmates released by the parole board and to those who are released because they have served their maximum sentence, less "good time." This latter group is also placed under community supervision until the expiration of their full term and is subject to the same restrictions. Where an assertion of this Report refers only to this group, they are called "conditional releasees."

service has no loan fund, and New York parolees are not eligible for unemployment benefits. Furthermore, the parole system does not encourage going on welfare because it contradicts the goals of self-sufficiency and dignity in the nonprison world. Not only does the parole service fail to provide adequate housing assistance, it often impedes a parolee's attempts to get settled because every proposed residence must be approved by the parole officer. The parolee's housing problems are further complicated by his ineligibility for public housing, at least in New York City.[23]

Unlike the rehabilitative objective, the law enforcement aim of the community supervision program is at least honored by a genuine effort at realization. Community supervision officers are urged to expend the greater part of their time and energy in trying to enforce the parole rules as embodied in the list which every parolee signs. This list is in the form of an agreement between the parolee and the parole board that the former will abide by the restrictions on his life imposed by the latter. The Correction Law specifies a number of conditions that may be imposed.[24] The parole agreement currently goes well beyond the minimal statutory provision, regulating virtually every aspect of a parolee's life.

Some of the more controversial conditions are: the prohibition against leaving the area of the state to which the parolee is released without the parole officer's permission; the requirement that a parolee must allow his parole officer to search him, or to visit him at home or at work, without prior notice; the limitation that a parolee may not associate with people who have a criminal record; the requirement that a parolee must consult with his parole officer before applying for a marriage license or changing his job or residence; and the requirement that a parolee must get permission from his parole officer to drive or own a car.

Parolees interviewed by the Citizens' Inquiry felt that these restrictions often unnecessarily inhibited their reintegration into society. In the New York metropolitan area—given the proximity of the Connecticut and New Jersey borders—the prohibition against driving and traveling inter-

---

23. See generally, Clark, *Crime in America* (New York: Simon & Schuster, 1970).

24. Section 215 of the New York Correction Law provides that

"The board shall adopt general rules with regard to conditions of parole and their violation and three members of the board may make special rules to govern particular cases. Such rules, both general and special, may include, among other things, a requirement that the parolee shall not leave the state without the consent of the board, that he shall, if eligible, reside in a suitable hostel or foster home, or that he shall, if eligible, reside in any suitable correctional facility, that he shall contribute to his own support in such hostel, foster home, or correctional facility, that he shall contribute to the support of his dependents, that he shall make restitution for his crime, that he shall, if there is a record, report or other evidence satisfactory to the board that he is addicted to the use of narcotic drugs, take clinic or similar treatment for narcotic addiction at a hospital or other facility where such treatment is available, that he shall abandon evil associates and ways, that he shall carry out the instructions of his parole officer and in general so comport himself as such officers shall determine."

state reduces a parolee's employment opportunities. The agreement, in general, denies the parolee what ordinarily would be basic constitutional guarantees to the right of privacy at home, on the job, and with respect to personal relations.

Furthermore, the comprehensiveness and vagueness of the conditions give parole officials enforcement leverage over the parolee, so that he is constantly at risk. In sum, the parole conditions are too numerous, coercive, and intrusive; their imposition seems more likely to hinder a parolee's integration into society than to help it.

After release, a parolee's principal contact with the parole system is through the community supervision parole officer, who is a college graduate with experience in social work, law enforcement, or law. The parole officer has a difficult role. He has two responsibilities: to assist parolees in adjusting to the outside world, and to prevent or punish parole violations and criminal activities. This means that the parole officer is to act as both social worker and policeman. It appears that he cannot fill either role very well.

As policeman, the parole officer is armed, authorized to search the parolee and his property, given power to restrict many aspects of his life, and charged with enforcing parole rules and initiating revocation proceedings if the rules are violated. He is statutorily classified, along with police and prison guards, as a "peace officer." [25]

As a social worker, he is supposed to counsel the parolee on basic social and financial problems. He may assist in finding a job or housing or drug therapy. He may mediate between the parolee and the agencies or organizations that he deals with. The two roles of the parole officer regularly conflict. He often must decide between an action which protects the community and one which aids the parolee. When such a situation arises, he is expected to choose the solution which he believes is most likely to protect the public. The conflict is apparent to parolees and precludes the development of a relationship of mutual trust.

New York's parole system emphasizes, more than in many jurisdictions, the role of law enforcement in community supervision. [26] This emphasis is misplaced for several reasons. For one thing, it is ineffective. Most unsuccessful parolees are apprehended by the police for a new offense before their parole officer has initiated parole revocation proceedings. Approximately half of New York parole revocations are initiated because of a new arrest. The law enforcement aspects of community supervision, when coupled with the impaired legal status of the parolee, also deny the parolee fundamental freedoms enjoyed by other citizens. Finally, the surveillance and the ever-present possibility that even minor conditions may be enforced to send a parolee back to prison can frustrate him in such a way as to increase his general alienation.

25. New York Crim. Proc. Law §§ 1.20(33)(i) and 140.25.

26. New York's parole agreement has more conditions than any other, according to a 1972 American Correctional Association study by William Parker.

Community supervision, in summary, does not assist the parolee and does not effectively protect the public. Scarce resources are spent on inept social services and ineffective enforcement of the parole agreement. The parole regulations become an albatross on the back of most parolees, actually impeding reentry into society.

Revocation

The basic coercive power of the community supervision program is the revocation of parole, followed by the parolee's return to prison for all or part of his sentence. Although the parole service maintains that this power is exercised fairly, parolees again are often treated as having none of the rights of ordinary citizens.

Revocation cuts across both the discretionary release and community supervision aspects of parole. Parole board members are ultimately responsible for deciding whether parole should be revoked in particular cases, and community supervision officers usually initiate and recommend a parolee's revocation. Because revocation leads back to prison, parolees live in terror of it.

The parole officer has enormous discretion in enforcing the parole agreement. The relevant statute provides that if the parole officer has "reasonable cause to believe that such [parolee] has lapsed, or is probably about to lapse, into criminal ways or company, or has violated the conditions of his parole in an important respect," [27] he is to report that to the parole board or its representative, who may then apprehend the parolee, or the officer may retake the parolee himself. Under the provisions of this statute, a parole officer may choose to overlook violations, and where a parolee has shown a generally good adjustment to the community, he often does so. When a violation of parole rules (often called a "technical violation") leads an officer to initiate revocation proceedings, it is often because he suspects that a parolee is "slipping," moving from a life that he thinks is fairly stable to one that seems to the officer more likely to bring about the commission of a crime. Other situations that parole officers deem appropriate for revocation proceedings are where a parolee is arrested, where he has absconded, or where he is convicted of a new felony. When a parolee is taken into custody as an alleged violator, he is held without any possibility of release, often for two or three months, pending his revocation hearing. [28]

In general, a parole officer prizes his wide discretion, and a certain amount of it is necessary to maintain the present system. Since the parole agreement contains so many technical rules, nearly every parolee

27. New York Correc.Law § 216.

28. See People ex rel. Calloway v. Skinner, 33 N.Y.2d 23, 347 N.Y.S.2d 178 (1973), which holds that (1) the right to bail is purely statutory in New York;

(2) a parole revocation proceeding is not a "criminal action or proceeding" within the meaning of the statute that governs bail; and (3) granting bail in parole revocation proceedings would create "insuperable problems."

violates one of them at some time. If a parole officer were obligated to recommend revocation every time he was aware of a rule violation, nearly all parolees would be returned to prison and then for only minor infractions.

The New York statute does not provide any due process safeguards for a parolee faced with revocation proceedings.[29] However, during the last few years, constitutional rulings of the United States Supreme Court and the New York Court of Appeals have begun to carve out some protection.[30] Taken together, these rulings have established, among other things, a two-step hearing process whereby the parole board determines whether or not the parole agreement has been violated. Recent decisions have also given the parolee the right to present witnesses, a limited right to confront witnesses against him, and the right to partial disclosure of information in the case file. While New York has complied in most respects with these rulings, it has refused to allow parolees to confront witnesses against them. In addition to providing parolees with procedural due process rights once revocation proceedings have begun, the judicial developments have also restrained parole officers somewhat in their decisions to recommend revocation.

The new due process rights are primarily important to the revocation process at its fact-finding stage. Once a finding of probable cause for a parole violation is made, parole board members must decide whether the violation is serious enough to warrant revocation, and, if so, whether to reincarcerate a parolee or return him to the community. They must make a prediction very similar to that made at the release stage, and their decision is the counterpart of judicial sentencing, albeit at a low level of visibility.

DEFECTS OF THE PAROLE THEORY

Parole rests on a set of assumptions popularly known as the treatment or rehabilitation theory. This theory, which gained wide currency in the nineteenth century and became the articulated goal of both sentencing and imprisonment, assumed that the cause of criminality was primarily a defect in the individual.[31] This defect, it was reasoned, could

29. The statute includes only a general grant of power to the parole board to revoke parole or conditional release (New York Correc. Law § 6a(2)). 7 New York State Code Rules & Regulations § 1.16 provides for the issuance of a parole warrant and the declaration of a delinquency where a parolee "fails to comply with the terms of his parole." Section 1.19 provides for representation by counsel, submission of evidence, and the presence of unsworn witnesses.

30. See People ex rel. Menechino v. Warden, Green Haven State Prison, 27 N.Y.2d 376, 318 N.Y.S.2d 449 (1971); Morrissey v. Brewer, 408 U.S. 471, 92 S.Ct. 2593 (1972); Gagnon v. Scarpelli, 411 U.S. 778, 93 S.Ct. 1756 (1973); and People ex rel. Calloway v. Skinner, 33 N.Y.2d 23, 347 N.Y.S.2d 178 (1973).

31. The "cause" of the individual's defect could be traced to external or societal reasons, or it might be traced to factors inherent in the individual. In either case, the person was impaired

be diagnosed and treated within a penal setting. The offender's response to treatment could be evaluated so that he could be released at the optimum moment of his rehabilitation (i. e., when he was least likely to commit another crime).

Under this theory, sentences had to provide for a flexible period of imprisonment, since the amount of time necessary for the offender's rehabilitation could not be predicted at the time of trial. In addition, prisons would have to provide treatment programs. Thus, a mechanism was needed to evaluate an offender's rehabilitation status in order to release him from prison at the optimal moment and to continue the rehabilitative process in the community. This mechanism is parole.

The announced goals of community supervision are: (1) to continue the treatment of the offender that was begun in prison by assisting him in his adjustment to the community, and (2) to protect the public from criminal activity by returning the offender to prison for violation of parole rules prior to the commission of a crime. To fulfill the latter goal, parole officers must identify parolees who are about to commit a crime; and the parole board, which possesses the final revocation authority, must agree with the parole officer's assessment and prediction.

Previous sections have discussed the gap between the reality of parole and its image. Instead of attempting to make carefully reasoned decisions based on an inmate's rehabilitation, the parole board actually uses a rule of thumb in setting the parole eligibility date. Members of the board speed through release interviews, reaching instant decisions that make no pretense at assessing the likelihood of an inmate's recidivism.[32]

The similarity between defendants granted parole and those denied it is striking enough to suggest that, despite its attempts at professionalism and competence, the parole board is unable to distinguish the rehabilitated from the nonrehabilitated. The community supervision program, instead of helping parolees adjust to nonprison society, is usually irrelevant and sometimes harmful. The parole service has not been able to fulfill its crime prevention function because of its inability to identify releasees who are about to endanger the public safety.

The usual response to the gap between the image and the reality of parole is to assume the validity of the theory and to recommend reforms in the practice. Typically, these reforms urge: (1) improving parole board decisions by requiring high qualifications for membership; (2) reducing the work load of the parole board to permit its members more

and the objective of correction was to somehow "repair" the individual. See Rothman, *The Discovery of the Asylum: Social Order in the New Republic* (Boston: Little, Brown & Co., 1971).

32. The language of "adjustment," "optimal time for release," or "incarceration has had its maximum value" may be used, but, as noted, the factors relied on, the rapidity of the decision, and the time to consider each case; (3) improving the comprehensiveness and accuracy of the information in each case file; (4) imposing some form of due process and review procedures to protect inmates against arbitrary and abusive action by board members; (5) developing specific written criteria to guide board members in making prediction decisions; (6) expanding the parole service and reducing the officer's case loads; (7) de-emphasizing law enforcement activity by parole officers, and (8) increasing social services for parolees.[33]

The practice of parole in New York diverges so widely from what is considered ideal that there is room for reform of the sort outlined above. The question, however, is whether the reform of parole in this fashion would actually change parole. If a system rests on invalid assumptions and has unrealistic goals, changes in practice will not remedy those defects. Concededly—and importantly—certain changes could add fairness to the system by distributing power more evenly, but the system would not likely be any more effective in achieving its overall objectives.

The parole system rests on the assumption that recidivism can be measurably reduced by exposing the offender, while in prison, to social programs such as education or vocational training or group therapy, or by giving him assistance in the community once he gets out. But the overwhelming evidence is that these programs and services are ineffective in reducing recidivism. A survey by Robert Martinson, a sociologist and former consultant to the New York State Office of Crime Control Planning, of all studies of rehabilitation programs undertaken around the country between 1945 and 1967 found that "the present array of correctional treatments has no appreciable effect—positive or negative—on the rates of recidivism of convicted offenders." [34]

A survey of studies of the California correctional system—which has instituted more sophisticated rehabilitation programs than New York— goes even further: "It is difficult to escape the conclusions that the act of incarcerating a person at all will impair whatever potential he has for a crime-free future adjustment and that, regardless of which 'treatments' are administered while he is in prison, the longer he is kept there the more he will deteriorate and the more likely it is that he will recidivate." [35]

Finally, even the "Preliminary Report to the Governor [of New York] on Criminal Offenders"—a report which completely endorsed the treatment model—admitted that "We are unable to state at the present time

use of arbitrary time periods suggest that these words are mere rhetoric.

33. For a recent version of these remedies, see National Advisory Commission on Criminal Justice Standards & Goals, *Corrections*, Standards 12.1–12.- 7.

34. Martinson, "The Paradox of Prison Reform—II: Can Corrections Correct?" New Republic, April 8, 1972, p. 14.

35. Robison and Smith, "The Effectiveness of Correctional Programs," 17 Crime & Delinquency 67 (1971).

[June 1968] with demonstrable certainty whether any particular treatment method is effective in preventing recidivism." [36]

Parole theory is further weakened by the fact that neither the parole board nor the parole officer seems able to predict the nature and likelihood of recidivism for inmates in general. High parole revocation rates—which indicate about 80 percent of the time that a new criminal offense has been committed—cast doubt on the efficacy of the parole board's predictions. The very small number of parolees for whom revocation proceedings are initiated before apprehension for a new offense suggests that the parole officers are equally unsure in their predictions. The state of the art of prediction is still too primitive to be used as justification for substantially restricting human freedom.

Even though the parole system is ineffective in meeting its stated goals, its continuation might be justified if parole fulfilled important alternative objectives. Again, it does not. The prospect of parole is not necessary to maintain prison discipline. Prison officials have many devices—good time credits, for example—which they can use as reward or punishment for that purpose. It is also commonly believed that the parole board reduces sentence disparities by paroling those whose offenses are similar after they have served comparable amounts of time. There is no hard evidence, however, that parole performs such a function. Even if such function were performed, we would not regard the mitigation of sentence disparities as a sufficient justification for an entire parole system, especially since that function could be achieved in other ways, such as appellate review of sentences, for example.

In addition to failing to fulfill its own goals or to fulfill an important alternative function, parole is oppressive and wasteful in its operation. Because parole is presently the inmate's most attractive exit from prison, its procedures have a great impact on inmate morale and behavior. Inmates know that the irrationality of parole decision-making keeps some of them in prison for reasons that do not promote any justifiable public policy. Parolees feel hindered in their adjustment to the community by parole restrictions, and some know they have been returned to prison for the flimsiest of reasons, while others know that they remain at large and might well have been reimprisoned.

Lastly, the parole system spends scarce tax dollars. While it is usually argued that the system actually saves the state money, that is true only if the alternative is imprisonment. If inmates were absolutely discharged from prison at a time when they otherwise would have been paroled, the state could save the $15 million now expended on parole, or it could use that money to provide badly needed services to ex-offenders.

36. New York State, Preliminary Report of the Governor's Special Committee on Criminal Offenders (1968) p. 51.

LONG–TERM RECOMMENDATIONS

The Citizens' Inquiry concludes that parole in New York is oppressive and arbitrary, that its stated goals are both contradictory and incapable of fulfillment, and that in its present form it is a corrupting influence in the criminal justice system. It should therefore be abolished. But abolition of the present system cannot occur within a vacuum. The following recommendations reflect the conclusion that parole is only one segment of an integrated process. Changing parole must also mean changing the other elements of the postconviction criminal justice system, if the outcome is to make our use of the criminal sanction more humane and more effective.

(1) The goals of rehabilitation as described in this summary, are unrealistic and should not shape sentencing and release decisions. At present, this society is not able to measurably reduce recidivism by exposing the offender to treatment or rehabilitation programs, either in prison or in the community. Discretionary release and compulsory community supervision, which rely on the rehabilitation theory, should therefore be discontinued.

(2) Sentences should be shorter and have a narrower range of indeterminacy. The criteria used to determine the length of terms and the justifications for indeterminacy must await further research. But certainly this study has concluded that a sentence structure based on the rehabilitation theory is groundless.

(3) The vast discretion involved in parole decision-making has been abused. In the light of past experience, the likelihood of basing the exercise of this discretion on rational criteria seems so low that it is tempting to suggest the elimination of all discretion from release procedures. However, until sentences are short and definite, some limited discretion over release will be necessary. There is need for the study of the appropriate overall sentencing and release process, but some of its qualities can be specified.

Its operations must be open to scrutiny to avoid the corrupting tendencies of discretionary power. It should favor the earliest possible release for the largest possible number of inmates, perhaps by requiring corrections officials to show cause why, at a certain point, an inmate should not be released. The present parole board should be dissolved, and release decisions should be made by citizens who are not part of the penal system but who are related to it by virtue of their contacts with inmates in out-of-prison situations, such as work-release or adult education programs. Those who decide should have varying race, class, and occupational backgrounds, and should include an inmate's peers. The decision-making process should provide customary due process protections. The release criteria should be matters of fact demonstrably related to a legitimate public purpose. Judicial review should be available for release decisions.

(4) New and diverse alternatives to incarceration should be developed and used. Confinement, when necessary, should be in small neighborhood facilities as little isolated from normal community activities as possible.

(5) Prison administration, release decisions, and post-release services must be open to public scrutiny. General public ignorance of prison life, release decision-making, and parole supervision has made it difficult to develop understanding of the penal system and a force for change. Only with greater public accountability will new and better programs and practices gain support.

(6) A wide range of programs should be offered to offenders before, during, and after incarceration. Participation in the programs should be voluntary at all times; presumably, one test of their effectiveness will then be evidence that many offenders use them. They should be paid for by the penal system but administered by people who provide similar kinds of service to ordinary citizens.

The programs should not be justified by a vague, condescending, and unmeasurable standard of rehabilitative value. They should be supported, instead, because our society believes that the opportunities they present to live as comfortably and productively as possible are worthwhile in and of themselves and should be shared equally by all citizens, whether they are criminal offenders or not.

(a) The ex-offender's most immediate need is for cash. He should receive financial aid, set at the minimum standard of living for his family size, for a period of several months after release from prison, when employment is not readily available and need exists. He should have access to low-interest loans for a lengthy period after direct aid is discontinued.

(b) Decent emergency housing should be available at no cost for the ex-offender's first days or weeks outside of prison. A sophisticated referral service should help him locate permanent housing, deal with housing agencies and management companies, and finance home purchases.

(c) Job training, with living wages, should be available, as well as employment counseling and referral. Where decent jobs are not available in the private sector, government should provide them. Current policies in both public and private job sectors that restrict ex-offenders from jobs should generally be abandoned.

(d) Educational opportunities should be available to inmates and ex-offenders on the same basis as students. Tutoring, aptitude testing, and financial aid will be necessary to help inmates and ex-offenders prepare for school, college, and vocational programs.

(e) Low-cost medical services should be offered to inmates and ex-offenders—both inside and outside the penal institutions. The services should include dental and psychiatric care, as well as programs for alcoholics and drug users.

(f) Both public and private legal services should be available to the offender, free or at low cost, from the moment of arrest until some time after release. Legal help should include representation of the client before agencies from which he may be eligible for benefits, such as welfare or workmen's disability.

One way to enlist an individual in whatever service programs are appropriate is to offer him, immediately after arrest or the issuance of a summons, the help of a community services adviser. This person should come from a socioeconomic background similar of that of the offender, and he should be fully prepared to act as his advocate in seeking help from the range of programs available. The adviser should have no enforcement role. If requested to do so by the offender, the adviser would keep in touch during incarceration and would assist with arrangements for family visits, out-of-prison activities, and preparations for the return home. When inmates are confined in neighborhood facilities, the adviser would work there and canvass the surrounding community for programs that the inmate can use. He would help the ex-offender with post-release problems for as long a period as requested. He would be supervised by an organization with the power to inspect prisons and report to the public on the problems of the penal system (perhaps an ombudsman organization based on the structure of the present New York State Commission of Correction). Present members of the parole service would have first priority for consideration as community service advisers.

TRANSITIONAL RECOMMENDATIONS

The long-term recommendations of this study will necessitate a lengthy period of change. It seems worthwhile, then, to try to articulate some of the desirable transitional steps, reforms which can be easily grafted onto the present parole system. They are not offered as substitutes for the changes discussed above, for they do not alter basic inadequacies of theory or practice. They are offered in the hope that they will insure fairness for inmates and that they will tend to expose and educate. It is crucial that the interim recommendations lead to further change and do not themselves come to symbolize an entrenched and inflexible system.

Our short-term recommendations for the decision-making aspect of the parole system are:

(1) At the setting of the minimum period of imprisonment by the parole board and at parole release interviews, an inmate should have the right:

(a) To be represented by retained or assigned counsel;

(b) To present witnesses on his own behalf;

(c) To examine personally or through counsel the entire case file prior to the release interview;

(d) To receive a statement of findings of fact and reasons for the decision within a short time of the interview;

(e) To receive a decision based on information disclosed to the inmate during the interview;

(f) To receive a written statement of the detailed and specific criteria which the parole board uses in deciding cases;

(g) To have judicial review of the substantive and procedural aspects of the decision.

(2) The burden of proof should be shifted so that it rests with the parole board to show why an inmate should not be released.

(3) Parole board hearings, records, and regular reports should be open and available to the press and public, subject only to the right of privacy of the individual involved to request secrecy as to details personal to him.

Short-term recommendations for the community supervision aspect of the parole system include:

(1) The length of time under community supervision should not exceed one year.

(2) The parole rules should be substantially reduced in number and simplified so that they are not coercive and do not permit a parole officer any more right to invade the privacy of a parolee than is constitutionally permissible in the case of ordinary law enforcement activities directed at persons not under correctional supervision. One set of sample parole rules might include requirements that the parolee:

(a) Seek and hold a job, or demonstrate another legal means of livelihood;

(b) Abide by the law; and

(c) Report regularly to the parole service.

(3) All law enforcement activities and authority of parole officers should be abolished.

(4) Parole should be revoked only when the parolee has committed and has been convicted of a new criminal offense of a magnitude that would ordinarily lead to incarceration.

(5) The law should provide each parolee with direct financial assistance comparable to unemployment or welfare benefits. These benefits should extend from release until another means of livelihood is established.

(6) Extensive social services, of the sort outlined as a long-term recommendation, should be provided on a voluntary basis to all parolees. Other government agencies, such as public housing authorities, civil service examiners, and welfare departments, should be prohibited from maintaining discriminatory bars against parolees.

(7) Inmates who are conditionally released should have their sentences credited with the time they spend in the community in the

event that they have their conditional release revoked and are returned to prison.

PAROLE THEORY AND OUTCOMES REEXAMINED *

The Report of the Citizens' Inquiry on Parole ** clearly moves on two levels. The first consists of a series of specific criticisms of the parole system of the State of New York as it now operates: Board members lack appropriate training, hearings are perfunctory, criteria are not specified, reasons for decisions are not given, rules are overly restrictive, parole officers fail to assist parolees, and they overemphasize surveillance and control activities. For the moment, I will leave to other commentators an assessment of the merits of those charges. What distinguishes this report, and will claim our attention here, is a second level of analysis which leads the writers to reject a variety of parole reforms—written criteria, increased social services, increased due process—except as they may be useful until more radical change is effected.

One wishes the report of the Citizens' Inquiry started with its conclusions and fully developed their implications, for at the end it is not at all clear that these "fundamental" reforms are better alternatives than the more modest, but more specific ones that were rather summarily dismissed. This is not said to depreciate the aims of those who worked on this report. Few dedicated to the ideals of a democratic society will not applaud the sentiment of the chairman of the group, Ramsey Clark, who, after reviewing the shortcomings of current parole practice, concluded: "Those who love justice, who believe violence is the ultimate human degradation, and who still want to love their country, must strive to change all this." [1] But the worth of a reform cannot be measured by the decency of the motives which gave rise to it. It must be finally judged by the degree to which it actually achieves those same standards of justice which the former Attorney General so fittingly invoked. A careful reading of this report leaves substantial doubts about how well the changes it proposes will reach the ends sought.

The authors of the Citizens' Inquiry assert that the reform of parole is not possible because the "system rests on invalid assumptions and has unrealistic goals." What should be made clear at once is that while the actual study may accurately portray current practices in New York, it is largely irrelevant to these more basic arguments. Efforts are made from time to time to draw on the study data to support the position that parole should be abolished, but they are inadequate to the task. The data simply do not bear with any decisiveness on the "faulty theory" and the "assumptions" upon which parole rests.

* Vincent O'Leary, *Criminal Law Bulletin*, Vol. II, No. 3, May-June 1975.

** See Preceding Section "Parole in Crisis."

1. Clark and Rudenstine, *Prison Without Walls, Report on New York Parole*, Citizens' Inquiry on Parole and Criminal Justice, Inc. (New York: Praeger Pubis-

The most important information used to support the proposition that parole cannot be reformed and must be abolished is inevitably drawn from other studies and reports. The purpose in underscoring this point is not to discredit the findings of the Citizens' Inquiry as they may apply to contemporary conditions in New York State. It is to make clear that with respect to the "abolish parole" arguments, we do not have a new, independent, empirical study. Instead, the writers use the backdrop of apparent abuses in New York to press for a nondiscretionary release [2] and nontreatment oriented correctional system very similar to that proposed in the publication, "Struggle for Justice," authored by a Quaker Committee in 1971.[3]

The conclusions reached do not necessarily follow from the situation portrayed in New York. Many alternative reforms obviously were possible, but these were not explored. Instead, the authors listed a few in a paragraph, dismissed them because of the need for "fundamental" change, and opted for eliminating the whole parole process. What the report fails to do is to trace out how this proposal would actually work and how it would yield more desirable results than the reforms that were rejected. Publicity has been focused on the committee's proposals, and to the extent that this encourages an interest in reform, it is salutory. However, a serious assessment of the fairness and feasibility of the proposals has not been measurably advanced, and it is important that this occur. What is involved in this report is not merely an argument about the form, practice, and organization of discretionary release and community supervision systems in lieu of prisons. At bottom is a question of the extent to which the principles upon which discretionary release and community supervision rest have any place in our criminal justice system.[4]

Obviously, the present limits of space do not allow for extended discussion of these matters. There appears in the Summary Report a section, entitled "Defects of the Parole Theory," which lists and describes as invalid at least five assumptions about parole. While the full report is more ambiguous in its attack on these assumptions, it may be useful to discuss briefly some of the issues raised. As we proceed, the lack of reliable data from the New York Report that touches on these assumptions will become increasingly clear. Also, some of the questions that

lishers, 1975) p. ix. This reference is to the full report of the study.

2. Although the proposed elimination of discretion is blurred by the recommendation that "citizens" replace the present parole board, in the context of the total report this is seen as a temporary measure until sentences are made sufficiently short. It might also be noted in passing that many parole boards in the United States are now made up of part-time members. There is little evidence that such citizen boards are

more effective than professional ones; if anything, the evidence lies in the opposite direction.

3. *Struggle for Justice* (New York: Hill & Wang, 1971).

4. The implications of these principles go far beyond parole. The worth of many diversionary programs—supervision in lieu of detention and probation, for example—must be inevitably discounted if they are accepted.

remain to be answered by the "abolish parole" advocates likewise will become apparent.

REDUCTION OF SENTENCE DISPARITIES

There is "no hard evidence" that the parole board "reduces sentence disparities by paroling those whose offenses are similar after they have served comparable amounts of time."

A review of the report of the Citizens' Inquiry reveals that the basis for this statement is not the result of a careful study of the personal and offense characteristics of offenders and the time they served before parole, but rather rests on a string of logical but increasingly attenuated deductions. They run somewhat as follows: Since the New York Parole Board now has the power to set *many* minimum sentences; and since it *tends* to set them at one-third the maxima; and since *most* inmates are paroled at the time of their first parole hearing, the board is not reducing "unwarranted" disparity in time served in prison among inmates.

To address this question with a degree of adequacy requires a fairly sophisticated statistical analysis. However, for various reasons, including the nonavailability of needed data, the Citizens' Inquiry staff did not undertake it. If they had, they might well have modified their conclusions. For example, I recently reviewed a soon-to-be-published report by one of my students, which employed rigorous statistical measures and compared minimum sentences fixed by the New York Parole Board as opposed to those previously fixed by judges. It showed a marked *decrease* in variations in minimum terms. Further, a recent doctoral dissertation, which investigated the effects of plea negotiation on time served in New York prisons, similarly demonstrated the regulating role played by the New York Board.[5]

But even if the decisions of the New York Board do not reduce the effects of disparate sentences by judges, the report does not address the implicit "theory" question—namely, "do centralized parole boards *in general* reduce disparities in time served?" When we look to data from several sources, the answer seems to be yes. For example, the information available to my colleagues and me when we prepared a report which covered all parole systems in the United States, supports the conclusion that if one discounts various legal restrictions, parole boards do dampen unexplained variations in time served.[6] The results of recent studies with the United States Parole Board, from which fairly precise decision scales

5. Hyun Joo Shin, *Analysis of Charge Reduction and Its Outcomes* (Unpublished Doctoral Dissertation, State University of New York at Albany, School of Criminal Justice, 1972).

6. Gottfredson, Neithercutt, Nuffield, and O'Leary, *Four Thousand Lifetimes: A Study of Time Served and Parole Outcomes* (Davis, California: National

have been developed, also give direct evidence of how a parole board can lessen disparity.[7]

It would be almost bizarre if a single body, which could affect the amount of time served in the prisons, did not achieve a greater degree of uniformity in its decision-making than hundreds of judges distributed widely across a state. One may not approve the characteristics of that uniformity, but the evidence certainly indicates that boards do achieve some consistency in decision norms.[8]

The central point is that a parole board can act as a significant balancing force in a state's sentencing system. The degree to which this is possible is complicated by a variety of statutory restrictions which cause disparities to be built into a system, but these can be removed. Further, the articulation of criteria, most notably undertaken by the United States Parole Board, demonstrates that parole boards can be useful instruments in the control of disparity.

Whatever its earlier history or the motivation for its establishment, today parole is an integral part of almost all sentencing systems, either serving or possessing the capacity to serve as a vehicle for modifying judicially imposed sentences. Responsible critics assume the burden of demonstrating that better and more workable alternatives exist which will provide for adjustments in time-served decisions by an impartial tribunal removed from the immediate passion of the courtroom. Appellate review of sentences is a frequently discussed option; however, this is not the place to debate the merits of that concept. It is the place to observe that the assumption that a parole board cannot diminish disparities is inaccurate. It is also the place to point out that while the Citizens' Inquiry Report indicates an awareness of the issue, no analysis is presented to justify in principle the elimination of a board in the executive branch sharing in decisions about the amount of time offenders should serve in prison.

PREDICTION OF RECIDIVISM

Neither a parole board nor a parole officer is "able to predict the nature and likelihood of recidivism for inmates in general."

This assertion is simply wrong. It is also one of the few times that the data on which the argument is based are directly presented. The table included in the report shows that there is no difference in outcome between those who are paroled by the New York Parole Board and those who are released by law under conditional supervision. These data supposedly illustrate the inability of board members to select those who are more likely to succeed on parole from those likely to fail.

Council on Crime and Delinquency Research Center, June 1973).

Council on Crime and Delinquency Research Center, 1973).

7. Gottfredson, Wilkins, Hoffman, and Singer, *The Utilization of Experience in Parole Decision Making, A Progress Report* (Davis, California: National

8. Gottfredson and Ballard, "Differences in Parole Decisions Associated with Decision Makers," 3 J. Research in Crime & Delinquency 112 (1966).

The problems with the table presented are threefold: (1) It does not include absconders; (2) it is for the first year, and less, of supervision; and (3) there are different months of exposure to supervision between parolees and conditional releasees. However, rather than argue these technical details, let us simply refer to a study, recently published by Peter Hoffman, which focuses directly on the issue posed by the Citizens' Inquiry and reaches precisely opposite conclusions. Hoffman, using an elaborate set of statistical controls and covering a longer period of supervision, declared:

> "[P]arolees do substantially better than mandatory releasees with more favorable outcomes. . . . [They] averaged 74% favorable outcomes compared to the 53% for mandatory releasees; 12% technical and absconding violations as compared to 19%; and only 14% new arrests compared to 28%." [9]

The fact is that most parole members can identify those factors which tend to be associated with relative success on parole, a finding duplicated previously by other parole studies. [10]

There are related issues, which the report touches only tangentially and which a serious assessment of the principle of discretionary release would be expected to explore. Perhaps one illustration will make the point. From time to time, the report obliquely questions whether there are any facts, not known at the time of sentencing, which improve our power of prediction about future criminal risk. The matter is never fully evaluated, one assumes, because the report later asserts (mistakenly, as we have seen) that no prediction is reliable. It is unfortunate because this is an issue of some importance in weighing the value of parole decision-making. To begin with, obviously, it is possible that facts related to parole outcome can be learned subsequent to sentencing. For example, it might not have been known that an offender had used narcotics, which is often associated with poor parole performance.

Aside from availability, there is the issue of whether facts not in existence at the time of sentencing (for example, having a job at the time of release from prison) can increase the reliability of our success estimates. Thus far, marginal gains in predictive accuracy have been shown to result from these kinds of variables, but they do exist, and relevant experiments combining clinical and statistical methods are under way. More to the point, newer methods of risk evaluation, which depend less on prior histories and more on controlled trial periods in the community through furloughs and similar devices, are rapidly coming into existence. [11]

9. Hoffman, "Mandatory Release, A Measure of Type II Error," 11 Criminology 547 (1974).

10. See, for example, O'Leary and Glaser, "The Assessment of Risk," *The Future of Parole*, ed. D. J. West (London: Gerald Ducksworth & Co., Ltd., 1972) p. 184.

11. Norval Morris underscores the value of such methods of risk assessment after trial in his recent work, *The Future*

The estimation of risk is much too complicated and too central a point to all criminal justice decision-making to be summarily dismissed in the style of the Citizens' Inquiry Report. The real questions relate to the proper uses of risk assessment in decision-making and how such assessment is to be controlled. To simply eliminate parole does not deal with the issue at all. For example, among the many questions which remain to be answered is: Which actors in the criminal justice system are more likely to be aware of new findings about risk and are more likely to stay abreast of techniques of risk assessment? A strong case can be made that, in principle, parole boards (or their functional equivalent) may be better placed to be aware of such information than, say, judges, for whom limited resources are available and whose professional interests are distributed far beyond the boundaries of this type of concern.

EFFECT OF TREATMENT ON RECIDIVISM

Recidivism cannot "be measurably reduced by exposing the offender, while in prison, to social programs . . . or by giving him assistance in the community once he gets out."

This is a pivotal argument raised by the Citizens' Inquiry Report. Despite its conclusive tone, however, many competent researchers would disagree. It is important to appreciate that there are at least two camps of criminologists. One side is roughly defined by Martinson and Robison, whose works are generously cited in the report and who assert that "no treatment works." The other side, which is not mentioned in the report, is represented by such writers as Glaser and Adams, who argue contrarily that while our research has been much too simplistic, there is good evidence that "different treatments work under some circumstances for various people." [12]

Putting aside an effort to resolve the relative merits of these conflicting positions, it is apparent that our knowledge about how to modify the behavior of offenders is limited. However, by itself, that concession does not answer the policy issue which needs to be addressed: To what degree should treatment remain a *goal* of the criminal justice system, even when the means of achieving it are imperfect?

How one sees the usefulness of discretionary release and community supervision may be quite different, depending on how that question is answered. The person accepting treatment as a goal is more apt, for

---

of Imprisonment (Chicago: University of Chicago Press, 1974).

12. See, for example, Robison and Smith, "The Effectiveness of Correctional Programs" 17 Crime & Delinquency 67 (1971), and Martinson, *The Treatment Evaluation Survey* (New York: Office of Crime Control Planning of the State of New York, 1971). In contrast, see Adams, "Measurement of Effectiveness and Efficiency in Corrections," *Handbook of Criminology* ed. Daniel Glaser (Chicago: Rand McNally Publishing Co., 1974) pp. 1021–1049, and Glaser, *Routinizing Evaluation: Getting Feedback on Effectiveness of Crime and Delinquency Programs* (Washington, D.C. : National Institute of Mental Health, H.E.W., 1973).

example, to favor activities yielding information about ways of reducing the chances an offender will commit new crimes after release from state control.   And the variability provided by a community supervision system is likely to be preferred to a system which narrows the options available for convicted persons, if only because of its greater potential to produce such information.

It is clearly beyond the bounds of this brief commentary to examine fully the merits and difficulties of employing treatment as a goal of the justice system.   That subject has taxed the skill of too many commentators to be dealt with offhandedly.   But at least one point will be made here because of its important implications—treatment as a goal can have an ameliorative as well as a punitive effect.

A major complaint against using the partial information available on treatment—a point made by the Citizens' Inquiry Report—is that some offenders will be unnecessarily treated and thus unfairly punished.   A recent study by Kozol and his associates demonstrates one facet of the problem.[13]   They reported that they were able to "treat" offenders so that they were sufficiently confident to recommend release for a significant number.   Subsequently, 92 percent remained at large without committing a serious offense in the next five years.   It so happened during this same period that a court ordered a group of inmates released whom Kozol and his associates felt had not been successfully treated and, therefore, they had recommended against their release.   Subsequently, almost 62 percent of these cases succeeded, a rate only one-third less than those successfully treated.   Critics made the obvious point: If the same proportions applied to subsequent groups, the result of allowing Kozol and his associates to retain offenders until they were deemed successfully treated was that for every inmate whose performance on release was improved, two were being retained unnecessarily and, therefore, unfairly.   This is a variant of the so-called "false-positive" argument.[14]

But the question is different if one asks if officials should have the authority to risk a reduction in time served below that which an offender ordinarily deserves in order to increase the probability that his behavior will be more law-abiding after release.[15]   Translating this into the case of Kozol, suppose that one knew that 92 percent of those recommended by Kozol and his associates would not commit serious offenses after release, a gain of some 30 percent over the level ordinarily expected.   It is necessary to hold all these offenders until they serve the full time they deserve, especially if there is a likelihood that there will be a decay in the

13. Kozol, Boucher, and Garofalo, "The Diagnosis and Treatment of Dangerousness," 18 Crime & Delinquency 372 (1972).

14. See, for example, Von Hirsch, "Prediction of Criminal Conduct and Preventive Confinement of Convicted Persons," 21 Buffalo L.Rev. 717 (1972).

15. Morris, n. 11 supra, makes this general point very well. It should be made clear that treatment is used here to include any acceptable measure which increases the offender's chance of avoiding future criminal behavior—not simply variations of psychotherapy.

percentage gained over the usual level of subsequent success? The Kozol data are simply illustrative; obviously, questions concerning the nature of the treatment and its voluntariness must be addressed. The point is— treatment always involves questions of probabilities and trade-offs, and it can mitigate as well as extend punishment.

One can avoid the inherent risks of treatment by arguing that as a matter of principle, estimates of future criminality should not affect our measures of dealing with the offender—only what he deserves should be involved. That position, however, will have difficulty in developing support unless it simultaneously carries the assurance that what is deserved is also sufficiently restrictive and lengthy to serve the interests of public safety. In fact, one of the dangers of using only that which is "deserved" as a sentencing principle is the likelihood that predictions of subsequent criminality will be "hidden" in the penalty system.

Concern about the future criminality of the convicted offender will continue to be an important part of our sentencing and correctional procedure for a long time to come. Indeed, note the words of the chairman of the Citizens' Inquiry in his eloquent introduction, "A parole service that offers cash, a choice of places to live, skilled jobs where attainable, mental and physical health services, schooling and other essentials to individual fulfillment, *can reduce crime*" (emphasis added).[16] The concern for crime control directed toward the individual offender is almost inevitable. The real issue is how to cope with it.

Whether one opts for "treatment," "deserts," or some hybrid, risks are involved. Those who advocated a treatment-incapacitative approach and established very long indeterminate sentences which lodged great power in a single sentencing and parole board, as in the State of California, failed to recognize the limitations of our knowledge about treatment and the dangers of great and uncontrolled discretion. Few commentators today support such a system. Many, instead, advocate a desert-treatment approach, with relatively short maximum sentences fixed by the court on the basis of what the offender deserves and within which treatment concerns might by played out.[17] The Report of the Citizens' Inquiry fails to examine this approach to minimizing the potential harshness of treatment while retaining its potential for amelioration. Its proposals are much more likely to produce a desert-incapacitation system which, by all odds, will yield a harsher and tougher penalty system than that envisioned by Mr. Clark.[18]

16. Clark, n. 1 supra, at ix.

17. See, for example, *Corrections Task Report*, National Advisory Commission on Criminal Justice Standards and Goals (Washington, D. C.: Gov't Printing Office, 1973). The reference here extends only to the ordinary term provisions, of course.

18. It might be noted that when one of Mr. Clark's successors, Mr. Saxbe, argued that "rehabilitation doesn't work," his call was not for shorter sentences, but tougher ones!

PAROLE SUPERVISION

Supervision does not provide community protection "because of the very small number of parolees for whom revocation proceedings are initiated before apprehension for a new offense."

The obvious problem with this assertion is that it fails to examine the question of how many parolees are arrested who are not subsequently revoked. That answer, of course, is many. As J. Edgar Hoover was so fond of pointing out, parolees as a group are highly arrest prone, and like Mr. Hoover, the Citizens' Inquiry does not pause long to examine the meaning of those arrests. For example, the report fails to deal with the question of how many parolees were arrested for serious crimes and how many were actually convicted of them. An important task of a parole agency is to monitor the quality of the many arrests to which the parolees are subjected and decide which warrant further investigation and constitute a possible basis for revocation of parole.

From the best data available, it appears that the number of parolees who are convicted of serious crimes or returned to prison in lieu of prosecution in the State of New York is lower than in many other jurisdictions. As a matter of fact, as the Citizens' Inquiry Report indicates, one of the criticisms made about the New York system is that it is overly diligent in seeking to suppress the number of offenses that parolees commit. As Studt has pointed out, a vague and general policy of surveillance is of doubtful effectiveness and may be counterproductive in the long term, but the evidence is fairly clear that close supervision can result in suppressing the commission of new offenses if it is pursued with sufficient vigor.[19]

Moving from the specific situation in New York to the level of general principle, a problem with the Citizens' Inquiry Report is underscored by the way in which a very neat dilemma is posed so that there is no way to demonstrate success in the crime-control function of parole. Thus, if a parolee commits a felony and is convicted, the parole system has failed because the public has not been protected; if a parolee is arrested but returned without a new conviction, the system has failed because the parolee has obviously been denied due process; and if a parolee is returned to prison for no arrests or convictions, the system has failed because such technical violations are inevitably the result of a parole officer's abuse of discretion.

19. See Studt, *Surveillance and Service in Parole* (Los Angeles: Institute of Government and Public Affairs, UCLA, 1972). According to the national reporting system for parole agencies, New York returned twice as many parolees to prison for technical violations as the national percentage. On the other hand, the national percentage for parolees returned for new crimes is 14 percent. The New York percentage is 9 percent, or 5 percent lower.

ABOLISHING PAROLE

Parole costs the state money "because if inmates were absolutely discharged from prison at a time when they otherwise would have been paroled, the state would have saved $15 million now expended on parole."

This may be one of the most crucial assumptions in the Citizens' Inquiry Report—namely, *if parole was to be abolished, there would be no increase in the time served in prison.* To get a better sense of the dimensions of that assumption, it might be useful to review some data relating to corrections in New York State. At the end of 1974, there were approximately *14,000* persons serving time in New York's prisons, and the budget, exclusive of capital construction costs, was well over $150 million. On the same date, there were another *14,000* offenders under parole supervision. The core of the Citizens' Inquiry is that all 14,000 persons on parole would be turned loose if parole were to be abolished.

This issue cannot be settled finally by speculation, but even the most optimistic reading of current evidence indicates that a sizable percentage of those under parole supervision would wind up in prison if parole were to be abolished. One should not forget that the most recent attempt to abolish parole in the State of New York was in the form of Governor Rockefeller's proposal to impose life sentences for drug offenders. The movement toward harsher penalties in New York is powerful, especially when crimes against persons are involved.[20] And it is precisely this type of offender who is found more commonly in New York prisons. In 1968, of the total number of inmates received, 31 percent were convicted of robbery; by 1972, the percentage had risen to over 40 percent. Clearly, there is a growing proportion of convicted offenders for whom the possibility of short prison terms *and* absolute discharge are very remote.

Parole, with its counterpart probation, has become the major system which permits a massive number of convicted persons to be placed on the streets while serving their sentences. Too few commentators appreciate this "managerial" aspect of parole administration and most ignore the elements of decision-making necessary to maintain significant numbers of offenders under sentence in the community. Such concerns are often disparaged as a kind of unhealthy emphasis on public opinion or are seen as an inappropriate, even slightly corrupt, attention to political issues. However, the recent attempt in New York to shift large numbers of mental hospital patients into the community without providing mechanisms to care for them, and the resultant public outcry, indicate the serious realities that must be dealt with successfully in shifting large numbers of persons from institutions to communities.

---

20. The 1973 New York legislature, for example, amended the Penal Code so that most offenders convicted of a felo- ny, particularly crimes against persons, who also have a prior felony conviction, *must* be sentenced to prison.

One of the most important current trends in correctional reform is the development of community alternatives for offenders, as opposed to an overreliance on prisons. When carefully examined, such alternatives closely resemble forms of parole or probation supervision. Putting aside for a moment whether or not a parole board should operate these types of programs, if the law were to allow only two choices—confinement in prison or total release without supervision—it will have removed from the hands of decision-makers an intermediate option which presently provides a major means of avoiding unnecessary incarceration. The most likely effect of the total abolishment of any form of parole in the State of New York would be a decisive increase in the number of persons in prisons, even if there was some diminution in the length of statutory sentences.

One final point needs to be underscored. Objections taken to the proposals of the Citizens' Inquiry does not mean an endorsement of contemporary sentencing and parole as we have known them. There is a good deal to criticize in the model of sentencing and parole that has been expounded and practiced in the United States, especially since the 1940s. Needed badly are creative experiments with a variety of alternatives. But to conclude that discretionary release and community supervision in any form should be dismissed out of hand is at least misguided and possibly quite dangerous. The really important questions which must be addressed are where to place decision-making authority and how to organize, limit, and control it.

The Citizens' Inquiry Report performed an important service in pinpointing an area of our criminal justice system urgently in need of reform. Their proposed solution has the surface appeal of dealing with a problem with one decisive stroke. But, as it stands, similar to so many previous correctional reforms, it also has the capacity of making the situation much worse. The problems are much too tough and too complicated to yield to swift and uncomplicated solutions.

ABOLISH PAROLE? *

Probably no component of corrections is under attack today more than the function of parole. My desk these days is a repository for an endless flow of critical articles, adverse court decisions, and bitter—sometimes savage—letters from convicts and their families, friends, and attorneys.

It used to be the prison—not long ago—that took all the heat for the shortcomings of corrections. But our society has worked through this issue and concluded by now, with considerable justification, that the prison is a hopeless place to undertake the rehabilitation of the criminal. Parole has now become the scapegoat of all of corrections' ills. There is

---

* Maurice Sigler, *Federal Probation*, June 1975. At the time of this writing Dr.   Sigler was Chairman of the U.S. Parole Commission.

little indication in the pile of paper on my desk that anyone remembers what the inmate did in the first place—or who put him in prison. It is the parole board who won't let him out, and the keeper of the keys has never been a popular figure in fiction or in fact.

Our society has its imperfections, and this is certainly true of the criminal justice system. Everyone knows how high the rate of reported crime is, and that the actual number of crimes that take place is three to five times higher than the number reported—but no one really blames the police or the prosecuting attorneys because the number of convictions is an insignificant fraction of either rate. Everyone knows that whatever sentence the convicted criminal receives—suspended sentence, probation, jail, or a long or short prison term—depends more on the particular judge handling the case than on any other factor, but only a few law school professors take particular note of this pervasive inequity. But it is the parole board, of all institutions in our society, that is supposed to be totally fair and just in its decisions.

The emotionalism that is associated with the current fashionable attack on parole is evident, for example, in a recent article (November 1974) in the *New York State Bar Journal*. The author, in a sharp paragraph summarizing the shortcomings of parole, concludes that on the basis of his studies and observations, the parole boards, among other things, do not have even "the commitment to perform (rationally or even equitably) the discretionary release function."

The parole board members that I know are not the irresponsible monsters that this passage would suggest. What it actually suggests is the lack of objectivity characterizing attacks on parole today.

I do not mean that parole should be sacrosanct; certainly it has its problems and deficiencies, and we need all the help and expertise we can get in resolving them. Yet our critics ought to be as fair about it as they want parole boards to be in the exercise of their responsibilities.

PAROLE A GENERATION AGO

Parole used to be pretty bad by today's standards, and perhaps it still is in some places. It also used to a tougher and harder world, and corrections itself, in the days when administrators had total discretion and the courts kept hands off, was tough and hard. It was a world of its own, sealed off from public scrutiny. I do not need to review the literature in this respect for the readership of Federal Probation.

My own career in corrections started in that world—some 36 years ago—as a prison guard. The "parole judge" of that day was an austere, unapproachable figure. He was one of the few persons from the outside world admitted to the prison, and preparations for his visit were those befitting a foreign potentate.

The hearing room was cleaned and dusted to antiseptic perfection. There was an enormous mahogany desk, and it was polished to a high sheen. Particular care was taken with the chrome-plated carafe and tray, and the fancy crystal glasses; they shone brilliantly. The carafe was filled with icewater, and it was replaced by an attendant every time the "judge" poured a glassful.

The part of the prison in which the hearing room was located was highly controlled; there had to be absolute quiet. The inmates to be heard were lined up outside the hearing room, and they had to stay rigidly in place without smoking or talking.

One at a time, the inmates were admitted to the room, and they stood stiffly before the desk. The "judge" asked each a question or two, and the hearing was concluded. If the inmate had more to say, he was cut off, and if necessary, a guard led him out.

The inmate had to remain in ignorance of his parole decision for weeks—often months. And when he got it, if it was a denial, there were no reasons of any kind given. All he got was a slip of paper with his name on it, and a terse "Parole denied." And there was nothing he could do to appeal the decision.

The "judge" often took pride in the number of cases he heard in one day. If the prison was located in a bad climate, or in an unattractive part of the country, the number of cases heard in one day tended to increase so he could get out of there. I have known of a "judge" to hear as many as 50 or 60 cases a day.

The "judge" often had his prejudices and peculiarities. If the inmate was less than perfect in his demeanor, or didn't exercise care in what he had to say, the "judge" might give him a severe lecture. Or the judge may have had certain types of cases he was hell on. I knew at least one "judge" who, for example, would never parole an inmate convicted of a Mann Act violation, and those were the days when the Mann Act was often used to sequester men whose across-state-line adventure involved only youthful romance. Other "judges" didn't like burglars, or car thieves, or income tax violators—or whatever.

Parole in those days should have been subjected to severe criticism, but it never was. Our modern critics would have had a field day.

CHANGES IN FEDERAL PAROLE

Parole has come a long way since then. The improvements came gradually over the years, but they were accelerated by the Morrissey v. Brewer decision and related court decisions of recent years. The Federal system has been particularly transformed, but many of the same changes have taken place in the states.

In the Federal system, the parole "judge" has gone. The members of the U.S. Board of Parole are policy-makers and administrators. Five of them head up our regional offices, and three are located in Washington.

The hearings are conducted by pairs of examiners—all of them chosen on the basis of extended experience in corrections. The hearing room no longer has the trappings of an august tribunal. The examiners borrow somebody's office while they are at the institution. The atmosphere is informal, and the inmate applicants for parole are given a full opportunity to make their case. If they wish, they may be accompanied by an advocate—family members, friends, prison supervisors, or attorneys.

A tentative decision is given to them on the spot, and if it involves a continuance to another hearing at a specified future date, or until their prison time is up, the reasons for this decision are discussed with them, and they are free to dispute the reasoning.

The U.S. Board of Parole, through a grant from the Law Enforcement Assistance Administration, and research done by the National Council on Crime and Delinquency, has developed a system of decision-making intended to bring about fairness and equity. When the application of this system results in a decision to parole, we of course encounter no accusations of unfairness. But when it results in a set-off for a future hearing, or no parole, inmates and their families and attorneys sometimes find it difficult to accept. This is understandable, no system that could possibly be devised could avoid it.

First, the examiner panel gives each case a salient factor score, ranging from zero to 11, with the higher the score, the better the prospects for successful completion of parole. The case gets points, or loses them, on the basis of such factors as prior convictions, prior commitments, education, employment history, marital status, etc. All of the factors were determined on the basis of research to have some predictability for success on parole.

The case is then given an offense severity rating—low, low moderate, moderate, high, very high, and greatest. This rating does not depend simply on the subjective judgment of the examiners. They are provided with a chart that lists offense categories under each severity rating.

Then, with the salient factor score, and the offense severity rating in hand, the examiners consult a second chart which indicates the amount of time an offender with a given background and salient factor score should serve for an offense of a given severity, assuming reasonably good institutional performance. For example, an offender with a salient factor score of 11 and an offense severity rating of low might be expected to serve 6 to 10 months before going out on parole. Or an offender with a salient factor score of 3 and a severity rating of very high may be expected to serve 55 to 65 months. For an offender with a severity rating of greatest, the most serious or heinous offenses, there is no maximum range stipulated.

For most offenders, the mix of salient factor score and offense severity rating involves a certain amount of risk in parole, and the system is intended to bring about a reasonable degree of fairness by insuring that they serve about the same amount of time as others in their situation.

But, for those cases where in the clinical judgment of the examiners the inmate has a much better prospect of success on parole than his score and rating suggests, the examiners can shorten the amount of time to be served below those specified by the guidelines. Or where the prospect of success on parole is much worse than that suggested by the score and rating, the examiners can extend the amount of time to be served beyond that specified.

Our statistics on the use of this system indicate that currently at initial hearings about 85 percent of the decisions are within the guidelines. About 9 percent are below the guidelines, and about 6 percent above.

The inmate gets a written decision within 15 working days of the hearing; if the decision is negative—a set-off or no parole—he is given the reasons in writing. If the chief hearing examiner or regional director does not agree with the recommendation of the examiners—and the recommendation is only tentative until they do—the regional director may modify the action or refer it to three members in Washington who constitute a National Appellate Board. The appeals board may vote either with the examiners or with the regional director, and a written decision is sent to the inmate.

If the decision received by the inmate is for a set-off, or no parole, or if he disagrees with the parole date, he may appeal that decision to the regional director. The regional director may advance a set-off up to six months, or change the salient factor score or offense severity rating, and adjust the set-off date accordingly. However, if he wishes to grant a parole where the examiners have denied one, or deny a parole where the examiners have recommended one, or if he wishes to advance a set-off date by more than 6 months, he must obtain the signature of another regional director. If he fails to obtain another signature, the examiner's recommendation stands.

If the inmate is then dissatisfied with the decision he gets as a result of his appeal to the regional director, he may appeal it to the National Appellate Board. This board may change the decision in some way, or affirm it. The parole decision is then final—short of going to the courts, which sometimes happens.

Again, our statistics show that currently appeals by inmates result in some form of relief—parole, advance set-off date and/or change in salient factor score or offense severity rating—about 25 percent of the time.

In certain cases—heinous or particularly notorious offenses, terms of 45 years or more, or where there is a high public interest—the guidelines procedure is used, but the decision is determined by vote of the regional director and two of the three members of the National Appellate Board. Appeal in these cases is directly to the appeals board.

In parole revocation cases, the procedure is too technical to be reviewed satisfactorily here, but it follows all of the due process safeguards set forth in the Morrissey v. Brewer decision—written notice of the claimed violations, disclosure of the evidence against the parolee, the right to present witnesses and documentary evidence, the right to confront and cross-examine adverse witnesses, written decisions, and written reasons for decisions. Not infrequently, the procedure results in no finding of revocation and the prompt reinstatement of the offender on parole, or in revocation accompanied by a reparole date.

All of the new procedures of course take time. No longer are 50 or 60 cases heard in one day. Our examiners try to hear 15 parole or revocation cases a day, but are averaging between 12 and 14; often this cannot be obtained without running through lunch and into the evening. The National Advisory Commission on Criminal Justice Standards and Goals in its 1973 *Corrections* report recommended an average of 20.

PROBLEM AREAS

A great deal has been done, but we still have problems. As in any other field, as fast as we resolve problems, new ones crop up. Sometimes the solutions to old problems in themselves create new problems.

The regionalization of the Board in 1974 has brought it into much closer proximity to inmates, their families and their attorneys, and the courts. Regionalization was intended to bring about a more expeditious delivery of decisions and services. But the new accessibility of the Board has in itself generated a workload and a variety of problems associated with individual cases that the Board has not previously experienced. At the moment, this rapidly increasing workload threatens to outstrip our capacity for dealing with it. Some of our staff, I am sure, feel that it has already done so. Because of the slower pace of the budgetary process, it will be some time before we can match resources with the demands upon them.

Our new rules and guidelines represent a sincere attempt to make our decision-making as fair and equitable as humanly possible. But already, these rules and guidelines are under attack by those who fail to make parole, or make parole as expeditiously as they would like. Although I am not unduly paranoid, I suspect that as long as there are inmates who do not make parole, any system we devise will be attacked. One issue at present is whether or not the Board should be under the Administrative Procedures Act, and subject its rule-making procedures to the provision of that Act. We have already had one adverse decision (Pickus v. U.S. Board of Parole), but the issue continues on its way up the laborious appellate process.

Perhaps the issue giving us the most trouble at the moment involves section 4208(a)(2) of our statute, under which the court imposes only a maximum term and leaves the matter of parole eligibility and release up to the Board. But there are those inmates, and those judges, who interpret the provision to mean that a sentence of this kind is supposed to result in early parole.

The judges who impose an (a)(2) sentence may have various things in mind. Some judges use it in all cases, regardless of the nature of the offense or the background of the offender. Other judges impose a long maximum (a)(2) sentence to satisfy public emotions, but anticipate that an early parole will soften the initial severity. Other judges use it to motivate the offender to work hard at his rehabilitation and earn an early release. Still other judges use it fully intending to turn the matter of eligibility and release entirely over to the Board.

But in most cases, we don't really know what the judges had in mind. Usually they do not state for the record what they had in mind when they imposed sentence. When they do, their views weigh very heavily on the decisions of the Board. Much of the controversy surrounding the use of the (a)(2) sentence would be eliminated if the judges would let us know what they had in mind when they imposed it.

In the past, the courts have taken us to task for not giving reasons for our decisions. Now that we give reasons, we sometimes get court orders stating that the reasons are inadequate or insufficient, and ordering new hearings. I fully agree that the Board ought to give sufficient and pertinent reasons for its decisions. But I find it difficult to understand why the Board should be singled out in this respect, when at the time most crucial for the offender—at sentencing—the courts give no reasons at all for the penalties they impose.

PAROLE COMPACT PROPOSAL

There is a feeling in some quarters, particularly among our critics in the academic community, that the solution to the problem of equitable parole decision-making lies in the so-called parole compact. Under this plan, the inmate, institution officials, and parole board representatives would sit down and work out a set of goals for the inmate to achieve— employment skills, education, therapy of various kinds—and when the inmate had achieved those goals, he would automatically be released.

This plan has a sensible sound to it. But it is far removed from the reality of offenders, institutions, and "treatment" programs. Anyone who has an extensive experience in working with offenders in prisons knows that there are inmates who could achieve almost any set of goals of this kind, but who would still be totally unready for release. I have known offenders who have picked up a half dozen trades during successive terms in prison, high school diplomas, and even college degrees, and who have participated in group therapy and counseling of various types, but still are dangerous people. When ultimately released, they lose no time in sticking up a bank or returning to their preferred variety of crime.

On the other hand, there are inmates who would not be able to meet such "treatment" goals, but who could be released with the expectation that they would never again get into trouble with the law. Many of them don't really need to meet such goals anyway. Some persons convicted of murder, for example, could be released as soon as they are convicted in court, and never get into trouble again. They remain in prison for a relatively long time because our society wants to demonstrate that it does not regard the taking of human life lightly.

A further flaw in the plan is that research so far has shown that prison "treatment" programs are singularly unsuccessful in bringing about the rehabilitation of anyone. Most prison administrators today would agree that the prison is well equipped to punish offenders, or to incapacitate them from the further commission of crimes while they are doing time—but they are not equipped to do much of anything else.

This is not to say that persons cannot come out of prison rehabilitated. Some of them do. Some of them mature naturally, just as the rest of us did in our earlier years. Some of them burn out; crime is a strenuous life, and it is no coincidence that statistics show that most crime is committed by relative youngsters. Others somehow see the light and make an abrupt change in their lifestyles; but this cannot be traced directly to formally established prison "treatment" programs.

The parole compact would formalize the "game" that some prisoners play—enrolling in various programs to make points toward parole. Prison educational departments are typically thronged with such offenders as professional con men, who are notoriously difficult to change. The "game" sometimes works—parole board personnel are human too, our critics notwithstanding, and given to sympathetic feelings. But to institutionalize the "game" in the form of the parole compact would be unfair to the public, which expects, if nothing else from the imprisonment of offenders, protection from further depredations. It would also be unfair to the inmates, and deeply increase their cynicism for law and order, for they know better than anyone else the mockery of so-called prison "treatment" programs.

ABOLISH PAROLE?

There is a vocal group who now say that the only solution is to do away with parole itself. There should be relatively short terms, graduated according to the seriousness of crimes. Offenders should know when they are sentenced exactly how long they will serve, and exactly when they will be released. The offender will not then have to do his time in uncertainty, dependent on the vagaries of the parole process.

Again, this proposal has a good sound to it. But like the parole compact, it ignores the realities.

The prisoners themselves would be unhappier with this plan than they have been with parole. No matter how short the term they may be sentenced to, they want to get out earlier (and I can't blame them). Even under the present system, and many of them do get short sentences, as soon as they are committed, they start exploring every possible avenue for bringing about an early release—appeals to the courts attacking their sentences or the conditions of their confinement, applications for executive clemency, pressures pleading their own ill health or the ill health of dependents—you name it.

It also ignores the realities of prison administration. If we are going to have prisons, we must give administrators the means by which to operate these prisons on a reasonably orderly basis. If prisoners are committed with fixed terms—with no time off for good behavior, and no eligibility for early release—there will be no incentive for the prisoners to behave themselves in confinement. Even under present circumstances, prisons are difficult enough to run, and some of them are impossible to run. My argument of course has been anticipated and condemned by those who advocate doing away with parole and instituting short, fixed terms, but nevertheless, it has validity. Under the proposed no-parole system, prisons would be worse hellholes than they are now—for prisoners and personnel alike.

The proposal ignores the realities of the legislative process. Most legislatures today, if they were to recodify their criminal statutes, would undoubtedly prescribe even longer maximums for many crimes. This has been the experience throughout the country when penal code revision has been under consideration. Penal codes are typically a mish-mash of conflicting penalties, some of them savage in their severity, and are undoubtedly in need of revision. But given the legislative temper—particularly with our shocking annual increases in crime rates—I see no hope that the penalties prescribed for crime can be as substantially eased across the board as those who advocate the abolishment of parole wish to bring about.

The abolish-parole people, for some reason, do address the basic problem that is handicapping a fully equitable application of the parole process—sentencing. The parole process is inseparable from the sentencing process.

SENTENCING AND PAROLE INTERRELATED

There is a vast literature in this country on the disparities, inconsistencies, and inequities of sentencing. With so many judges, with so many different personalities and philosophies, and with so much discretion in the sentencing process, it is inevitable that the quality of justice should be so uneven.

Every day, a parole board sees sentences that are too long, and others that are too short—given the nature of the offenses and the backgrounds of the offenders. One judge may impose a year for bank robbery—another 25 years—and others somewhere in between, on offenders whose crimes and backgrounds are relatively similar. And so it goes with other crimes.

One judge may send an offender to prison for psychiatric treatment—although that is the last place where he will get it. Another may commit an offender to learn a trade, but there is no evidence that even learning a trade will turn him away from crime. Still another will commit an offender purely for the sake of punishment—and that the offender will get—but how much punishment is enough?

Some offenders should be paroled right away, but their sentences are so long that the parole board has no authority to do it. Other offenders should never be paroled, but their sentences are so short that they get out soon anyway. With so much variation in sentences, and the purpose of sentences, regardless of circumstances, it is difficult for prison administrators to determine exactly what should be done with a large proportion of their populations.

Somehow or another, a parole board is expected to bring some kind of order out of this chaos, and make fair and evenhanded decisions that will minimize the disparities and take into consideration what it guesses to be the intention of the sentencing judges, what it knows about the problems of prison administrators, and what in its judgment is in the best interests of public safety and protection.

Professor Norval Morris, in his recent book, *The Future of Imprisonment,* writes that "our sentencing practices are so arbitrary, discriminatory, and unprincipled that it is impossible to build a rational and humane prison system upon them," and that "there is at present such a pervading sense within prison of the injustice of sentencing that any rehabilitative efforts behind the walls are seriously inhibited." Even given the inconsistencies of the sentencing process, I do believe that the solution lies in abolishing it, or taking the authority away from the courts.

There are various ways in which the courts can retain their sentencing discretion and yet minimize the disparities that are now so prevalent. The literature deals fully with them—sentencing institutes, sentencing panels in multi-judge courts, the use of sentencing criteria, judicial visits to institutions, appellate review of sentences, and others. The National Advisory Commission on Criminal Justice Standards and Goals has outlined a number of them. Some have been implemented here and there.

The fairness of the parole process depends almost directly on the fairness of the sentencing process. Much has been done to improve parole, and I would be the first to say that the courts have been extremely influential in this respect. And more can be done to improve parole, but again we need the help of the courts. If they can make their sentencing decisions more consistent and let us know the reasons for the decisions they do make, we can make parole much fairer to all concerned. I know that the courts really want to make sentencing much more equitable, and despite the emotionalism of some of our critics, we in parole also have a commitment to make a continuing effort to bring about further improvements in what we do.

To those who say "let's abolish parole," I say that as long as we use imprisonment in this country, we will have to have someone, somewhere, with the authority to release people from imprisonment. Call it parole— call it what you will. It's one of those jobs that has to be done.

REVOCATION OF PAROLE: THE LEGACY OF MORRISSEY V. BREWER *

* * *

To an even greater extent that in the case of imprisonment, probation and parole practice is determined by an administrative discretion that is largely uncontrolled by legal standards, protections or remedies. Until statutory and case law are more fully developed, it is vitally important within all of the correctional field that there should be established and maintained reasonable norms and remedies against the sort of abuses that are likely to develop where men have great power over their fellows and where relationships may become both mechanical and arbitrary.[2]

This quotation from the American Correction Association's (ACA) Manual of Correctional Standards used by Justice Douglas in his separate opinion in Morrissey v. Brewer[3] sets out the theme of this paper. The American Correctional Association has been a leader in the field of developing modern penology. The fact that the *Morrissey* decision comes as a culmination of a movement toward granting parole revocation hearings rather than a forerunner is partly attributable to the enlightened efforts of members of ACA.[4]

The formulators of policy must be encouraged to move ahead vigorously toward achieving a greater measure of human dignity and freedom within the bounds of the need to balance the competing ideals of the struggle to control and reduce crime on the one hand, and the need to rehabilitate the offender on the other. Coupled with this dichotomy is society's increasing, and probably long overdue, concern for the victims of crime. In this maelstrom of competing ideals, goals and concerns, the modern correctional officer must tred lightly yet with a strong sense of direction.

---

* *Proceedings* of the 105th Annual Congress of Corrections, American Correctional Association, Louisville, Ky., 1975. Paper delivered by Jack E. Farley.

2. Id. at 500 n. 13.

3. Id.

4. Id. at 499 n. 11.

"Criminologists have argued that effective rehabilitation of criminals must include creating respect for the rules and procedures of the legal system. Any such respect, however, is threatened by a process that ignores the protections laymen, including lawbreakers, associate with justice."[5] "A prisoner does not shed" basic constitutional "rights at the prison gate. Rather, he 'retains all the rights of an ordinary citizen except those expressly, or by necessary implication, taken from him by law.' "[6]

> When the prison gates slam behind an inmate, he does not lose his human quality; his mind does not become closed to ideas; his intellect does not cease to feed on a free and open interchange of opinions; his yearning for self-respect does not end; nor is his quest for self-realization concluded. If anything, the needs for identity and self-respect are more compelling in the dehumanizing prison environment.[7]

It is in this context that the *Morrissey* decision should be viewed. It is a challenge, not a roadblock. It is a window, not a mirror. It is a beginning, not an end.

Our Constitution does not require all that is or may be deemed socially desirable.[8] Many constitutional scholars have determined that its function as interpreted by the Supreme Court should be *de minimis.*[9] Thus the fundamental fairness embodied in the two-step hearing process of *Morrissey* may well be viewed as a point of embarkation for providing procedural due process in other areas of corrections.

One area of particular concern was only touched lightly in *Morrissey,*[10] drawn fairly well in Gagnon v. Scarpelli,[11] then the canvass torn and thrown out completely in Wolff v. McDonnell.[12] Our present inquiry might well be stated: *Quo vadem* right to counsel?

---

5. Van Dyke, *Parole Revocation Hearings in California: The Right to Counsel,* 59 Calif.L.Rev. 1215, 1223 (1971).

6. Procunier v. Martinez, 416 U.S. 396, 422–23 (1974) (separate opinion) (Marshall, J.) quoting, Coffin v. Reichard, 143 F.2d 443, 445 (6th Cir. 1944).

7. Procunier v. Martinez, supra, at 428 (separate opinion) (Marshall, J.). See also, Note, *An Endorsement of Due Process Reform in Parole Revocation: Morrissey v. Brewer,* 6 Loyola, Los Angeles L.Rev. 157 (1973); Loewenstein, *Accelerating Change in Correctional Law: The Impact of Morrissey,* Clearinghouse Review 528 (Jan. 1974); Fisher, *Parole and Probation Revocation Procedures after Morrissey and Gagnon,* 65 J.Crim.L. & C. 46 (1974);

Cassan, *The "Morrissey" Maelstrom: Recent Developments in California Parole and Probation Revocations,* 9 San Fran.L.Rev. 43 (1974).

8. Reynolds v. Sims, 377 U.S. 533, 625–26 (1964) (dissent) (Harlan, J.).

9. See, e. g., Goldberg v. Kelly, 397 U.S. 254, 271–279 (1970) (dissent) (Black, J.).

10. Morrissey, supra n. 1, at 489.

11. Gagnon v. Scarpelli, 411 U.S. 778, 783–791 (1973).

12. Wolff v. McDonnell, 418 U.S. 539 (1974).

MORRISSEY—GAGNON DECISIONS

Revocation of parole or probation, though not a part of criminal prosecution, deprives an individual of his conditional liberty.[13]   Such liberty "includes many of the core values of unqualified liberty and its termination inflicts a 'grievous loss' on the parolee and often on others." [14]   Therefore, through the holding of Morrissey v. Brewer,[15] such liberty is within the protection of the Fourteenth Amendment and can be terminated only by due process of law.[16]

Morrissey required that a parolee who is charged with violation of parole must be given two separate and distinct hearings.[17]   The first hearing is in the nature of a preliminary hearing where it is decided if there is probable cause or reasonable grounds to believe there has been a parole violation.   The determination at this hearing must be made by a person not directly involved with the case.   For this hearing, the parolee must be given notice of the place and purpose of the hearing and the alleged parole violations.   At this stage the parolee can speak in his own behalf, can present relevant documents and individuals, and on request can question adverse witnesses where this creates no risk of harm to the witnesses.   The hearing officer must make a digest of the evidence presented, and based on that evidence, must decide the issue of probable cause stating the reasons and evidence relied on.[18]

The second hearing is more comprehensive and must be afforded within a reasonable time to the parolee who requests it, and "must lead to a final evaluation of any contested relevant facts and consideration of whether the facts as determined warrant revocation."   At this time, the parolee must be given the opportunity to be heard, and to show he either did not violate his parole conditions, or if he did there were mitigating reasons for doing so.[19]

For the second hearing, the minimum requirements of due process mandate that the parolee be afforded written notice of the alleged parole violations, disclosure of adverse evidence, an opportunity to be present

---

13. Morrissey v. Brewer, supra n. 1, at 480. The liberty of a parolee is conditional in the sense that he has conditions of parole which restrict his freedom.

14. Id. at 482.

15. Id.

16. Id. at 482.   In determining what process is due, the Court determined that the state had a number of interests to be considered.   "Given the previous conviction and the proper imposition of conditions, the state has an overwhelming interest in being able to return the individual to imprisonment without the burden of a new adversary criminal trial if in fact he has failed to abide by the conditions of his parole."   Id. at 483.

17. Id. at 485 & 489.

18. The Court indicated in *Morrissey* that due process seems to require this initial inquiry be held at or reasonably near the area of the alleged parole violation or arrest "and as promptly as convenient after arrest while information is fresh and sources are available."   Id. at 485.

19. Id. at 488.

and to be heard via presentation of witnesses and documents, cross-examination of adverse witnesses where there is no good cause to prevent this, a hearing body which is neutral and detached from the case, and a written finding of this body as to the reasons for their decision and the evidence they have relied on. Evidence admissible at this hearing is not restricted to evidence admissible at trial. Since these inquiries are narrow they should also be flexible.[20]

After having firmly established in *Morrissey* that an alleged parole violator does have, after all, many constitutional safeguards available to him, including the most basic of all, the right to be heard,[21] in *Gagnon* the Supreme Court through the words of Justice Powell eschewed the logical implications of *Morrissey* and retreated to the Betts v. Brady [22] case-by-case test for determining whether the alleged parole or probation violator is entitled to counsel at his hearing.[23] Although he acknowledged that this test has been "rejected in favor of a per se rule"[24] in Gideon v. Wainwright[25] (which requires counsel in felony cases,) Justice Powell concluded (inexplicably, at least to this writer) that neither *Gideon* nor *Argersinger*,[26] (the case which established right to counsel whenever an accused faces confinement) showed that "a case by case approach to furnishing counsel is necessarily inadequate to protect constitutional rights asserted in varying types of proceedings . . . ."[27] Justice Powell then proceeded to set out in great detail what he determined to be the "critical differences" between criminal trials and probation or parole revocation hearings.[28] He concluded that most of the time counsel will not be necessary but "there will remain certain cases in which fundamental fairness—the touchstone of due process—will require that the State provide at its expense counsel for indigent probationers or parolees."[29]

Because of the vagaries of fact situations Justice Powell said that no firm guidelines could be set out but he decided to try it any way:

> Presumptively, it may be said that counsel should be provided in cases where, after being informed of his right to request counsel, the probationer or parolee makes such a request, based on a

20. Id. at 488–489.

21. Goldberg v. Kelly, supra n. 9, at 267.

22. Betts v. Brady, 316 U.S. 455 (1942): Interestingly enough, at least one circuit (the Fourth) prior even to Morrissey, had specifically rejected the case by case test and also construed Mempa v. Rhay to support dictum to the effect that probation revocation was a "stage of criminal proceedings," thus "appointment of counsel for an indigent is required at *every stage* of a criminal proceeding where *substantial rights* of a criminal accused may be affected," Hewett v. North Carolina, 415 F.2d 1316, 1322 (4th Cir. 1969).

23. Gagnon, supra n. 11, at 788.

24. Id.

25. Gideon v. Wainwright, 372 U.S. 335 (1963) (right to counsel in felony cases).

26. Argersinger v. Hamlin, 407 U.S. 25 (1972), (right to counsel in all cases where accused faces confinement).

27. Gagnon, supra n. 11, at 788.

28. Id. at 788–89.

29. Id. at 790.

timely and colorable claim (i) that he has not committed the alleged violation of the conditions upon which he is at liberty; or (ii) that, even if the violation is a matter of public record or is uncontested, there are substantial reasons which justified or mitigated the violation and make revocation inappropriate, and that the reasons are complex or otherwise difficult to develop or present. In passing on a request for the appointment of counsel, the responsible agency also should consider, especially in doubtful cases, whether the probationer appears to be capable of speaking effectively for himself. In every case in which a request for counsel at a preliminary or final hearing is refused, the grounds for refusal should be stated succinctly in the record.[30]

It seems very likely that Justice Powell did indirectly what he believed he should not do directly, that is, determine that every alleged probation or parole violator is entitled to counsel at his or her revocation hearing. A true picture of the background, education, and usual lack of articulateness of the average probationer or parolee [31] would strongly suggest that this result is greatly preferable to the case by case approach.[32]

DIVERGENCE OF WOLFF V. McDONNELL

In Wolff v. McDonnell,[33] the Court took a different tack in dealing with questions arising out of prison disciplinary proceedings. Though finding that many of the procedural due process rights of *Morrissey-Gagnon* must be observed, such as, advance notice of the alleged violation, a written statement of the findings of facts,[34] the right to call witnesses in one's own behalf and to present documentary evidence in one's defense,[35] Justice White, writing for the Court, decided that whether to allow confrontation and cross-examination should be left to the discretion of prison authorities,[36] and, though he found that due process of prison disciplinary proceedings is a developing concept, he decided there is no absolute right to counsel in prison disciplinary proceedings.[37] Utilizing the balancing of interests test, the Court determined that "insertion of counsel into the disciplinary process would inevitably give the proceedings a more adversary cast and tend to reduce their utility as a means to

30. Id. at 790–91.

31. See, e. g., Stevenson v. Reed, 391 F.Supp. 1375, 1379 nn. 3 & 4 with accompanying test (N.D.Miss.1975).

32. Oddly enough, however, the *Stevenson* court, supra n. 31, holds that adequate law libraries rather than appointed counsel are a sufficient mechanism for providing access to the courts even in view of the fact that the inmates at Parchman, Mississippi major prison facility generally had poor educational backgrounds.

33. Wolff, supra n. 12.

34. Id. at 564–565.

35. Id. at 566.

36. Id. at 567–568.

37. Id. at 569–570.

further correctional goals.[38]   Justice White also alluded to problems of delay and difficulties in obtaining sufficient numbers of counsel.[39]

A definition of the balancing test in *Morrissey* and *Gagnon* appears to be the safety of society versus the welfare of the individual convicted of crime.   The high purpose of parole as set out in *Morrissey* and quoted in *Gagnon* is "to help individuals reintegrate into society as constructive individuals as soon as they are able   .   .   ." [40]   By implication the desired result is the rehabilitation of the convicted person.

The test in *Wolff*, however, is a much narrower concept: the state correctional authority versus the inmate.[41]   The Court stated the use of counsel would tend to reduce the utility of disciplinary proceedings in attaining correctional goals.   In this context, it is not entirely clear how the Court would define these goals though they are apparently not so altruistic as those in *Morrissey-Gagnon*.

Traditionally, of the triumvirate of correctional goals, namely, retribution, deterrence and rehabilitation, the latter is in its ascendancy. "Rehabilitation is the only one of these three philosophies that is both consistent with the spirit of a democratic culture and protective of the public: rehabilitation is an effort so to deal with a law violator that he will not commit further crime." [42]   If it is true that even prison discipline has as its main objective the rehabilitation of the prisoner,[43] then fundamental fairness would seem to be the touchstone of due process both inside institutions as well as outside.   It follows that there is no valid correctional goal, in the broader sense, to be served by denying counsel to inmates in prison disciplinary proceedings,[44] or at the very least some form of adequate counsel substitute.[45]

Beside the fact that "due process" would seem to require counsel for the convicted person at parole and probation revocation hearings, as well as at prison disciplinary hearings, the prolixity of issues, the lack of schooling and articulateness on the part of many convicted persons, and the need to prevent the arbitrary exercise of power would seem equally to make the right to counsel at such hearings a fundamental precept.[46]   As

38. Id. at 570.

39. Id.

40. Morrissey, supra n. 1, at 477; Gagnon, supra n. 11, at 783.

41. Wolff, supra n. 12 at 560.

42. Sands v. Wainwright, 357 F.Supp. 1062, 1094–95 (M.D.Fla.1973).   Judge Scott presents a stunning tour de force in analyzing due process applications in prison disciplinary proceedings.   This opinion predates even *Gagnon*.

43. Id. at 1095.   Judge Scott quotes with approval from the American Correc-

tional Association's Manual of Correctional Standards 347 (1954).

44. Cf. Palmigiano v. Baxter, 487 F.2d 1280, 1291–92 (1st Cir. 1973) vacated, 418 U.S. 908, on remand, 510 F.2d 534 (1974).

45. Clutchette v. Procunier, 510 F.2d 613 (9th Cir. 1975).   Prior to Wolff, the Ninth Circuit had held there was a somewhat broader right to counsel substitute, 497 F.2d 809, 821–22 (9th Cir. 1974).

46. Cf. United States ex rel. Bey v. Connecticut State Board of Parole, 443 F.2d 1079, 1087–88 (2nd Cir. 1971); vacated as moot, 404 U.S. 879 (1971).   The

the Supreme Court indicated in Powell v. Alabama, "[t]he right to be heard would be, in many cases, of little avail if it did not comprehend the right to be heard by counsel." [47]　It has not been sufficiently demonstrated that there is any truly overriding state interest to be served by proceedings so summary in nature as to deny right to counsel.

RIGHT TO COUNSEL: PROBATION AND PAROLE REVOCATION HEARINGS

After reviewing its prior decision in the light of *Morrissey* and *Gagnon*, at least one state's highest court has determined that "those involved in parole revocation can take no other course than to appoint counsel in all cases and to have a full-blown trial for every alleged charge of parole violation." [48]　The Supreme Court of Indiana decried the use of the "case-by-case" test on the grounds that the law has always "abhorred" such a test and litigants ought not to be subjected to the uncertainties of "depending on the personal thinking of those who happen to be judges at the time." [49]

The United States Court of Appeals for the Second Circuit has amply explained the need for counsel in the *Bey* case. [50]

A lawyer's training particularly suits him to analyze and organize for the benefit of an impartial tribunal evidentiary matter bearing on the occurrence or non-occurrence, as well as the significance, of past events. [51]

A "trained lawyer might well" show "mitigating circumstances and hidden significance" not readily apparent on the face of a probation officer's report. [52]　For example, if *Bey* had had counsel at this revocation hearing he might have been able to belie any sinister significance to his allegedly carrying a "dagger" when in reality it was only a hunting knife found in a box under some clothes in Bey's closet.　The Court was compelled to recognize "the necessity for the aid of counsel in marshalling the facts, introducing evidence of mitigating circumstances and in general aiding and assisting the defendant to present his case." [53,54]

In 1967, a comparatively early date in the development of due process in parole and probation revocation proceedings, one court decided, even before Mempa v. Rhay "that counsel [at a probation revocation hearing] is not only desirable but is so essential to a fair and trustworthy hearing

recent National Advisory Commission on Criminal Justice Standards and Goals adopted Corrections Standard 12.4 which calls for counsel to be allowed or provided for indigents at parole revocation hearings.

47. Powell v. Alabama, 287 U.S. 45, 68–69 (1932).

48. Russell v. Douthitt, 304 N.E.2d 793, 794 (Ind.1974).

49. Id.

50. Bey, supra n. 46, at 1087–88.

51. Id.

52. Id.

53. Id. at 1088, quoting Mempa v. Rhay, 389 U.S. 128, 135 (1967).

54. *Mempa*, supra.

that due process of law when liberty is at stake includes a right to counsel." [55] Counsel would see to it that the relevant facts were disclosed, "vague and insubstantial allegations discounted, and irrelevancies eliminated." [56] The court went on to state that where probationer was allowed to bring in retained counsel then equal protection gave an indigent probationer a right to appointed counsel. [57]

In at least one jurisdiction the right to counsel at probation and parole revocation hearings has been established by court rule. [58] In another, the right, at least to retained counsel, has been established by parole board rule. [59]

Some states have by statute permitted counsel at parole revocation hearings and the Court of Appeals of Michigan has held that the constitutional right to equal protection of the laws means that indigent persons must be appointed counsel where a parolee "of means" was allowed counsel. The Court went on to hold that the Michigan Department of Corrections had to bear the cost of the appointed counsel until the state legislature could "otherwise provide." [60]

At least one court has determined that "efficient administration of justice" requires counsel at parole and probation revocation hearings and sets out with characteristic thoroughness exactly why counsel is necessary:

> A violation may be of such little consequence that a probationer may not even be aware of his transgression. An explanation of his intents and motives might well establish that he was not volitionally guilty of any misconduct. However, he too often lacks the training and poise to present to either his probation officer or the court his explanation in a persuasive manner, although perhaps because the stakes are high. Trained counsel, in such circumstances, "can help delineate the issues, present the

---

55. Perry v. Williard, 427 P.2d 1020, 1022 (Ore.1967).

56. Id.

57. Id.

58. See State v. Settle, 512 P.2d 46, 49 (Ariz.1973).

59. See Ex parte Laird, 305 So.2d 357 (Miss.1974) (hearing officer violated parole board will by not allowing retained counsel to participate in probation revocation hearing).

60. People v. Mash, 45 Mich.App. 459, 206 N.W.2d 767 (Mich.1973); See also, Callison v. Michigan Dept. of Corrections, 56 Mich.App. 260, 223 N.W.2d

738 (Mich.1974) (indigent not only entitled to counsel at parole revocation proceeding but he must be informed of the right); Accord, Dillenburg v. Morris, 84 Wash.2d 353, 525 P.2d 770 (Wash. 1974); In *Callison* the alleged parole violator had committed another offense while on parole but the court said he was entitled to and needed counsel to explain mitigating circumstances, Id. at 740. In Florida a state statute apparently permitted retained counsel at parole revocation hearings and the Court, concluded, prior to *Gagnon*, that equal protection required appointment of counsel for indigents, Cottle v. Wainwright, 477 F.2d 269 (5th Cir. 1973), vacated, 414 U.S. 895, 94 S.Ct. 221 (1973) (for reconsideration in light of *Gagnon*).

factual contentions in an orderly manner, conduct cross-examination, and generally safeguard the interests of" his client.[61]

The Court of Appeals of New York has determined that their state constitution insures a parolee his right to counsel at least at the final parole revocation hearing.[62]

Applying *Gagnon* precisely in 1974, Judge Swinford, late federal district judge in Eastern Kentucky, determined that an alleged parole violator was entitled to counsel where state parole authorities had not complied with *Morrissey* requirements in the parole revocation hearing and in view of the fact the alleged violator had denied breaching conditions of his parole.[63]

Another case arising out of the Eastern District of Kentucky, Preston v. Piggman, gave the Sixth Circuit an opportunity to apply almost every requirement of *Morrissey* as well as hold specifically via *Gagnon* that the alleged parole violator was entitled to counsel.[64] Although hewing close to the particular facts the court's decision in *Preston* has application to any situation where a Parole Board does not give an alleged parole or probation violator sufficient opportunity to explain his conduct even where, as in *Preston*, the parolee has admitted having violated the conditions of his parole.[65] The Court noted that the state parole board's practice, as evidenced by testimony of the parole board chairman, of revoking parole for every parole violation "clearly runs counter to the dictates of the Court in *Morrissey* . . . ."[66] Judge Miller, speaking for the court, held that the case clearly fitted the *Gagnon* criteria for appointment of counsel in view of the many factors of mitigating quality which would require counsel in order to be "thoroughly explored."[67]

DISCIPLINARY PROCEEDINGS

A prisoner's interest in good time credits and any disciplinary proceeding concerning such credits "has real substance and is sufficiently embraced within Fourteenth Amendment 'liberty' to entitle him to those minimum procedures appropriate under the circumstances and required

---

61. People v. Vickers, 105 Cal.Rptr. 305, 503 P.2d 1313, 1321 (Calif.1973) quoting, Goldberg v. Kelly, 397 U.S. 254, 270–271 (1970). The Supreme Court of California relied heavily on *Morrissey* in this pre-*Gagnon* decision since *Morrissey* applied only prospectively.

62. People ex rel. Calloway v. Skinner, 33 N.Y.2d 23, 300 N.E.2d 716, 718–719 (N.Y.1973); See also, People ex rel. Combs v. LaVallee, 29 A.D.2d 128, 286 N.Y.Supp.2d 600 (N.Y.Sup.Ct., App. Div.1968); People ex rel. Donohoe v. Montanye, 35 N.Y.2d 221, 318 N.E.2d 781 (N.Y.1974). In *Donohoe* the Court overturned on state constitutional

grounds a state parole board rule that barred counsel at parole revocation hearings of parolees convicted of crime while on parole.

63. Forbes v. Roebuck (sic), 368 F.Supp. 817 (E.D.Ky.1974) (parolee not in custody at time of alleged local hearing).

64. Preston v. Piggman, 496 F.2d 270 (6th Cir. 1974).

65. Id. at 274.

66. Id. at 275 n. 1.

67. Id. at 275.

by the Due Process Clause to insure that the state-created right is not arbitrarily abrogated."[68]

In Wolff v. McDonnell,[69] the Supreme Court determined that there is no constitutional requirement that the *Morrissey-Scarpelli* procedures be followed in all respects in state prison disciplinary proceedings.[70] The Court perceived a qualitative and quantitative difference between loss of good time and the revocation of parole or probation.[71]

Even though *Wolff* held that the Constitution did not mandate that counsel be present at prison disciplinary hearings, later cases have found situations which require counsel's presence at such proceedings.

The Federal District Court in Roberts v. Taylor[72] found that when a prisoner is charged with violations of prison disciplinary rules, and as a result of these same actions state criminal proceedings have been commenced he must be afforded the right to the presence of a "non-participating legal advisor" during the disciplinary hearing.[73] Counsel is only allowed to assist the inmate by aiding him in preparing his case, and also by advising him during the hearing. *Roberts* also held that where an inmate has been arraigned on state criminal charges, has invoked his fifth amendment privilege at the disciplinary hearing and such invocation was relevant to the determination of the validity of the disciplinary charges, then this inmate is entitled to a grant of use immunity.[74]

In Aikens v. Lash[75] the United States Court of Appeals for the Seventh Circuit determined, contrary to *Wolff*, that a prison disciplinary board must give written reasons to an inmate when they deny him the right to cross-examine witnesses.[76] This is the only way that the sound-

---

68. Wolff v. McDonnell, supra n. 12, at 557.

69. Id.

70. Id. at 560. As far as the Court is concerned due process does not involve a set of procedures which inflexibly apply to all possible situations. See, Cafeteria Workers v. McElroy, 367 U.S. 886 (1961).

71. There are qualitative and quantitative differences for the prison inmate since

. . . the deprivation of good time is not the same immediate disaster that the revocation of parole is for the parolee. The deprivation, very likely, does not then and there work any change in the conditions of his liberty. It can postpone the date of eligibility for parole and extend the maximum term to be served, but it is not certain to do so, for good time may be restored. Even if not restored, it cannot be said with certainty that the actual date of parole will

be affected; and if parole occurs, the extension of the maximum term resulting from loss of good time may affect only the termination of parole, and it may not even do that. The deprivation of good time is unquestionably a matter of considerable importance. The State reserves it as a sanction for serious misconduct, and we should not unrealistically discount its significance. Wolff, supra n. 12, at 561.

72. 390 F.Supp. 705 (D.R.I.1975).

73. Id. at 710. The court felt that any other holding would unnecessarily impede the disciplinary hearing.

74. See, Palmigiano v. Baxter, 510 F.2d 534 (1st Cir. 1974).

75. 514 F.2d 55 (7th Cir. 1975).

76. See also, Clutchette v. Procunier, 510 F.2d 613 (9th Cir. 1974). Clutchette also found that:

ness of the disciplinary board's use of discretion can be reviewed and subjected to meaningful scrutiny.

These court decisions subsequent to *Wolff* have found that the process due an inmate charged with disciplinary violations is more than that required by *Wolff*. Future changes in prison environments may require that the prison inmate be afforded even greater procedural safeguards in disciplinary hearings.

PAROLE RECISSION

The requirements of *Morrissey* with regard to the minimal due process requirements in parole revocation proceedings have been extended to parole recissions.[77] Where the potential parolee has been assigned a release date, he has more than just "a mere anticipation of hope of freedom."[78] The California Court observed that "[b]ecause the nature of the inquiry [at parole recissions] is nearly identical to that of a normal parole revocation, and because the interest in conditional liberty is in many ways as valuable and would inflict a similar 'grievous loss' if terminated, the same procedures and rights should be insured."[79] In addition, the conditional right to counsel provided under *Gagnon* has been extended to parole recissions.[80] In at least one case this right to counsel was based on the state's constitution.[81]

OTHER PROCEDURAL SAFEGUARDS NECESSITATING COUNSEL

In depreciating the need for counsel at revocation hearings, the Supreme Court in *Gagnon* observed that "formal procedures and rules of evidence are not employed" at such hearings.[82]

This premise, however, is susceptible to severe criticism in view of the rapid development in state and federal courts of procedural and evidentiary safeguards designed to insure fair and just revocation hearings for all probationers and parolees.

A prisoner subject to removal of one or more privileges (1) must be given notice of intent to remove one or more stated privileges, (2) together with a statement of grounds for removal, (3) at a reasonable time before discipline is imposed, and (4) must be given an opportunity to respond before such discipline is imposed.

The Court in *Wolff* stated that they did not suggest that the due process procedures required by *Wolff* were also necessary for imposition of less grievous penalties such as the loss of privileges.

77. Batchelder v. Kenton, 383 F.Supp. 299 (C.D.Calif.1974).

78. Id. at 301–302.

79. Id. at 302.

80. Id.; Gee v. Brown, 120 Cal.Rptr. 876, 534 P.2d 716, (1975) modified on denial of rehearing, 122 Cal.Rptr. 231, 536 P.2d 1017. The second opinion of the California Supreme Court signaled a retreat from Federal constitutional grounds to the state constitution. *Morrissey* standards have also been extended to revocation of work release, State ex rel. Djonne v. Schoen, 217 N.W.2d 508 (Minn.1974).

81. Gee v. Brown, supra, 536 P.2d 1017 (1975).

82. Gagnon v. Scarpelli, supra n. 11, at 789.

HEARSAY EVIDENCE

The use of "hearsay evidence" to substantiate a parole or probation revocation has been condoned in some jurisdictions as compatible with the due process requirement of fundamental fairness.[83] When, however, the hearsay evidence is "unreasonably abundant and its substantive reliability highly suspect," a revocation decision founded on such evidence will be vitiated for lack of due process of law.[84]

Since the revocation hearing "is to determine the fact of parole [or probation] violation," [85] hearsay evidence may be regarded as insufficient proof to sustain the deprivation of a man's liberty.[86]

A prohibition against the use of "hearsay evidence" appears mandated by the confrontation and cross-examination requirement of *Morrissey* unless "the hearing officer specifically finds good cause for not allowing confrontation." [87]

UNCONSTITUTIONALLY OBTAINED EVIDENCE

Although numerous courts have held that evidence illegally seized from a probationer or parolee is admissible at his revocation hearing,[88] recent decisions have eroded the certainty of that principle.[89] A parole or probation officer may be exempt from the probable cause and warrant requirements of the Fourth Amendment, but his conduct in a particular case may be "so unreasonable" as to render the search and seizure unconstitutional. For example, a parole officer's search of a parolee's residence, when the officer had "nothing in the way of subjective information to justify the search," rendered the search "unreasonable." [90]

Furthermore, at least one jurisdiction has ruled that evidence obtained through an unconstitutional search and seizure is incompetent to prove any fact in court whether the proceeding be a trial or revocation hearing.[91]

83. Hyser v. Reed, 318 F.2d 225 (D.C. Cir. 1963), cert. denied 345 U.S. 957, (1963); Arciniega v. Freeman, 439 F.2d 776, 777 (9th Cir. 1971).

84. State v. Caron, 334 A.2d 495, 498 (Me.1975).

85. *Morrissey*, supra n. 1, at 499, separate opinion by Douglas, J.

86. People v. Lewis, 28 Ill.App.3d 777, 329 N.E.2d 390 (Ill.1975).

87. *Morrissey*, supra n. 1, at 489; State v. Miller, 42 Ohio St.2d 102, 326 N.E.2d 259 (Ohio 1975).

88. United States v. Hill, 447 F.2d 817, 819 (7th Cir. 1971); United States v. Brown, 488 F.2d 94, 95 (5th Cir. 1973); United States v. Farmer, 512 F.2d 160, 162–163 (6th Cir. 1975); State v. Caron, supra n. 84.

89. Latta v. Fitzharris, 521 F.2d 246 (9th Cir. 1975).

90. Coleman v. Smith, —— F.Supp. —— (W.D.N.Y.1975), 17 Cr.L. 2306 (July 16, 1975).

91. Michaud v. State, 505 P.2d 1399 (Okla.Ct.Crim.App.1973).

DOUBLE JEOPARDY

Often the conduct which allegedly violates the terms of the parole or probation constitutes a separate crime. Even when the parolee probationer has been acquitted at a criminal trial of the charged offense, the state may be permitted to revoke parole or probation on the basis of the same evidence which was insufficient to sustain a conviction.[92] A contrary result has been reached by relying on the principle of collateral estoppel, an aspect of the Fifth Amendment guarantee against double jeopardy. Collateral estoppel simply means that "when an issue of ultimate fact has been determined by a valid and final judgment, that issue cannot again be litigated between the same parties in any future lawsuit." [93] Consequently, a probationer's acquittal at a criminal trial would preclude the state, under the doctrine of collateral estoppel, from relitigating the same questions of the probationer's misconduct in a subsequent proceeding to revoke his probation.[94]

BURDEN OF PROOF

Although the *Morrissey* decision does not explicitly delineate the burden of proof in a parole revocation hearing, the opinion does note that the informal hearing must be "structured to assure that the finding of a parole violation will be informed by an accurate knowledge of the parolee's behavior." [95]

The probationer/parolee is not necessarily clothed in the presumption of innocence at the revocation hearing.[96] And, unlike a criminal proceeding, the degree of proof required for parole or probation revocation is less than guilt beyond a reasonable doubt.[97] The standard of proof applied may vary from evidence which "reasonably satisfies" [98] the court of a violation to "a preponderance of the evidence." [99]

Logically, the burden of proof, at least to the point of establishing a *prima facie* violation, must rest on the party seeking to revoke the parole or probation. When neither side introduces any evidence at a revocation

---

92. Standlee v. Smith, 83 Wash.2d 405, 518 P.2d 721 (Wash.1974).

93. Ashe v. Swenson, 397 U.S. 436, 443, (1970).

94. People v. Grayson, 58 Ill.2d 260, 319 N.E.2d 43 (Ill.1974). "[I]t would be unseemly for the probation court to conclude, counter to the result of a criminal trial, that an offense has occurred and that it could provide the basis for a revocation." American Bar Association *Standards Relating to Probation*, § 5.3, commentary.

95. *Morrissey*, supra n. 1, at 484.

96. United States ex rel. Mason v. Amico, 360 F.Supp. 1344 (W.D.N.Y.1973); In Re Whitney, 421 F.2d 337 (1st Cir. 1970).

97. State v. Kuhn, 81 Wash.2d 648, 503 P.2d 1061, 1062 (Wash.1972); State v. Wilhite, 492 S.W.2d 397, 399 (M.App. 1973); United States v. D'Amato, 429 F.2d 1284 (3rd Cir. 1970).

98. State v. Kuhn, supra, 503 P.2d at 1062.

99. People v. Grayson, supra n. 94, at 45.

hearing, due process is not satisfied and a decision to revoke is unjustified.[100]

CONCLUSIONS

No matter how one classifies parole or probation revocation or prison disciplinary proceedings, it is clear that to abrogate a convicted person's status, be it parole, probation, or even prison yard privileges, is a sufficient diminution of liberty to fall within the penumbra of the Fourteenth Amendment guarantee of due process. It seems equally clear that the right to counsel is a basic safeguard for providing this constitutional guarantee. Procedural due process without counsel is an empty promise in most instances. There is no doubt that right to counsel is as precious to convicted persons as it is to free men.

PAROLE REVOCATION DECISIONMAKING: PRIVATE TYPINGS AND OFFICIAL DESIGNATIONS *

Revocation rates are frequently employed as a means of measuring the effectiveness of various parole and probation programs, with lowered rates heralded by program directors as testimony of organizational proficiency. In the research that follows, we will not be evaluating program effectiveness per se, but will focus on how revocation-related decisionmaking occurs. Our data suggest that if one is to use revocation rates as a measure of program success, one should be highly conscious of the processes by which decisions to revoke parolees are made. While known infractions draw attention to the parolee and make his status as a parolee problematic, violations are subject to multiple interpretations and the seriousness of a given offense can be readily defined away. The decision to revoke a parolee reflects the agent's personal orientations and his perception of self-accountability to the goals, and personnel of the system in which he works. Revocation is not a structured response to parole violations; it is a socially influenced definition.

The present research is based on a general model of labeling (Prus, 1975a). In this model, four basic processes are seen as describing how persons come to be socially defined: (1) "typing" or private classification of persons (targets) by some agent; (2) "designating" whereby the typing agent reveals his attributions of the target to others; (3) "assessing" whereby those learning of the agent's typing of the target determine if the designations are target appropriate; and (4) "resistance" whereby persons exposed to the agent's definitions of the target, finding these inappropriate to the target, challenge those target definitions (Prus, 1975b). The target may learn of the designation and participate in assessing and resisting activities in the same way as any other audience.

---

100. People ex rel. Warren v. Mancusi, 40 App.Div.2d 279, 339 N.Y.S.2d 882 (N.Y.App.Div.1973).

* Robert C. Prus and John R. Stratton, *Federal Probation*, March 1976.

The research reported here focuses on the first two stages of the labeling model as they pertain to a parole officer *typing* his parolees as "revocables" and officially *designating* them in terms of his private evaluations. The decision to revoke a parolee actually involves two decisions: (1) whether a man "deserves" to be revoked; and (2) whether revocation proceedings should be initiated. Although other researchers (e. g., Pownall, 1963; Reed and King, 1966; Battaglia, 1968; Robison and Takagi, 1968; Irwin, 1970; and Dembo, 1970, 1972) have contributed to our understanding of parole revocation decisionmaking, without reference to this two-step sequence, it is felt that a delineation of the elements involved in making these two decisions is crucial, if the revocation process is to be more fully understood. In this article, the relationship between these two decisions and the agents' orientational framework is examined.

METHODS

This study involved all 45 parole agents in a midwestern state. Data were collected from the agents in a variety of ways including questionnaires, interviews, and observation. In addition, some records were analyzed and immediate supervisors and higher administrative personnel were interviewed. There is considerable objective and subjective data to indicate that this particular agency would be considered both professional (standards and training) and strongly rehabilitative in its orientation.

In the questionnaire agents were provided with four cases in the form of vignettes. Each case involved two separate incidents, one being a more serious version of the other. For each case, agents were asked to indicate for each condition whether or not they thought the man should be revoked (private typing), and what their official response would be.[1]

When percentage differences and correlational coefficients are examined the discrepancy between private typings and official designations becomes apparent. Parole agents indicated that they would officially revoke only 50 percent of those they privately felt should be revoked under the less serious conditions, and 61 percent of those they thought

---

1. (Private Typings)

Do you think his parole should be revoked?

1. __ I definitely feel it should be revoked.
2. __ I strongly feel it should be revoked.
3. __ I feel it probably should be revoked.
4. __ I feel it probably should *not* be revoked.
5. __ I strongly feel it should *not* be revoked.
6. __ I definitely feel it should *not* be revoked.

(Official Responses)

What action would you take in this case? (as multiple responses were possible, the most serious response was coded).

1. __ do nothing.
2. __ counsel him.
3. __ warn him.
4. __ "chew him out."
5. __ put him in jail for about __ days.
6. __ send him an official reprimand.
7. __ recycle him.
8. __ revoke him.

should be revoked under the more serious conditions. The zero order correlations between private typings and official designations were .35 and .57 for the less and more serious conditions, respectively. Agents were acting more consistently with their private typings when the parolee infraction was more serious. While agents' typings (private definitions) seem to bear some relationship to their designations (public definitions), there seems to be considerable "screening" occurring between their private definitions and their official designations.

The agents were asked on the questionnaire to provide reasons for the decisions they reached for each case. Followup interviews and field observations also provided insight into the concerns influencing decisions. From these data, we have uncovered two sets of underlying concerns which seem vital to the understanding of parole revocation. While private definitions and official designations are somewhat related, they are contingent on notably different concerns, for unlike private definitions, official responses place the agent in a situation of accountability so that the consideration of costs and rewards of various options become more prominent. The underlying orientations affecting private definitions are considered first, followed by those which might prevent their being translated directly into official (public) designations.

PRIVATE DEFINITIONS

Five concerns seem basic to agents' private typings of parolees as candidates for revocation. These are:

(1) Protecting society (is the man a threat to the community?).

(2) Gaining cooperation (can I work with him?).

(3) Protecting the parolee (from others, and even my own biases).

(4) Rehabilitating the parolee (change his orientations to life).

(5) Maintaining the parole system (meet expectations of superordinates).

Protection of society may well be the most important consideration in privately typing a parolee a revocation candidate, for it is typically only after one gets into trouble with the police, or other persons in the community, that the agent comes to consider him in a revocation context. In this context, seriousness of the incident would seem an important variable, however, it seems that much of the impact of seriousness is moderated by other concerns, such as parolee attributed responsibility for the event, victim antagonism toward the parole officer, and the agent's concern with rehabilitating the parolee.

The second concern, that of gaining parolee cooperation, is an important one in influencing the extent to which parolee incidents are defined as serious. Cooperation concerns reflect not only past behavior on the part of the parolee, but also what the agent feels he may expect from a parolee in the future. When a parolee is seen as willing to cooperate even via a promise of future cooperation, an agent will often excuse what he might otherwise define as a relatively serious infraction. Since parole is not a voluntary status, and as agents encounter resistance from parolees, obtaining a desired form of cooperation can negate even relatively serious incidents. We should note that cooperation, on the part of the parolee, provides partial validation of the parole agent's role, as well as an indication of personal respect. Rehabilitation programs can now be more easily implemented and the agent's task becomes a little easier. A blatant lack of cooperation, on the other hand, could be interpreted as indicating a dangerous parolee, one who respected neither the agent, nor the system; one who could not be worked with; and one whose presence threatened the very nature of the agent's job. While no agents were encountered who appeared to be "trying to get a man," some agents did indicate that they were waiting for particular parolees to get into serious trouble so that they could revoke them. By contrast, those parolees defined as cooperative ("a success in the making?") appeared to have much of the seriousness of their infractions defined away.

Another concern which appears operative in private revocation definitions is that of protecting parolees. Somewhat unexpectedly questionnaire responses revealed strong concerns for protecting parolees. This concern was also reflected in interviews and field observations. Midstate agents appeared suspicious of reports from citizens, family members, employers, and police, when these reports reflected unfavorably on their parolees. Before an incident was seriously considered, agents would attempt to verify the credibility of their sources, looking for "evil" motives and/or victim-precipitated situations. Some agents seemed willing to act once the credibility of the complainant was established; others, however, upon establishing credibility, would insist on proof of the level necessary for acceptance in a courtroom. In these instances the agent would operate as a "public relations" man, attempting to "cool out" complainants by offering to arrange for restitution and/or jailing the parolee for a few days if they wouldn't press charges.

The concern for protecting parolees seems to have three foundations. First, is the feeling that "these are my guys, I've got to take care of them." Second, there is a concern for success; a feeling that parolee failures reflected agent incompetence. The third consideration is concern with balancing justice. The first factor, the "mother hen" approach, seemed to operate when agents felt close to their men and when they defined their parolees as somewhat helpless or "dumb," persons not fully responsible, or in a disadvantaged position. The success concern did not require personal intimacy, but might be likened to playing a game, with agents having to get their entry past the obstacles and "home-free" in order to win. The third component reflected justice concerns. Being allowed some discretion in the handling of cases some agents tried to restore the balance of justice. When a particular parolee was seen to have received a "bum rap," or when the agent thought a parolee would be prosecuted too vigorously, he might tolerate incidents from this parolee which he would not tolerate from others. Overall there seemed a tendency to consider prison terms as too long, and to feel that society owed the fellow who had been in jail longer a few more indiscretions than persons who had served short terms. In endeavoring to be fair, some agents acknowledged going against their better judgment in not revoking certain parolees, for fear that they might be doing so out of personal bias. In addition, cases were encountered where parole agents transferred parolees to other agents because the parolee had accused them of being unfair or because there was evidence of a "personality conflict." These transfers, although relatively infrequent, usually took place when the agent was about to revoke the man. There was surprising little carry-over of reputational effects. The second agent seemed to make a deliberate attempt to "start clean" with the parolee; the transfer provided a new set of tolerances and chances.

The fourth concern affecting private assessments was that of wanting to rehabilitate all parolees. Unlike the "mother hen" approach, which involves bailing parolees out of current problem situations, the rehabilitation approach assumes that there is something wrong with the parolee, and then attempts to remedy this defect. Basic to this approach, in the parole context, is the notion that anybody can be changed, if the agent is given enough time and can find the right program. A strong commitment to this perspective leads to an extreme reluctance to accept revocation as an alternative, even in private typings. Most agents seem to recognize extensive rehabilitation as idealistic but many still strive to try to realize this outcome in each of their parolees. One finds that their parolees are shuffled from program to program, after each "mess up," over the duration of their parole period, to ultimately be released as a "success." Optimism seems a central ingredient of a rehabilitation perspective. After viewing these people being channeled through a variety of programs, one might conclude that these parolees were "working" the rehabilitation scene considerably more than it was working on them. In those areas in which there were a larger number of available programs, this tendency was even more pronounced. Situations were also encountered where other agencies and help sources competed with one another for a chance to salvage parolees whom the agent had put in jail for a few days while deciding what to do with him. Some parolees are apparently quite resourceful in finding "sponsors," to "cool out" the parole agent.

The fifth concern influencing the agents' private typings of parolees in a revocation context, is the obligation the agent feels he has towards the parole system. We found the agents to be not only conscientious in making decisions, but also quite sensitive to the opinions of their supervisors, and to agency policies. Evidence of this was seen in questionnaire responses, as well as in the field. Where parole agent roles are defined in terms of rehabilitation goals, and where organizational policy is to reduce revocation rates, these considerations operate as deterrents to the defining of parolees as revocation candidates, even at a private level. This research has led us to be most sensitive to the impact of organizational ideology on the making of deviants.

OFFICIAL DEFINITIONS

While agents are seen to be influenced by the organizational ideology in their private definitions, the impact of the system becomes considerably more noticeable in the shift from private to official definitions. Taking a cognitive "screening" perspective, an effort will be made to indicate those factors which appear to operate as filters between the two sets of definitions. The earlier mentioned concerns affecting private typings are still relevant, but when it comes time to make a revocation definition public, other issues become prominent. The following concerns operate to reduce the likelihood that a private definition of a parolee, as a revocation candidate, will become an official definition:

(1) Perceived likelihood of a successful revocation.

(2) Perceived personal cost of revocation attempt.

(3) Perceived threat to agent's status as a "successful" agent.

(4) Beliefs regarding acceptability of prison.

The agents' anticipation of a successful revocation seemed to heavily influence their decisions to make a private revocation decision known to others. To this end, agents were concerned with showing: (1) that they had highly credible evidence; (2) that the parolee exhibited a persistent pattern of "criminality"; and (3) that in spite of their total and consistent efforts to help him, he would not try to help himself. Agents contemplating a revocation, therefore: review the parolee's background (outstanding qualities may work against the revocation); maintain chronological listings of all parolee activities; conduct investigations; and try to involve other community agencies ("see, nobody could work with this man!"). In general, where agents perceive conditions which might mitigate against their revocation definitions being accepted, they are reluctant to ask for revocation, even when they strongly feel a parolee should be returned to prison. Further, in cases where agents have had previous revocations turned down, the consequence of this has been to make out only these agents, but their office mates as well, more reluctant to ask for revocations.

Beyond the problematics of getting a revocation when it is desired, it should also be noted that processing a revocation, from the agent's point of view, can be time consuming and costly, relative to gains. As one of the agents put it, "no one pats you on the back for a revocation," and if one considers following the path of least resistance, revocations are deterred. By requesting a revocation, an agent not only opens himself to a considerable amount of paperwork, but also to conflicts which ensue from his labeling endeavors. Assuming that his supervisor forwards his request, the agent may be concerned about being prepared to face the subsequent hearing, and the possibility of being "grilled" and humiliated by the parolee's defense counsel. Further, issues of racial prejudice, and/or civil rights, may lead agents to anticipate certain undesired legal complications; and even should such claims be proven unfounded, agents feel that they may have negative consequences for their career advancement.

Figure 1. The career of a revocation definition

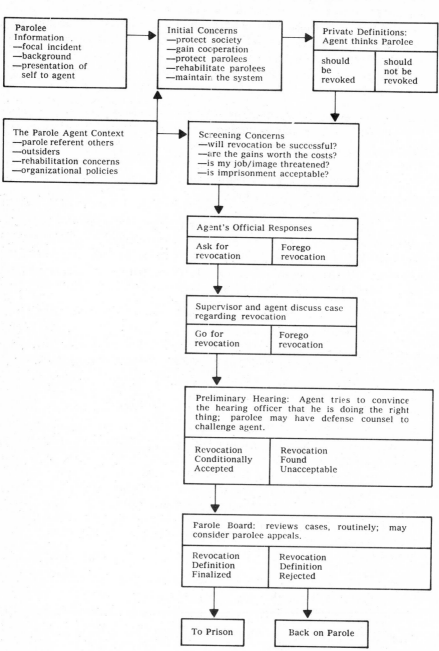

[B6531]

Another concern, and one which seems to affect agents who have been active in requesting revocations, is the concern that they may be attaining an undesirably high personal rate of revocation. These agents are not concerned with the difficulty of revoking someone at this point, but they are concerned over what another revocation will do to their image within the organization. The impression was created that they felt job security was tied to having acceptable individual revocation rates. Agents felt that those who counted in the organization, lacking other criteria, tended to evaluate on the basis of their revocation rates. There was the feeling among the agents that those agents who revoked over 10 percent of their cases were suspected of not performing their jobs adequately.

The preceding three concerns reflect system-based resistances agents may experience in trying to implement their decisions. The last concern reflecting uncertainty regarding the value of imprisonment represents a more personalized orientation, and one that seems to occur most frequently among agents taking a rehabilitation stance. Realizing that their action (to revoke) can have widespread effects on the life of the parolee, some agents consider the implications of revocation (i. e., incarceration) to be so undesirable as to lead them to avoid official revocation designations, even though they feel that the man should be revoked. Finally, it should be noted that in returning a man to prison, the agent not only admits that he failed with this parolee but he also foregoes other opportunities to work with and possibly "save" him.

The diagram on page 354 attempts to place these underlying dimensions in the context of a career notion of parolee definitions. It is useful in providing an overview of the total definitional process. As can be seen, the final parolee definition reflects a routing of revocation definitions through several negotiation points. The agent arrives at a private assessment of a parolee relative to revocation. If he decides the man should be revoked, he then asks himself if this is possible, given the nature of the parole situation and the system within which he works. Where revocation is seen as a good possibility which does not entail any great personal loss, he may decide to make his private assessment known to others. The first critical negotiation occurs when the agent seeks the approval of his supervisor. If, after this first negotiation, the parolee is still considered a revocation candidate, the request will be processed to the parole board for further processing (negotiation) of parolee status. If the revocation recommendation is not turned down at any of these points, it becomes a finalized official definition.

SUMMARY AND CONCLUSIONS

While the personal orientations of parole agents are important in determining their private definitions of parolees as warranting revocation, it appears that we should be very sensitive to subsequent cognitive screening processes as agents endeavor to create official parolee definitions consistent with those they consider most desired by the organizational network to which they find themselves accountable. This, to us, is suggestive of a fundamental issue concerning the meaning of revocation rates relative to system effectiveness. Do lowered revocation rates reflect improved supervision and effective parolee rehabilitation programs or do they reflect coping behavior on the part of agents to maintain their jobs and the system in which they operate? It is only by examining the processes by which revocations occur that we may begin to evaluate system effectiveness. To this end, we have delineated a model which would allow researchers to inquire more fully into the processing of revocations.

NOTES

Battaglia, Carmello

1968—"Deviant Behavior of Parolees and the Decision-Making Process of Parolee Supervisors." Doctoral Dissertation. Florida State University.

Circourel, Aaron

1968—*The Social Organization of Juvenile Justice.* New York: Wiley.

Dembo, Richard

1970—"Orientation and Activities of the Parole Officer." Doctoral Dissertation. New York University.

1972—"Orientations and Activities of the Parole Officer," *Criminology,* 10:193–215.

Irwin, John

1970—*The Felon.* Englewood Cliffs, N.J.: Prentice-Hall.

Pownall, George A.

1963—"An Analysis of the Role of the Parole Supervision Officer." Doctoral Dissertation. University of Illinois.

Prus, Robert C.

1973—"Revocation Related Decision-Making by the Parole Agent: A Labeling Approach." Doctoral Dissertation. University of Iowa.

1975a—"Labeling Theory: A Reconceptualization and a Propositional Statement on Typing," *Sociological Focus,* 8:79–96.

1975b—"Resisting Designations: An Extension of Attribution Theory into a Negotiated Context," *Sociological Inquiry,* 45:3–14.

Reed, John P. and Charles E. King.

1966—"Factors in the Decision Making of North Carolina Probation Officers," *Journal of Research in Crime and Delinquency,* 3:120–128.

Robinson, James and Paul T. Takagi

1968—"The Parole Violator as an Organizational Reject," pp. 233–54 in R.M. Carter and L.Y. Wilkins (eds.), *Probation and Parole.* New York: Wiley.

TOPICS FOR THOUGHT AND DISCUSSION

1. List and explain at least four ways in which parole and pardon differ.

2. Briefly discuss the evolution of parole from its roots in the mid-nineteenth century, to its introduction in America in New York.

3. Chief credit for developing an early parole system is due Alexander Maconochie. What were his contributions?

4. Define and discuss the concepts of "transportation" and "ticket-of-leave".

5. What was the "Elmira system"? What is its importance to our criminal justice system today?

6. Discuss some of the concerns of parole authorities which may influence the release decisionmaking.

7. What are some "models" by which paroling authorities may be organized? Discuss the pros and cons of each. Which model of organization does the National Advisory Commission on Criminal Justice Standards and Goals recommend? Why?

8. What are the provisions for parole revocation mandated by the U. S. Supreme Court in Morrissey v. Brewer?

9. *Morrissey* left some issues still unresolved. What are some of these issues. Have subsequent Court decisions solved some of these deficiencies?

10. What are the Uniform Parole Reports? Discuss this system of reporting national parole statistics and its value.

11. Discuss the current "crisis" in parole. What are the issues?

12. Report the points of view of proponents of both sides of the current controversy of the validity of parole as it exists today.